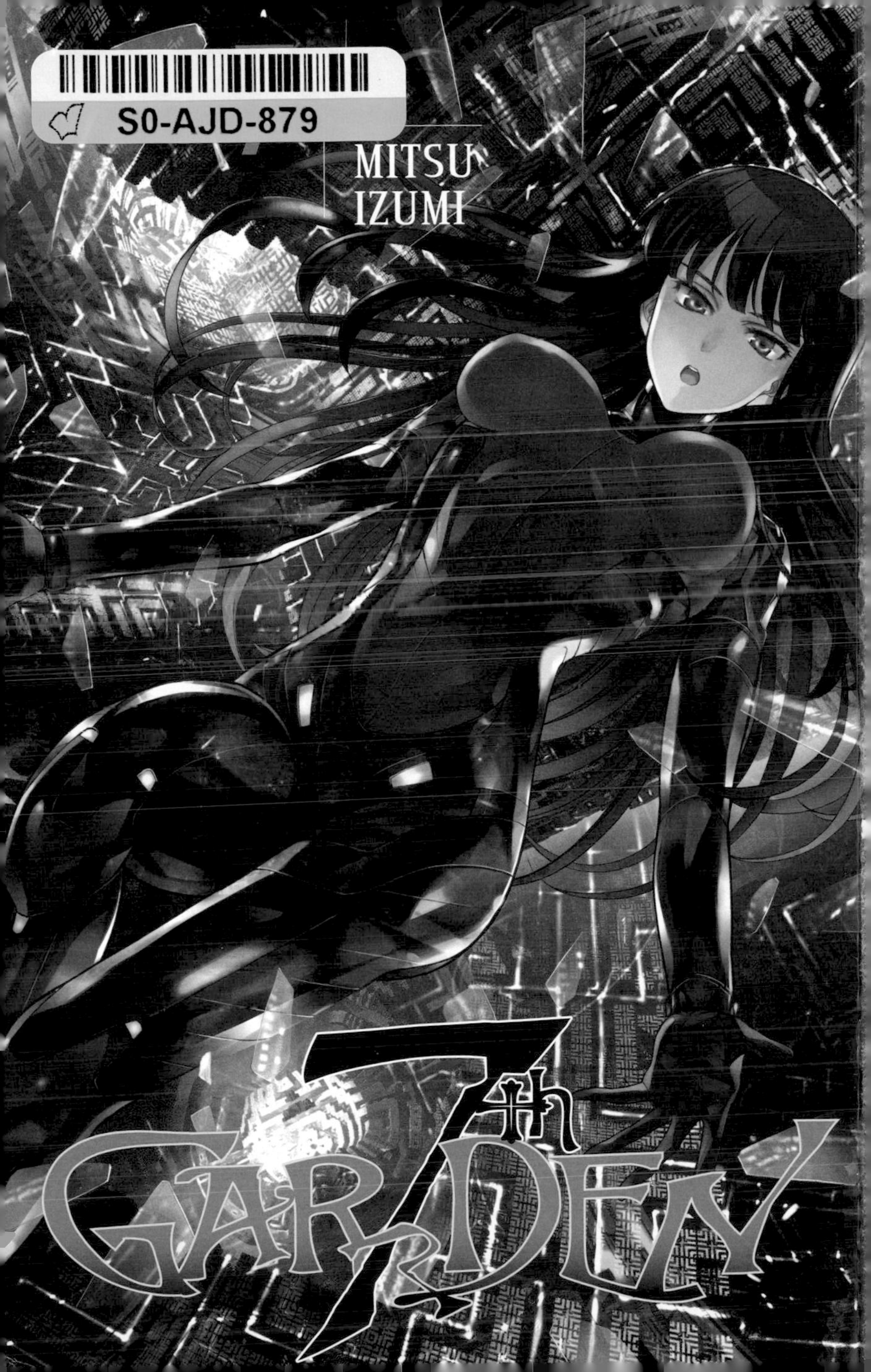
MITSU
IZUMI
7th
GARDEN

The fifth angel...

...shone the light of the stars into the darkness of the sky...

...to safeguard all of God's creatures.

7thGARDEN

CONTENTS

root. 25

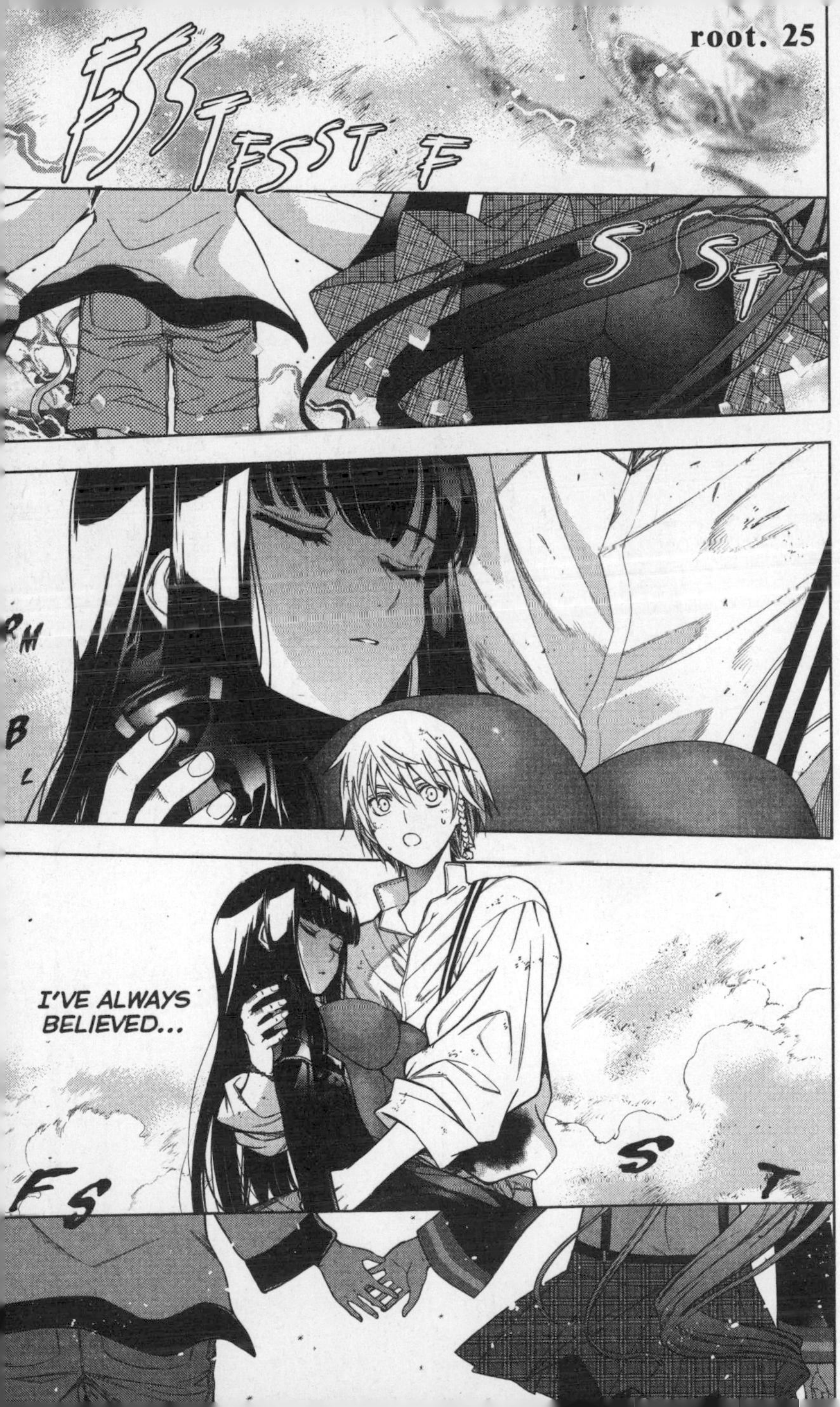
FSST
FSST
F
S ST
I'VE ALWAYS BELIEVED...
S T
FS

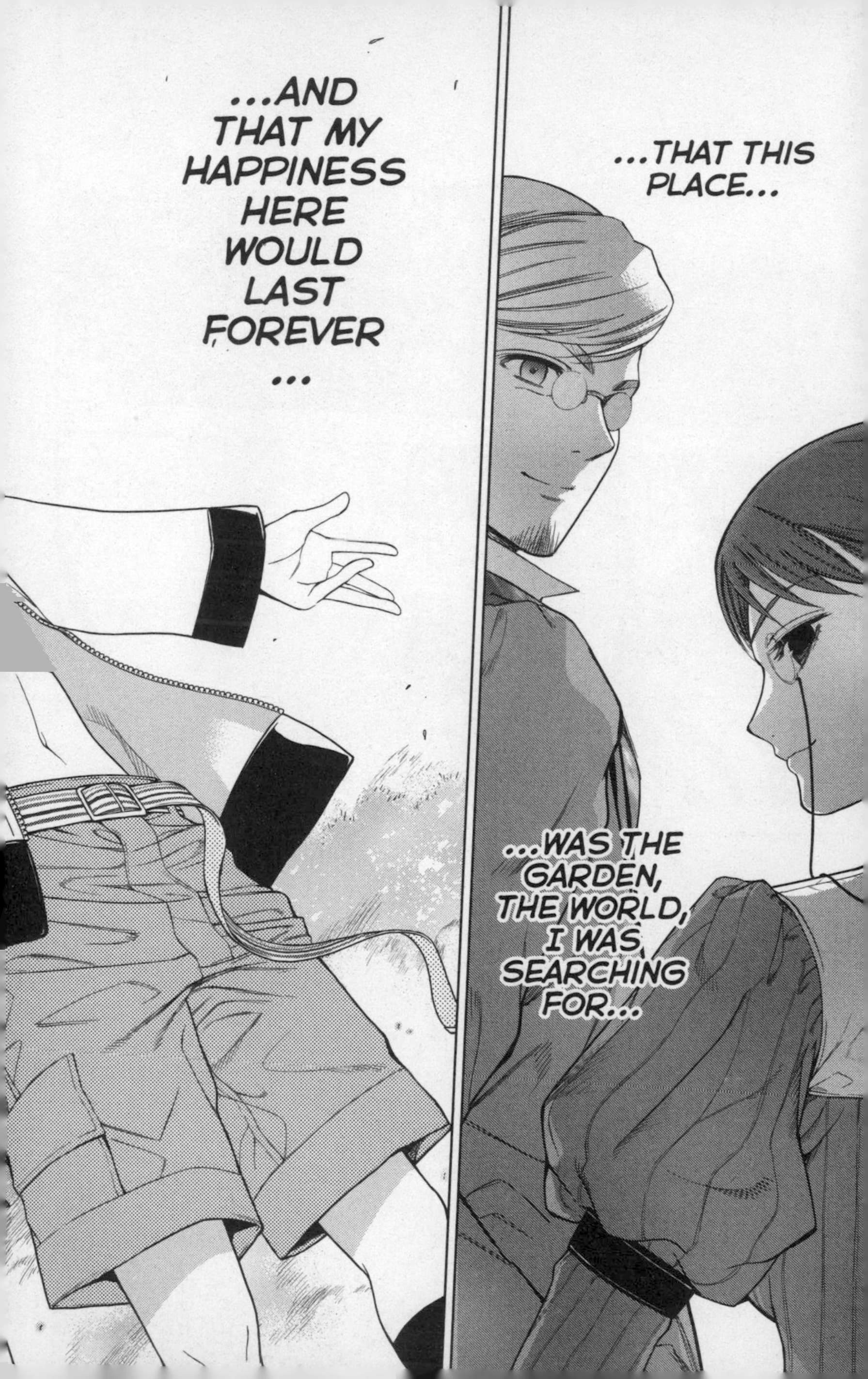
...THAT THIS PLACE...
...WAS THE GARDEN, THE WORLD, I WAS SEARCHING FOR...
...AND THAT MY HAPPINESS HERE WOULD LAST FOREVER...

root. 25 Cross Heart

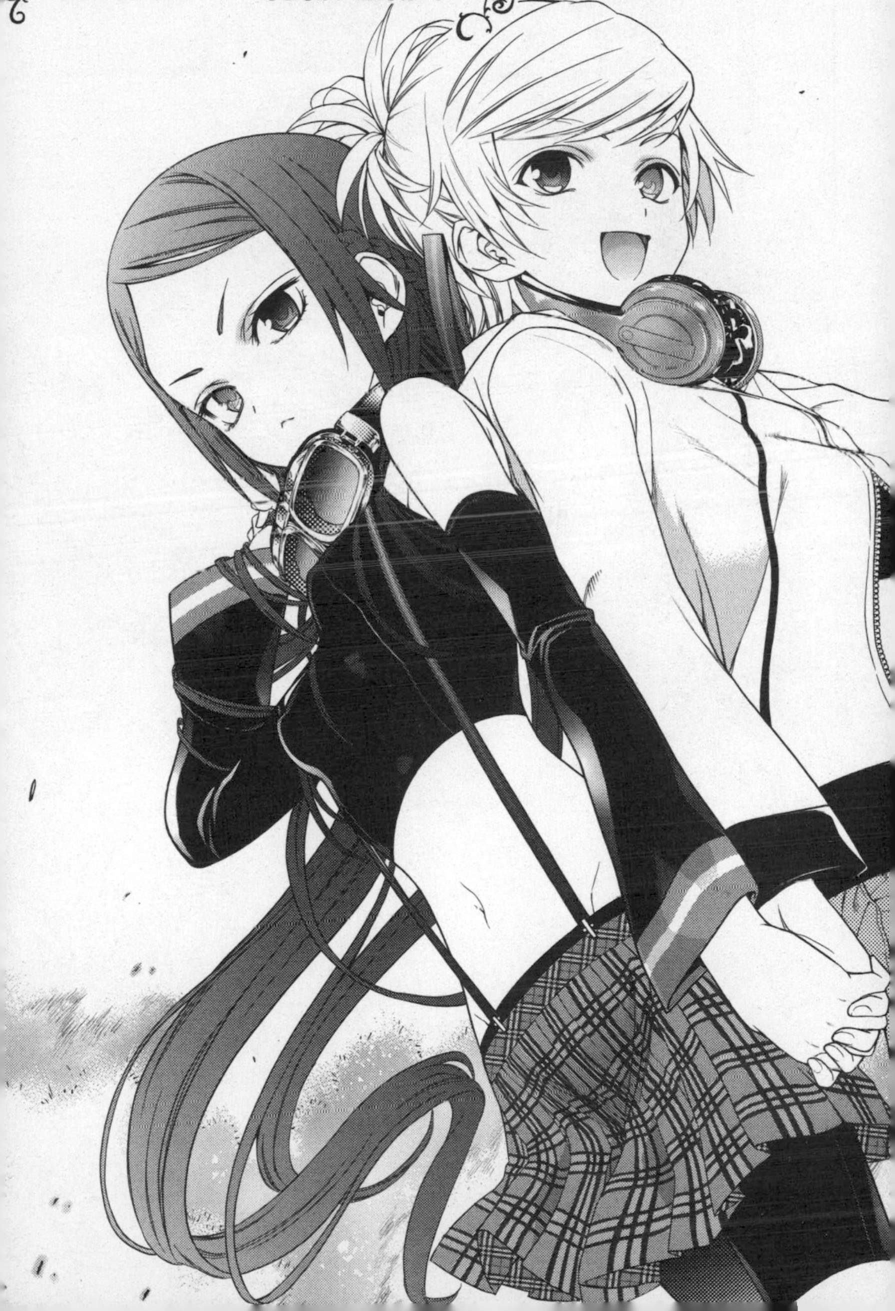

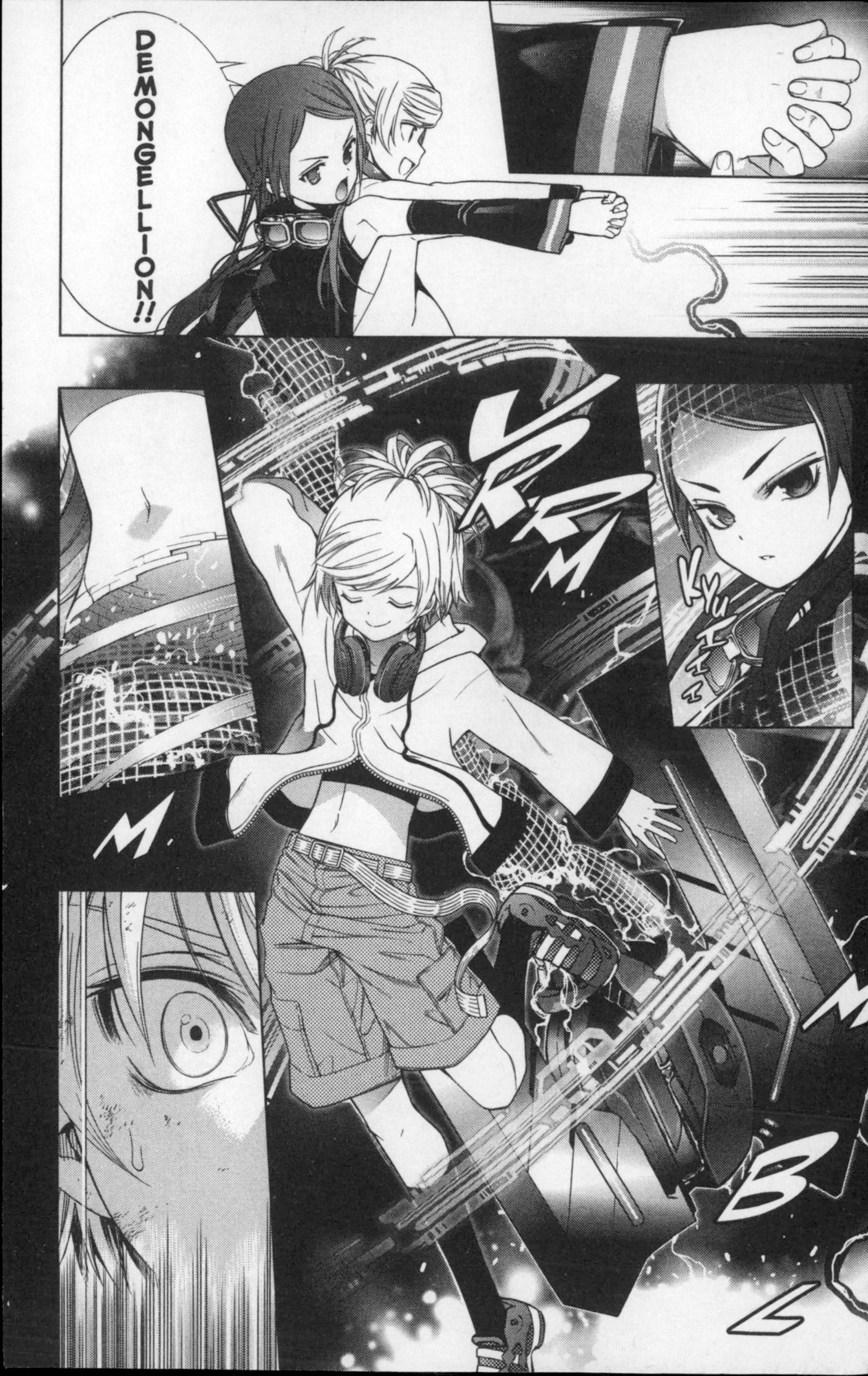
DEMONGELLION!!
KYUIIII

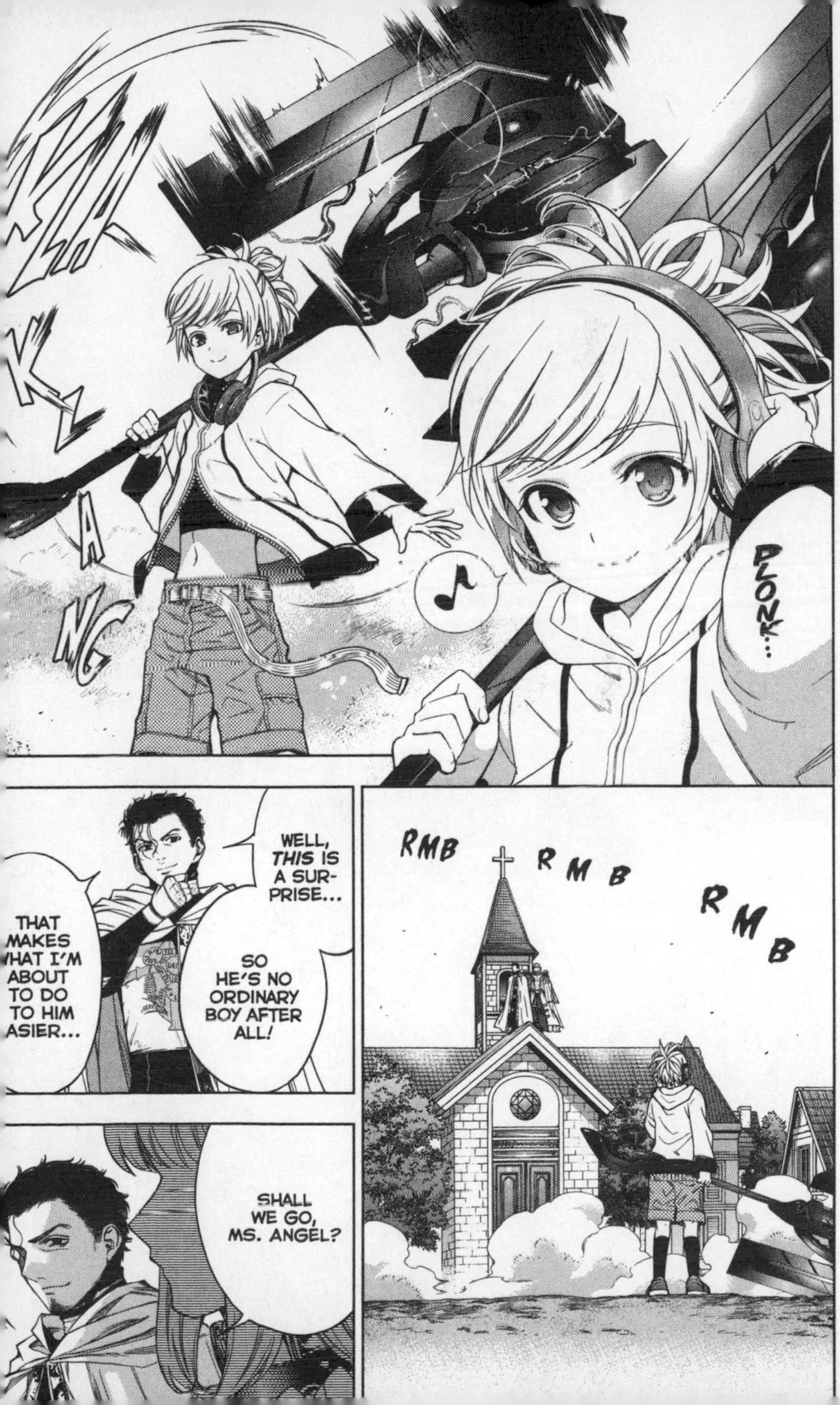

♪
PLONK...
RMB
RMB
RMB
WELL, THIS IS A SURPRISE...
SO HE'S NO ORDINARY BOY AFTER ALL!
THAT MAKES HAT I'M ABOUT TO DO TO HIM ASIER...
SHALL WE GO, MS. ANGEL?

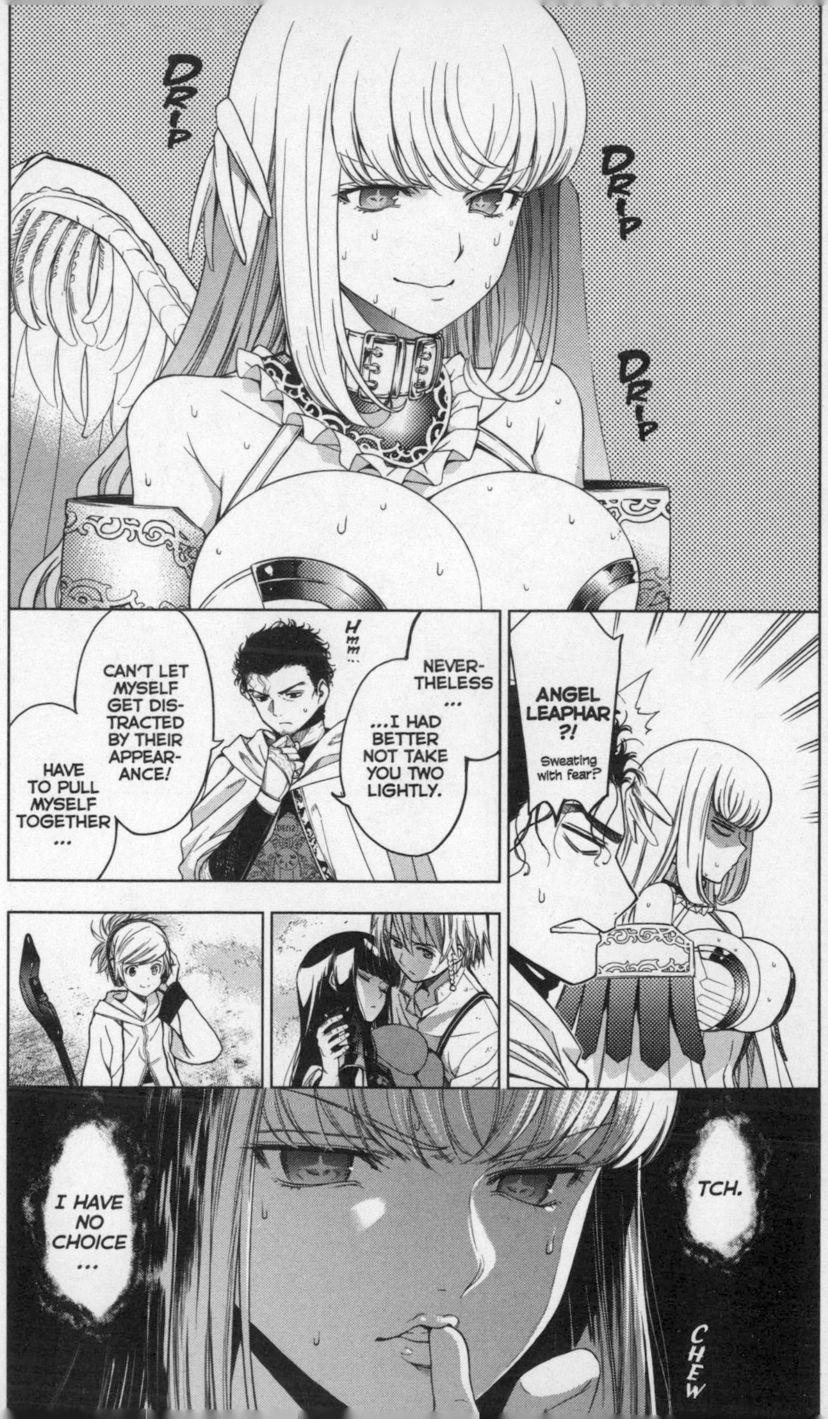
DRIP
DRIP
DRIP
ANGEL LEAPHAR?!
Sweating with fear?
Hmm...
NEVER-THELESS...
...I HAD BETTER NOT TAKE YOU TWO LIGHTLY.
CAN'T LET MYSELF GET DIS-TRACTED BY THEIR APPEAR-ANCE!
HAVE TO PULL MYSELF TOGETHER...
TCH.
CHEW
I HAVE NO CHOICE...

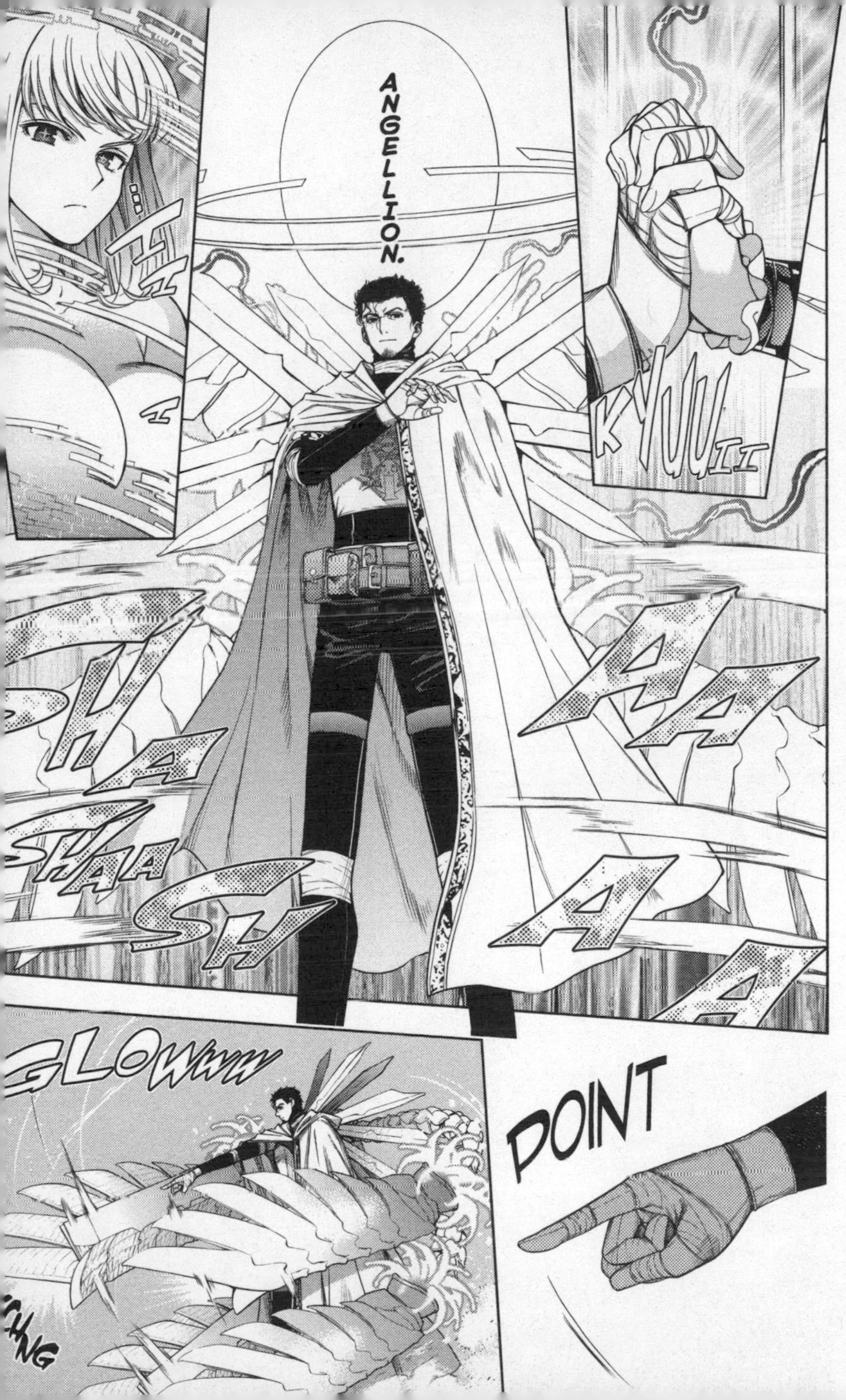
KYUUII
ANGELLION.
...
SHAA
SHAASH
AAAA
POINT
GLOWWW

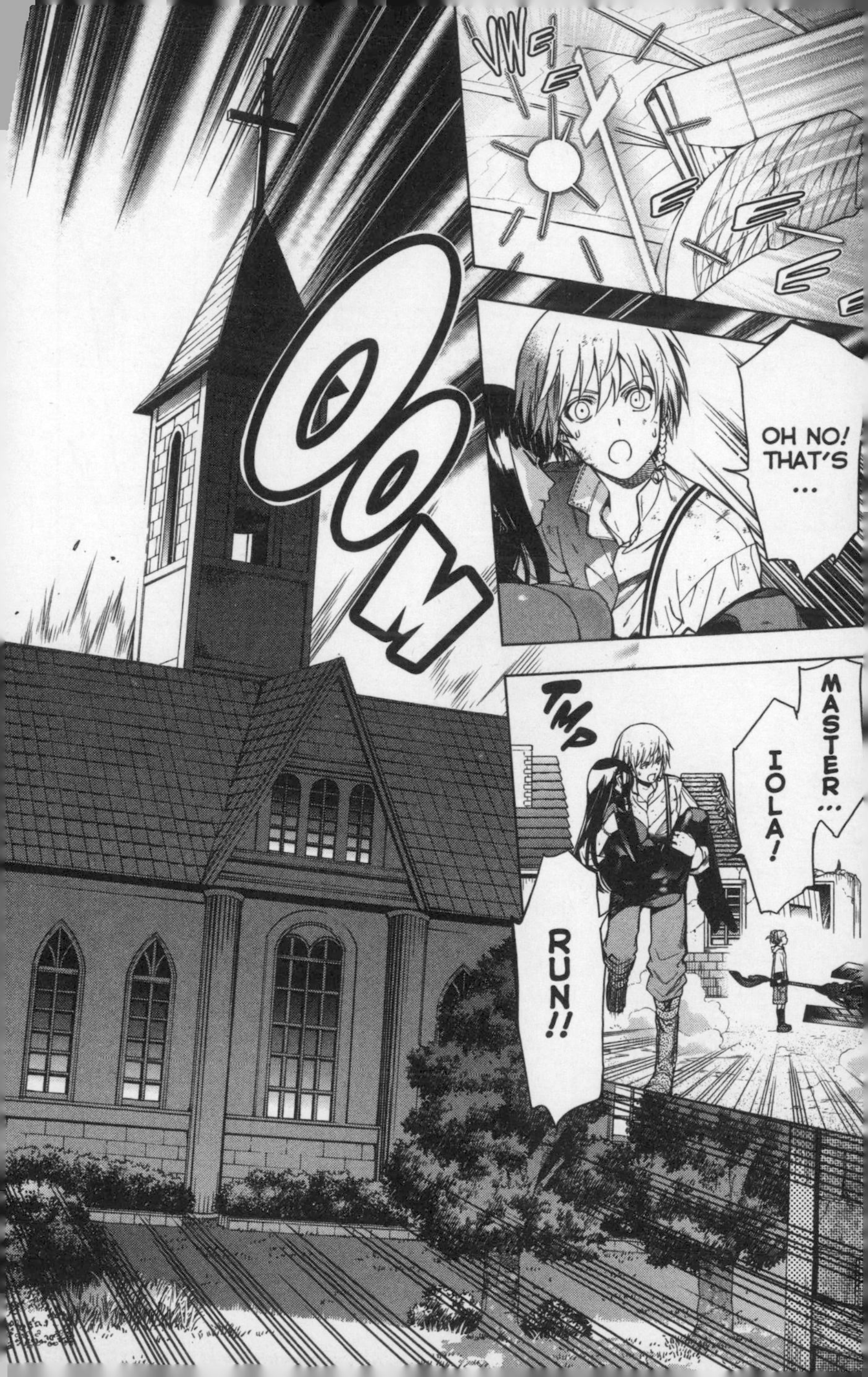
VWEEEEEEE
OH NO! THAT'S ...
MASTER ... IOLA!
TMP
RUN!!
BOOM

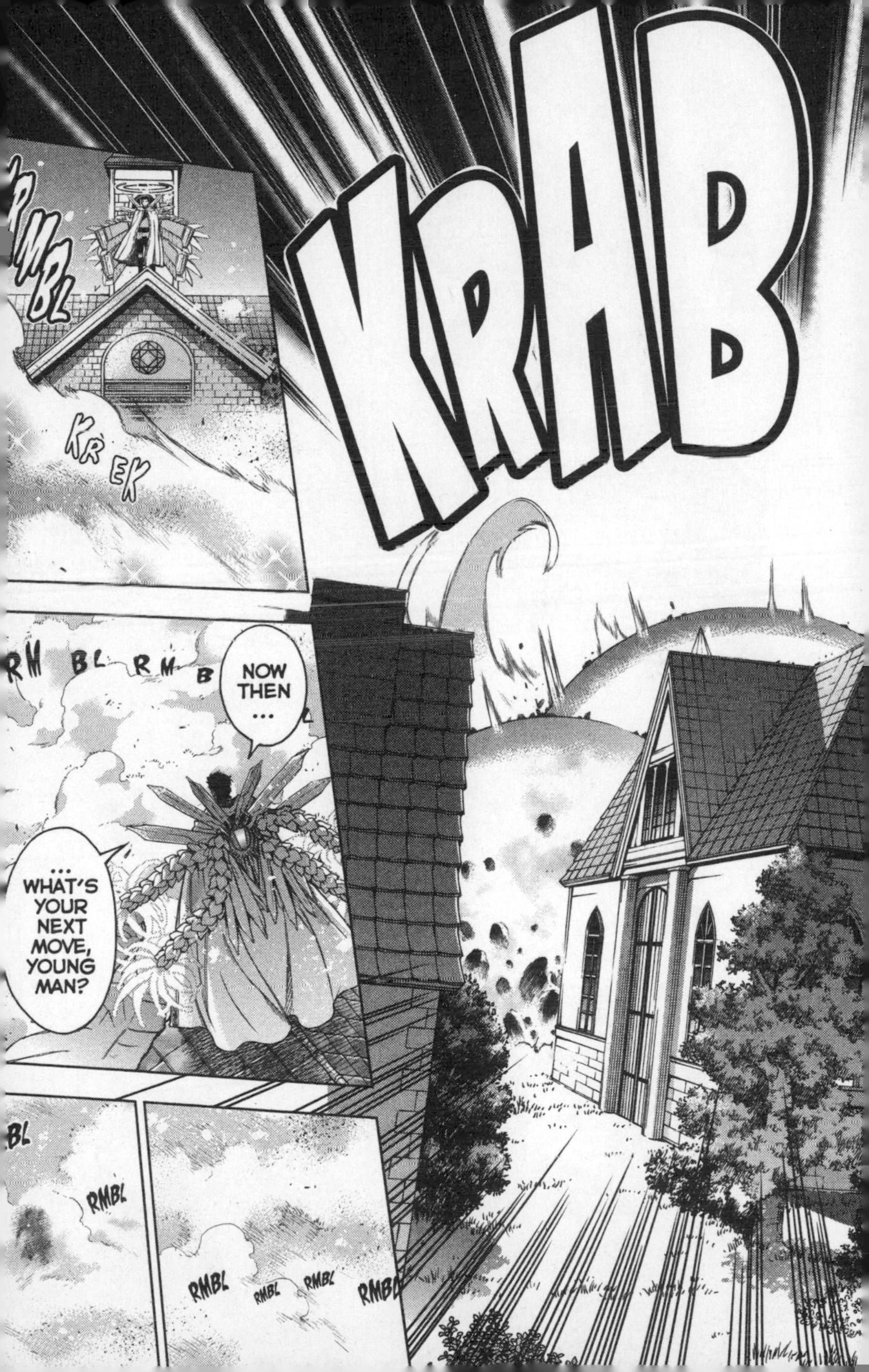
KRAB
KREK
NOW THEN ...
... WHAT'S YOUR NEXT MOVE, YOUNG MAN?
RMBL
RMBL
RMBL
RMBL
RMBL

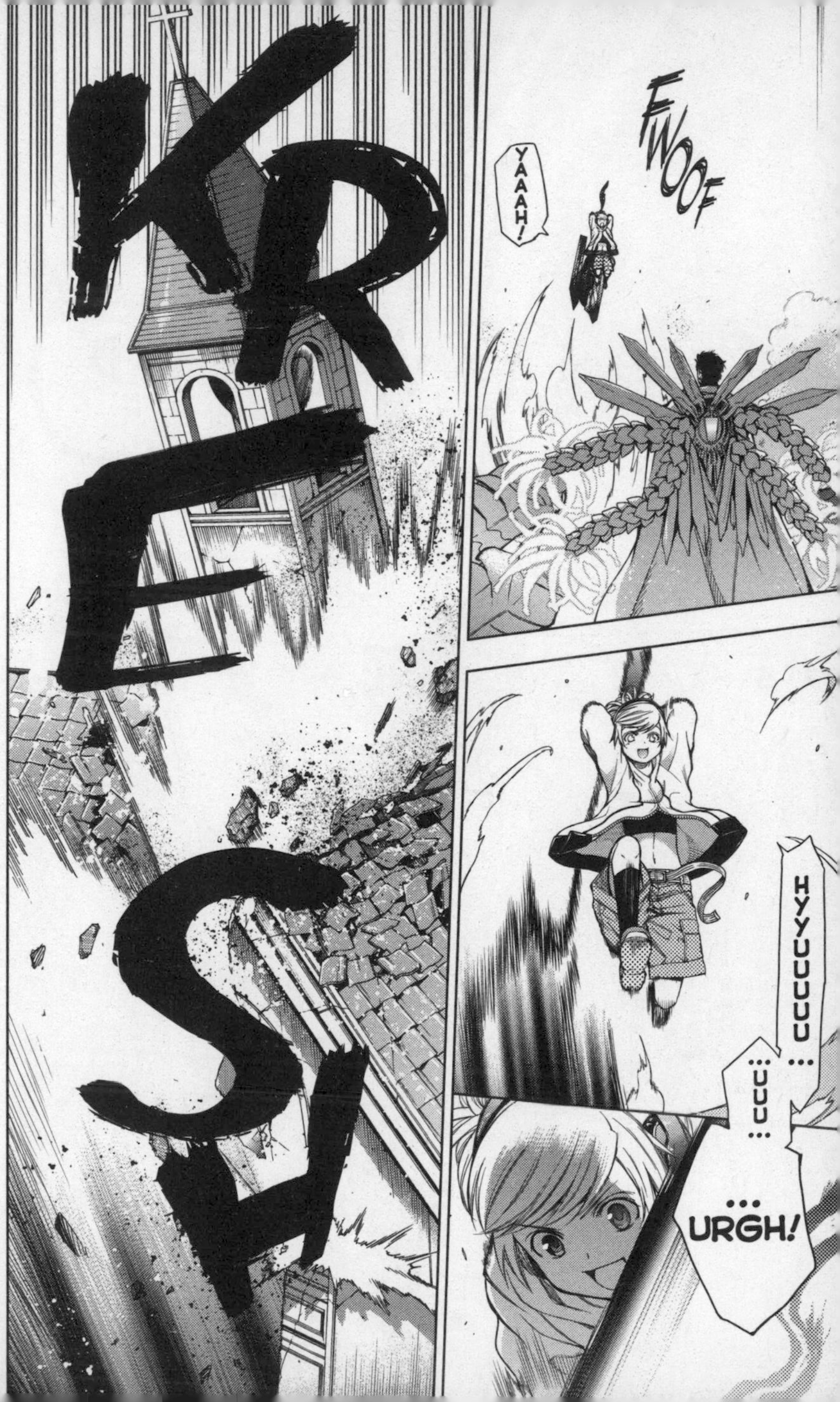
FWOOF
YAAAH!
HYYUUUUU...
...UUU...
...URGH!
KRESH

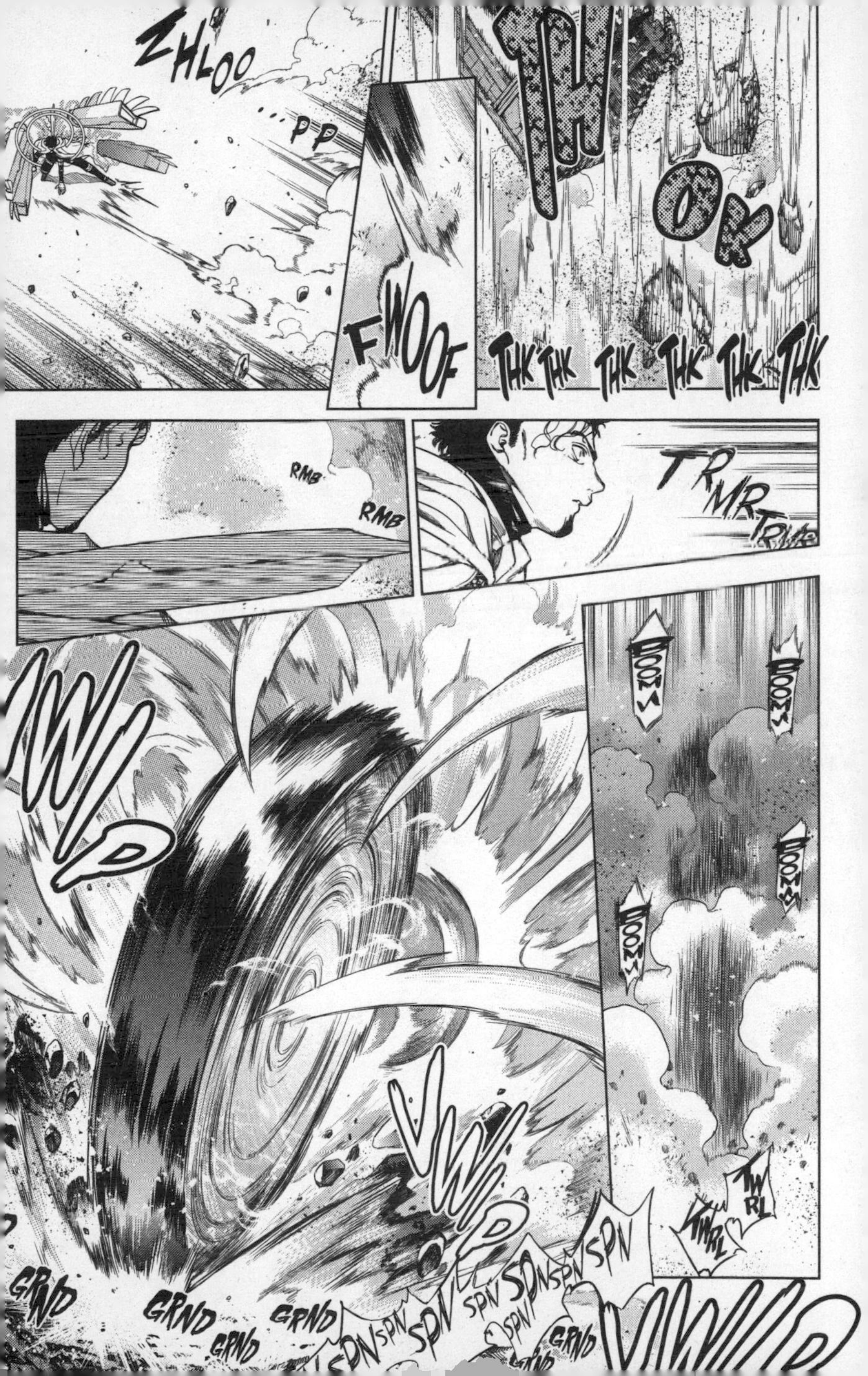
THOK
THK THK THK THK THK THK
FWOOF
ZHLOO
...PP
TRMR TRMR
RMB
RMB
BOOMM
BOOMM
BOOMM
BOOMM
TWRL
TWRL
VWWIP
SPN SPN SPN SPN SPN SPN SPN SPN
VWIP
GRND GRND GRND GRND GRND GRND
WHIP

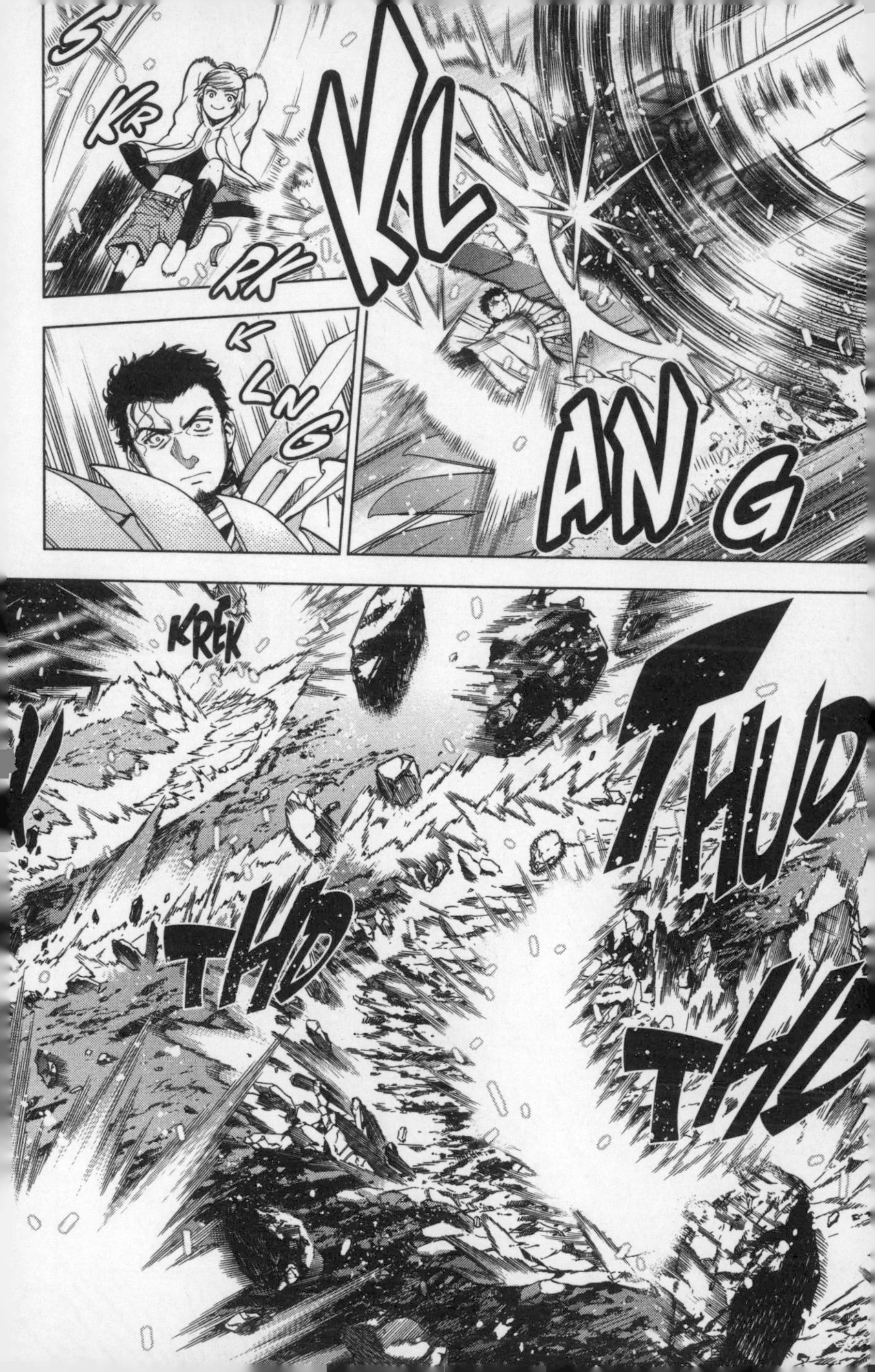

KL
ANG
S
KR
RK
K
LNG
THUD
KREK
THD

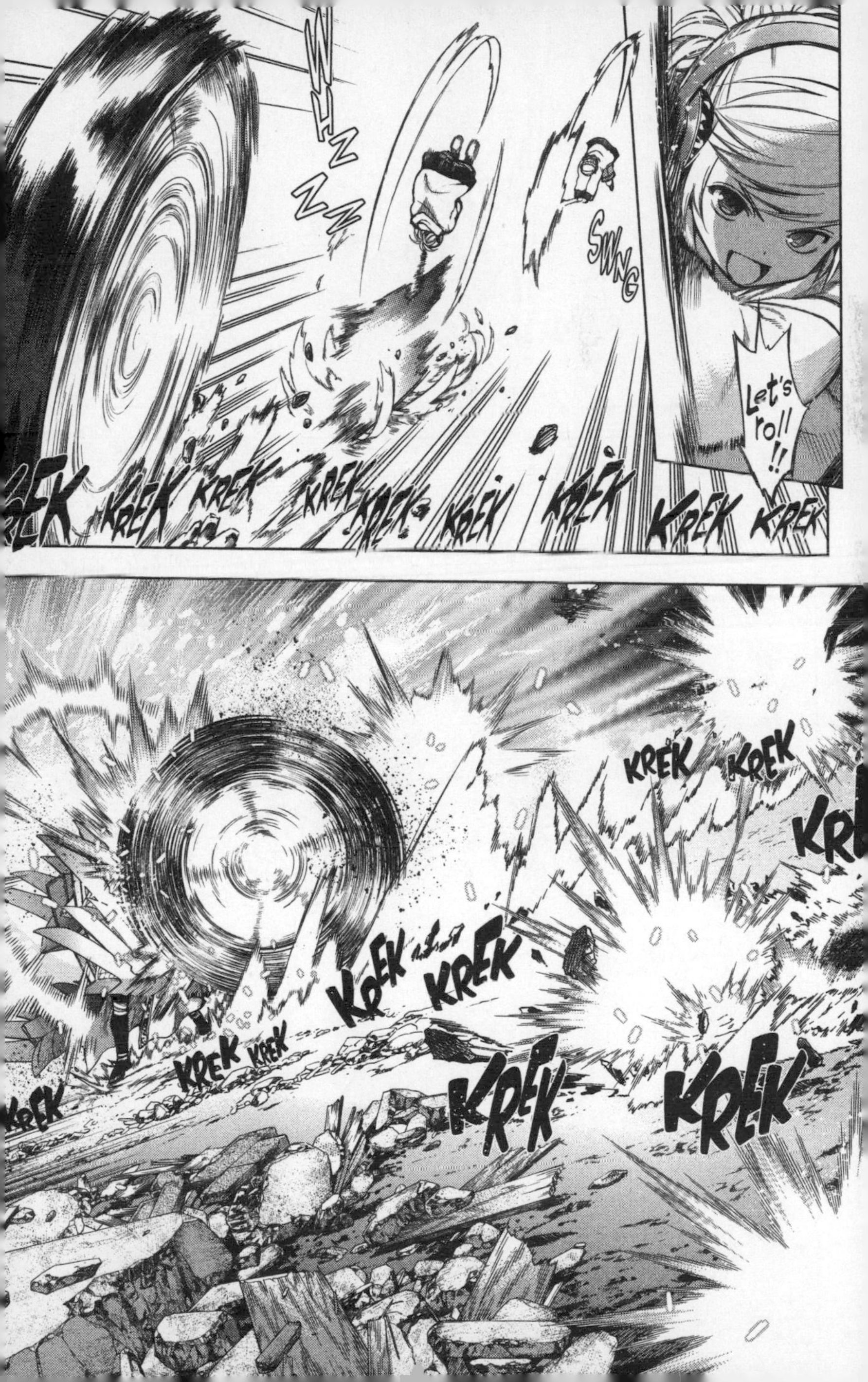
Let's roll!!
SWING
WHZZZ
KREK KREK KREK KREK KREK KREK KREK KREK KREK
KREK KREK
KREK
KREK KREK
KREK KREK
KREK
KREK KREK

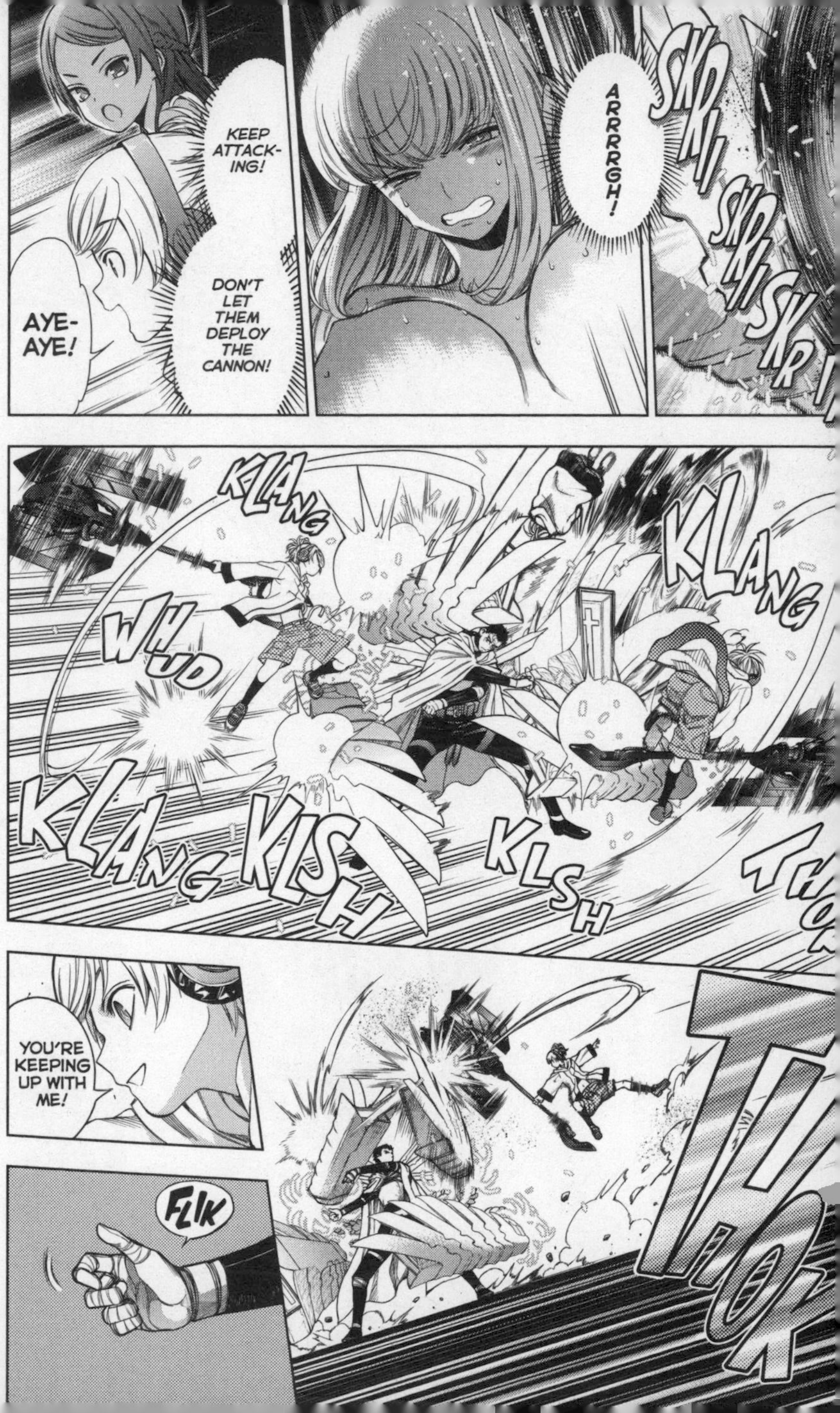
SKRI SKRI SKRI SKRI
ARRRRGH!
KEEP ATTACK-ING!
DON'T LET THEM DEPLOY THE CANNON!
AYE-AYE!
KLANG
KLSH
KLANG
WHUD
KLISH
KLANG
THOK
YOU'RE KEEPING UP WITH ME!
FLIK

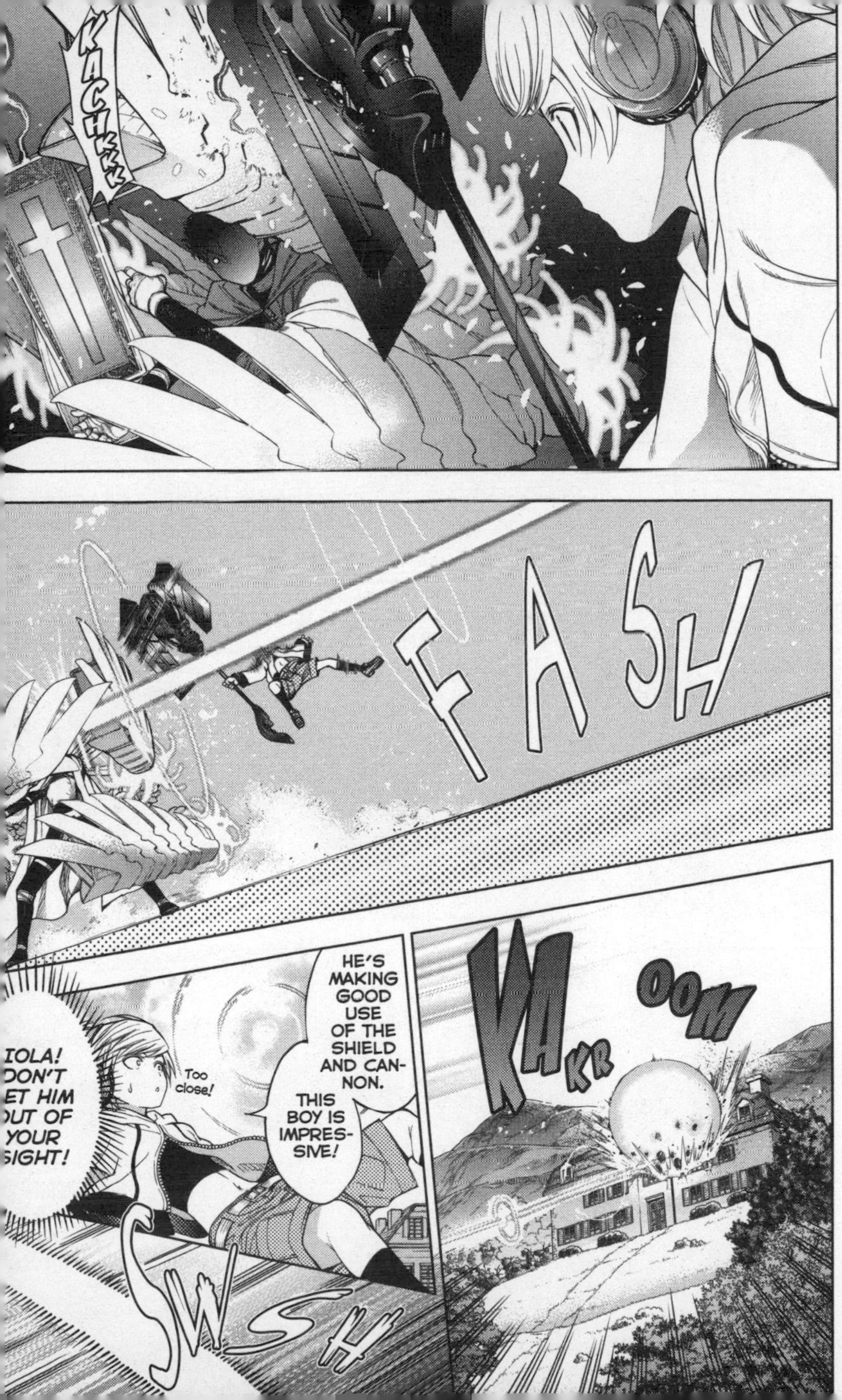
KACHKKK
FASH
KAKROOM
HE'S MAKING GOOD USE OF THE SHIELD AND CANNON.
THIS BOY IS IMPRESSIVE!
Too close!
IOLA! DON'T ET HIM OUT OF YOUR SIGHT!
SWSH

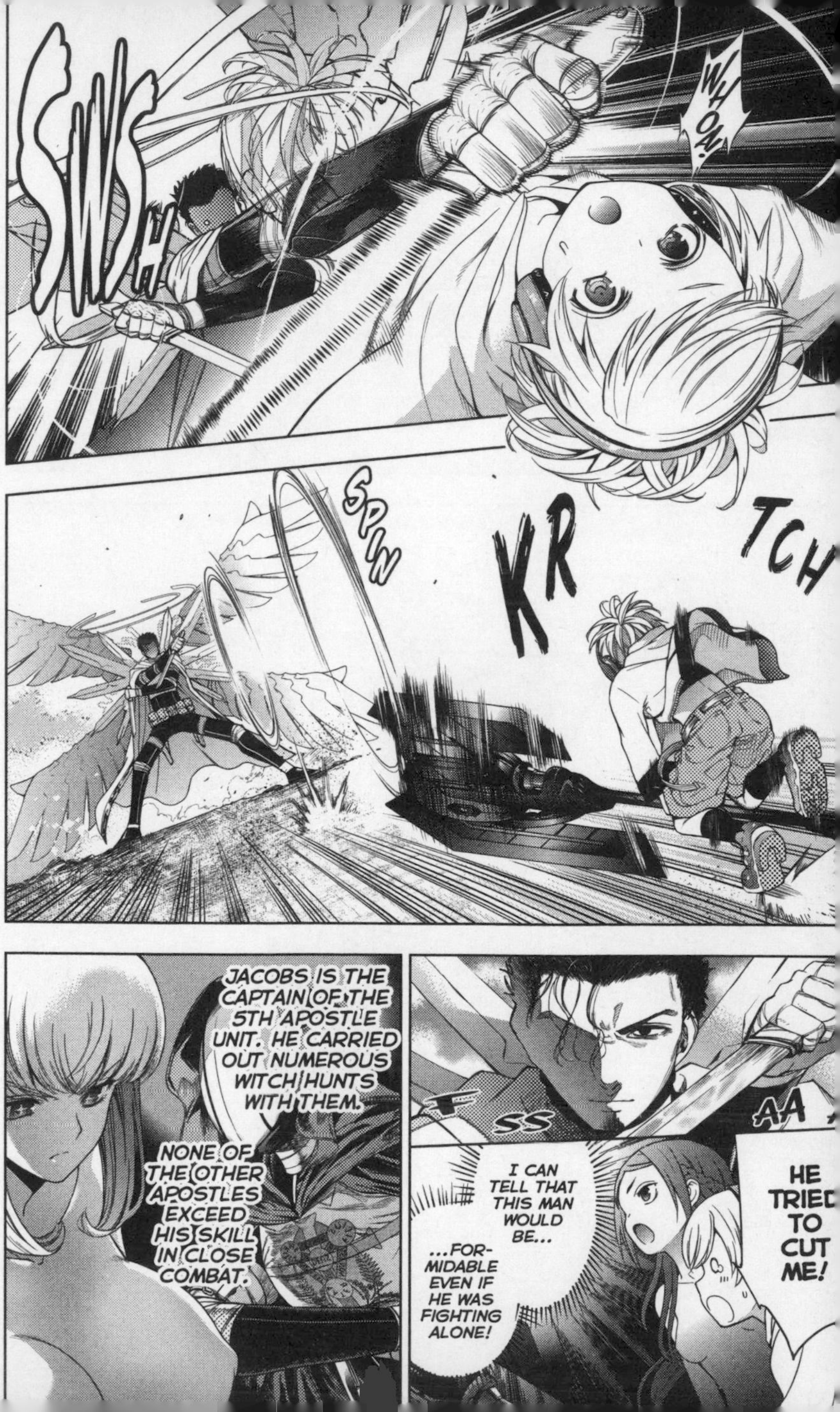
WHOOM!
SWSH
KR TCH
SPIN
FSS
AA
HE TRIED TO CUT ME!
I CAN TELL THAT THIS MAN WOULD BE...
...FORMIDABLE EVEN IF HE WAS FIGHTING ALONE!
JACOBS IS THE CAPTAIN OF THE 5TH APOSTLE UNIT. HE CARRIED OUT NUMEROUS WITCH HUNTS WITH THEM.
NONE OF THE OTHER APOSTLES EXCEED HIS SKILL IN CLOSE COMBAT.

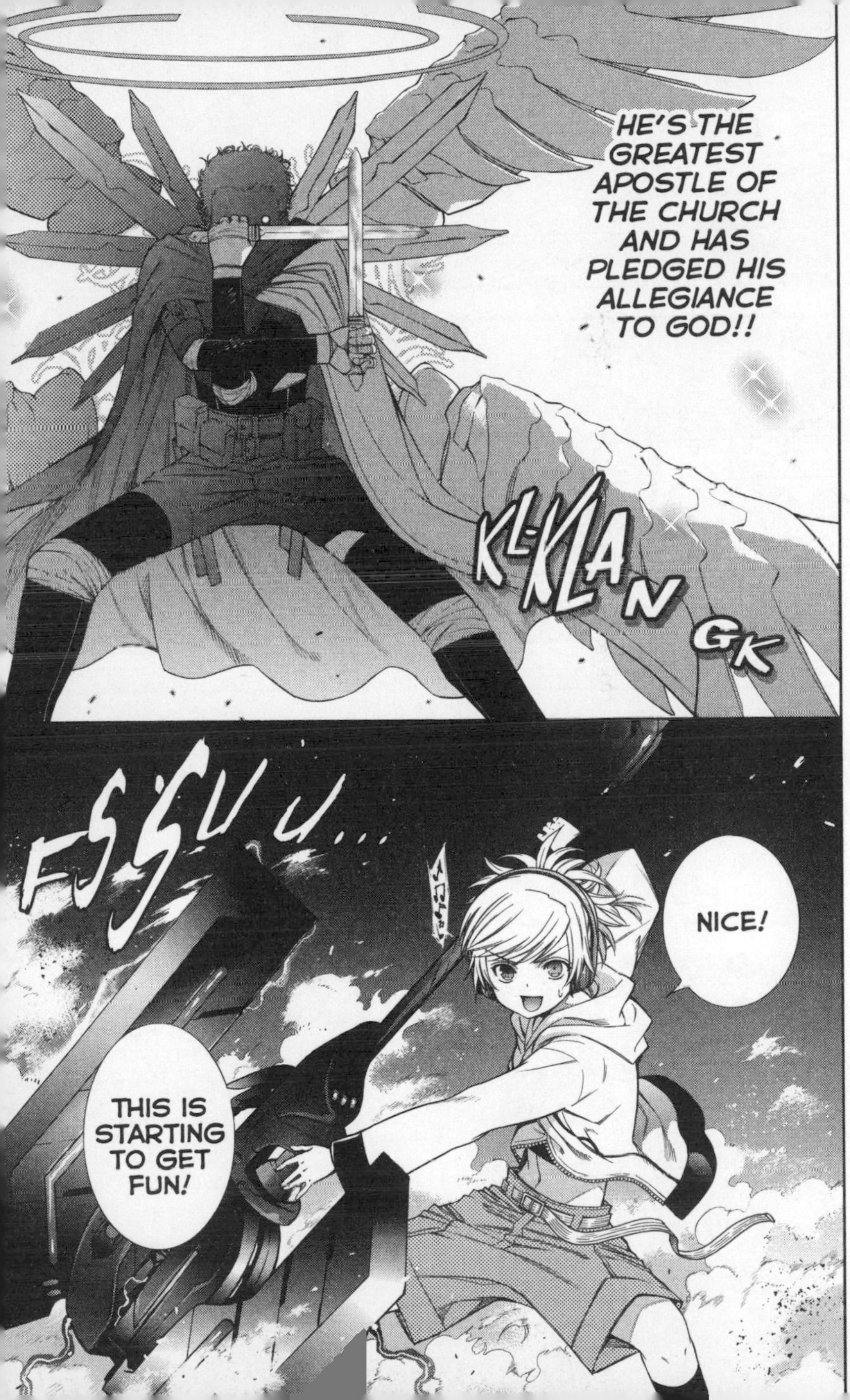
HE'S THE GREATEST APOSTLE OF THE CHURCH AND HAS PLEDGED HIS ALLEGIANCE TO GOD!!
KL-KLANNGK
FSSUU...
NICE!
THIS IS STARTING TO GET FUN!

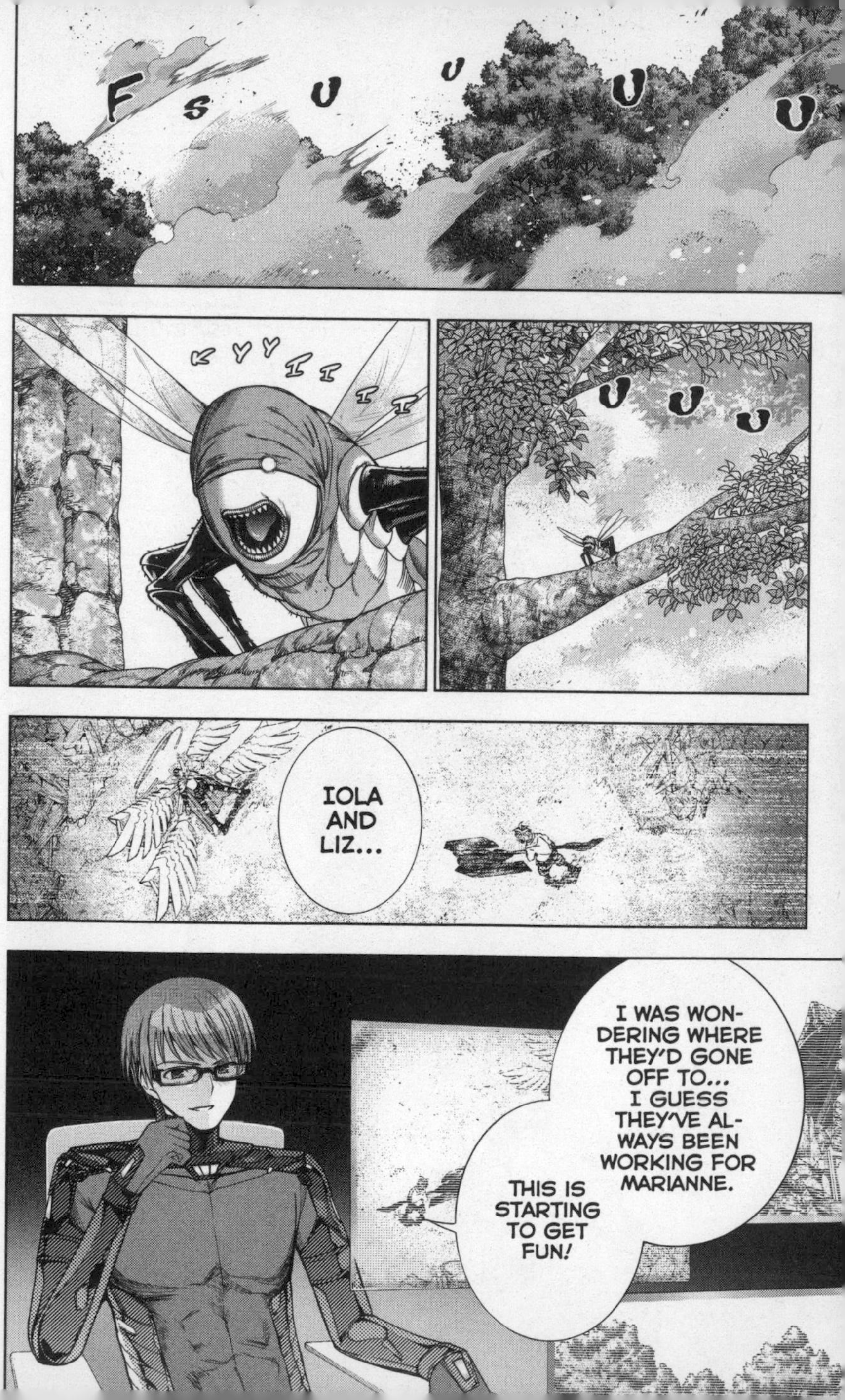
FSUUUU
UUU
KYYIIII
IOLA AND LIZ...
I WAS WONDERING WHERE THEY'D GONE OFF TO... I GUESS THEY'VE ALWAYS BEEN WORKING FOR MARIANNE.
THIS IS STARTING TO GET FUN!

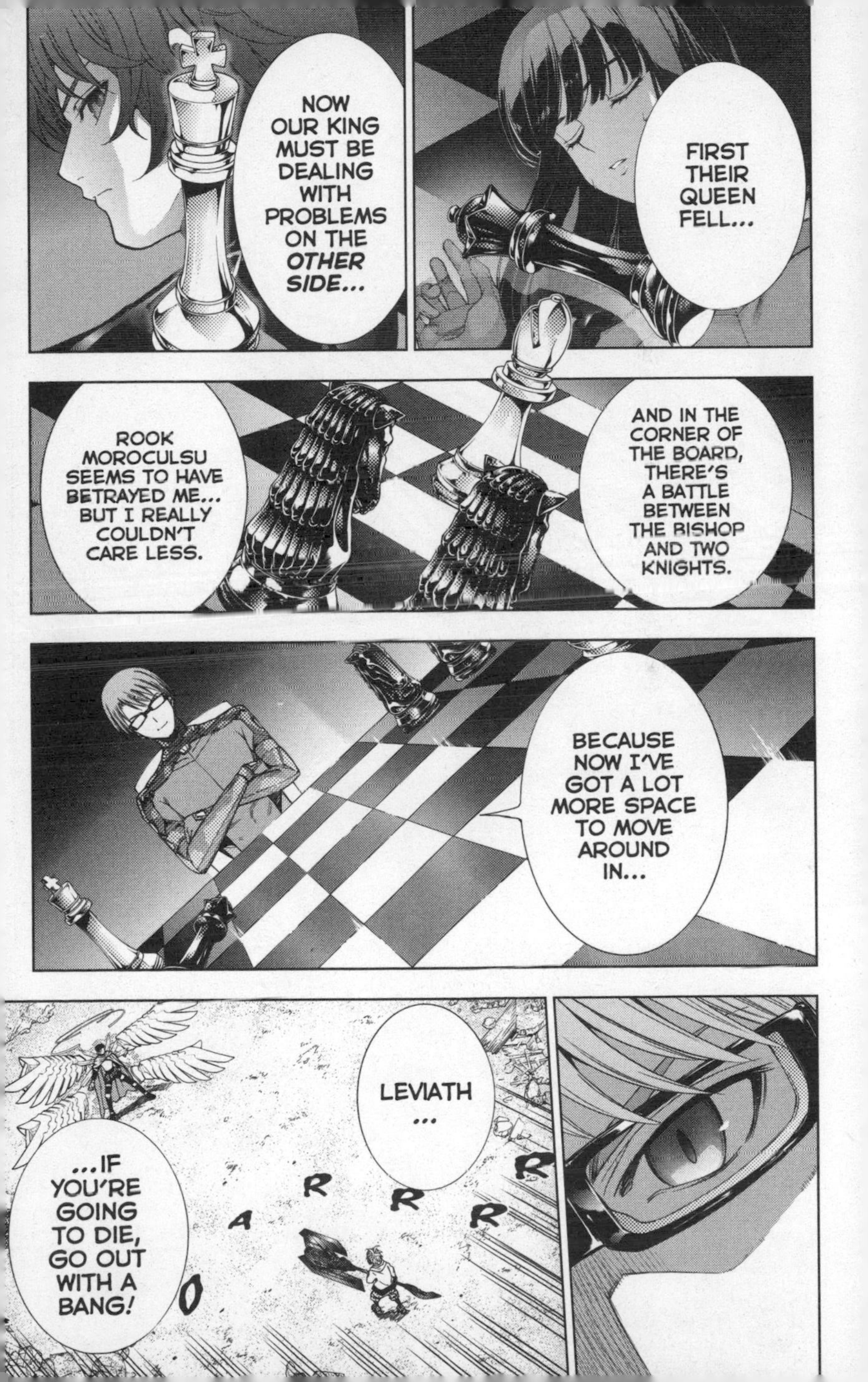
FIRST THEIR QUEEN FELL...
NOW OUR KING MUST BE DEALING WITH PROBLEMS ON THE *OTHER* SIDE...
AND IN THE CORNER OF THE BOARD, THERE'S A BATTLE BETWEEN THE BISHOP AND TWO KNIGHTS.
ROOK MOROCULSU SEEMS TO HAVE BETRAYED ME... BUT I REALLY COULDN'T CARE LESS.
BECAUSE NOW I'VE GOT A LOT MORE SPACE TO MOVE AROUND IN...
LEVIATH...
OARRRR
...IF YOU'RE GOING TO DIE, GO OUT WITH A BANG!

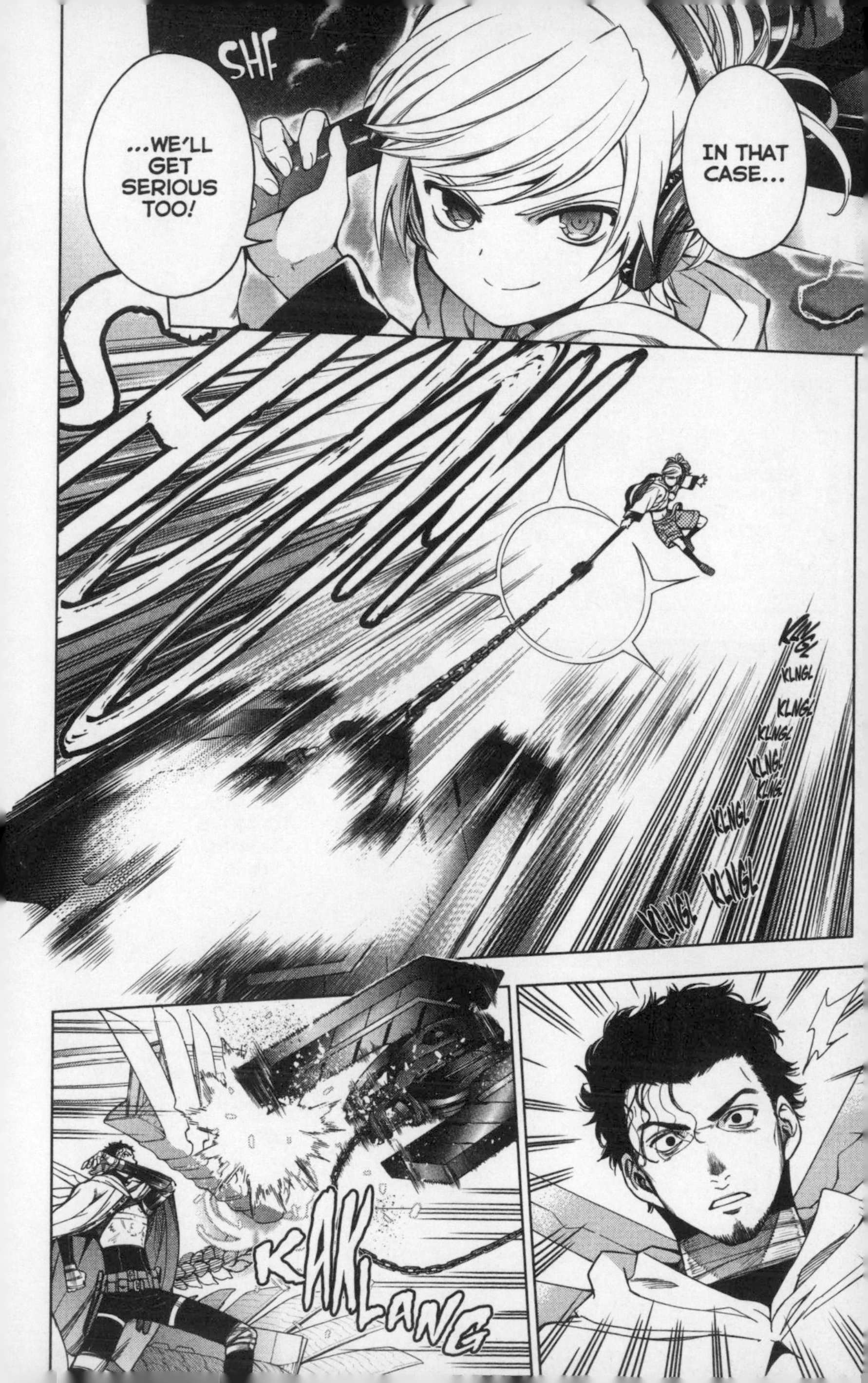
IN THAT CASE...
SHF
...WE'LL GET SERIOUS TOO!
KLNGL
KLNGL
KLNGL
KLNGL
KLNGL
KLNG
KLNGL
KLNGL
KLNGL
KAKLANG

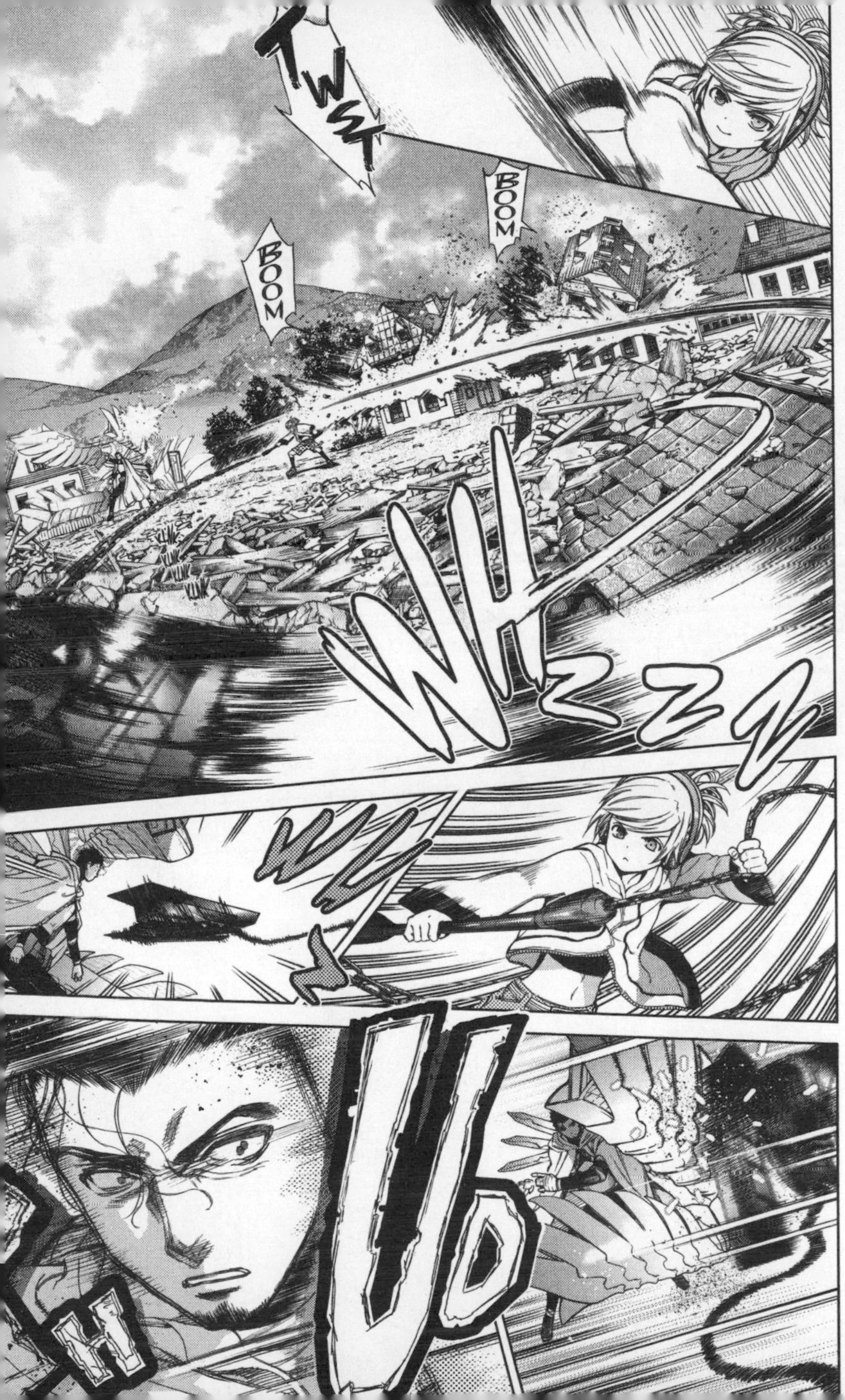
TWST
BOOM
BOOM
KLINK
KLINK
KLINK
KLINK
WHZZZN

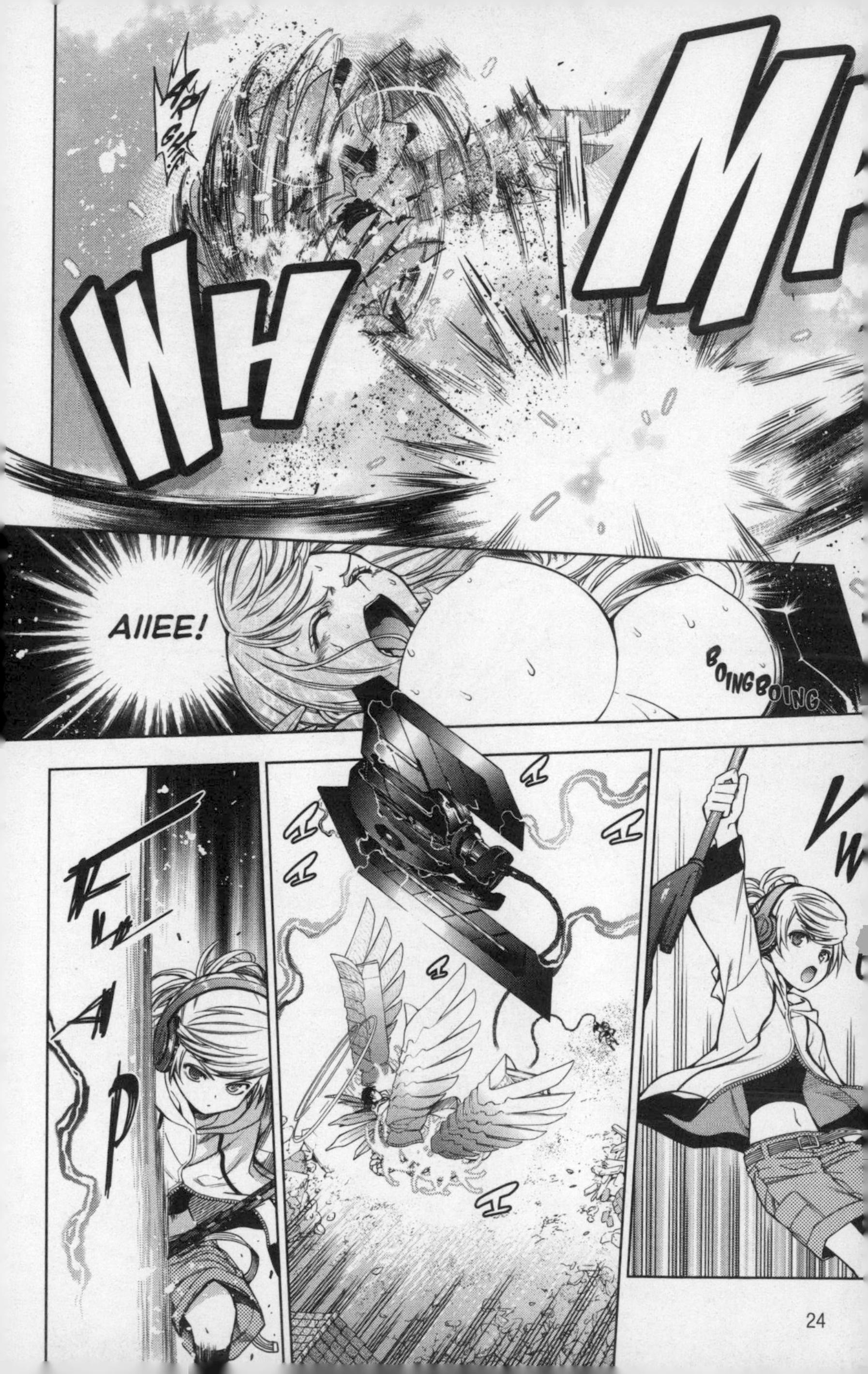

M
WH
ARGH!!
BOINGBOING
AIIEE!

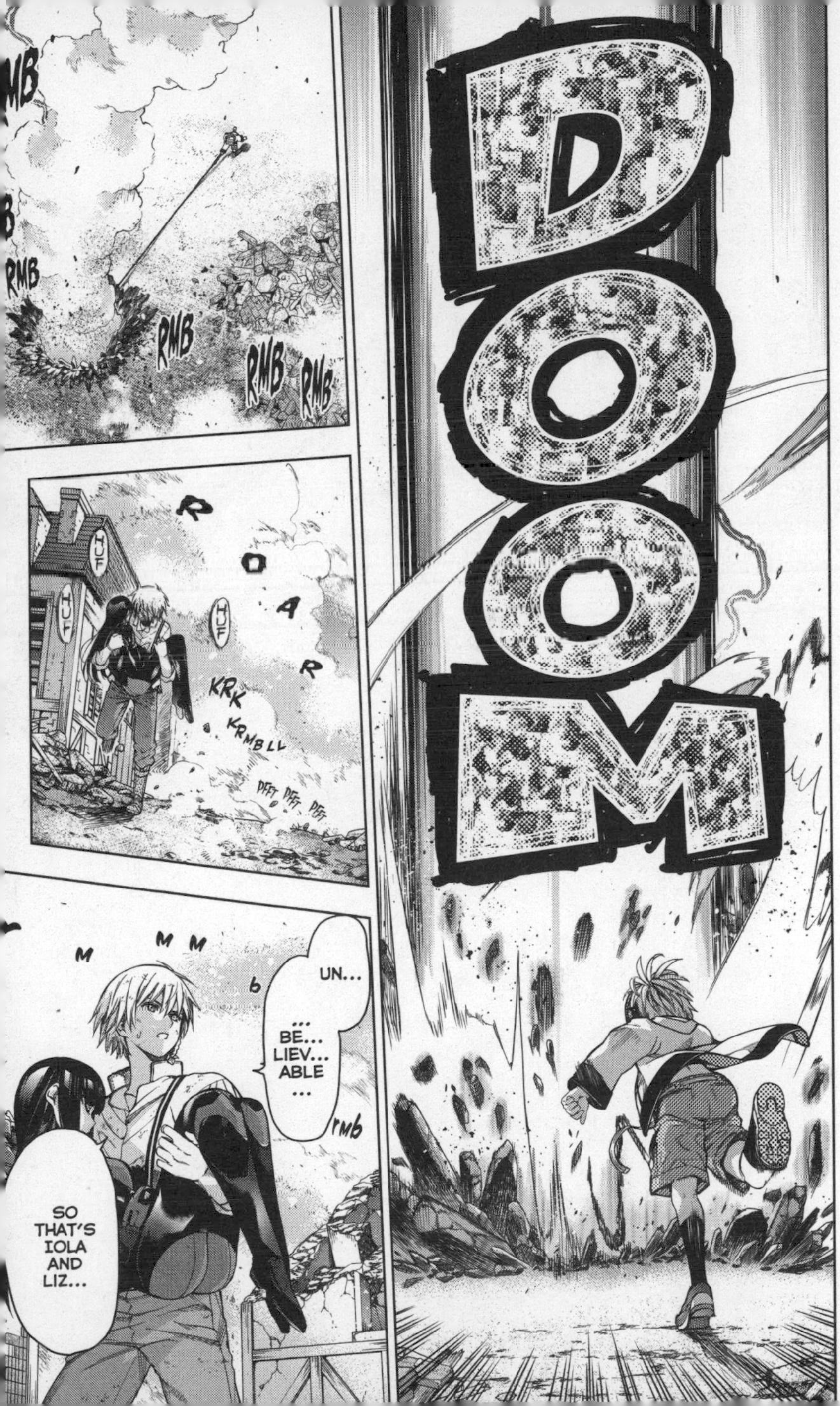
DOOM
RMB
RMB
RMB
RMB
RMB
RMB
ROAR
HUF
HUF
HUF
KRK
KRMBLL
PFFT PFFT PFFT
MMMb
UN...
... BE... LIEV... ABLE ...
rmb
SO THAT'S IOLA AND LIZ...

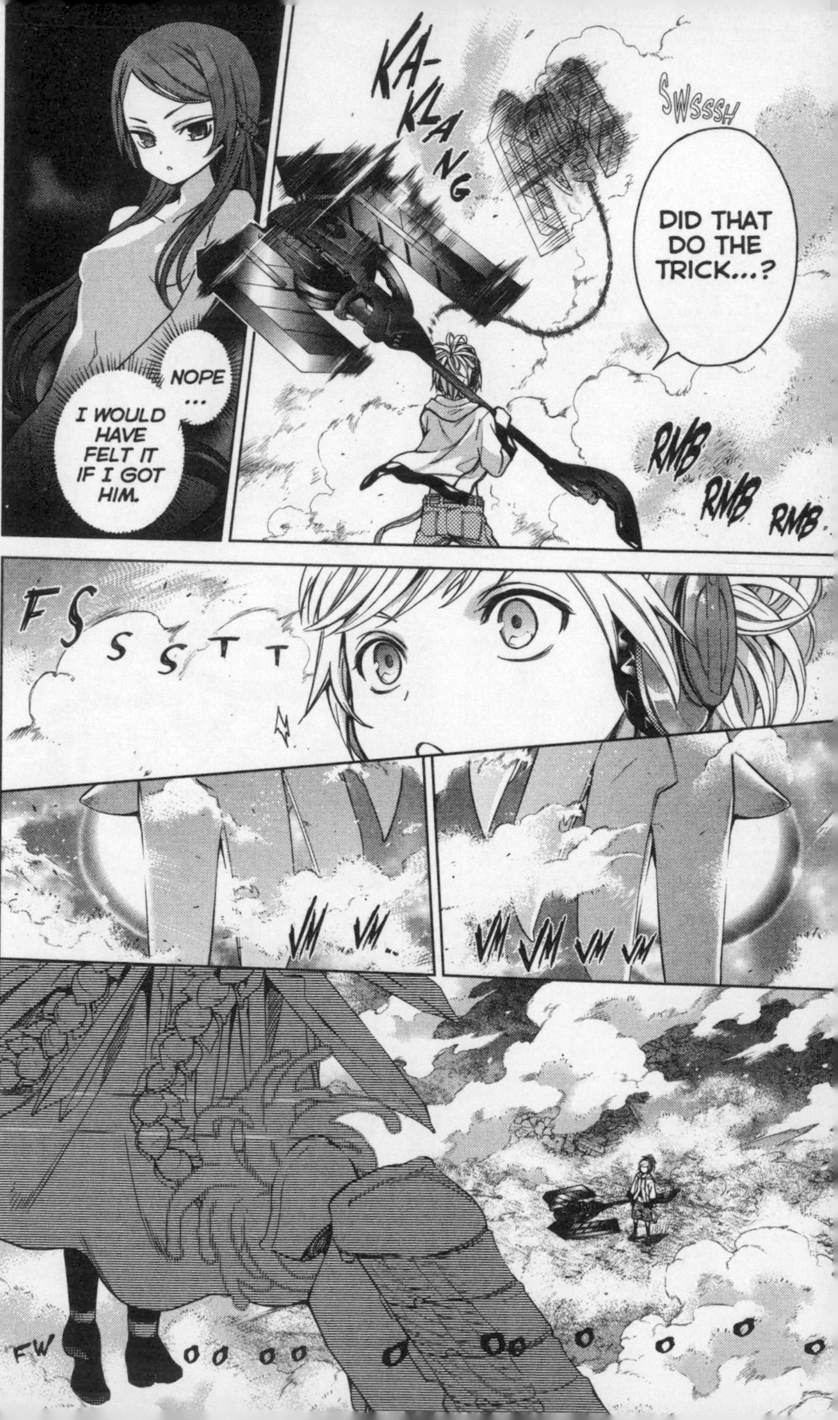
KA-KLANG
SWSSSH
DID THAT DO THE TRICK...?
RMB RMB RMB
NOPE...
I WOULD HAVE FELT IT IF I GOT HIM.
FSSSTTT
VM VM VM VM
VM VM..
FWOOOOOOOOOOOO

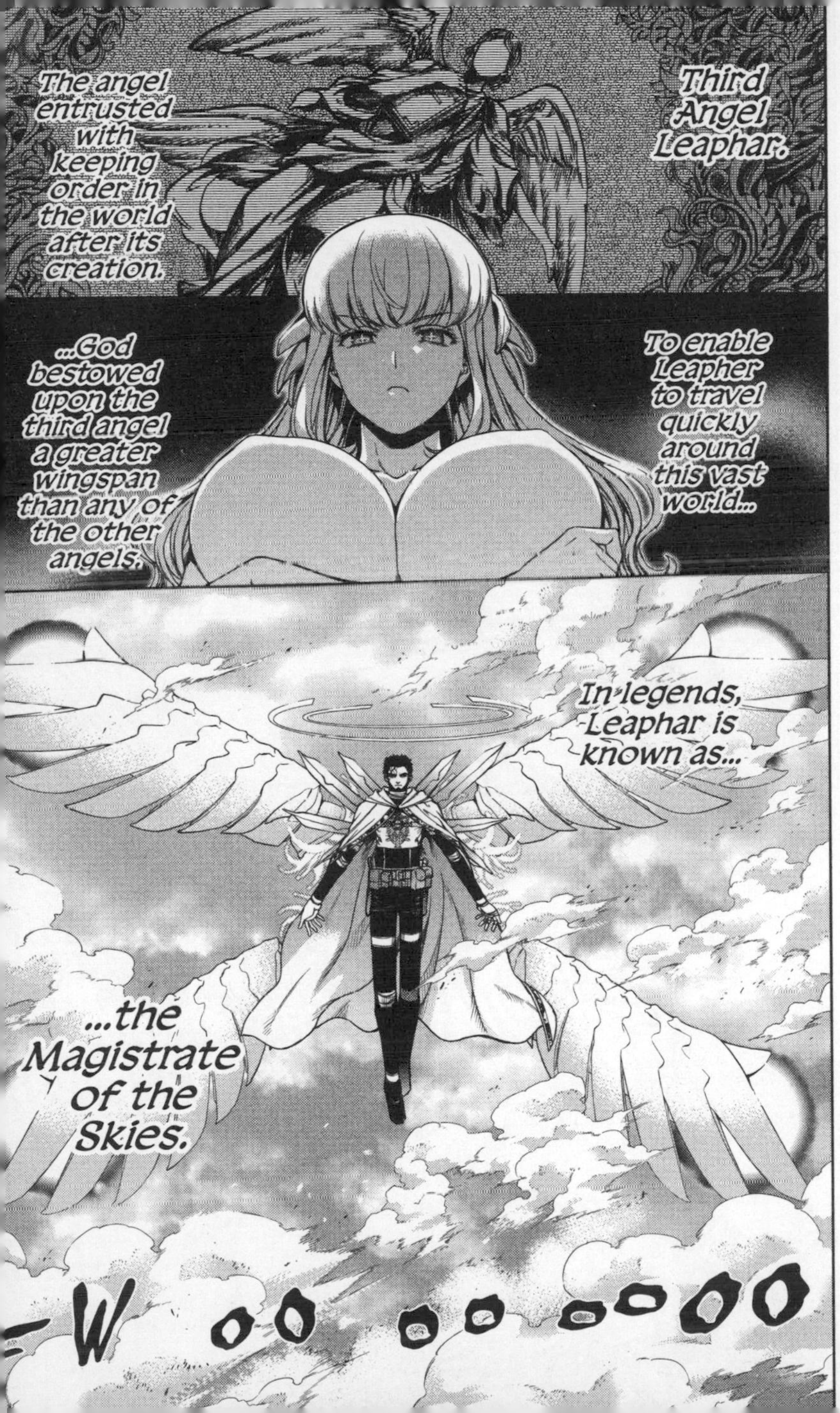
Third Angel Leaphar.
The angel entrusted with keeping order in the world after its creation.
To enable Leapher to travel quickly around this vast world...
...God bestowed upon the third angel a greater wingspan than any of the other angels.
In legends, Leaphar is known as...
...the Magistrate of the Skies.
Woooooooooo

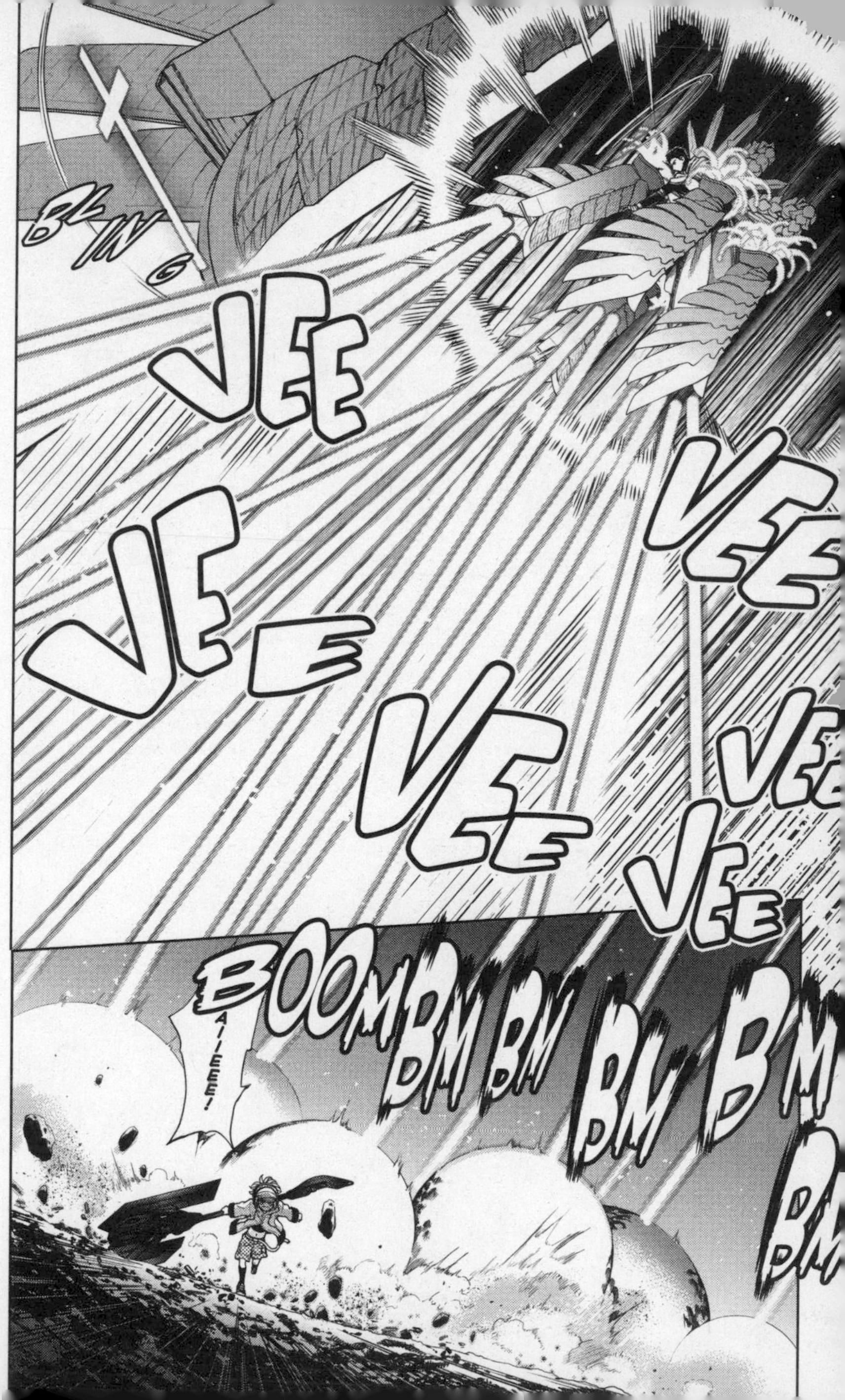
VEEE
BLING
VEEE
VEEE
VEE
VEEE
VEEE
BOOM
BM BM BM BM BM BM BM
AIIEEE!

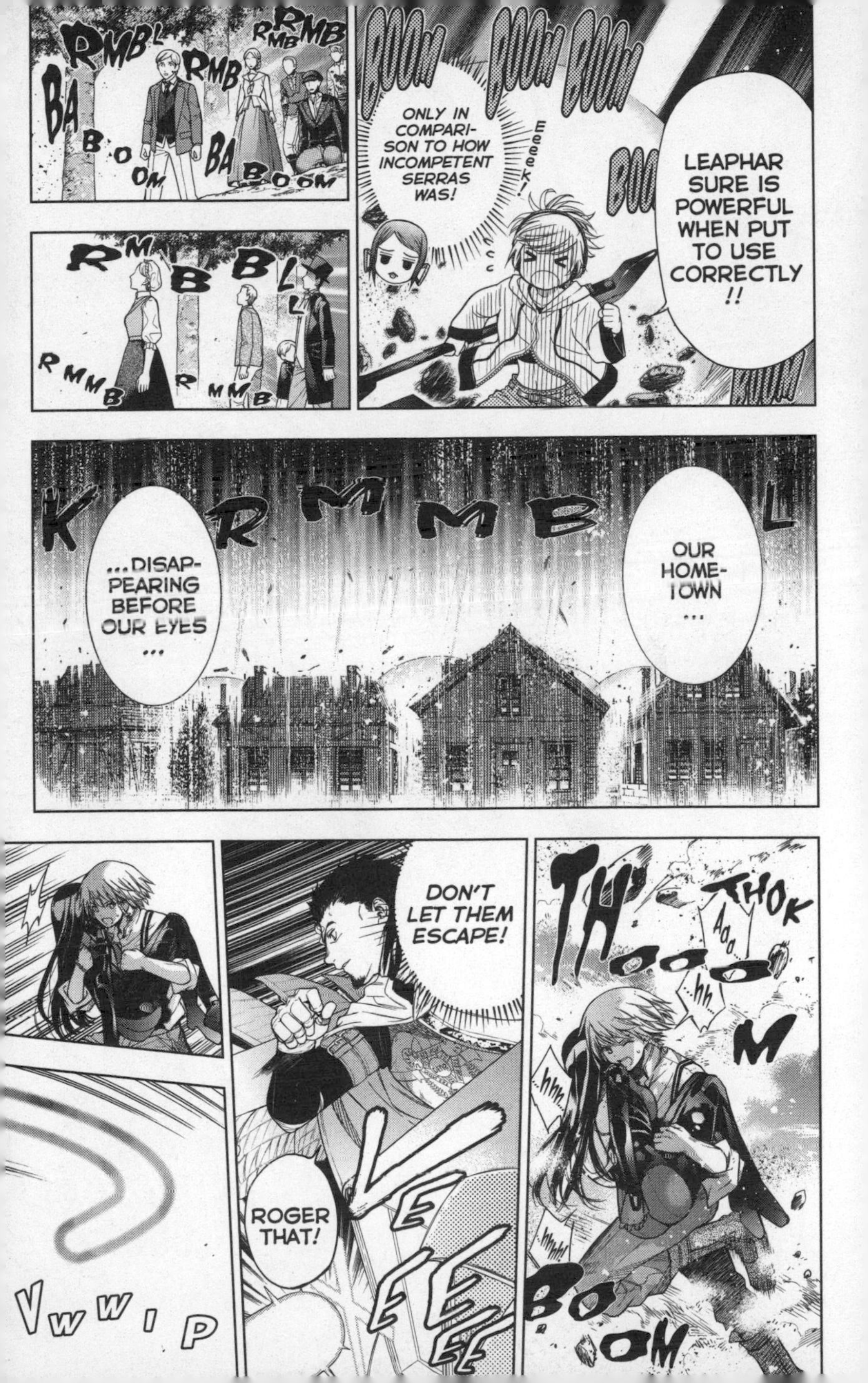
BOOOM BOOOM BOOOM
LEAPHAR SURE IS POWERFUL WHEN PUT TO USE CORRECTLY!!
ONLY IN COMPARISON TO HOW INCOMPETENT SERRAS WAS!
Eeeek!
RMBL RMB RMB
BA BOOM BA BOOM
RMBBL
RMMB RMMB
KRMMBL
OUR HOME-TOWN...
...DISAP-PEARING BEFORE OUR EYES...
THOK
THOOOM
Aaa...
...hh
BOOM
DON'T LET THEM ESCAPE!
ROGER THAT!
VWWIP

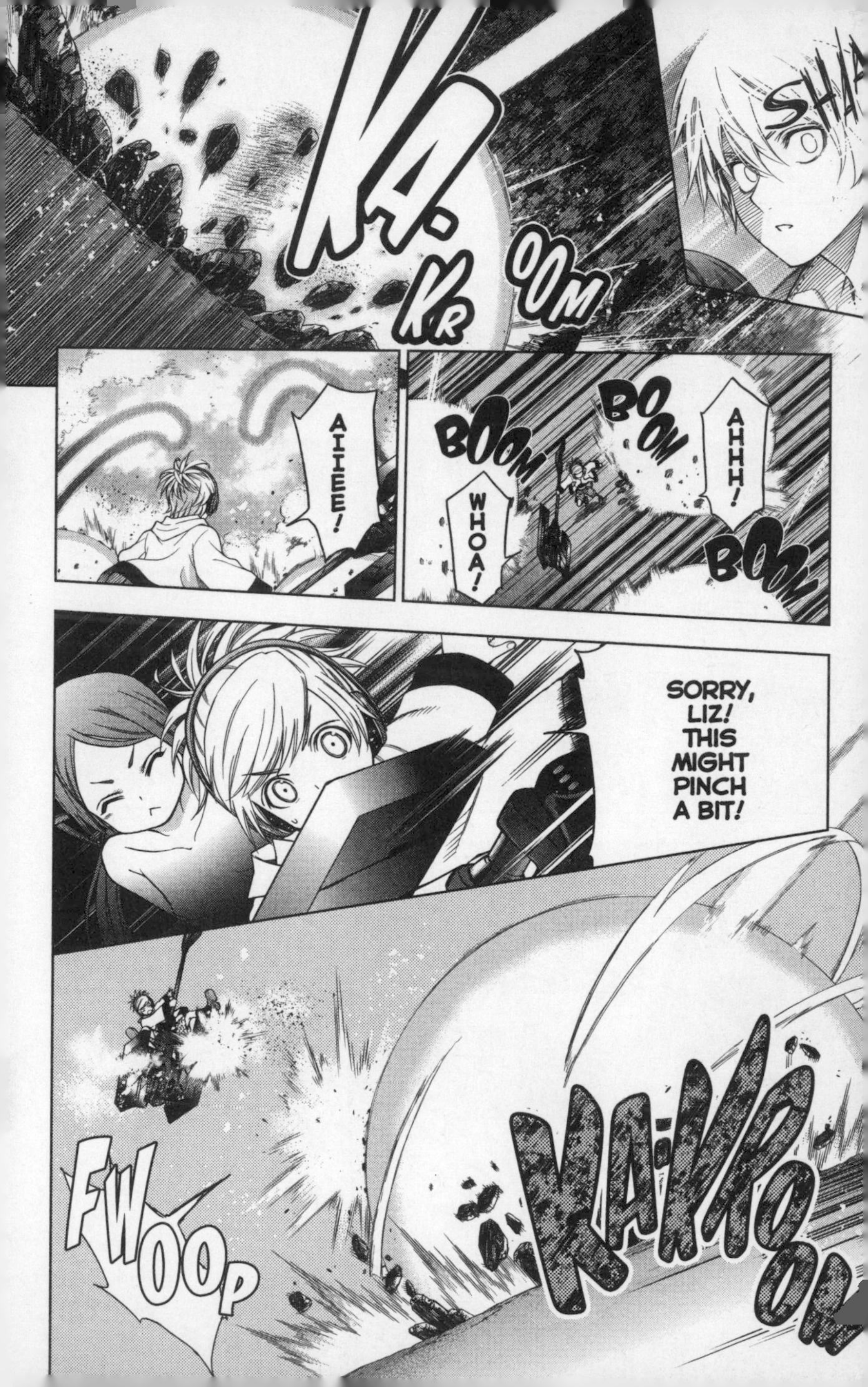
SHA
KAKROOM
AHHH!
BOOM
BOOM
BOOM
WHOA!
AIIEEE!
SORRY, LIZ! THIS MIGHT PINCH A BIT!
KAKROOM
FWOOP

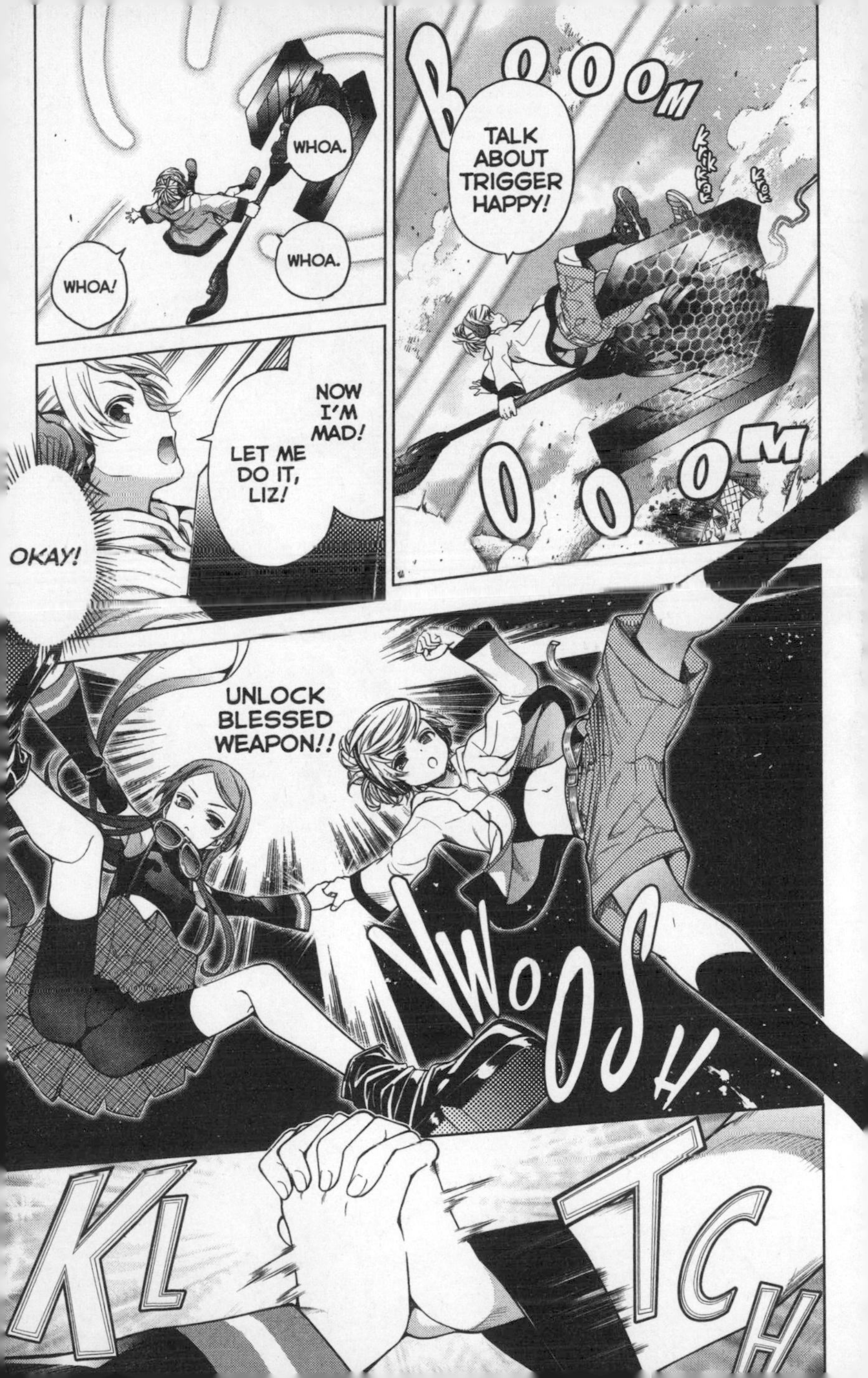
BOOOM
TALK ABOUT TRIGGER HAPPY!
BOOOOM
WHOA.
WHOA.
WHOA!
NOW I'M MAD!
LET ME DO IT, LIZ!
OKAY!
UNLOCK BLESSED WEAPON!!
VWOOSH
KLTCH

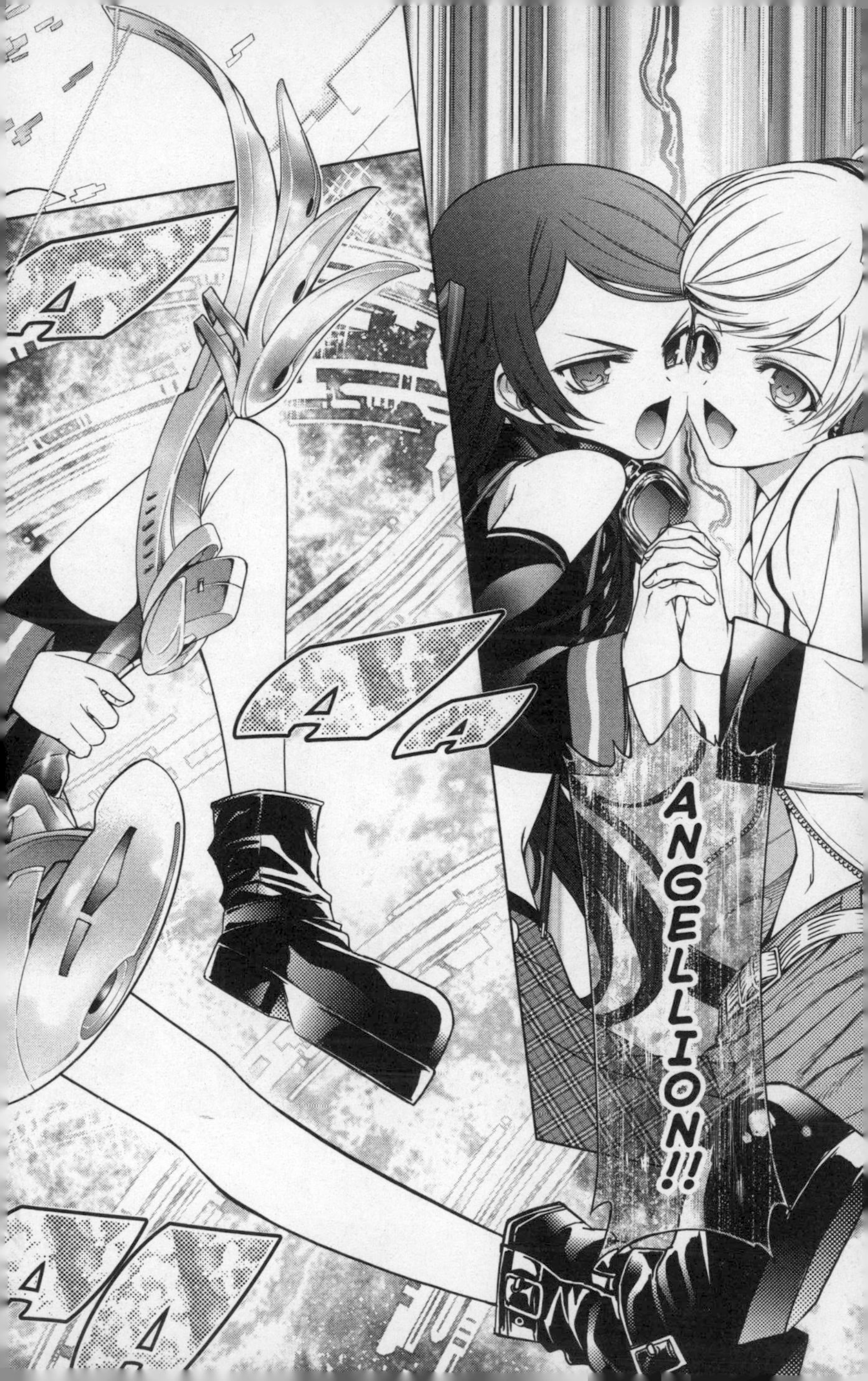
ANGELLION!!

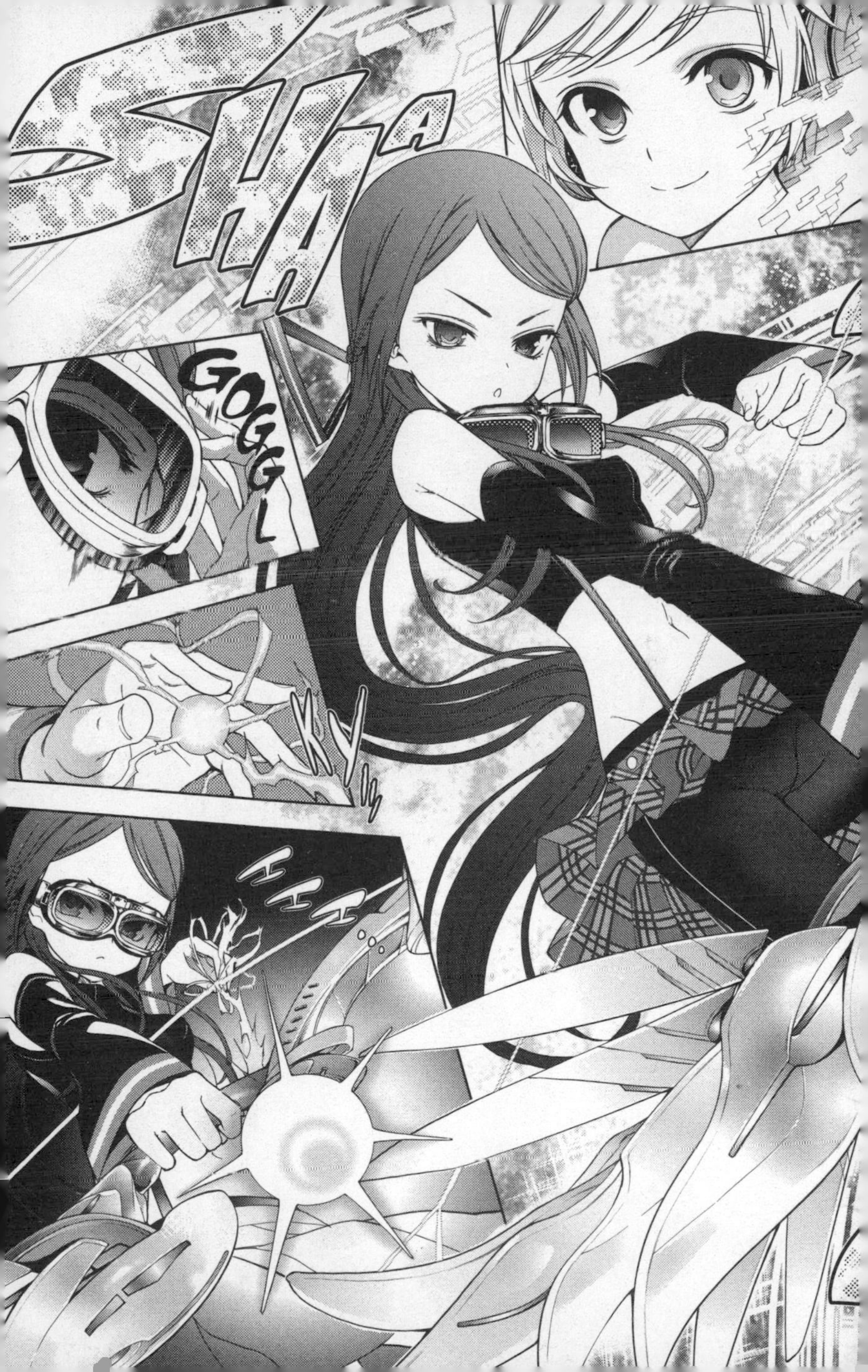
SHAA
GOGGL

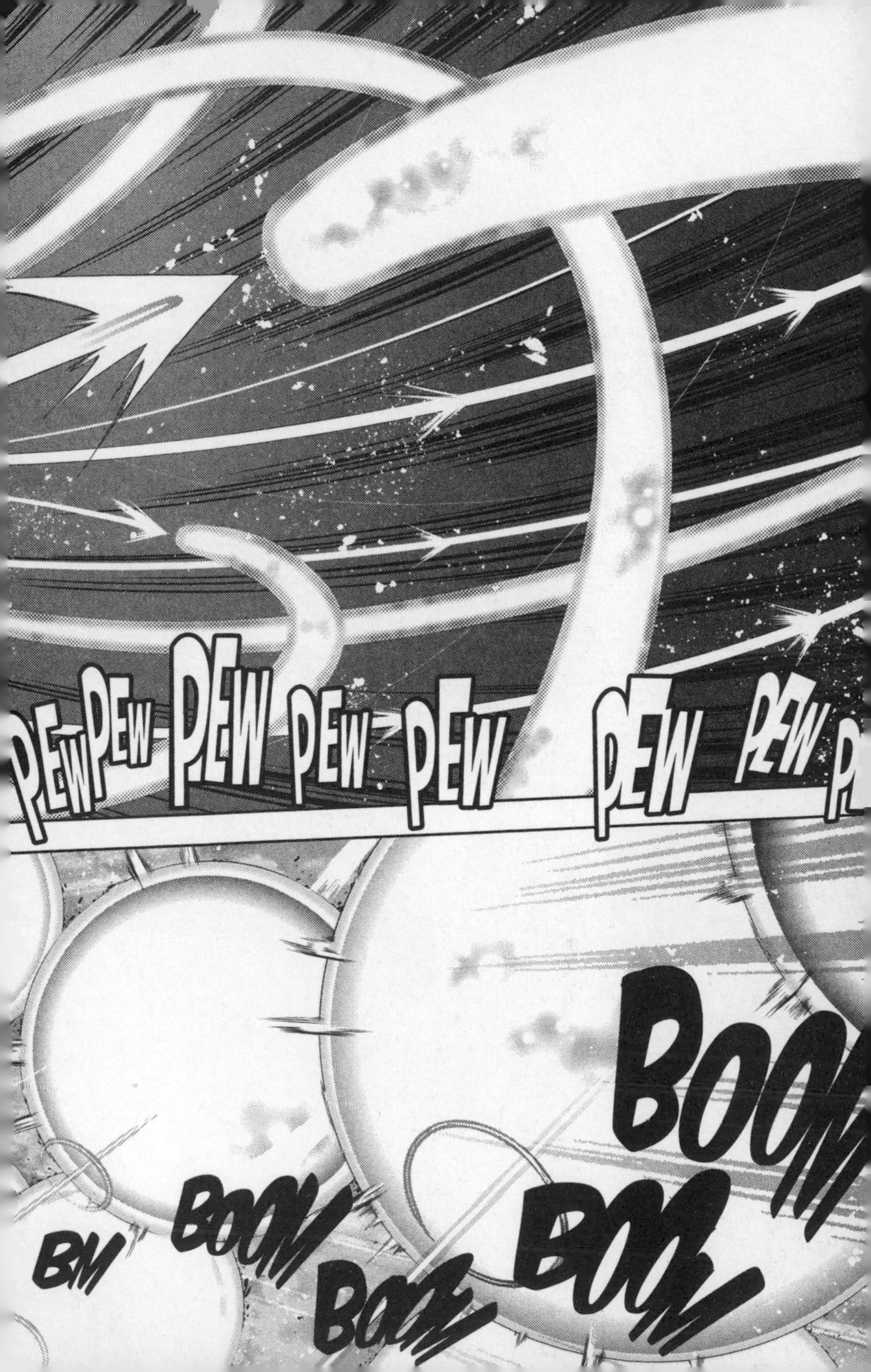
PEW
PEW
PEW
PEW
PEW
PEW
PEW
BOOM
BOOM
BOOM
BOOM
BM

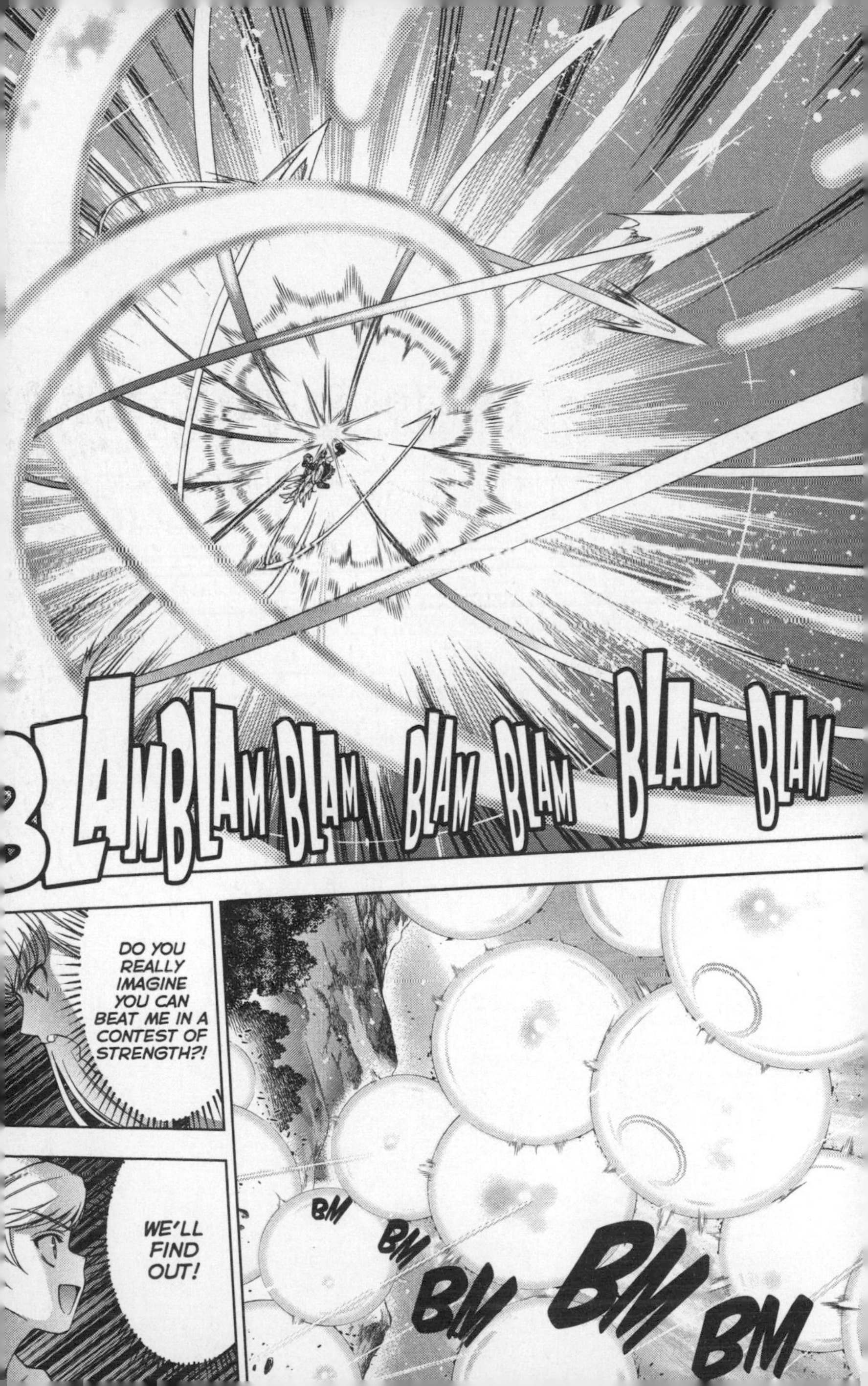
BLAM BLAM BLAM BLAM BLAM BLAM BLAM
DO YOU REALLY IMAGINE YOU CAN BEAT ME IN A CONTEST OF STRENGTH?!
BM BM BM BM BM
WE'LL FIND OUT!

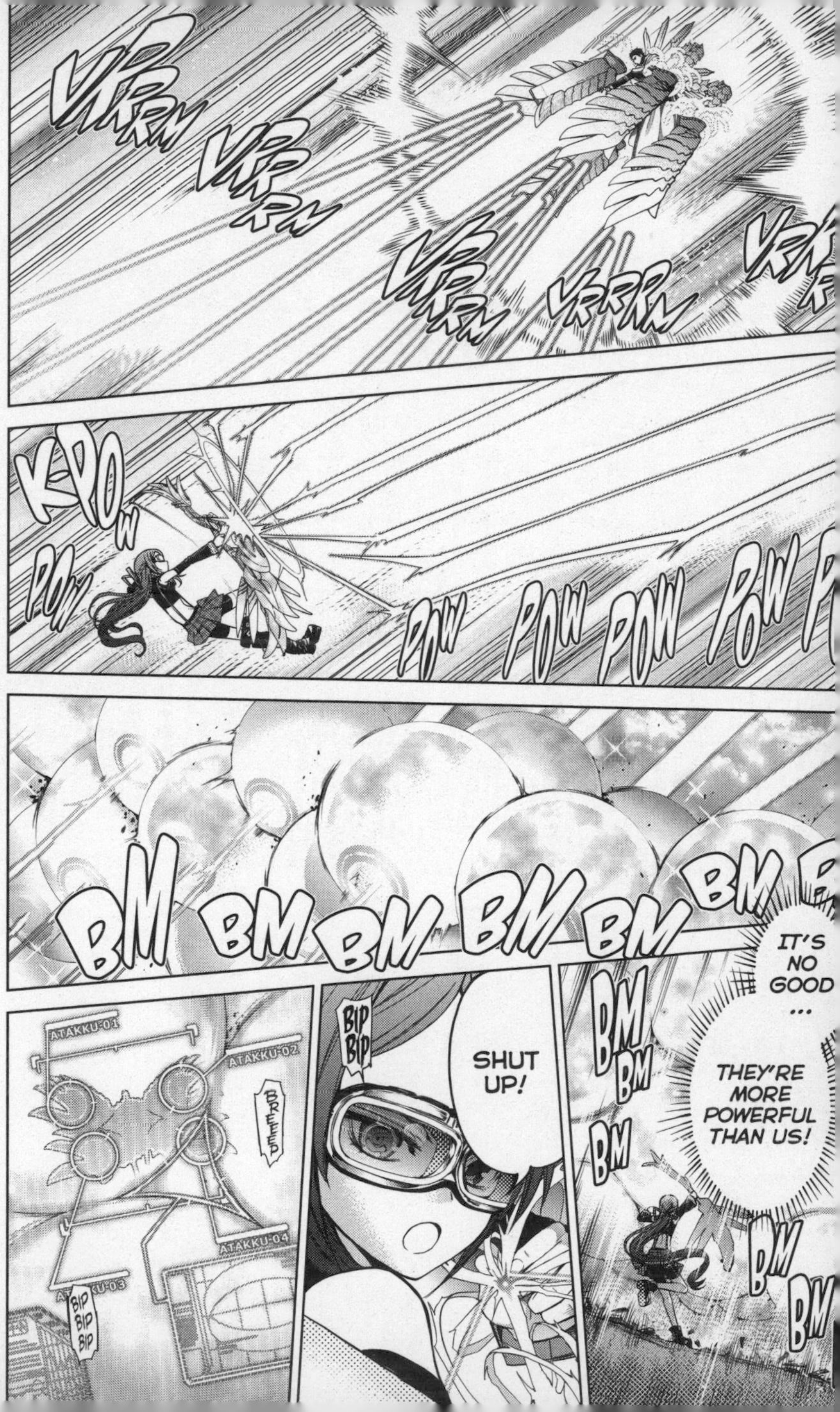
VRRRM
VRRRM
VRRRM
VRRRM
K-POW
POW
POW POW POW POW
BM BM BM BM BM BM
IT'S NO GOOD...
THEY'RE MORE POWERFUL THAN US!
BM BM
BM
BM BM
BIP BIP
SHUT UP!
ATAKKU-01
ATAKKU-02
BREEP
ATAKKU-04
ATAKKU-03
BIP BIP BIP

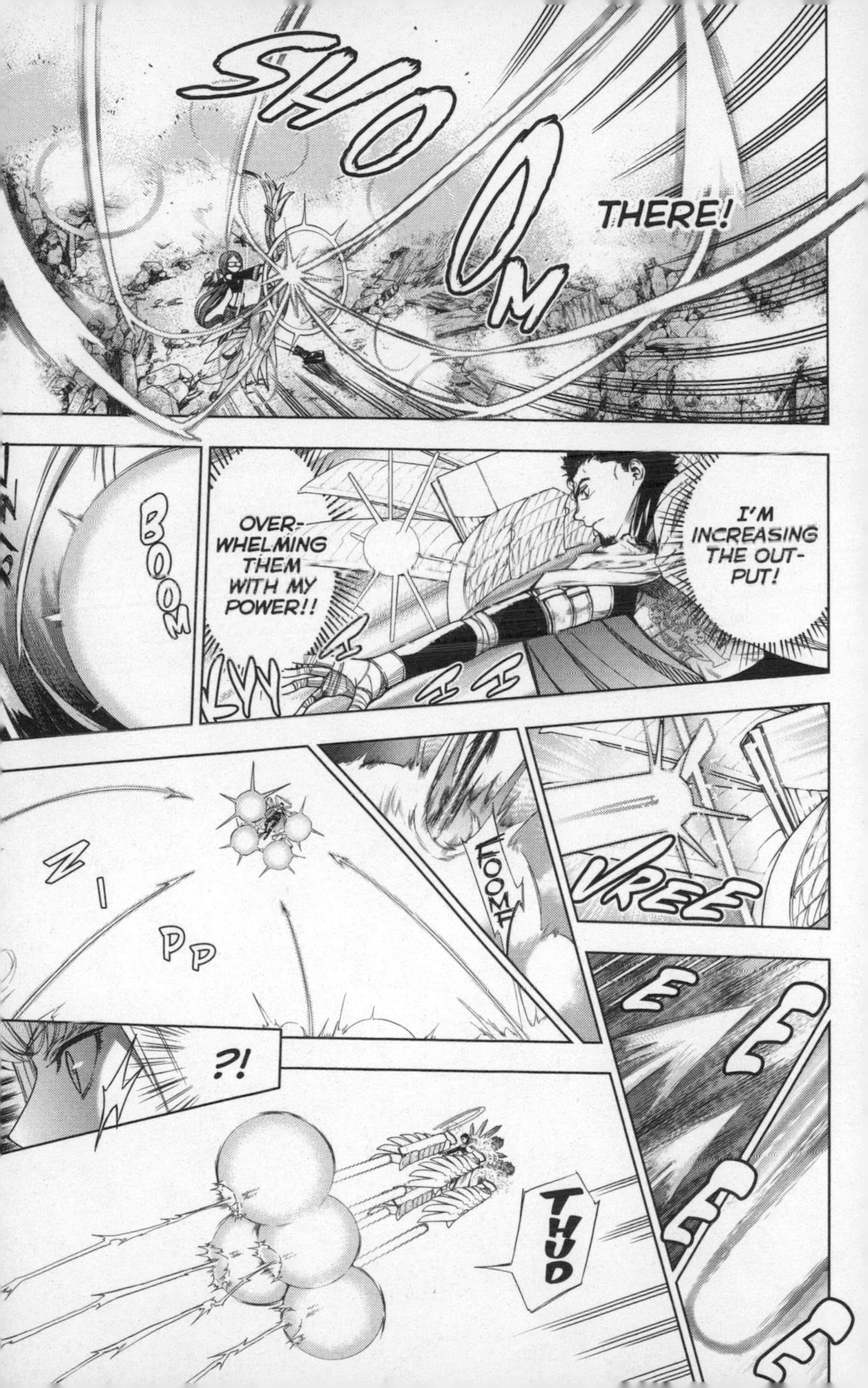
SHOOM
THERE!
I'M INCREASING THE OUT-PUT!
OVER-WHELMING THEM WITH MY POWER!!
BOOM
VREE
EEEEEEE
FOOMF
ZIPP
?!
THUD

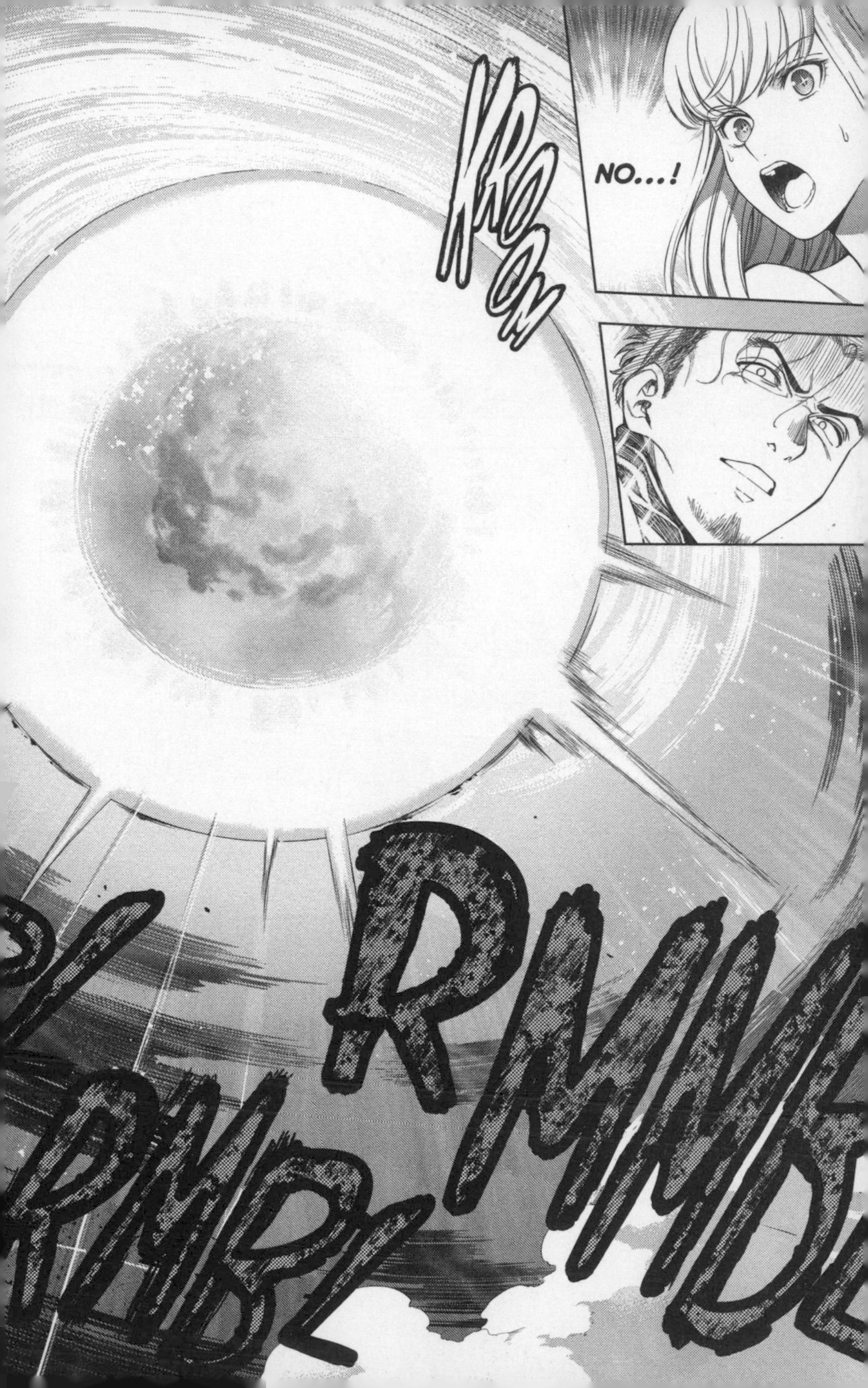
NO...!

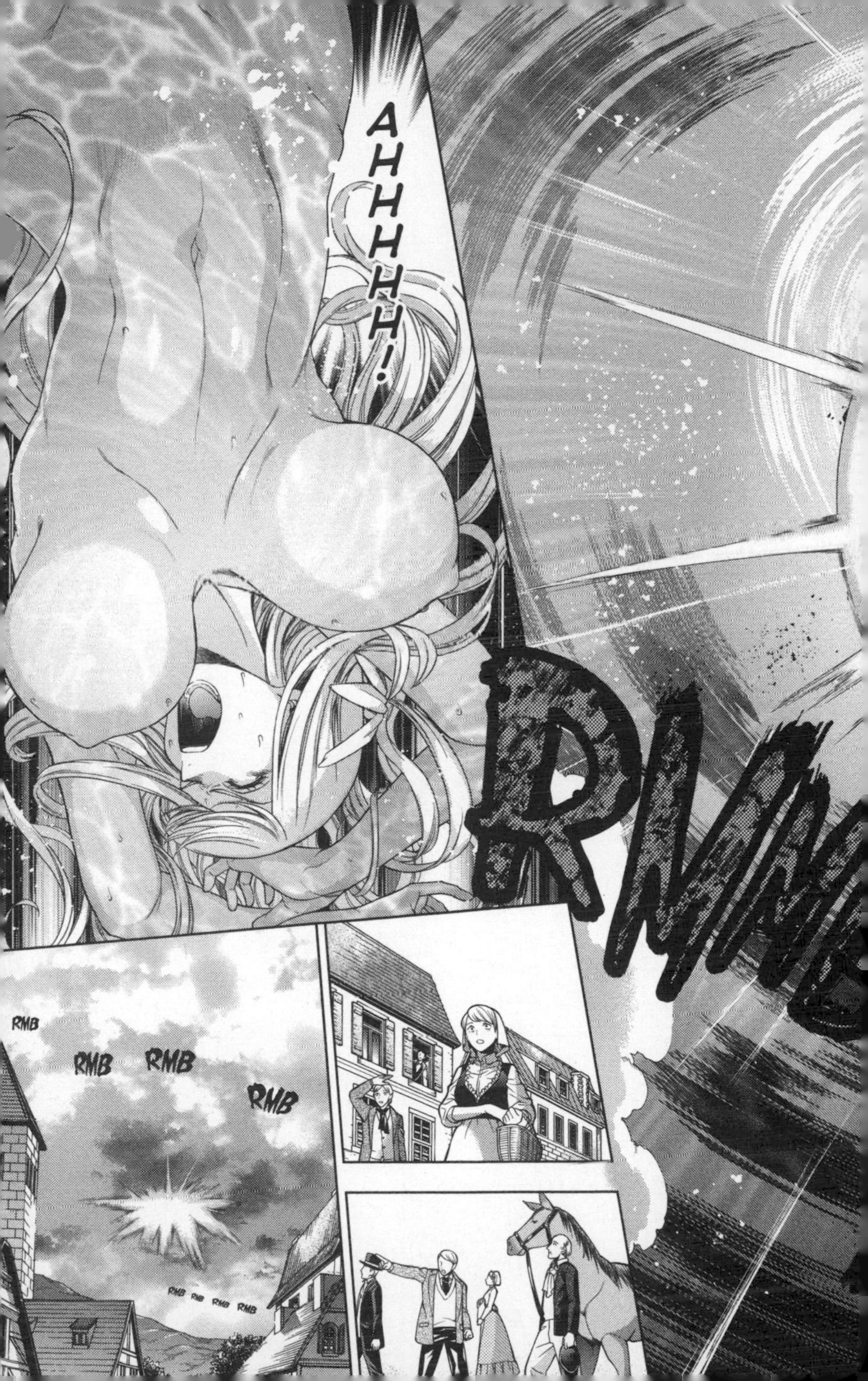
AHHHHH!
RMB
RMB RMB
RMB
RMB RMB RMB RMB

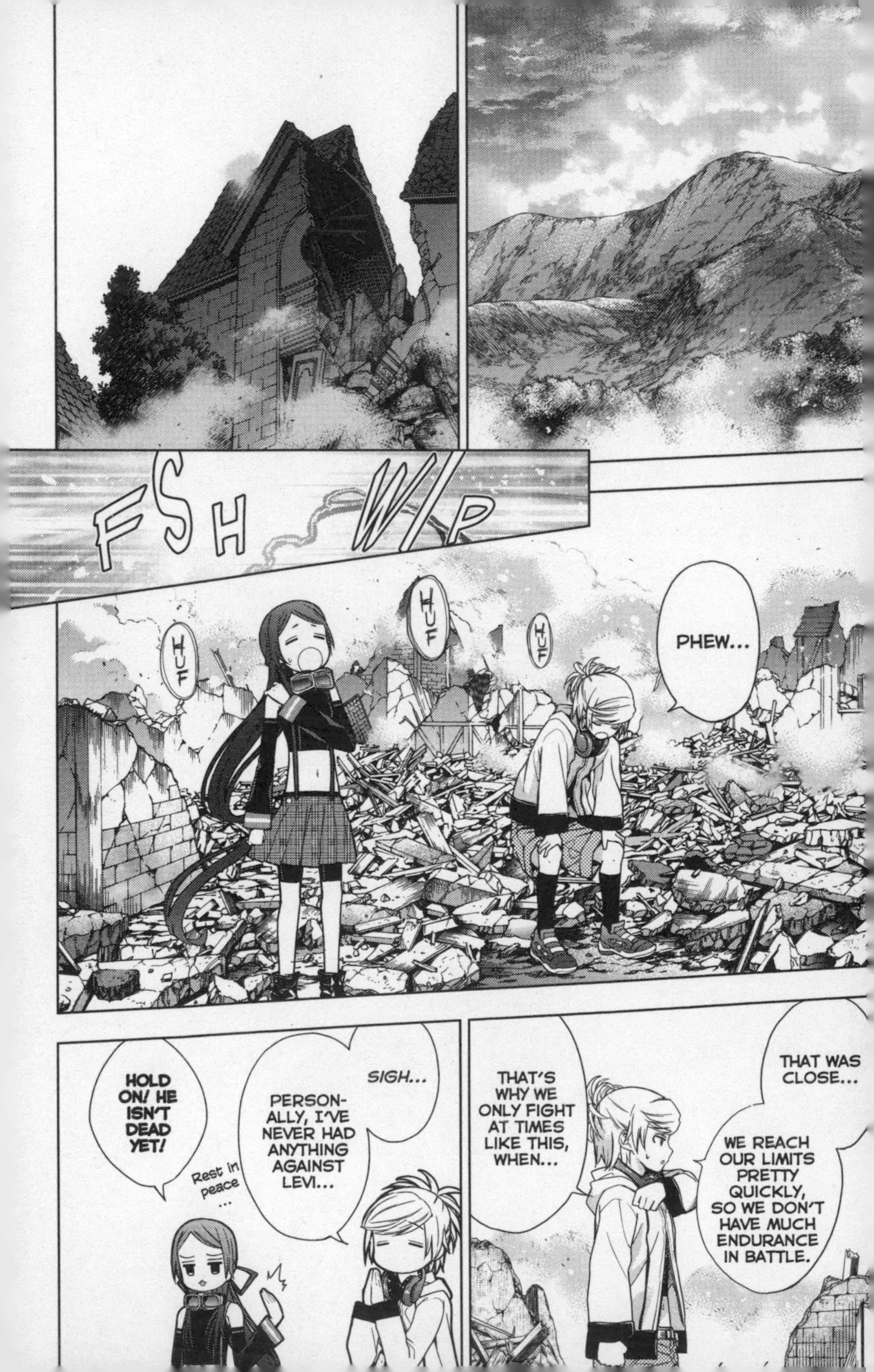
FSH
WHIP
PHEW...
HUF
HUF
HUF
THAT WAS CLOSE...
WE REACH OUR LIMITS PRETTY QUICKLY, SO WE DON'T HAVE MUCH ENDURANCE IN BATTLE.
THAT'S WHY WE ONLY FIGHT AT TIMES LIKE THIS, WHEN...
SIGH...
PERSON-ALLY, I'VE NEVER HAD ANYTHING AGAINST LEVI...
Rest in peace ...
HOLD ON! HE ISN'T DEAD YET!

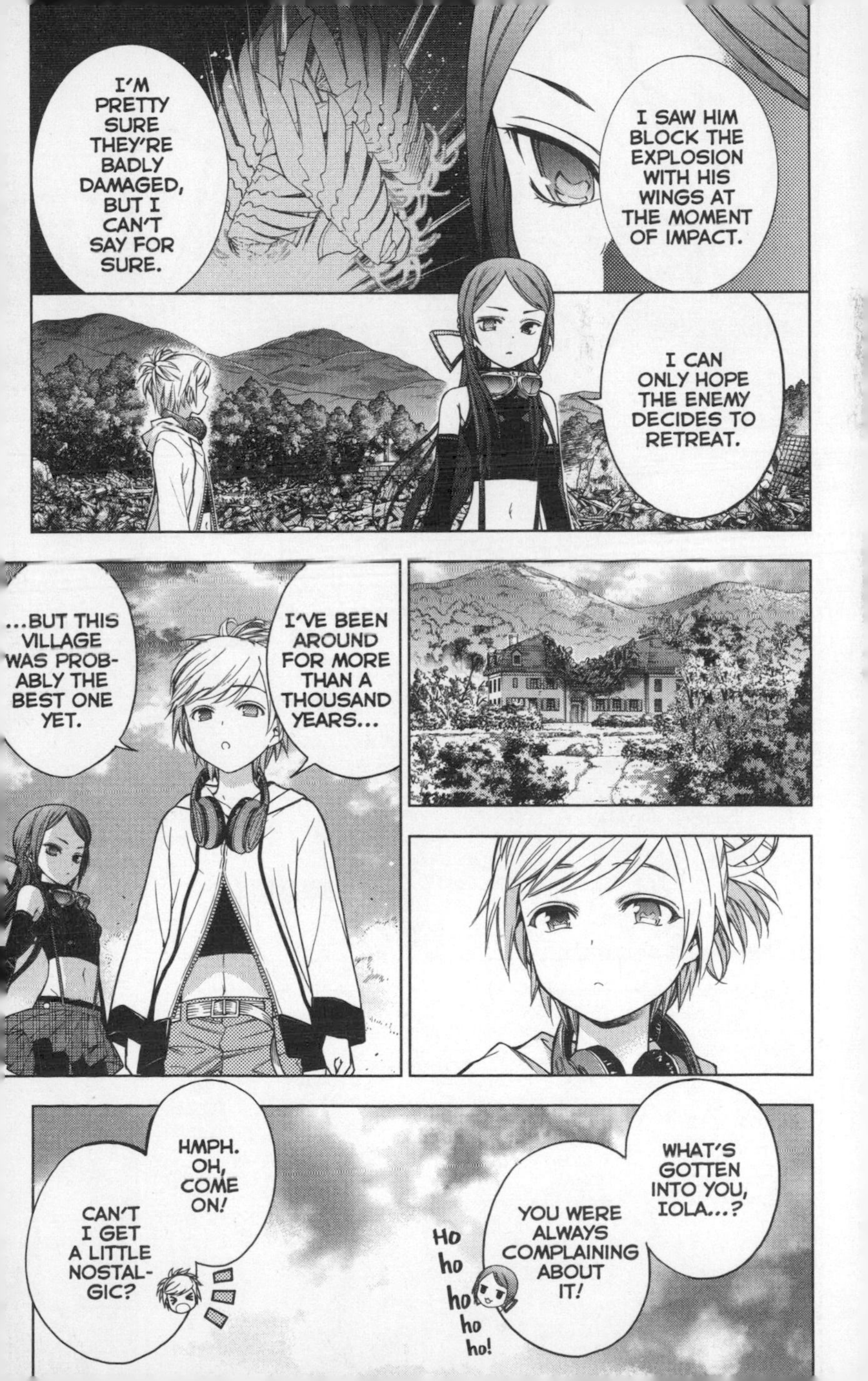
I SAW HIM BLOCK THE EXPLOSION WITH HIS WINGS AT THE MOMENT OF IMPACT.
I'M PRETTY SURE THEY'RE BADLY DAMAGED, BUT I CAN'T SAY FOR SURE.
I CAN ONLY HOPE THE ENEMY DECIDES TO RETREAT.
I'VE BEEN AROUND FOR MORE THAN A THOUSAND YEARS...
...BUT THIS VILLAGE WAS PROBABLY THE BEST ONE YET.
WHAT'S GOTTEN INTO YOU, IOLA...?
YOU WERE ALWAYS COMPLAINING ABOUT IT!
Ho ho ho ho ho!
HMPH. OH, COME ON!
CAN'T I GET A LITTLE NOSTALGIC?

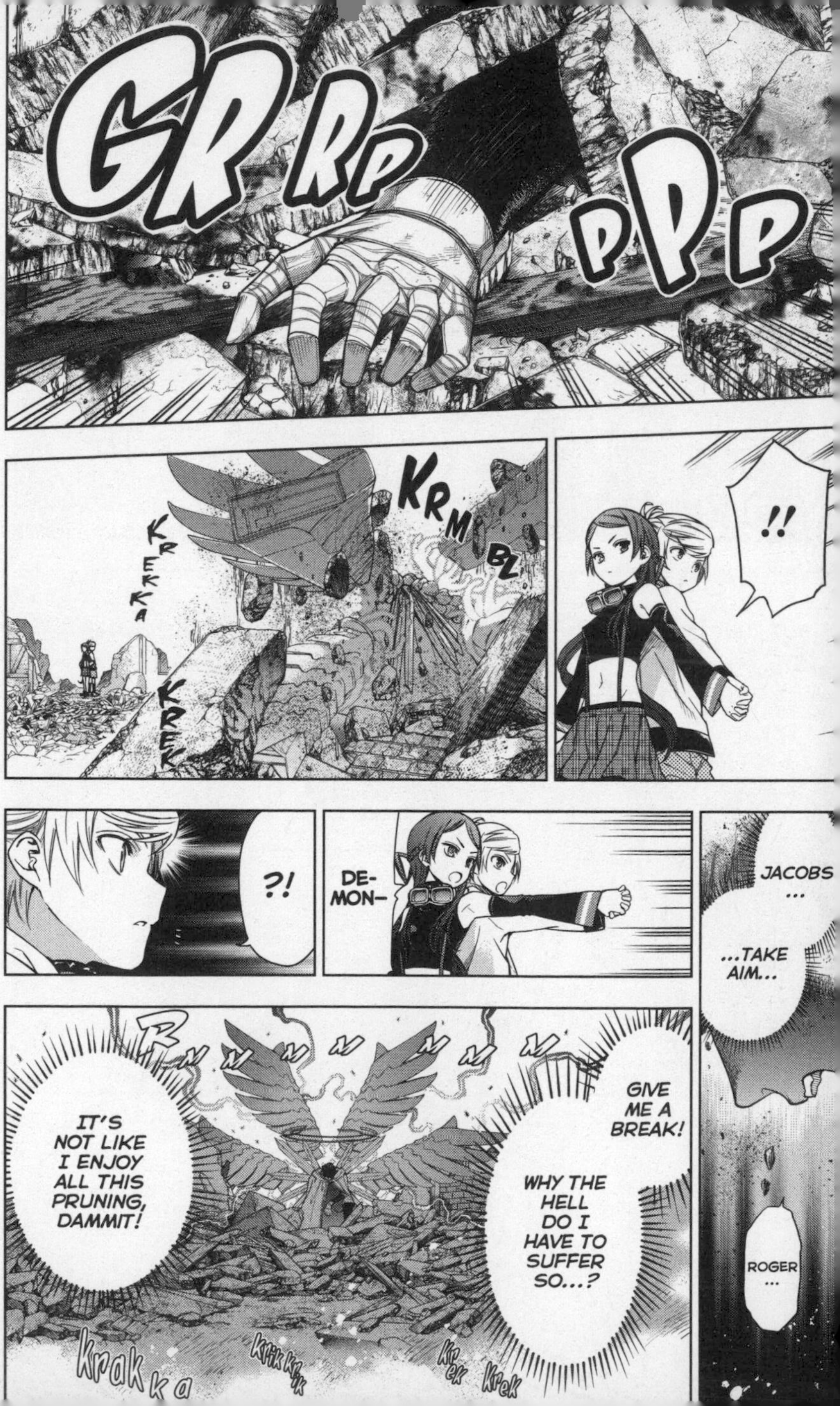
GRRP
PPP
!!
KRMBL
KREKKA
KREK
JACOBS...
...TAKE AIM...
ROGER...
DE-MON-
?!
RNNMMMM
GIVE ME A BREAK!
WHY THE HELL DO I HAVE TO SUFFER SO...?
IT'S NOT LIKE I ENJOY ALL THIS PRUNING, DAMMIT!
Krek Krek
Krik Krik
Krakka

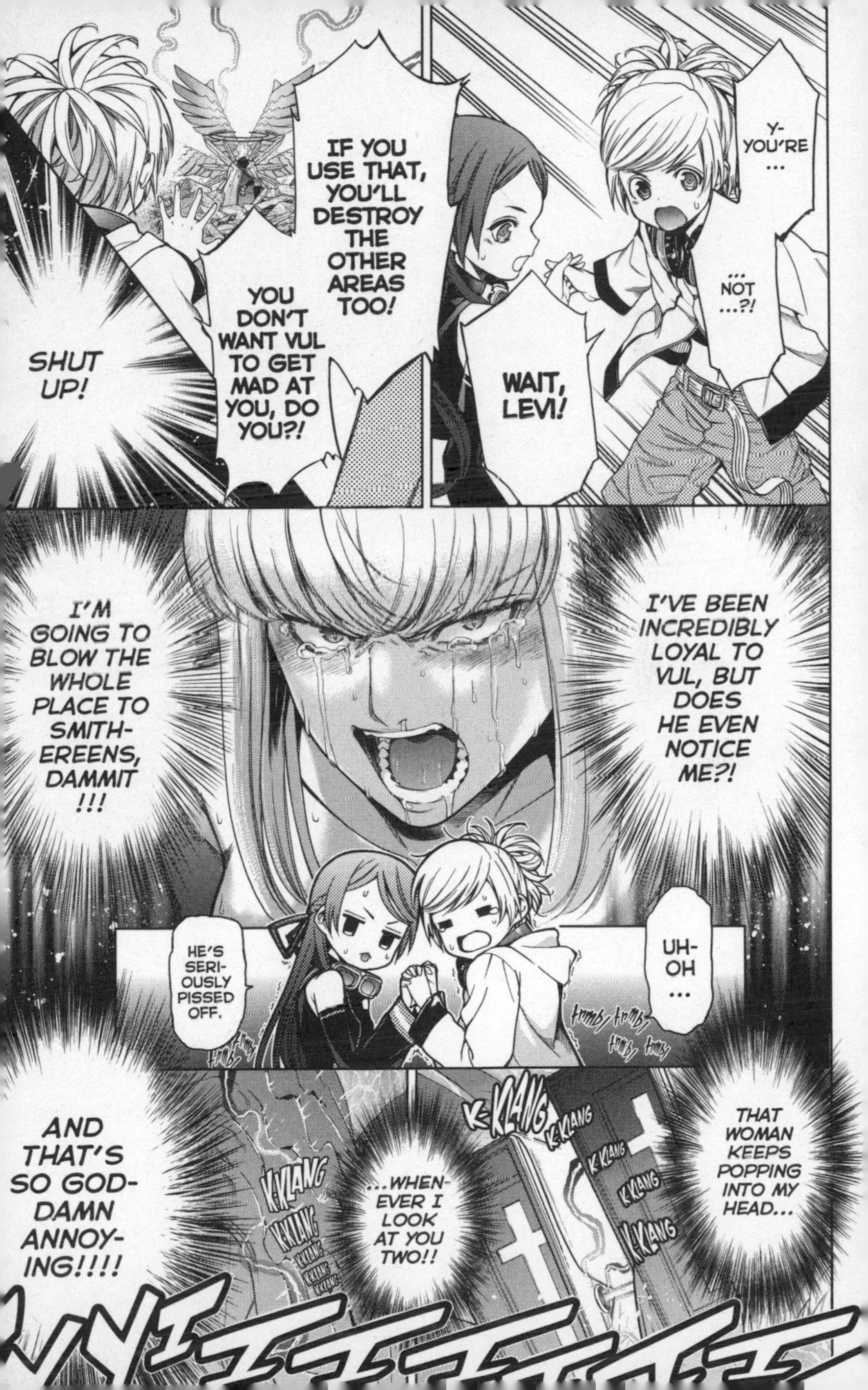
Y-YOU'RE ...
... NOT ...?!
WAIT, LEVI!
IF YOU USE THAT, YOU'LL DESTROY THE OTHER AREAS TOO!
YOU DON'T WANT VUL TO GET MAD AT YOU, DO YOU?!
SHUT UP!
I'VE BEEN INCREDIBLY LOYAL TO VUL, BUT DOES HE EVEN NOTICE ME?!
I'M GOING TO BLOW THE WHOLE PLACE TO SMITH-EREENS, DAMMIT!!!
UH-OH ...
HE'S SERI-OUSLY PISSED OFF.
K-KLANG K-KLANG K-KLANG K-KLANG K-KLANG
THAT WOMAN KEEPS POPPING INTO MY HEAD...
...WHEN-EVER I LOOK AT YOU TWO!!
K-KLANG K-KLANG
AND THAT'S SO GOD-DAMN ANNOY-ING!!!!
VNIIIIIIIIII

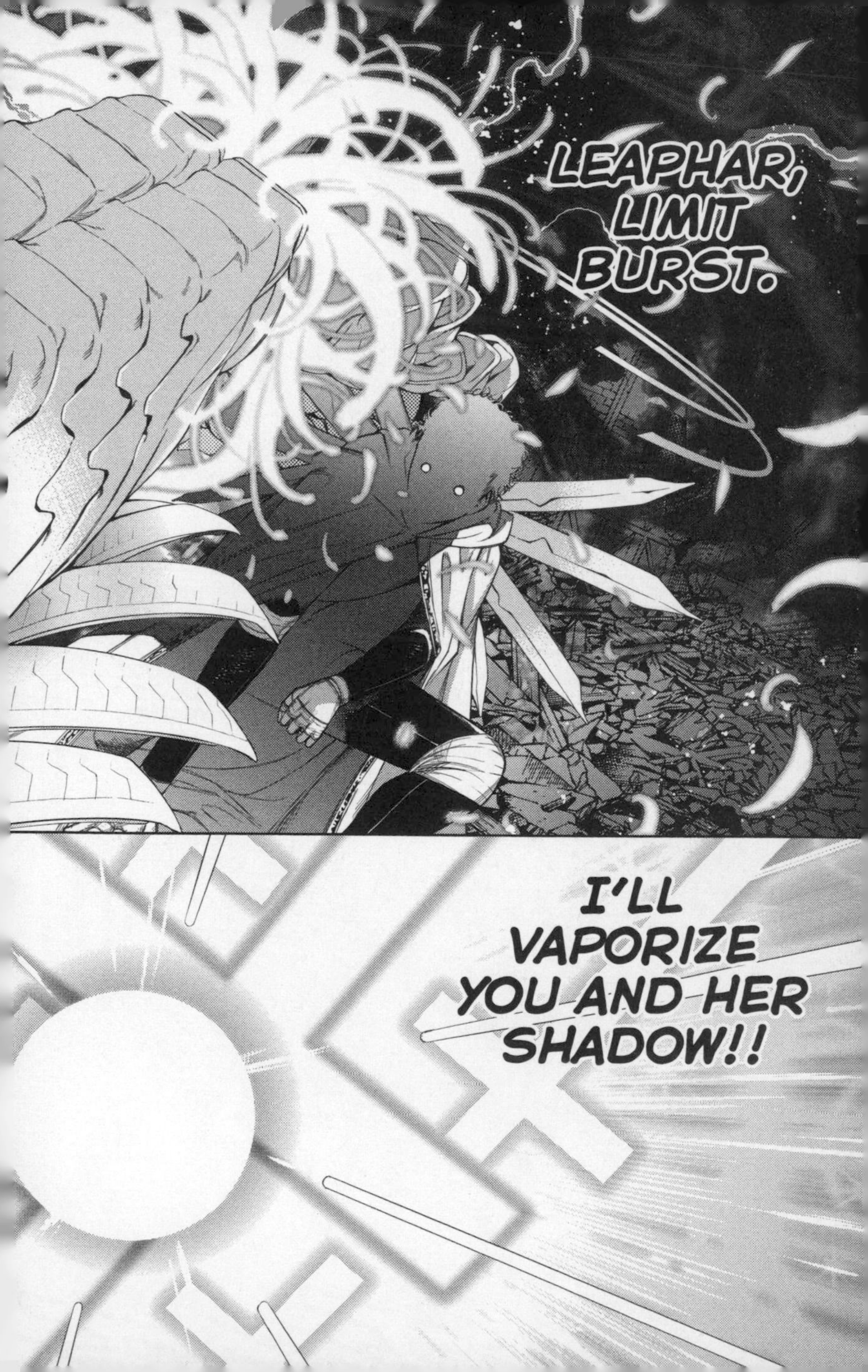
LEAPHAR, LIMIT BURST.
I'LL VAPORIZE YOU AND HER SHADOW!!

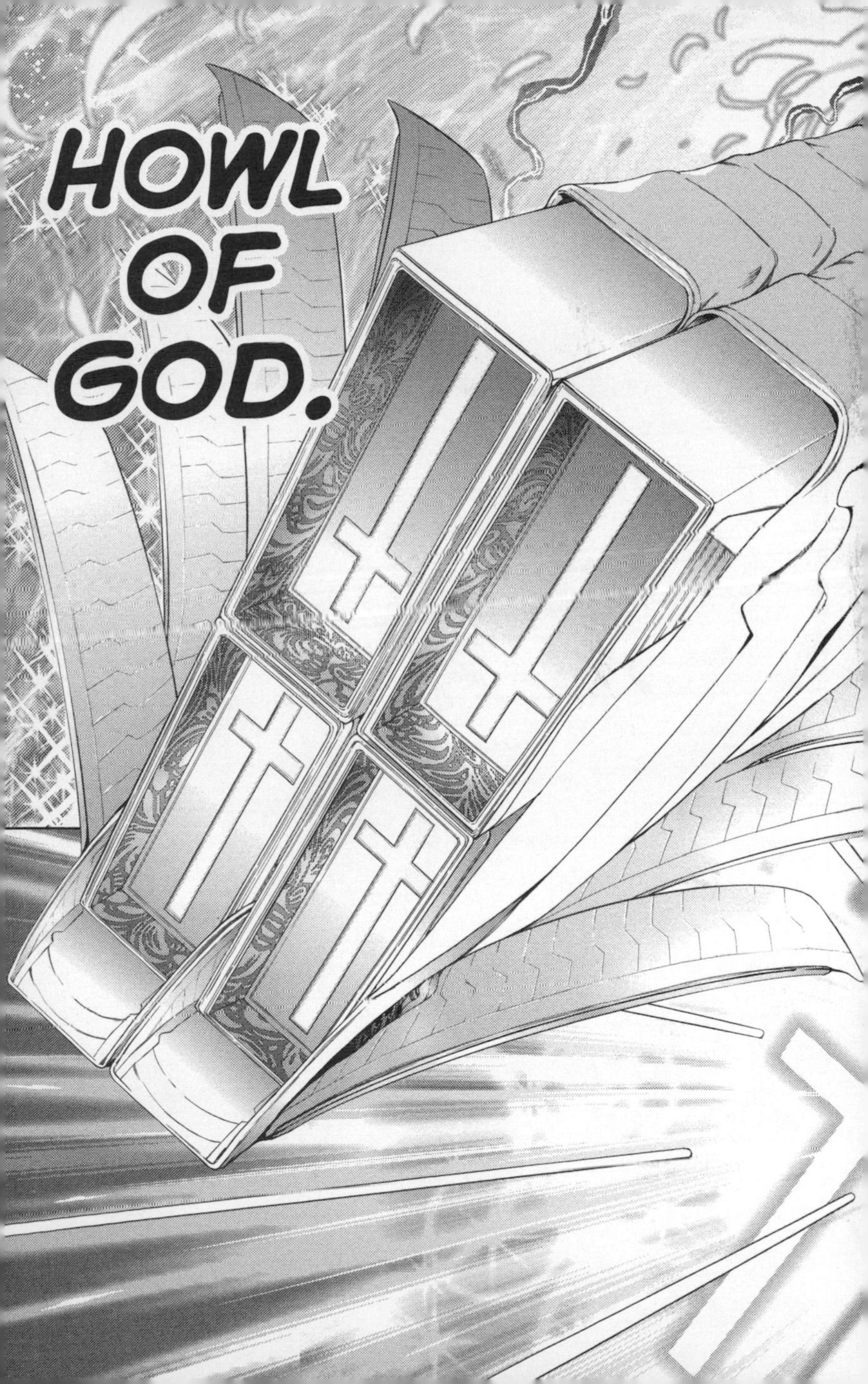
HOWL OF GOD.

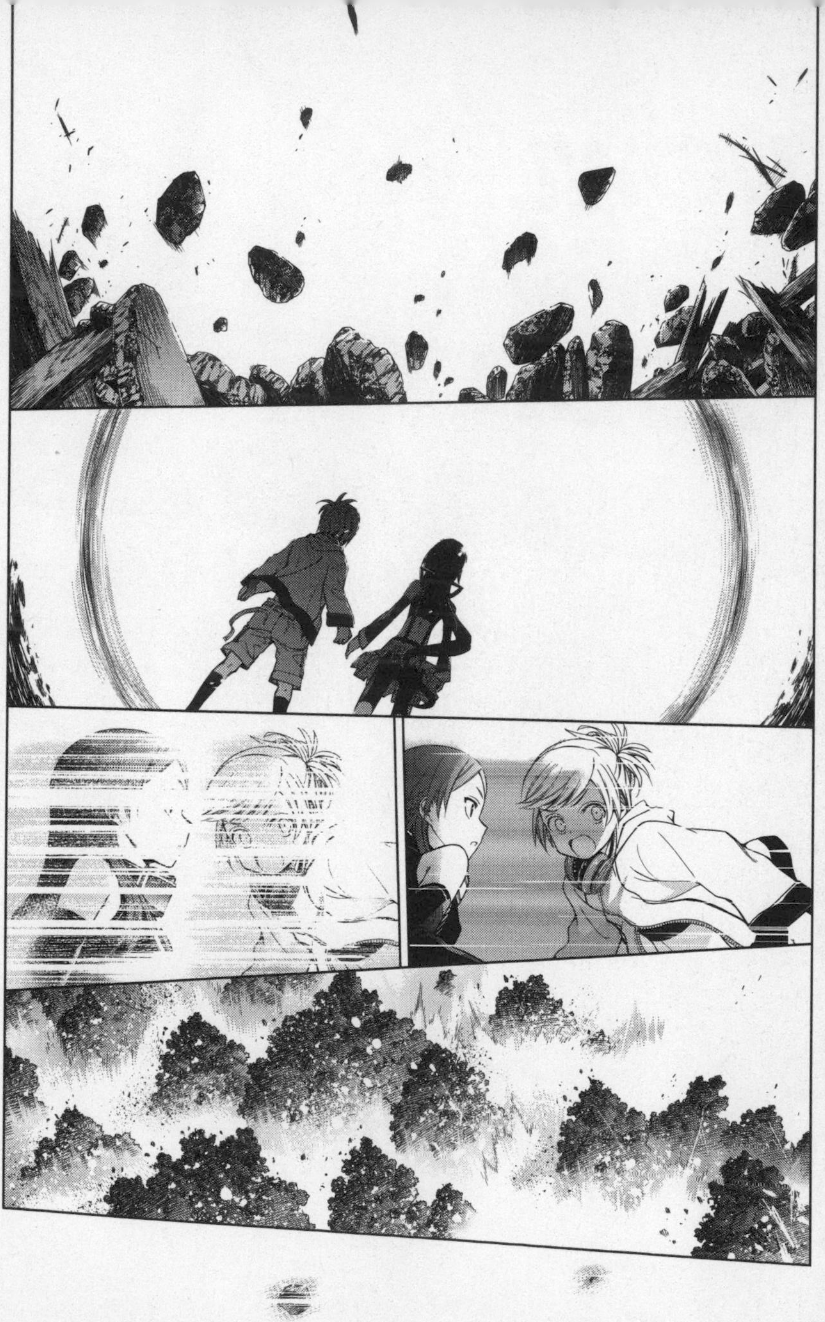

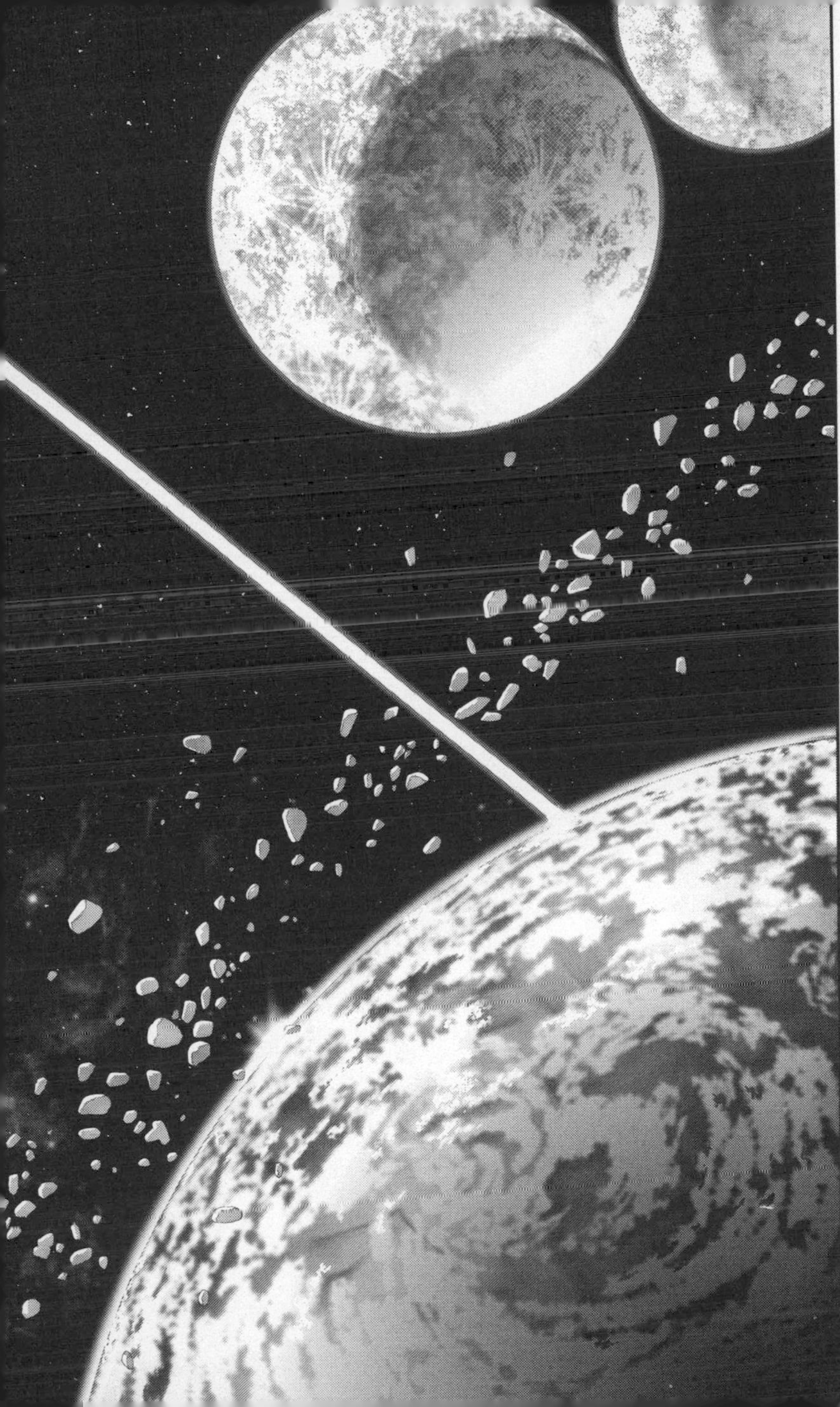

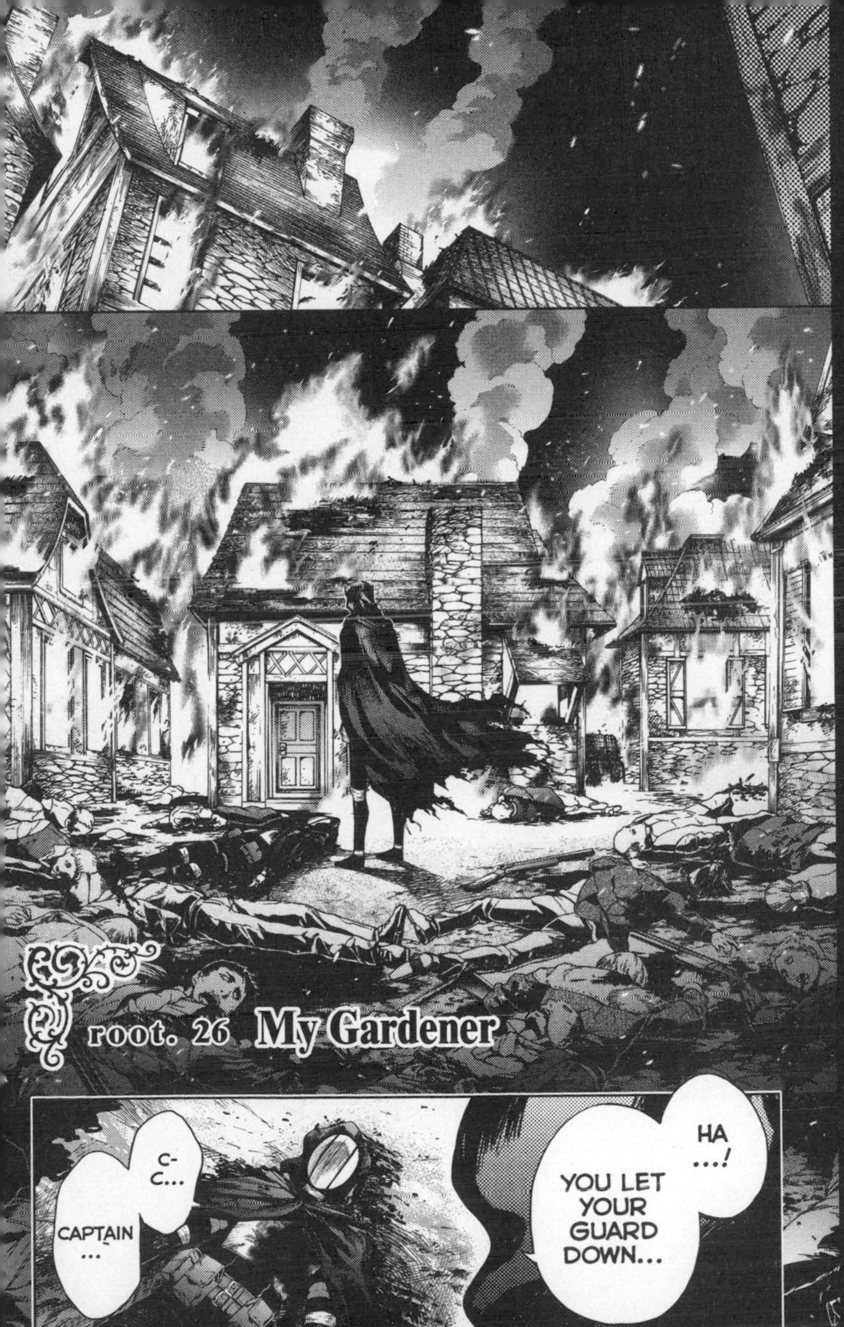
root. 26 My Gardener
HA ...!
YOU LET YOUR GUARD DOWN...
C- C...
CAPTAIN ...

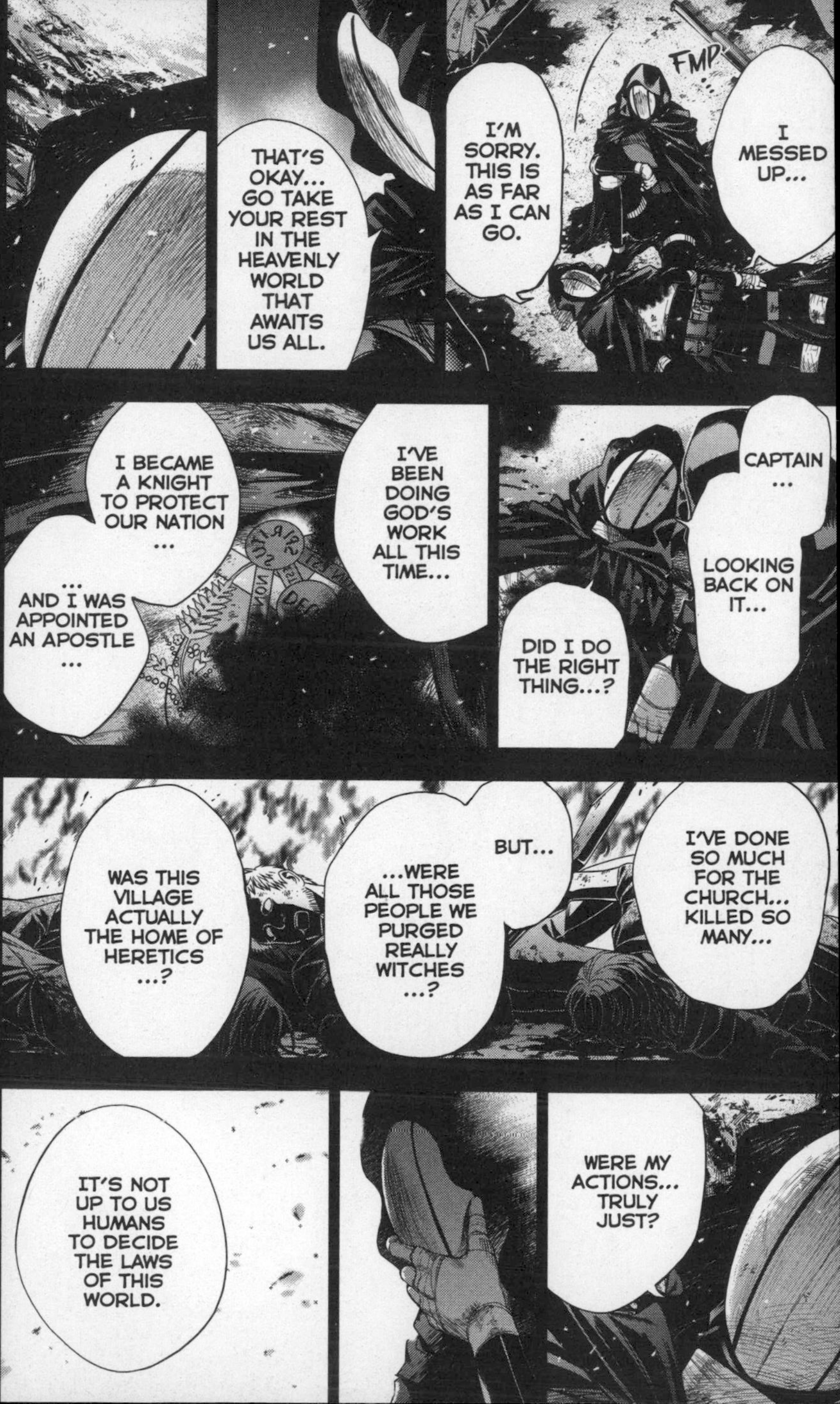

FMP
I MESSED UP...
I'M SORRY. THIS IS AS FAR AS I CAN GO.
THAT'S OKAY... GO TAKE YOUR REST IN THE HEAVENLY WORLD THAT AWAITS US ALL.
CAPTAIN ...
LOOKING BACK ON IT...
DID I DO THE RIGHT THING...?
I'VE BEEN DOING GOD'S WORK ALL THIS TIME...
I BECAME A KNIGHT TO PROTECT OUR NATION ...
... AND I WAS APPOINTED AN APOSTLE ...
I'VE DONE SO MUCH FOR THE CHURCH... KILLED SO MANY...
BUT...
...WERE ALL THOSE PEOPLE WE PURGED REALLY WITCHES ...?
WAS THIS VILLAGE ACTUALLY THE HOME OF HERETICS ...?
WERE MY ACTIONS... TRULY JUST?
IT'S NOT UP TO US HUMANS TO DECIDE THE LAWS OF THIS WORLD.

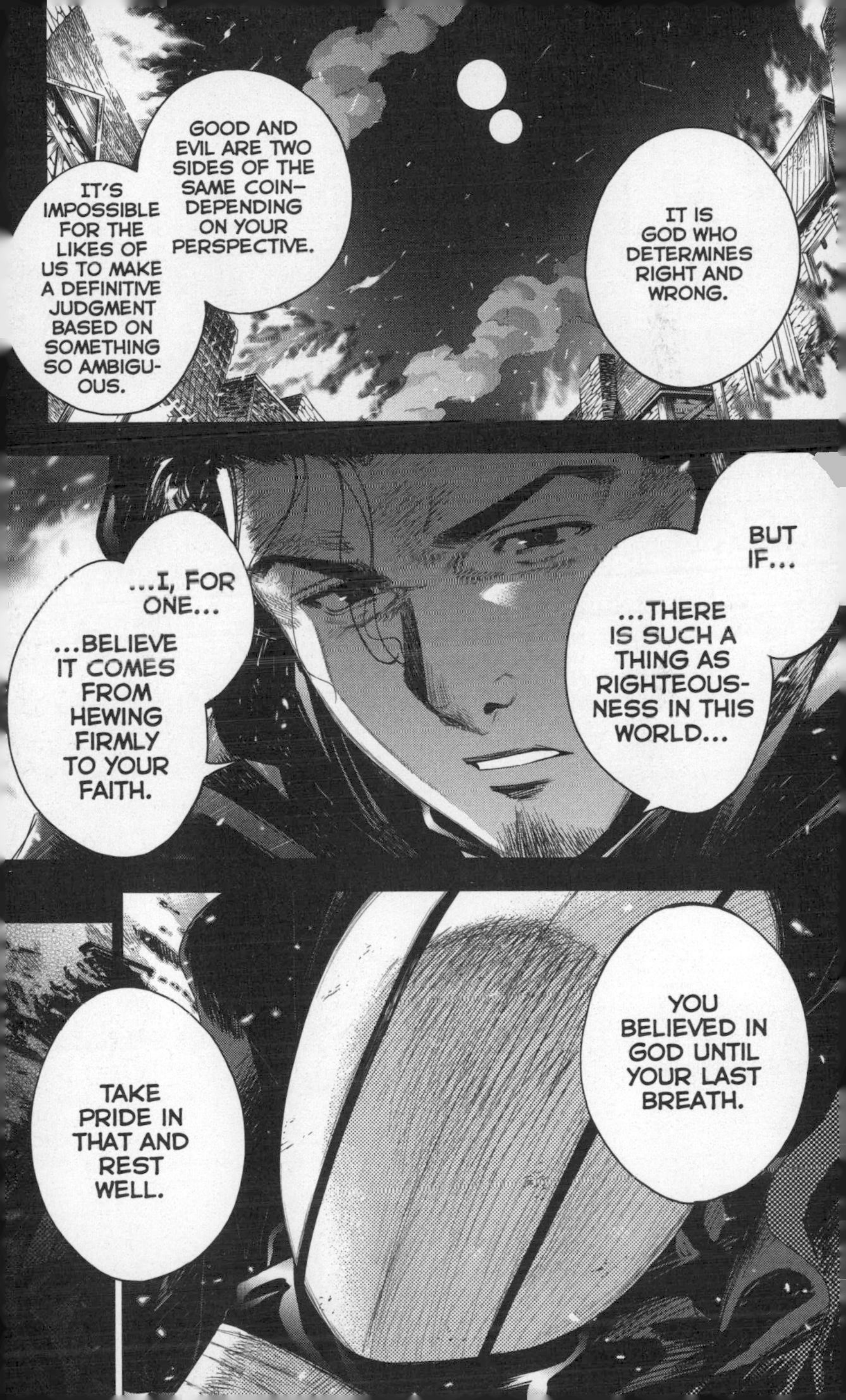
IT IS GOD WHO DETERMINES RIGHT AND WRONG.
GOOD AND EVIL ARE TWO SIDES OF THE SAME COIN— DEPENDING ON YOUR PERSPECTIVE.
IT'S IMPOSSIBLE FOR THE LIKES OF US TO MAKE A DEFINITIVE JUDGMENT BASED ON SOMETHING SO AMBIGU- OUS.
BUT IF...
...THERE IS SUCH A THING AS RIGHTEOUS- NESS IN THIS WORLD...
...I, FOR ONE...
...BELIEVE IT COMES FROM HEWING FIRMLY TO YOUR FAITH.
YOU BELIEVED IN GOD UNTIL YOUR LAST BREATH.
TAKE PRIDE IN THAT AND REST WELL.

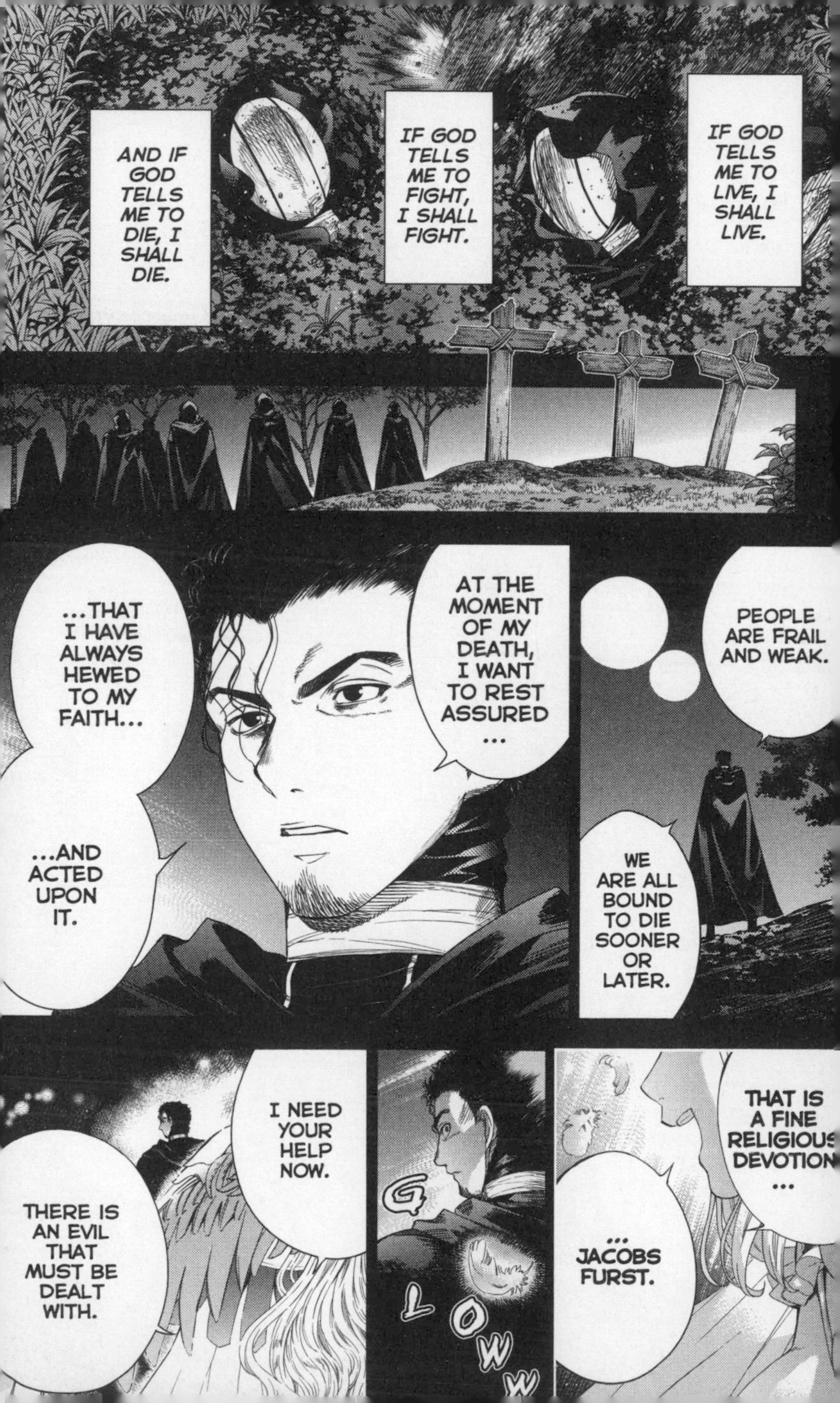
IF GOD TELLS ME TO LIVE, I SHALL LIVE.
IF GOD TELLS ME TO FIGHT, I SHALL FIGHT.
AND IF GOD TELLS ME TO DIE, I SHALL DIE.
PEOPLE ARE FRAIL AND WEAK.
WE ARE ALL BOUND TO DIE SOONER OR LATER.
AT THE MOMENT OF MY DEATH, I WANT TO REST ASSURED ...
...THAT I HAVE ALWAYS HEWED TO MY FAITH...
...AND ACTED UPON IT.
THAT IS A FINE RELIGIOUS DEVOTION ...
... JACOBS FURST.
GLOWW
I NEED YOUR HELP NOW.
THERE IS AN EVIL THAT MUST BE DEALT WITH.

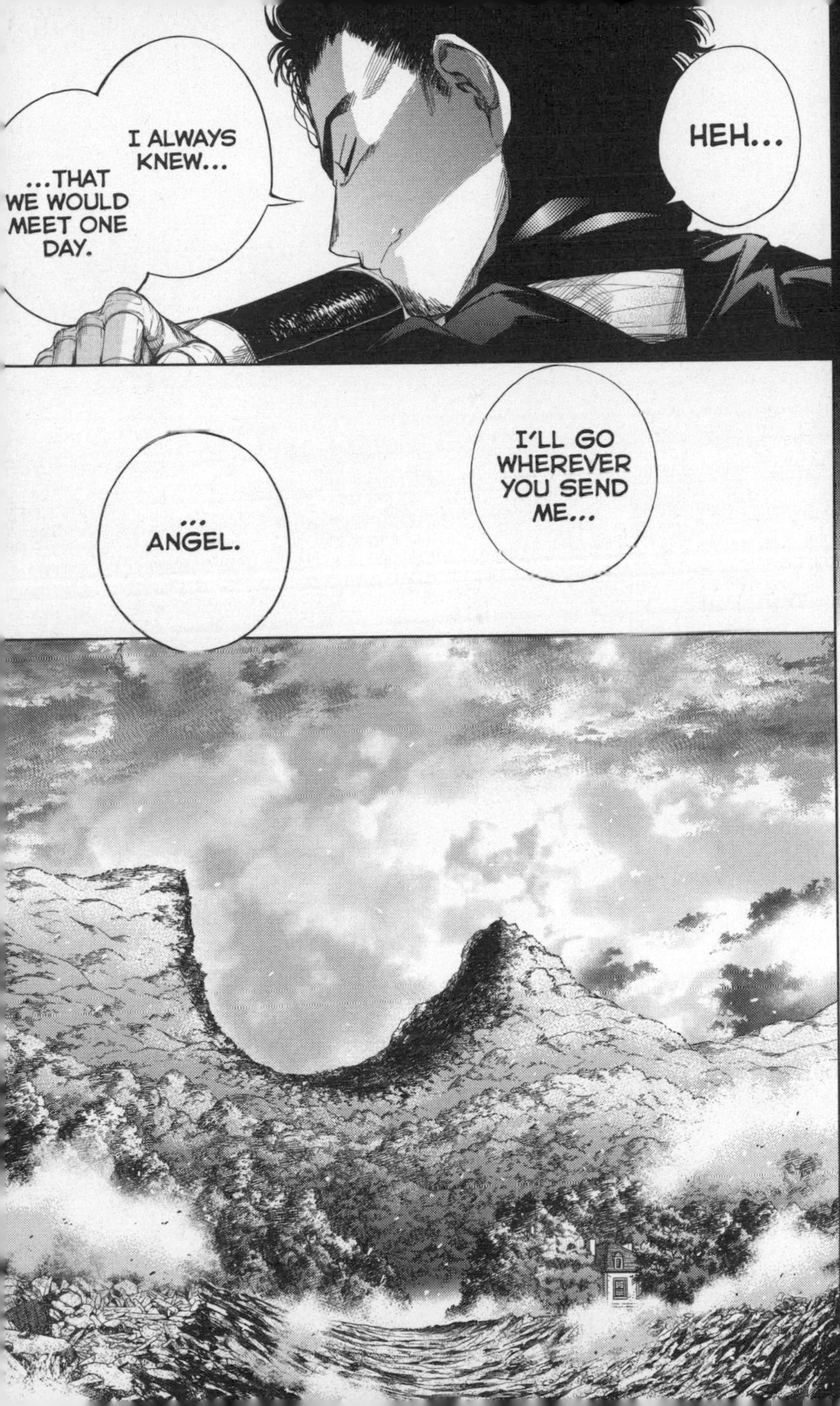
HEH...
I ALWAYS KNEW...
...THAT WE WOULD MEET ONE DAY.
I'LL GO WHEREVER YOU SEND ME...
... ANGEL.

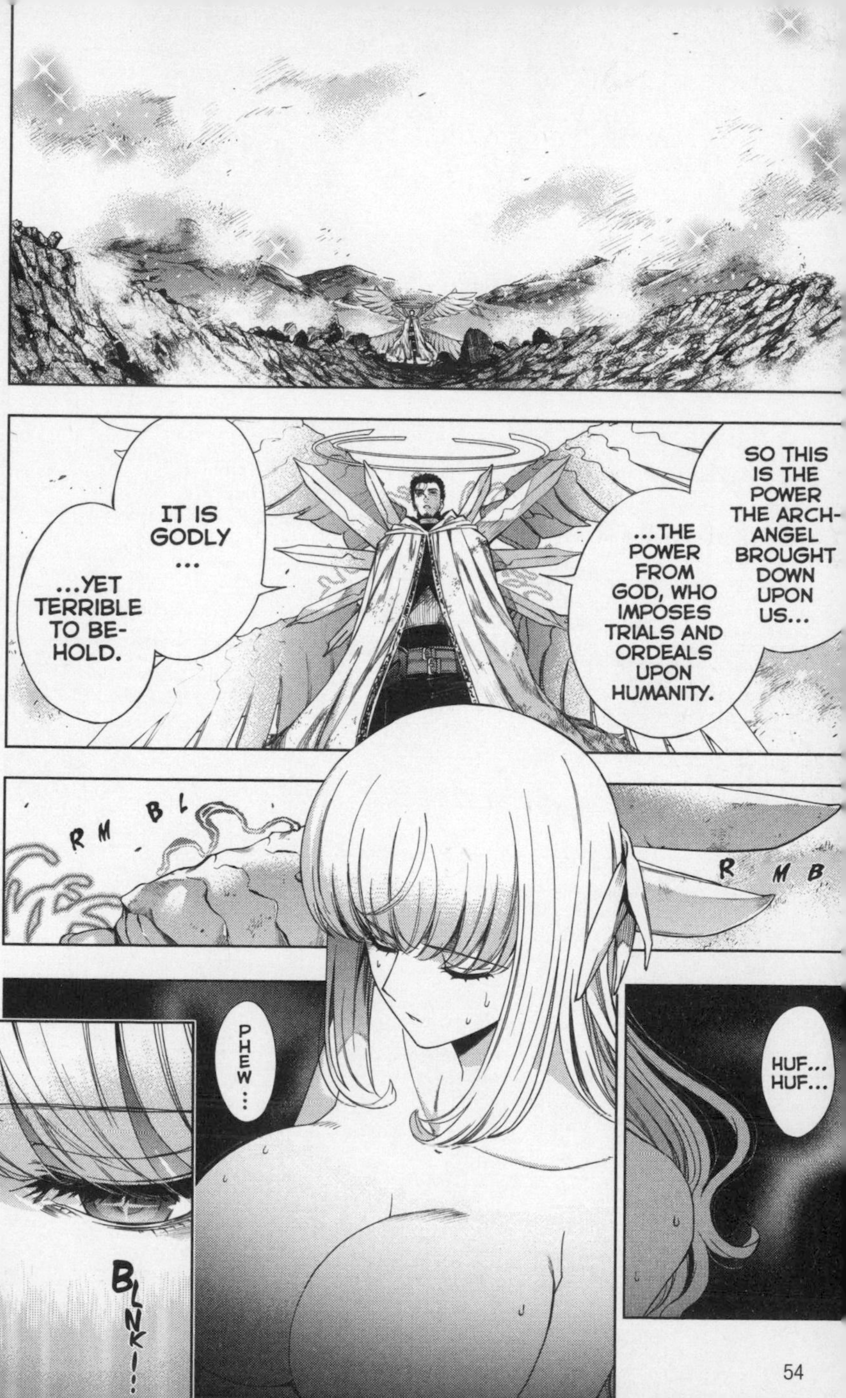
SO THIS IS THE POWER THE ARCH-ANGEL BROUGHT DOWN UPON US...
...THE POWER FROM GOD, WHO IMPOSES TRIALS AND ORDEALS UPON HUMANITY.
IT IS GODLY ...
...YET TERRIBLE TO BE-HOLD.
RMB
RMBL
HUF... HUF...
PHEW...
BLNK!!

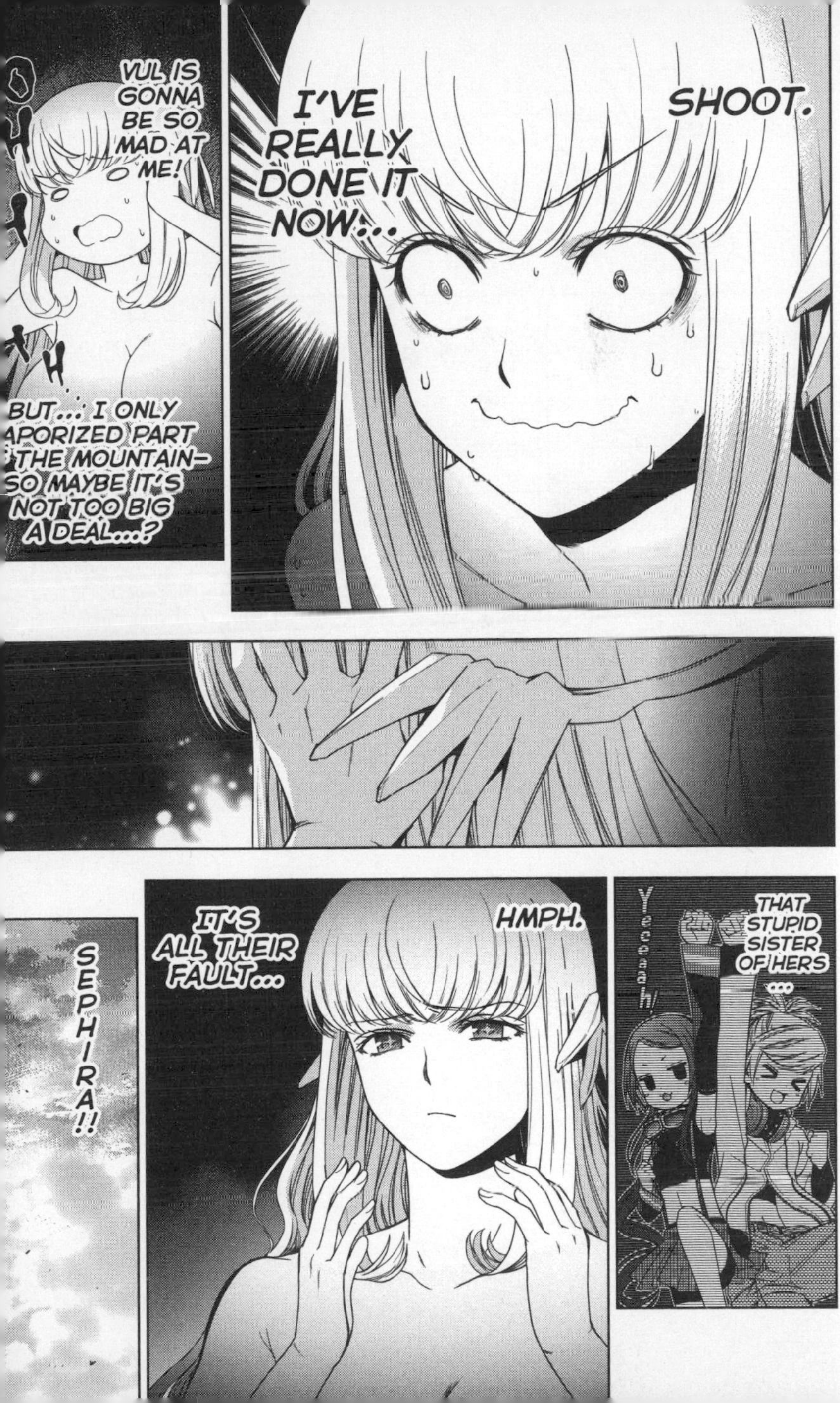
SHOOT.
I'VE REALLY DONE IT NOW...
VUL IS GONNA BE SO MAD AT ME!
BUT... I ONLY APORIZED PART THE MOUNTAIN— SO MAYBE IT'S NOT TOO BIG A DEAL...?
THAT STUPID SISTER OF HERS...
Yeeeaah!
HMPH.
IT'S ALL THEIR FAULT...
SEPHIRA!!

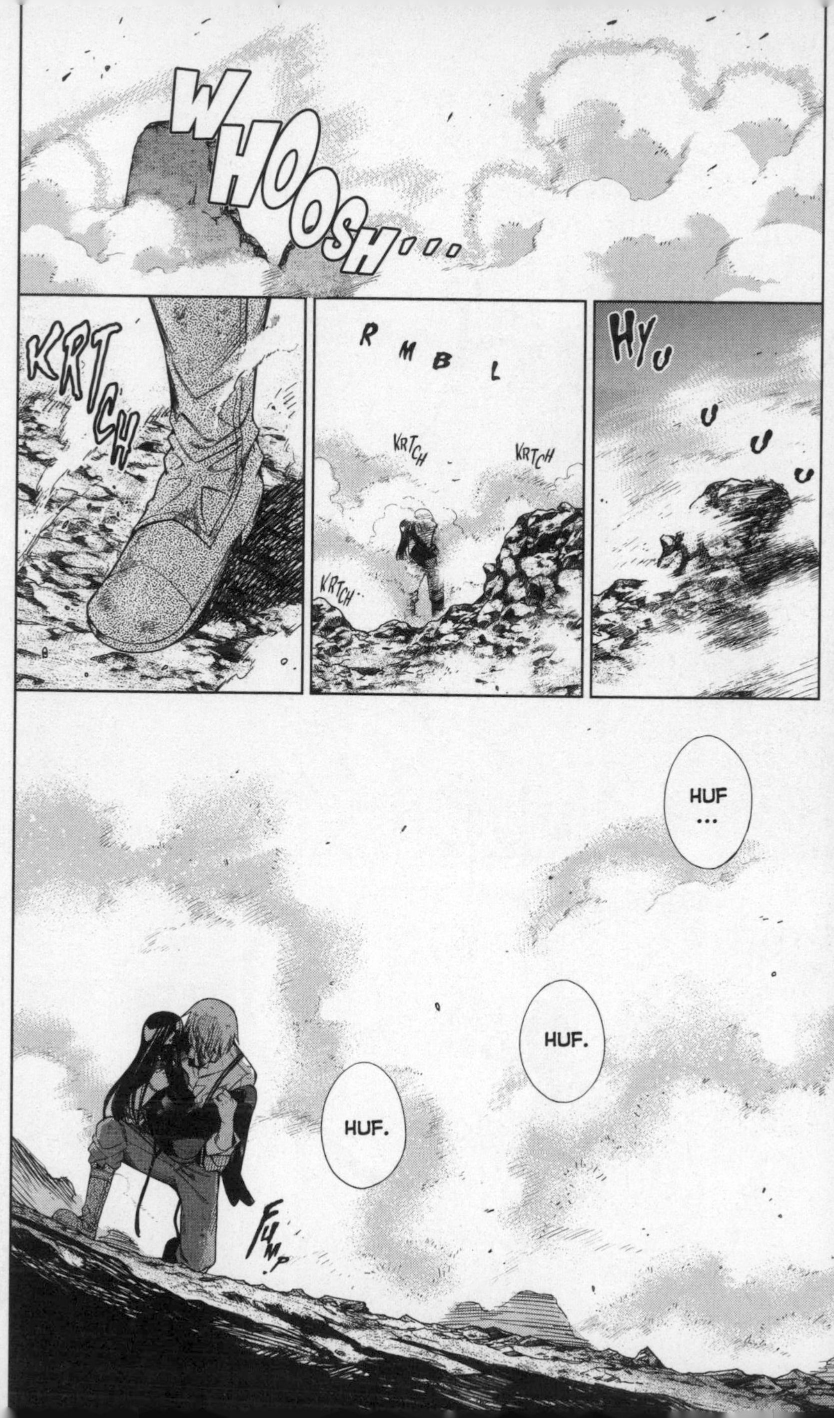
WHOOSH...
HYUUUUU
RMBL
KRTCH
KRTCH
KRTCH
KRTCH
HUF...
HUF.
HUF.
FUMP!

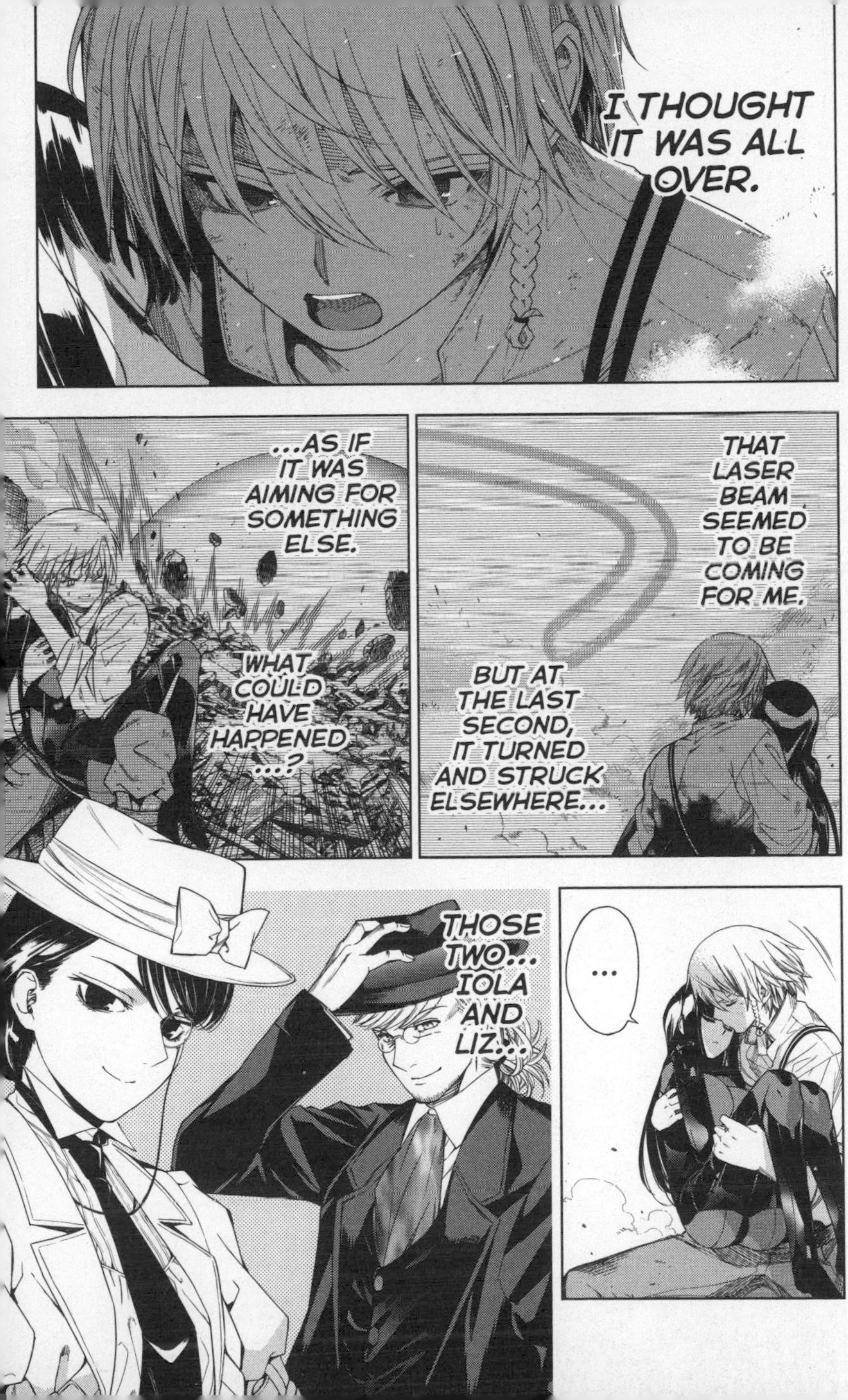
I THOUGHT IT WAS ALL OVER.
THAT LASER BEAM SEEMED TO BE COMING FOR ME.
BUT AT THE LAST SECOND, IT TURNED AND STRUCK ELSEWHERE...
...AS IF IT WAS AIMING FOR SOMETHING ELSE.
WHAT COULD HAVE HAPPENED ...?
...
THOSE TWO... IOLA AND LIZ...

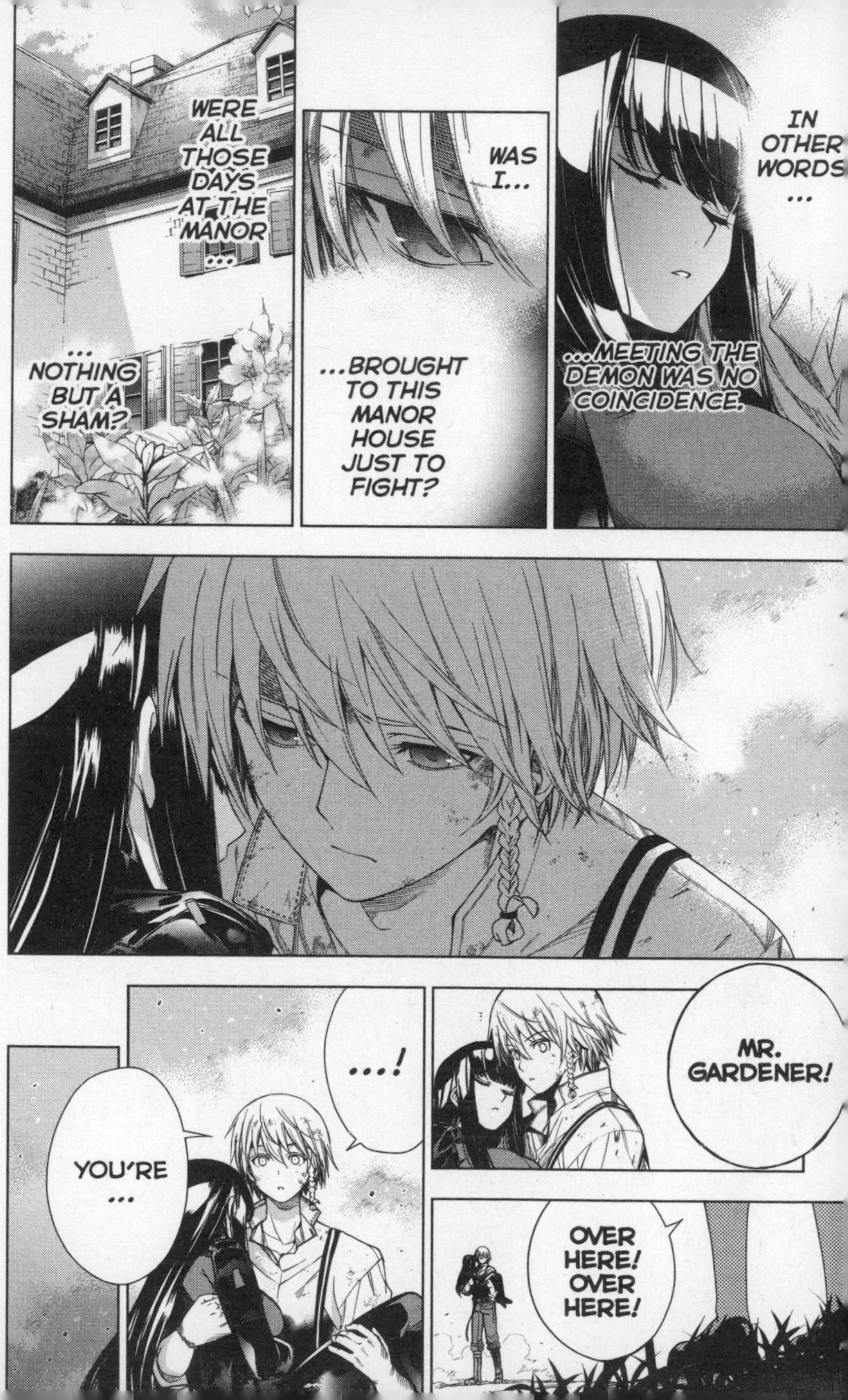
IN OTHER WORDS...
...MEETING THE DEMON WAS NO COINCIDENCE.
WAS I...
...BROUGHT TO THIS MANOR HOUSE JUST TO FIGHT?
WERE ALL THOSE DAYS AT THE MANOR...
...NOTHING BUT A SHAM?
MR. GARDENER!
OVER HERE! OVER HERE!
...!
YOU'RE ...

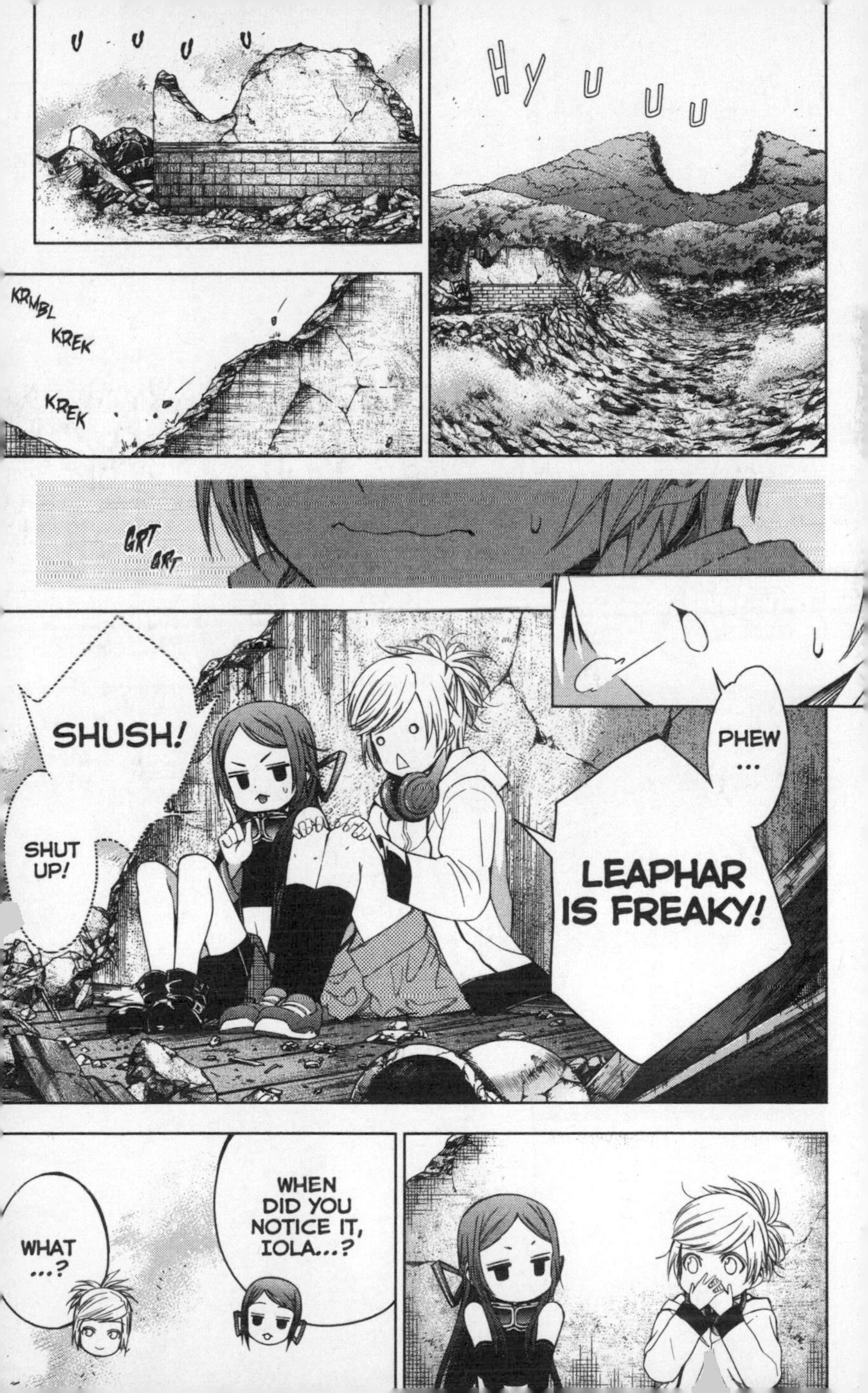
HYUUUU
UUUU
KRMBL
KREK
KREK
GRT GRT
PHEW...
LEAPHAR IS FREAKY!
SHUSH!
SHUT UP!
WHEN DID YOU NOTICE IT, IOLA...?
WHAT...?

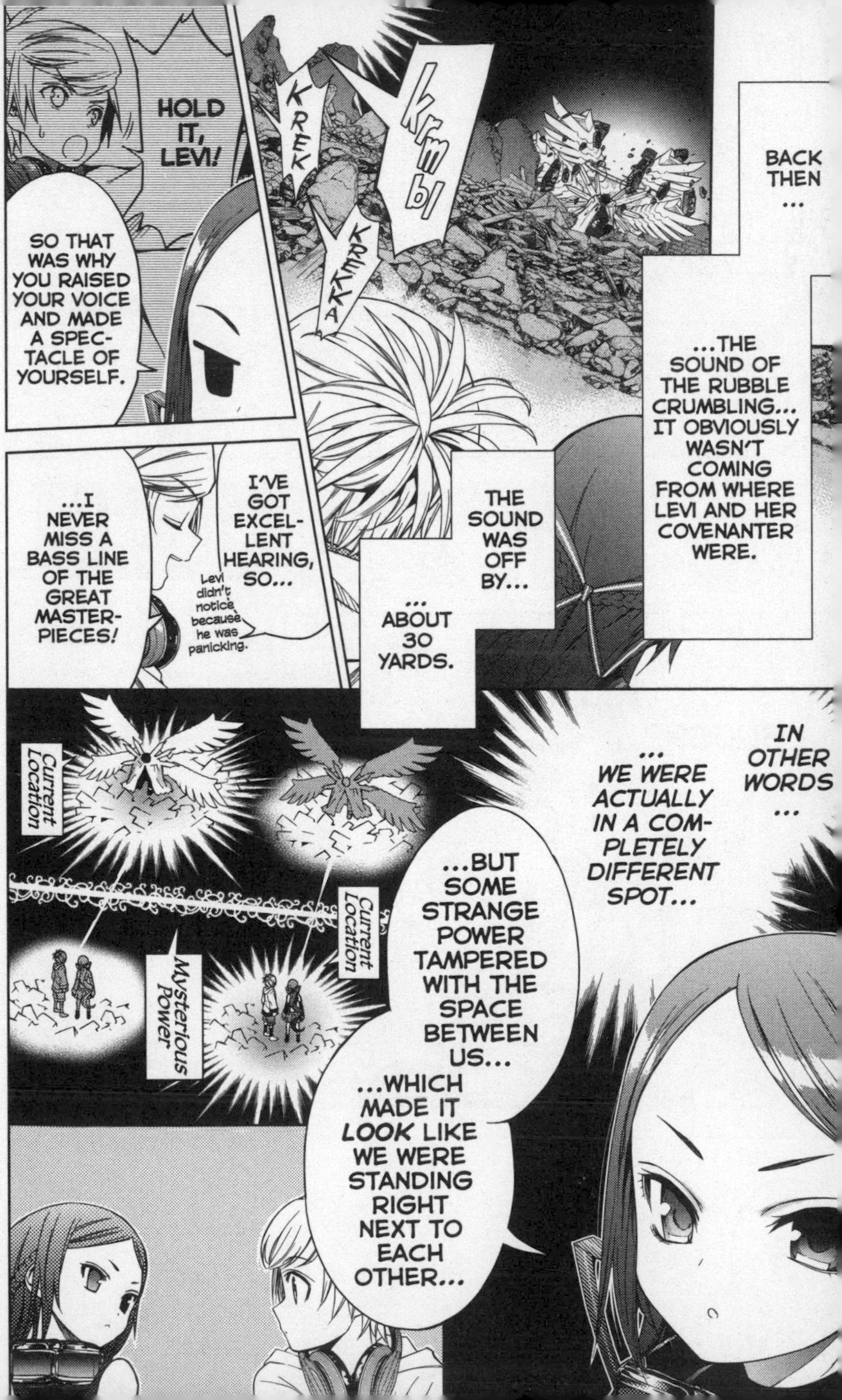
BACK THEN ...
krmbl
KREK
KREKKA
...THE SOUND OF THE RUBBLE CRUMBLING... IT OBVIOUSLY WASN'T COMING FROM WHERE LEVI AND HER COVENANTER WERE.
HOLD IT, LEVI!
SO THAT WAS WHY YOU RAISED YOUR VOICE AND MADE A SPEC-TACLE OF YOURSELF.
THE SOUND WAS OFF BY...
...ABOUT 30 YARDS.
I'VE GOT EXCEL-LENT HEARING, SO...
...I NEVER MISS A BASS LINE OF THE GREAT MASTER-PIECES!
Levi didn't notice because he was panicking.
IN OTHER WORDS ...
...WE WERE ACTUALLY IN A COM-PLETELY DIFFERENT SPOT...
...BUT SOME STRANGE POWER TAMPERED WITH THE SPACE BETWEEN US...
Current Location
Current Location
Mysterious Power
...WHICH MADE IT *LOOK* LIKE WE WERE STANDING RIGHT NEXT TO EACH OTHER...

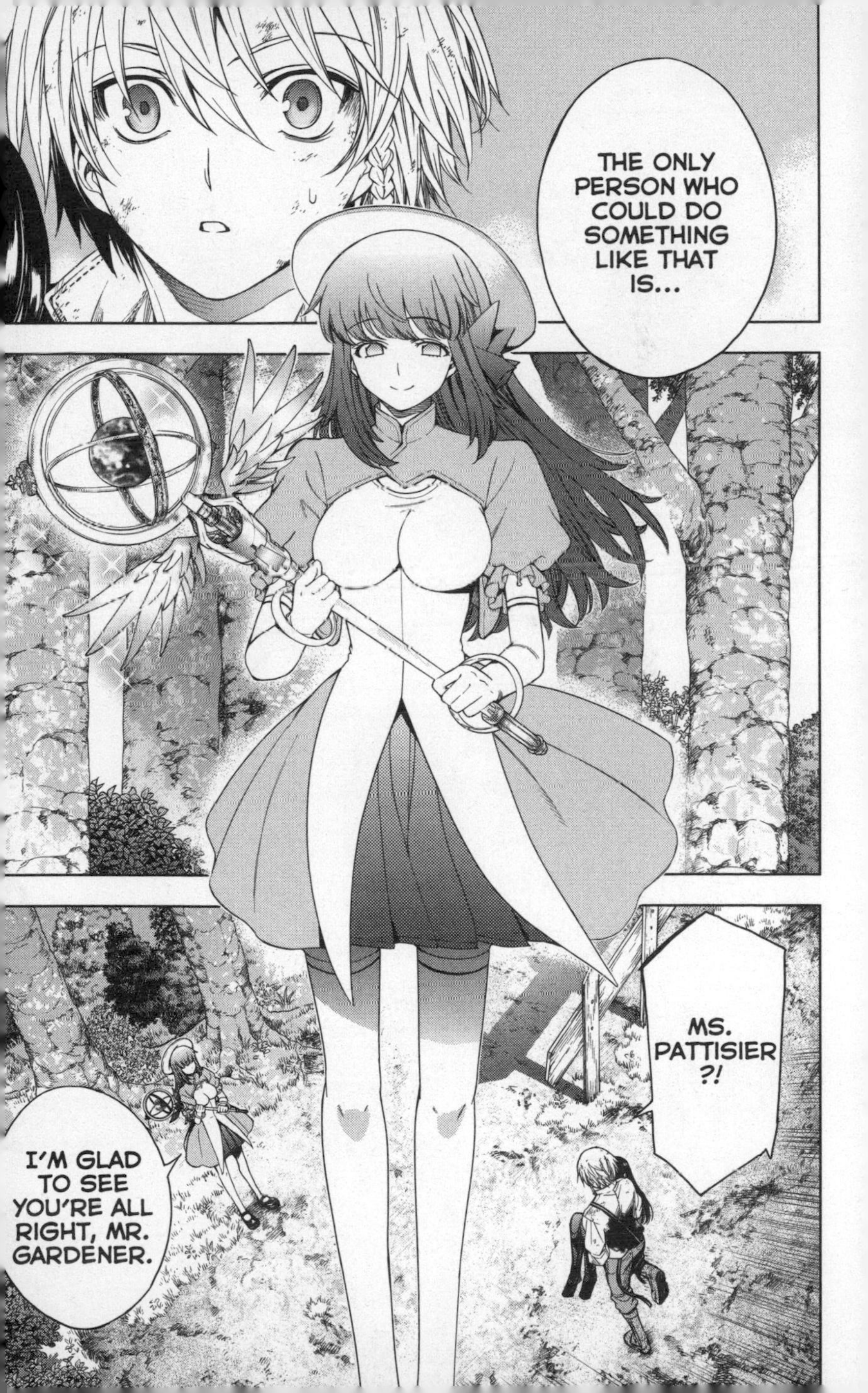
THE ONLY PERSON WHO COULD DO SOMETHING LIKE THAT IS...
MS. PATTISIER?!
I'M GLAD TO SEE YOU'RE ALL RIGHT, MR. GARDENER.

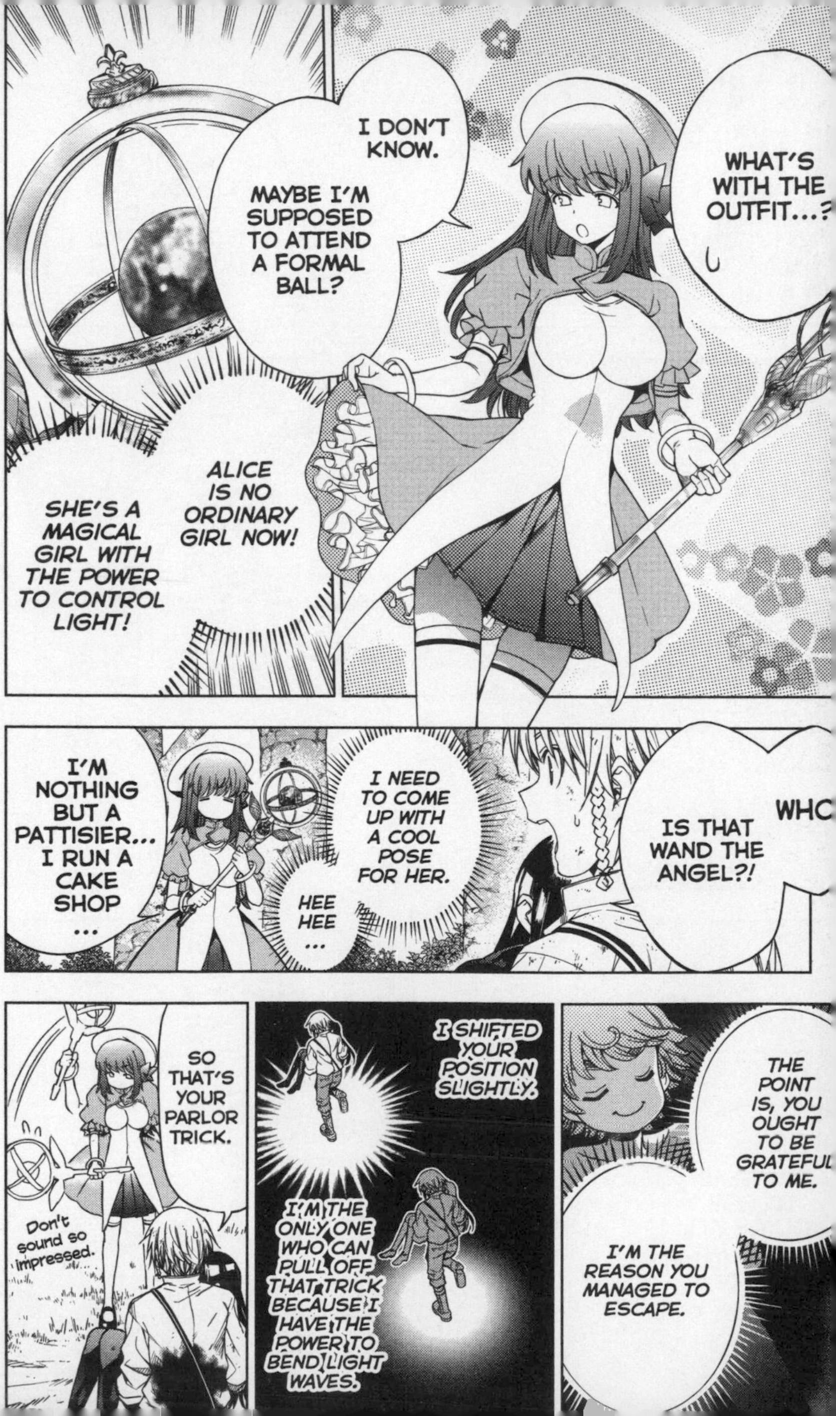
WHAT'S WITH THE OUTFIT...?
I DON'T KNOW.
MAYBE I'M SUPPOSED TO ATTEND A FORMAL BALL?
ALICE IS NO ORDINARY GIRL NOW!
SHE'S A MAGICAL GIRL WITH THE POWER TO CONTROL LIGHT!
IS THAT WAND THE ANGEL?!
I NEED TO COME UP WITH A COOL POSE FOR HER.
HEE HEE ...
I'M NOTHING BUT A PATTISIER... I RUN A CAKE SHOP ...
THE POINT IS, YOU OUGHT TO BE GRATEFUL TO ME.
I'M THE REASON YOU MANAGED TO ESCAPE.
I SHIFTED YOUR POSITION SLIGHTLY.
I'M THE ONLY ONE WHO CAN PULL OFF THAT TRICK BECAUSE I HAVE THE POWER TO BEND LIGHT WAVES.
SO THAT'S YOUR PARLOR TRICK.
Don't sound so impressed.

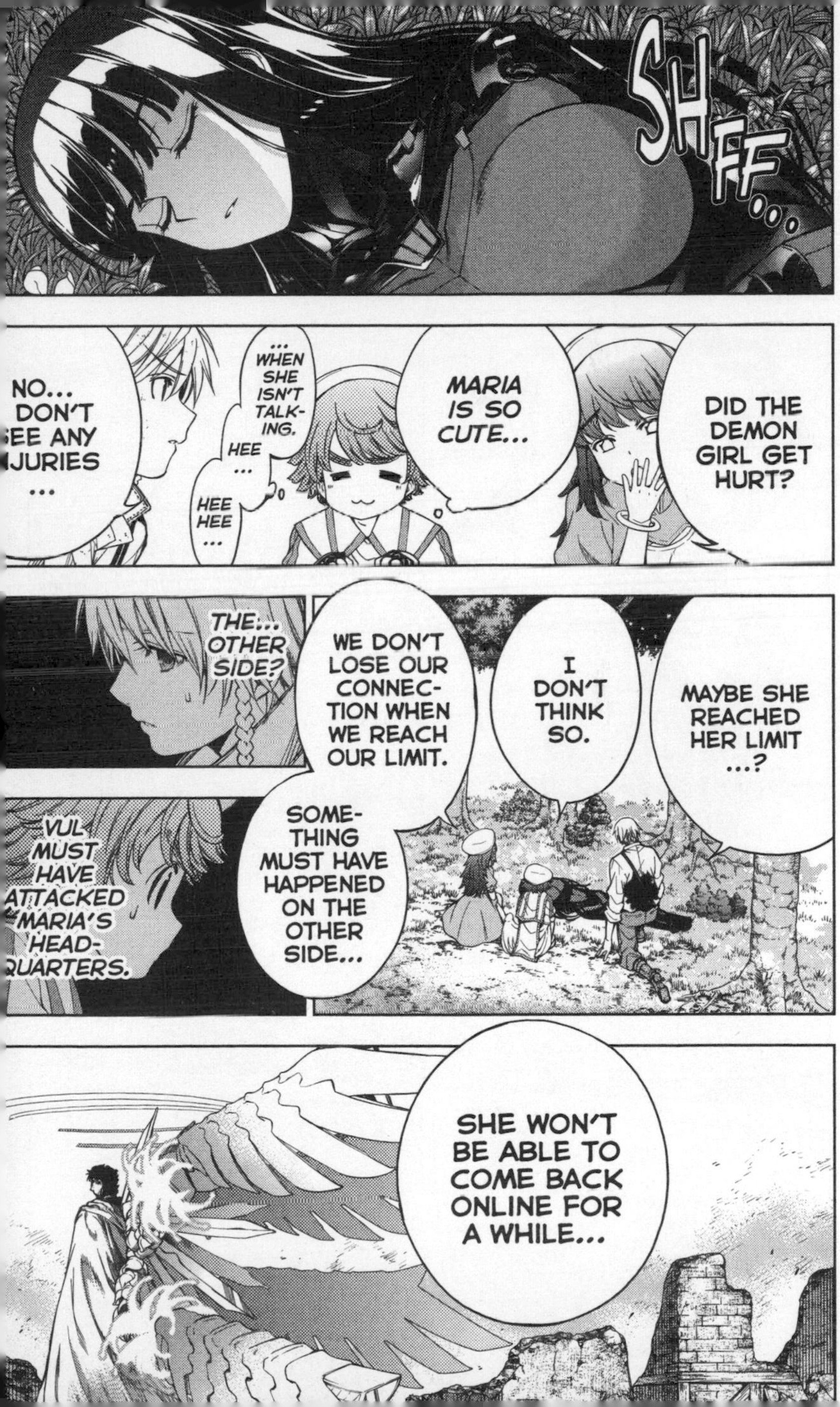
SHFF...
DID THE DEMON GIRL GET HURT?
MARIA IS SO CUTE...
...WHEN SHE ISN'T TALK-ING.
HEE... HEE HEE...
NO... DON'T EE ANY JURIES ...
MAYBE SHE REACHED HER LIMIT ...?
I DON'T THINK SO.
WE DON'T LOSE OUR CONNEC-TION WHEN WE REACH OUR LIMIT.
SOME-THING MUST HAVE HAPPENED ON THE OTHER SIDE...
THE... OTHER SIDE?
VUL MUST HAVE ATTACKED MARIA'S HEAD-QUARTERS.
SHE WON'T BE ABLE TO COME BACK ONLINE FOR A WHILE...

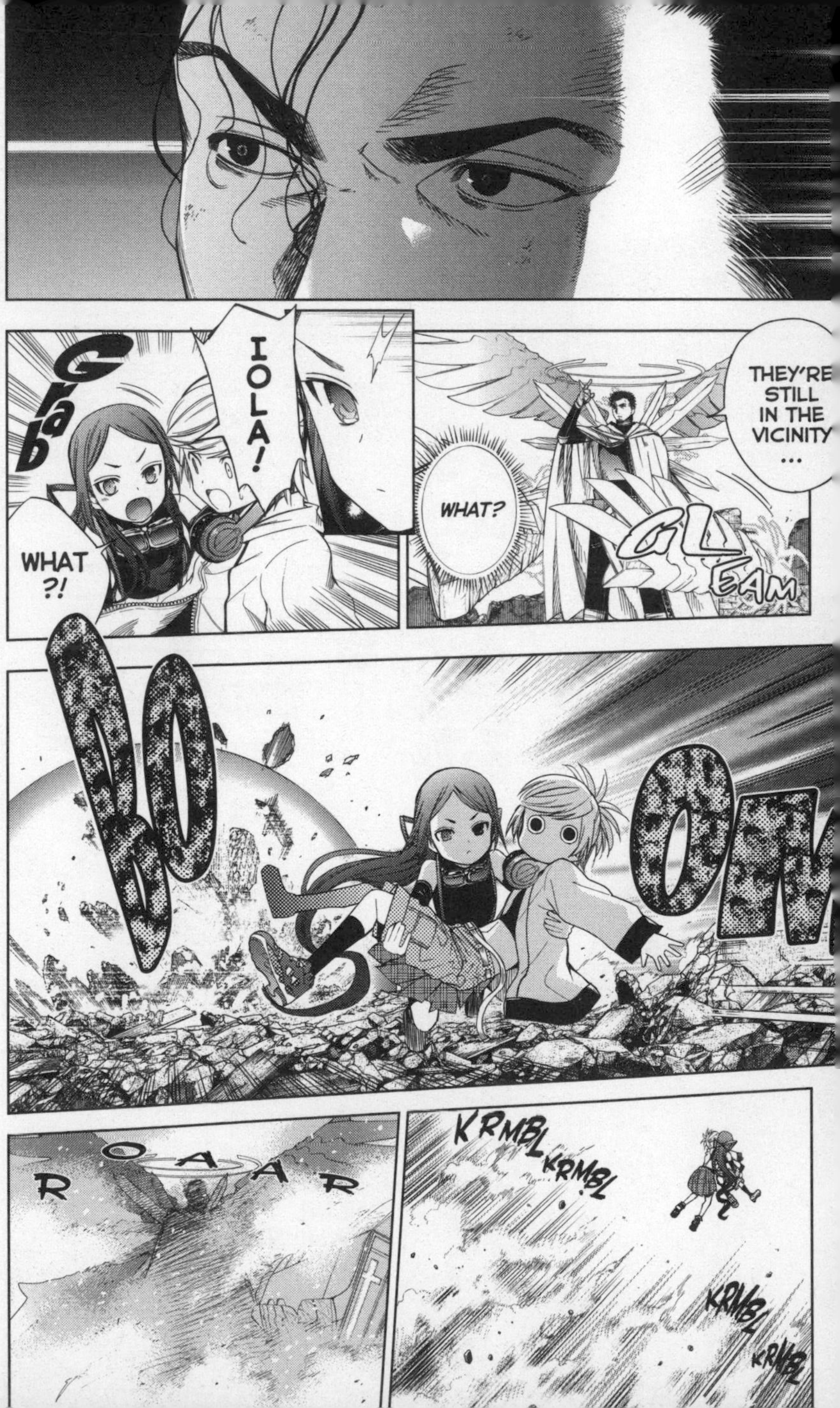
THEY'RE STILL IN THE VICINITY...
WHAT?
GLEAM
IOLA!
Grab
WHAT?!
BOOM
KRMBL
KRMBL
KRMBL
KRMBL
ROAAR

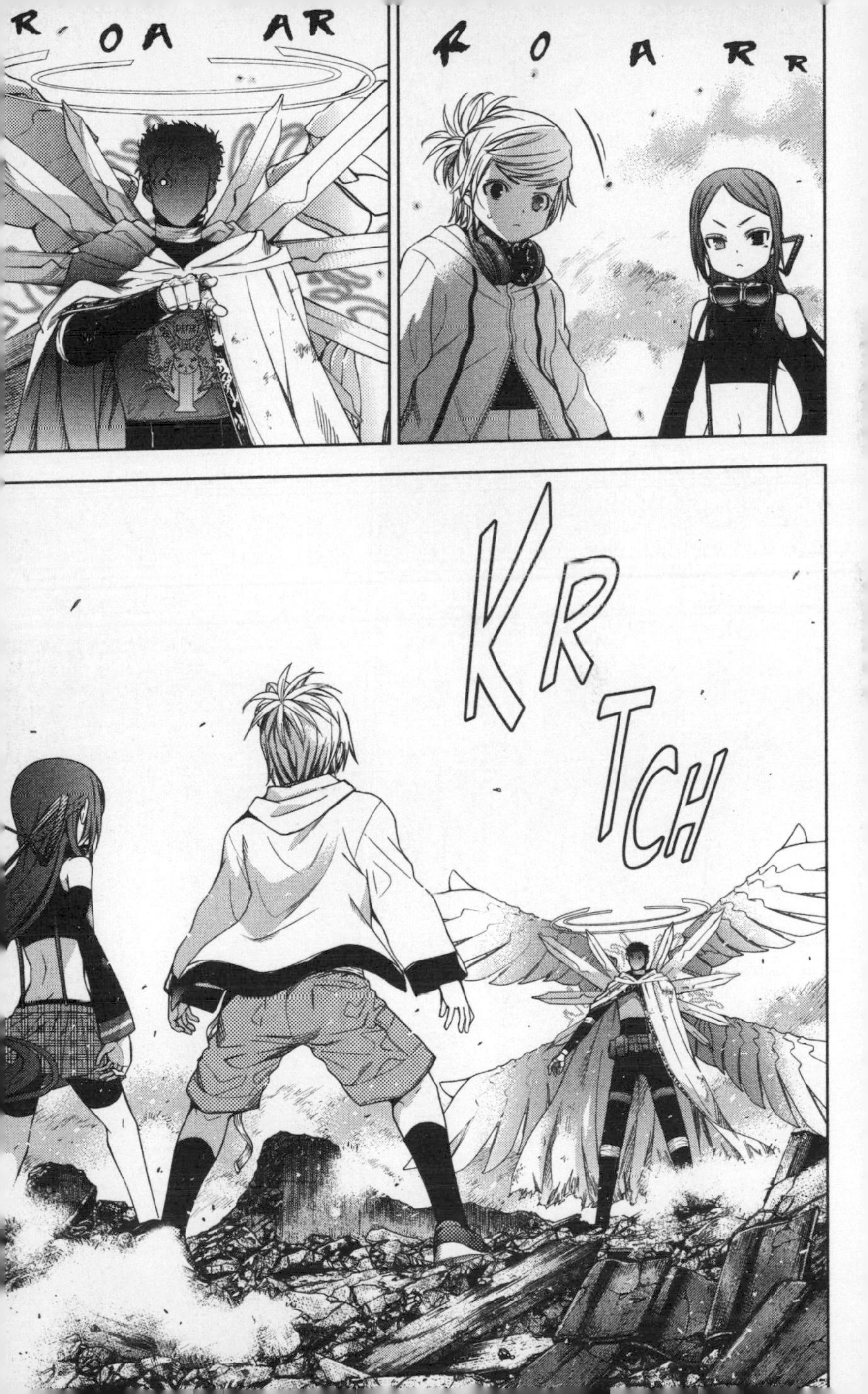
ROARR
ROAAR
KRTCH

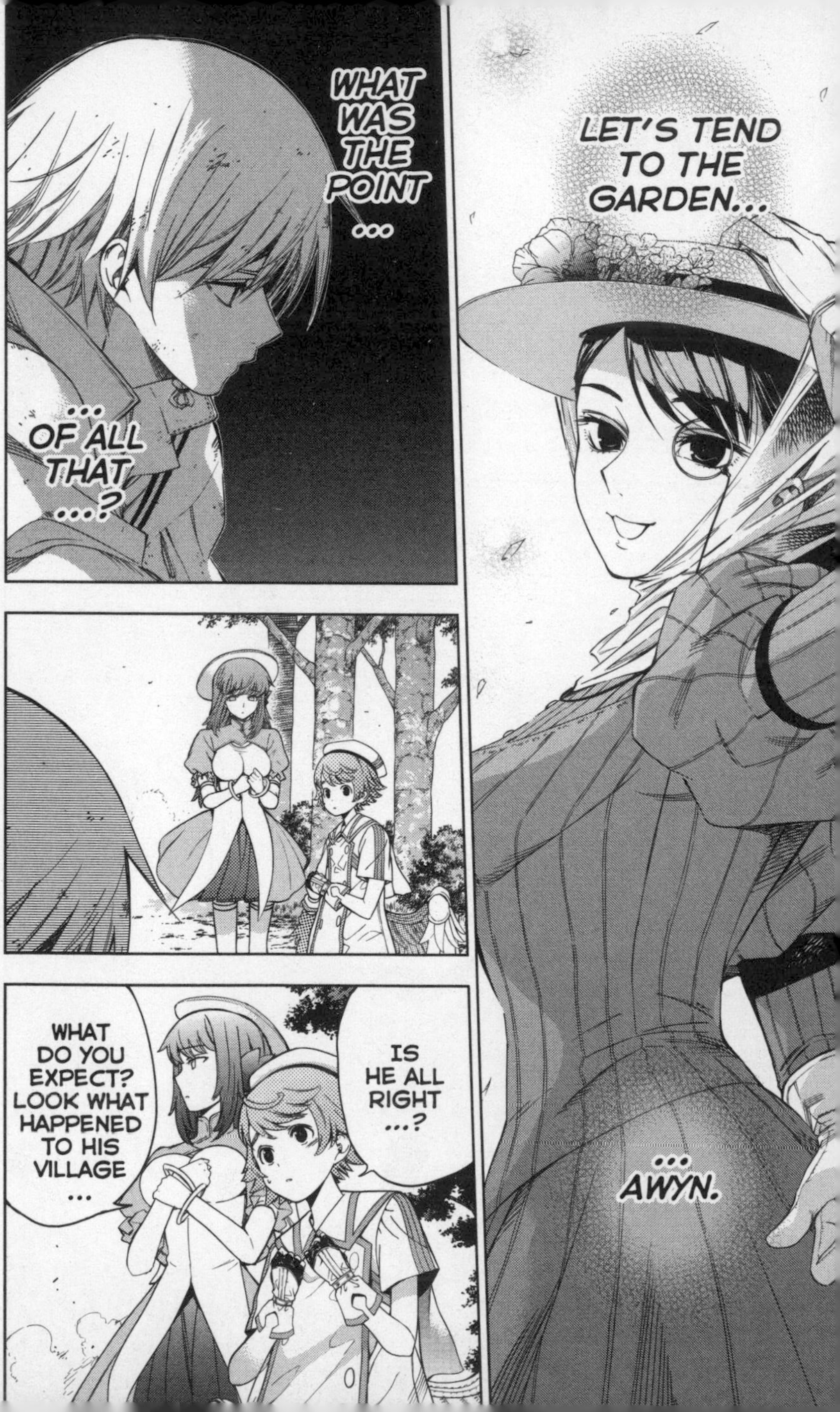
LET'S TEND TO THE GARDEN...
... AWYN.
WHAT WAS THE POINT ...
... OF ALL THAT ...?
IS HE ALL RIGHT ...?
WHAT DO YOU EXPECT? LOOK WHAT HAPPENED TO HIS VILLAGE ...

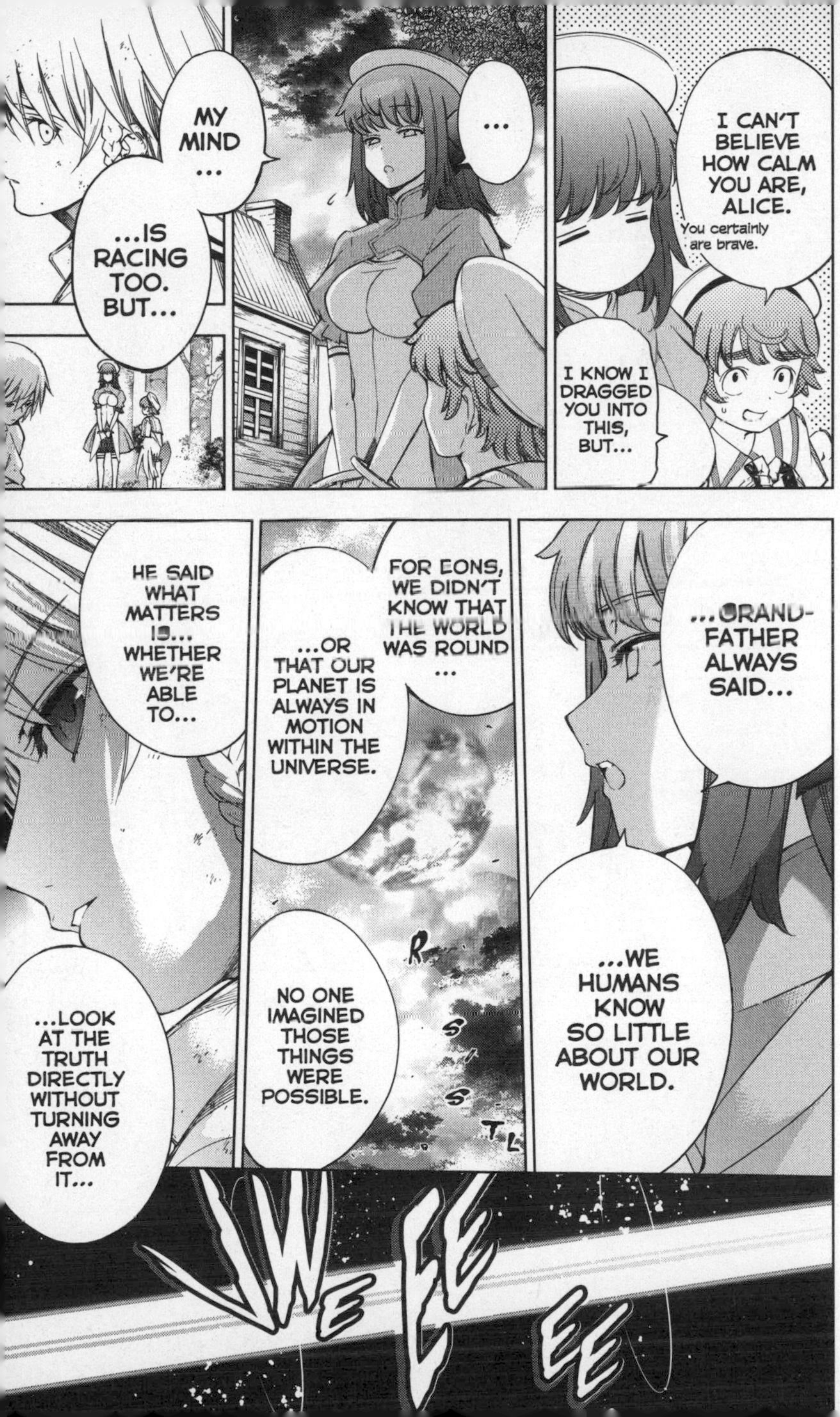
I CAN'T BELIEVE HOW CALM YOU ARE, ALICE.
You certainly are brave.
I KNOW I DRAGGED YOU INTO THIS, BUT...
...
MY MIND ...
...IS RACING TOO. BUT...
...GRAND-FATHER ALWAYS SAID...
...WE HUMANS KNOW SO LITTLE ABOUT OUR WORLD.
FOR EONS, WE DIDN'T KNOW THAT THE WORLD WAS ROUND ...
...OR THAT OUR PLANET IS ALWAYS IN MOTION WITHIN THE UNIVERSE.
NO ONE IMAGINED THOSE THINGS WERE POSSIBLE.
RSSSTL
HE SAID WHAT MATTERS IS... WHETHER WE'RE ABLE TO...
...LOOK AT THE TRUTH DIRECTLY WITHOUT TURNING AWAY FROM IT...
WEEEE

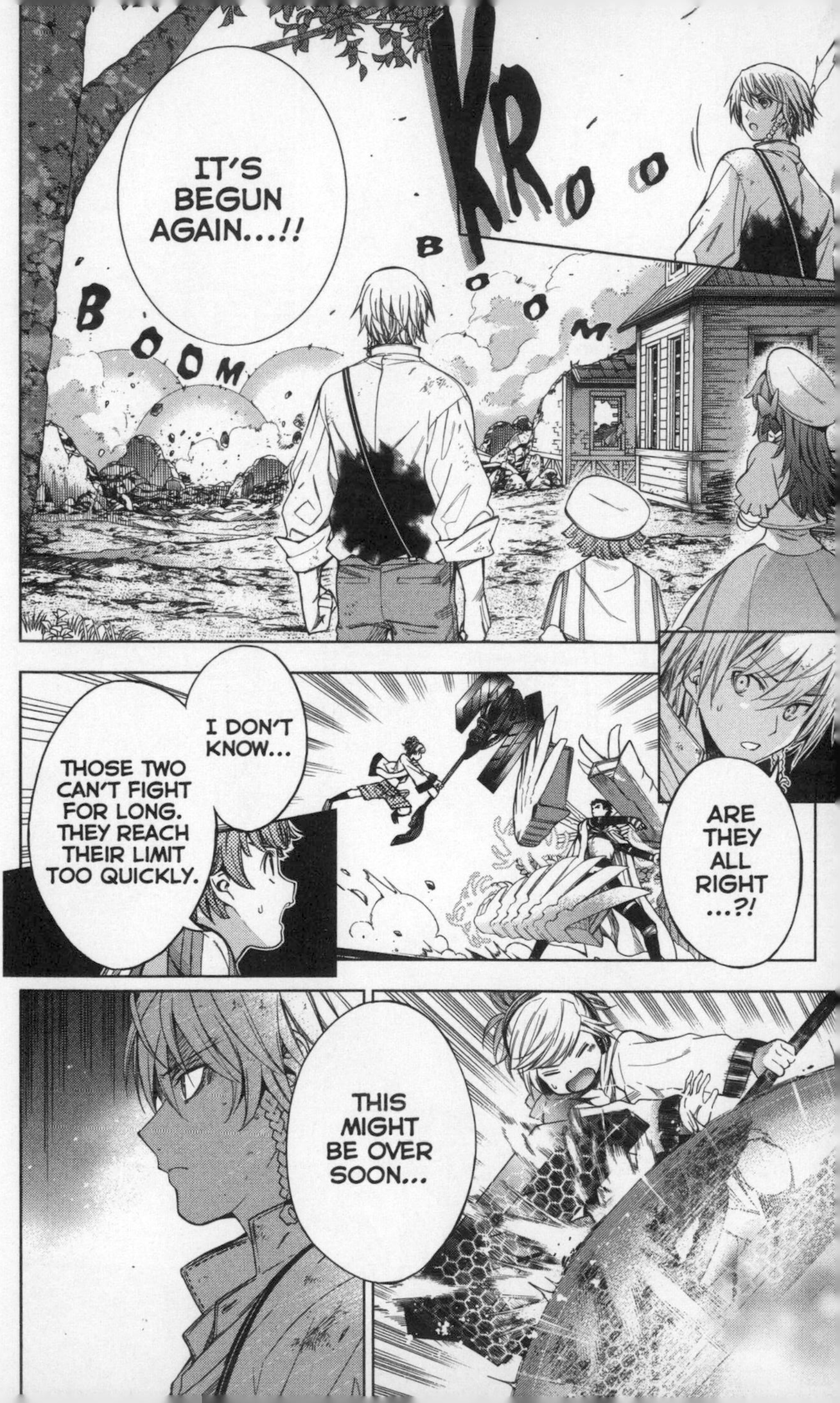
KROOO
IT'S BEGUN AGAIN...!!
BOOM
BOOM
BOOM
ARE THEY ALL RIGHT ...?!
I DON'T KNOW...
THOSE TWO CAN'T FIGHT FOR LONG. THEY REACH THEIR LIMIT TOO QUICKLY.
THIS MIGHT BE OVER SOON...

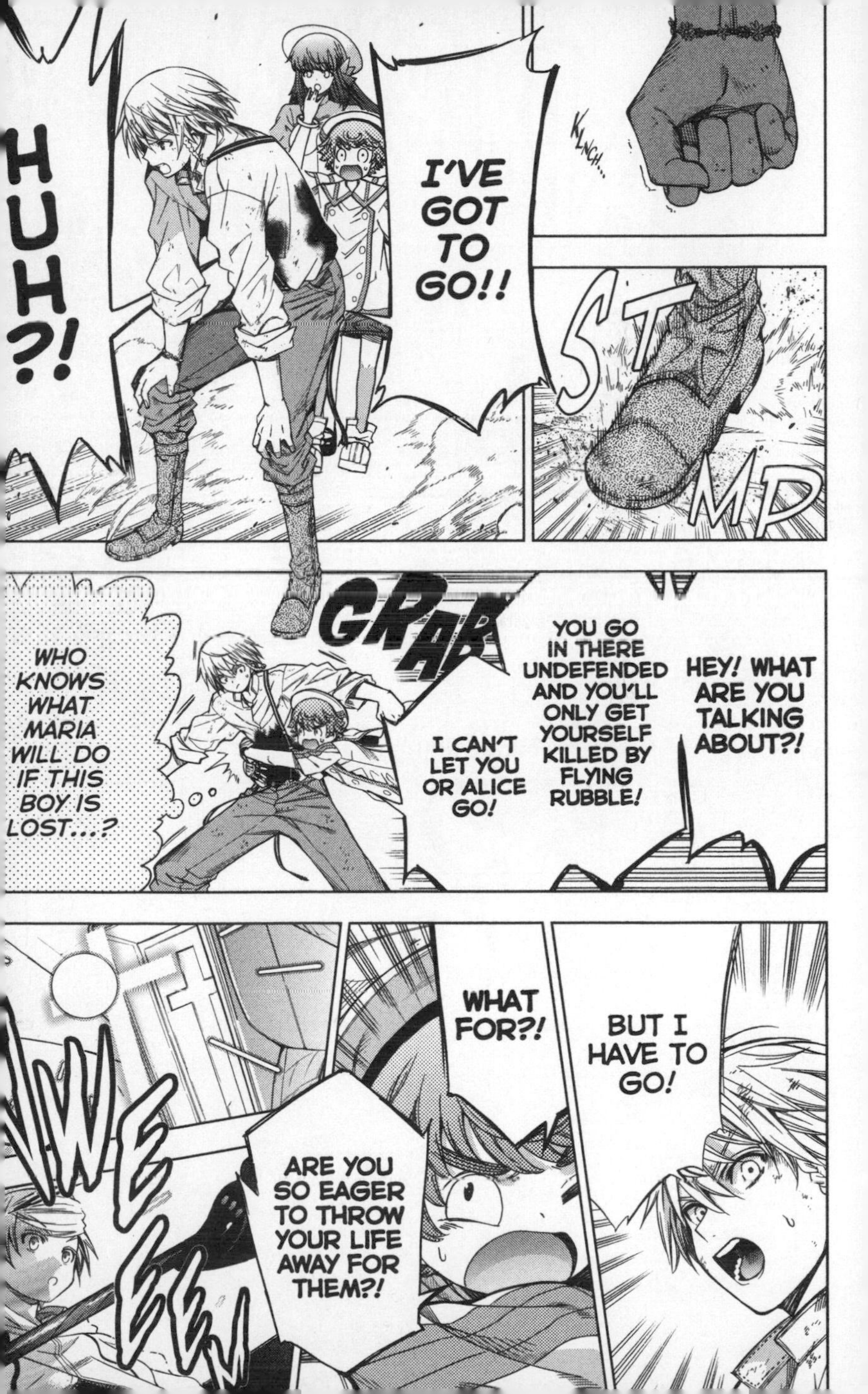
KLNCH...
STMP
I'VE GOT TO GO!!
HUH?!
HEY! WHAT ARE YOU TALKING ABOUT?!
YOU GO IN THERE UNDEFENDED AND YOU'LL ONLY GET YOURSELF KILLED BY FLYING RUBBLE!
I CAN'T LET YOU OR ALICE GO!
GRAB
WHO KNOWS WHAT MARIA WILL DO IF THIS BOY IS LOST...?
BUT I HAVE TO GO!
WHAT FOR?!
ARE YOU SO EAGER TO THROW YOUR LIFE AWAY FOR THEM?!

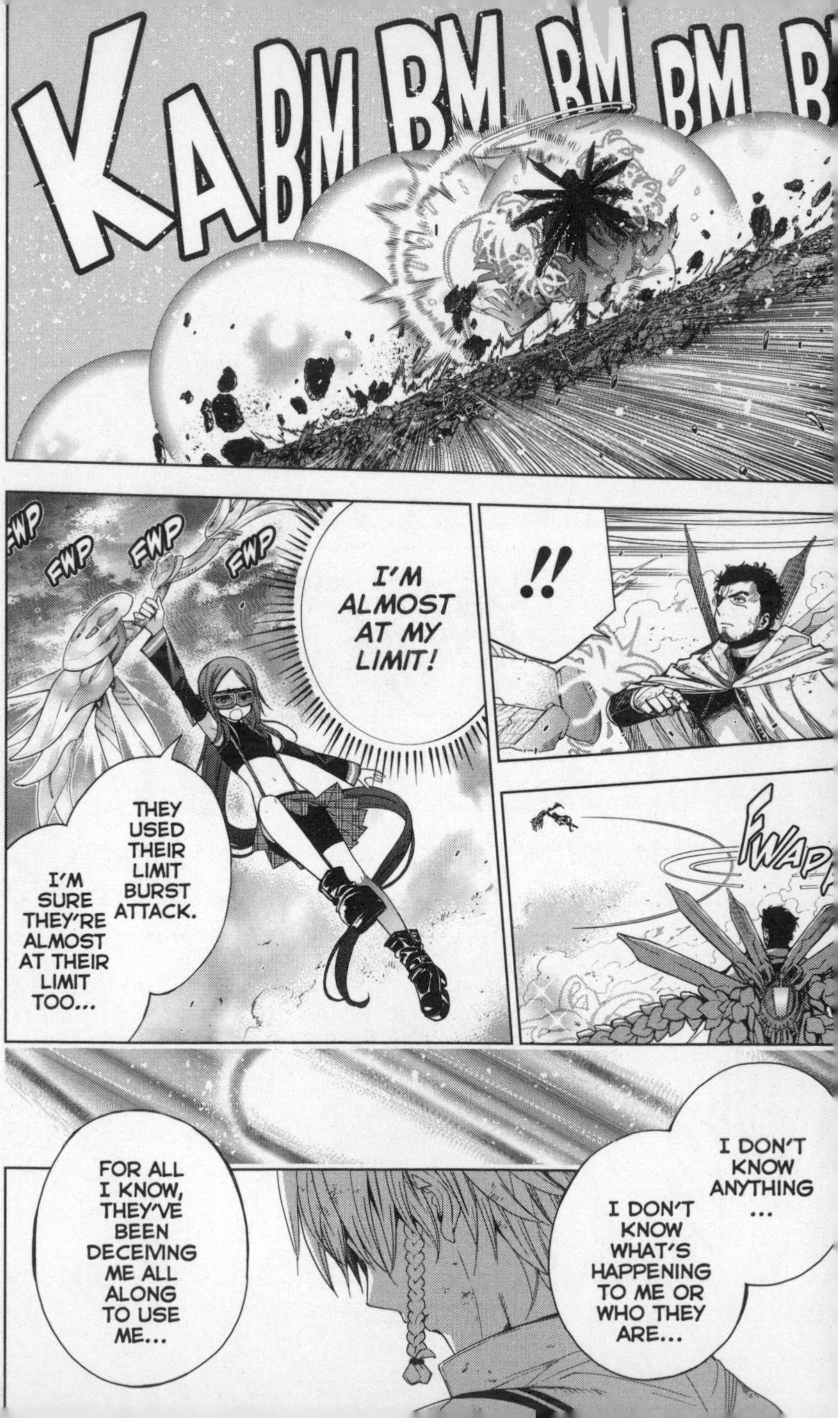
KABM BM BM BM
!!
FWAP
FWP FWP FWP FWP
I'M ALMOST AT MY LIMIT!
THEY USED THEIR LIMIT BURST ATTACK.
I'M SURE THEY'RE ALMOST AT THEIR LIMIT TOO...
I DON'T KNOW ANYTHING...
I DON'T KNOW WHAT'S HAPPENING TO ME OR WHO THEY ARE...
FOR ALL I KNOW, THEY'VE BEEN DECEIVING ME ALL ALONG TO USE ME...

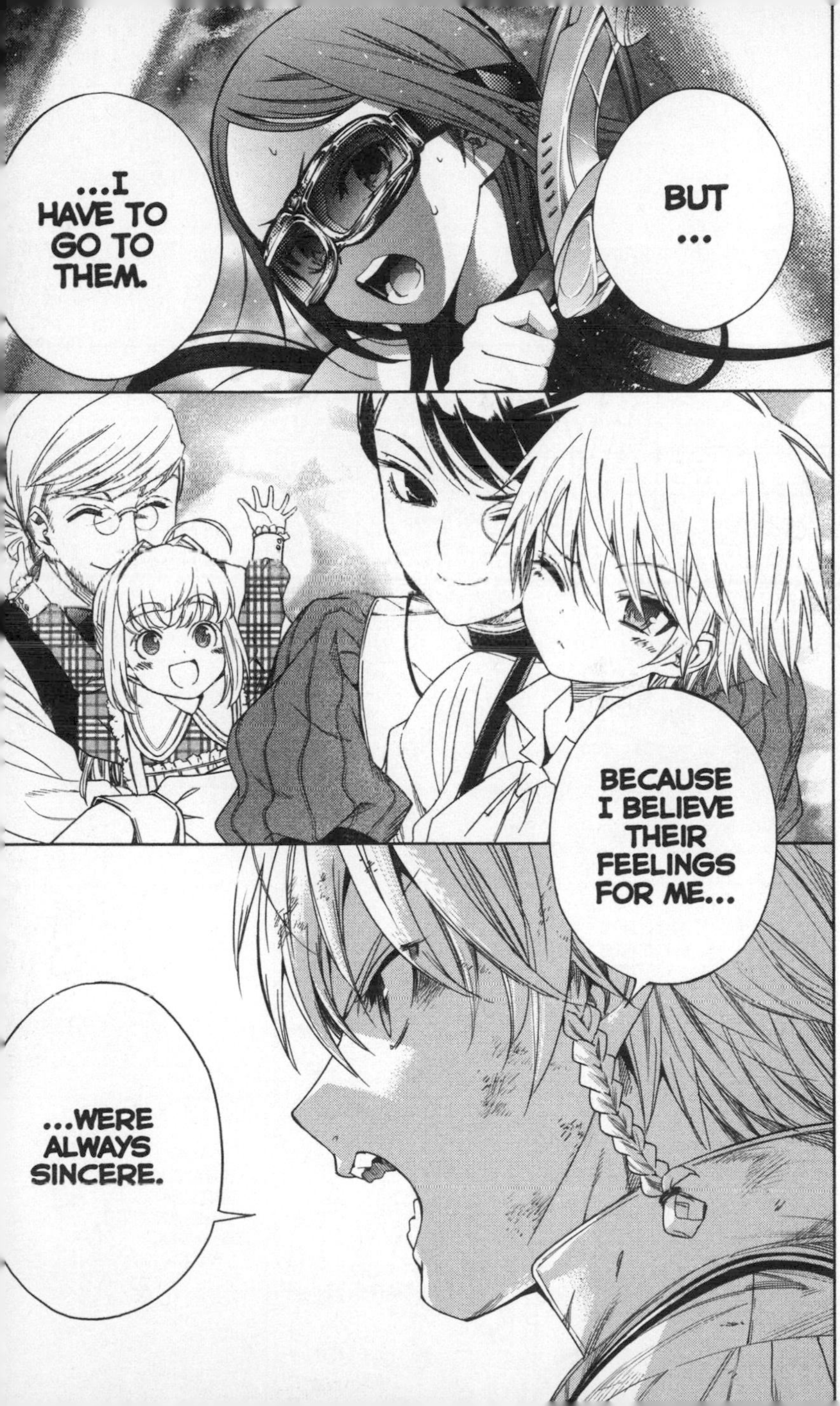
BUT ...
...I HAVE TO GO TO THEM.
BECAUSE I BELIEVE THEIR FEELINGS FOR ME...
...WERE ALWAYS SINCERE.

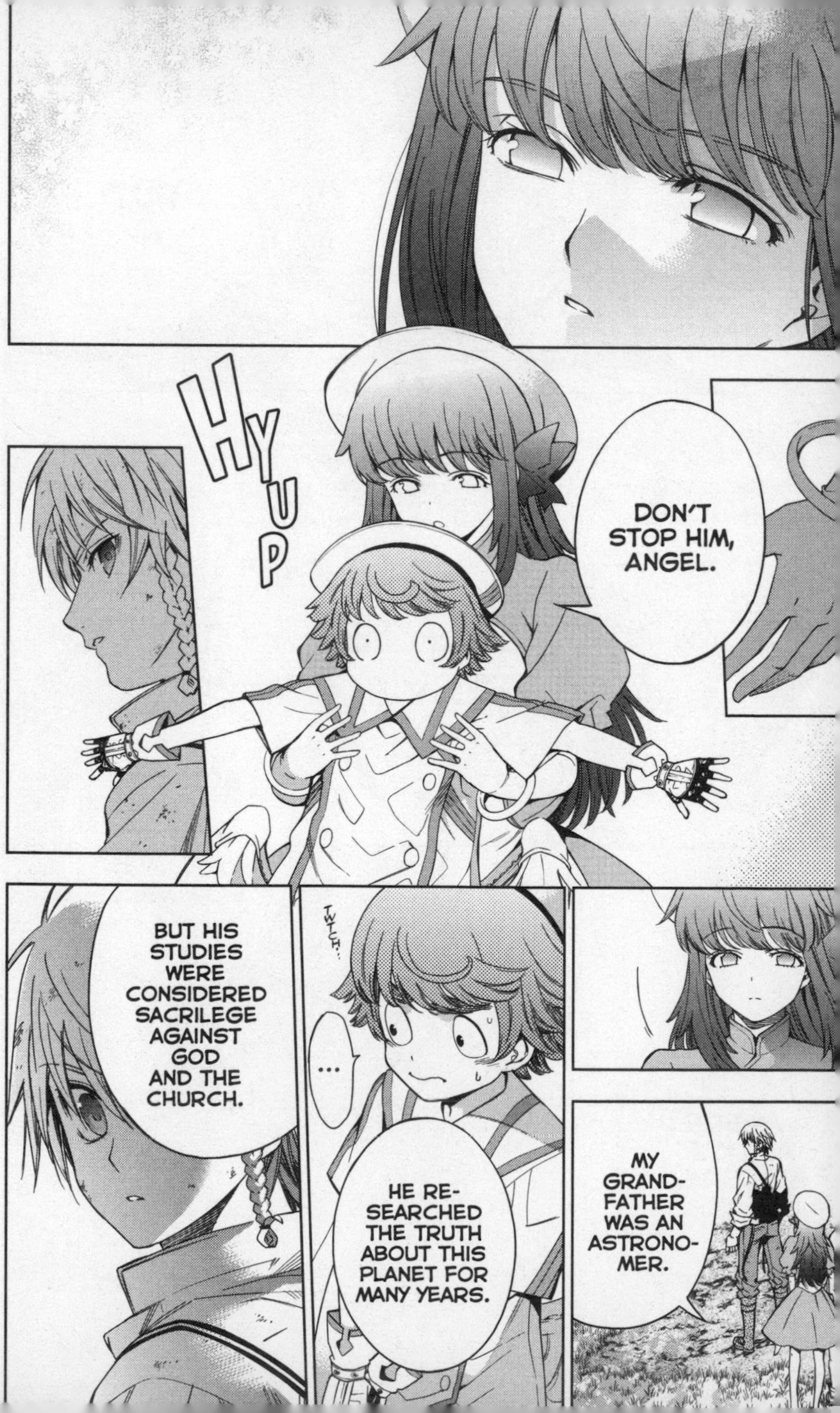
DON'T STOP HIM, ANGEL.
HYUP
MY GRAND-FATHER WAS AN ASTRONO-MER.
TWITCH..
...
HE RE-SEARCHED THE TRUTH ABOUT THIS PLANET FOR MANY YEARS.
BUT HIS STUDIES WERE CONSIDERED SACRILEGE AGAINST GOD AND THE CHURCH.

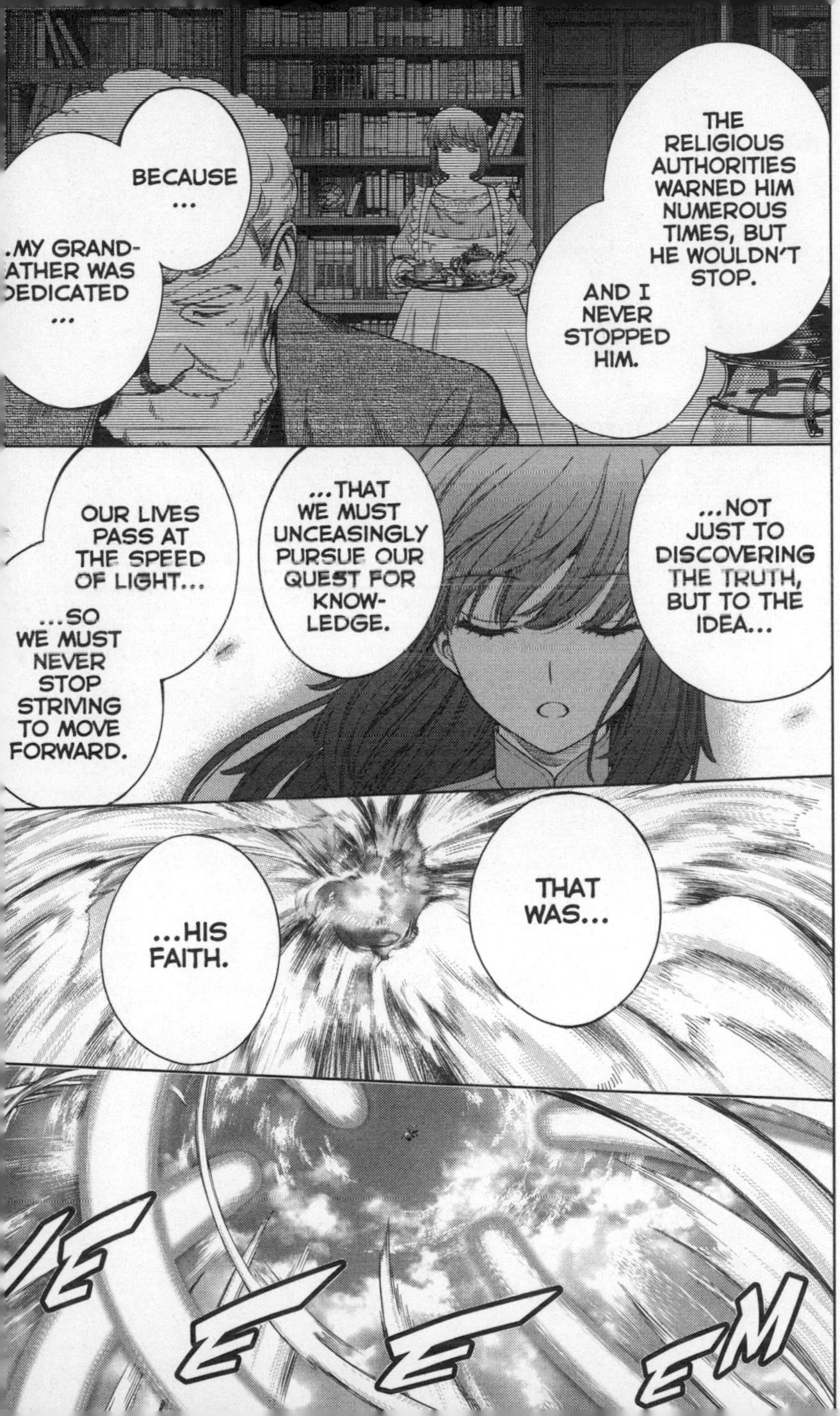
THE RELIGIOUS AUTHORITIES WARNED HIM NUMEROUS TIMES, BUT HE WOULDN'T STOP.
AND I NEVER STOPPED HIM.
BECAUSE...
.MY GRAND-ATHER WAS DEDICATED ...
...NOT JUST TO DISCOVERING THE TRUTH, BUT TO THE IDEA...
...THAT WE MUST UNCEASINGLY PURSUE OUR QUEST FOR KNOW-LEDGE.
OUR LIVES PASS AT THE SPEED OF LIGHT...
...SO WE MUST NEVER STOP STRIVING TO MOVE FORWARD.
THAT WAS...
...HIS FAITH.
IEEE-EM

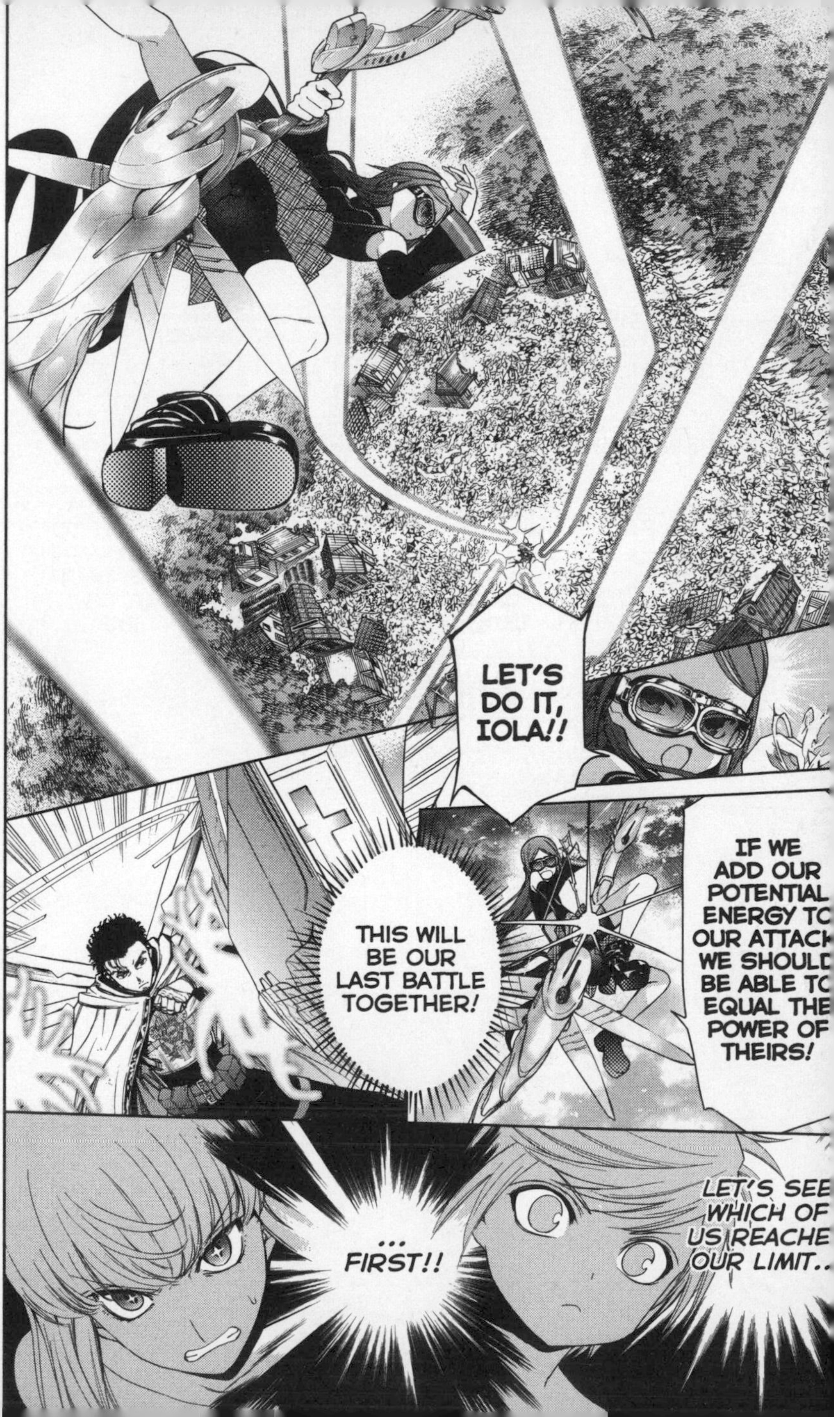
LET'S DO IT, IOLA!!
IF WE ADD OUR POTENTIAL ENERGY TO OUR ATTACK WE SHOULD BE ABLE TO EQUAL THE POWER OF THEIRS!
THIS WILL BE OUR LAST BATTLE TOGETHER!
LET'S SEE WHICH OF US REACHE OUR LIMIT...
... FIRST!!

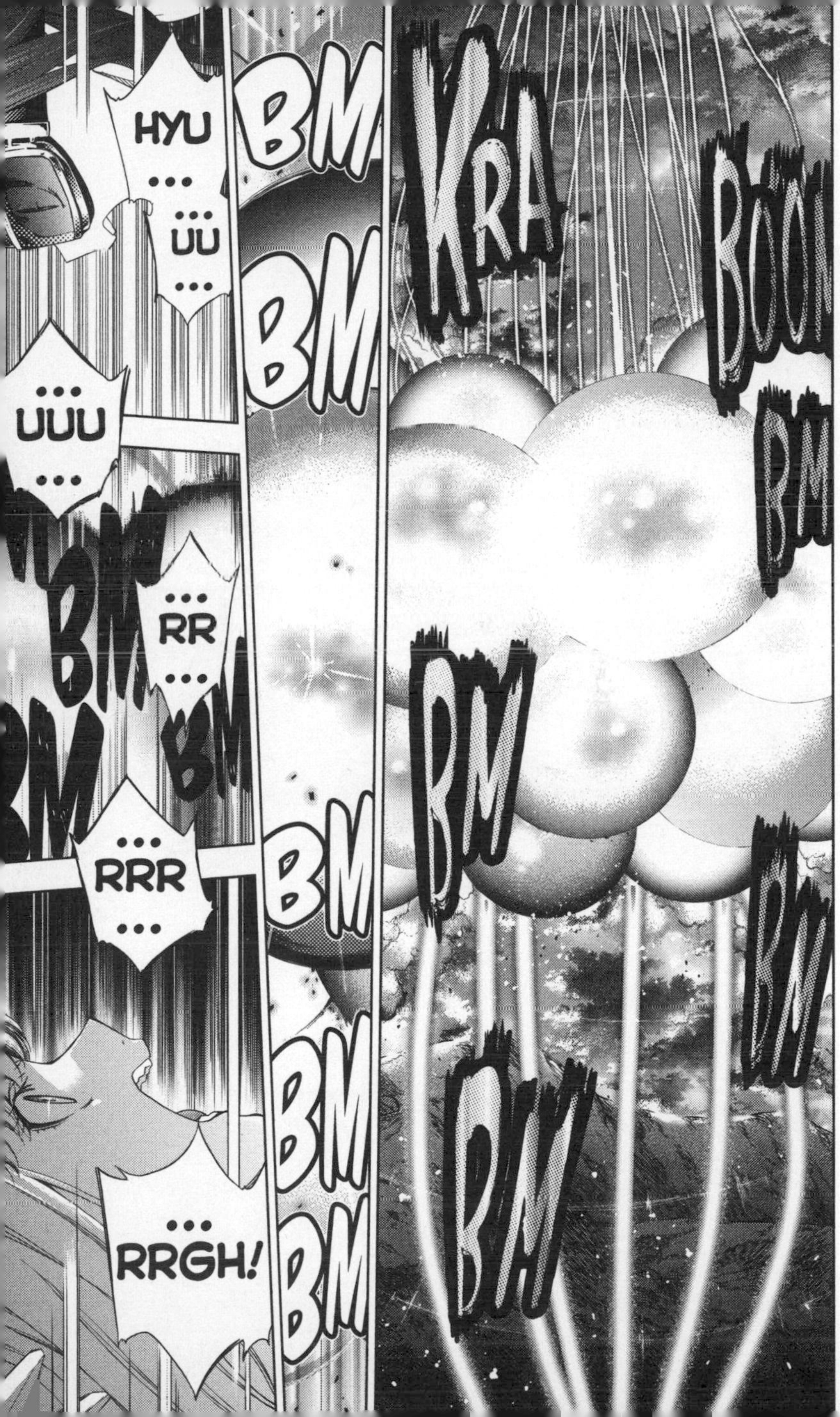
KRA
BOO
BM
BM
BM
BM
BM
BM
BM
BM
BM
HYU ... ...UU ...
...UUU...
BM
BM
BM
BM
...RR...
...RRR...
...RRGH!

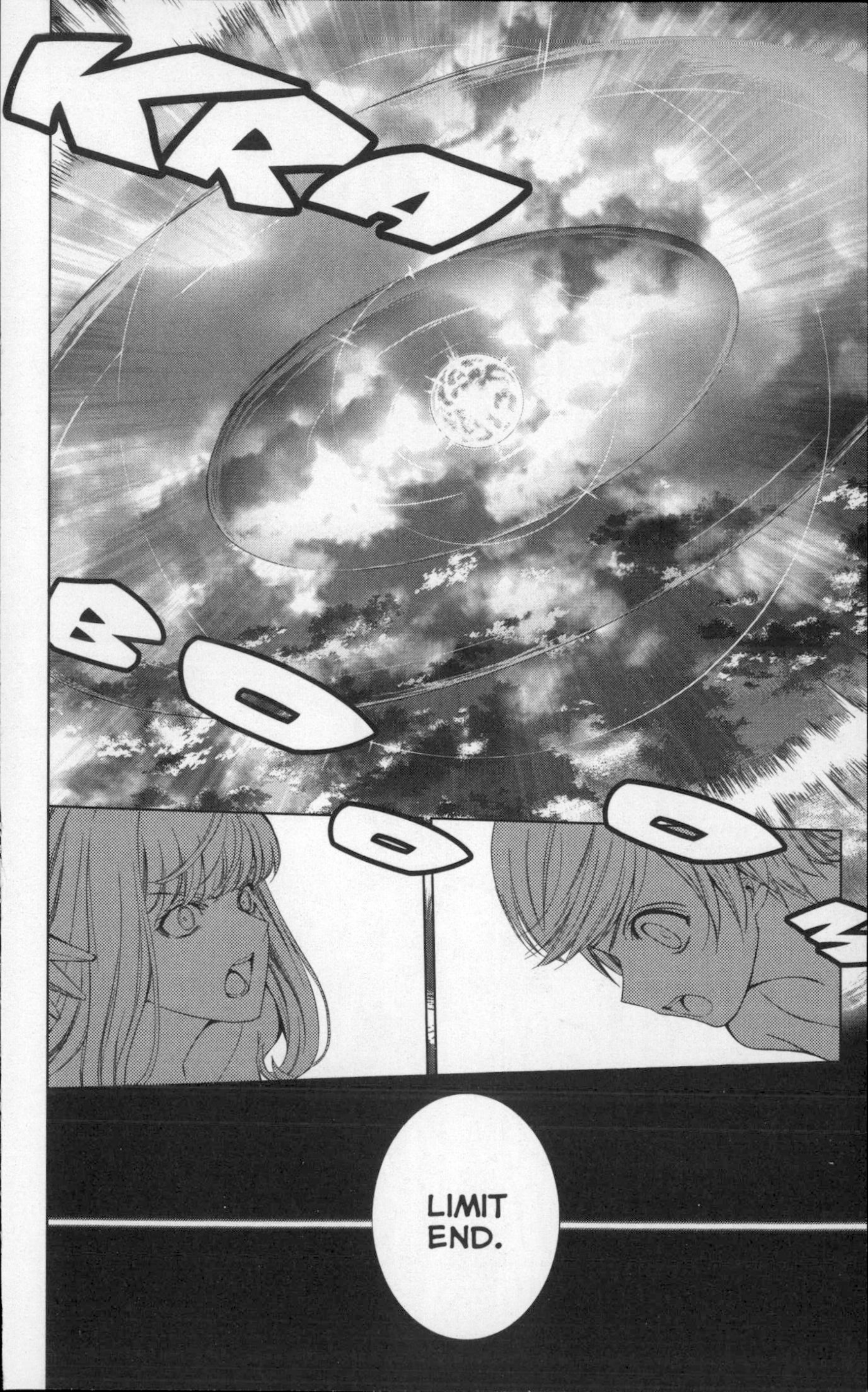
KRA
BOOOM
LIMIT END.

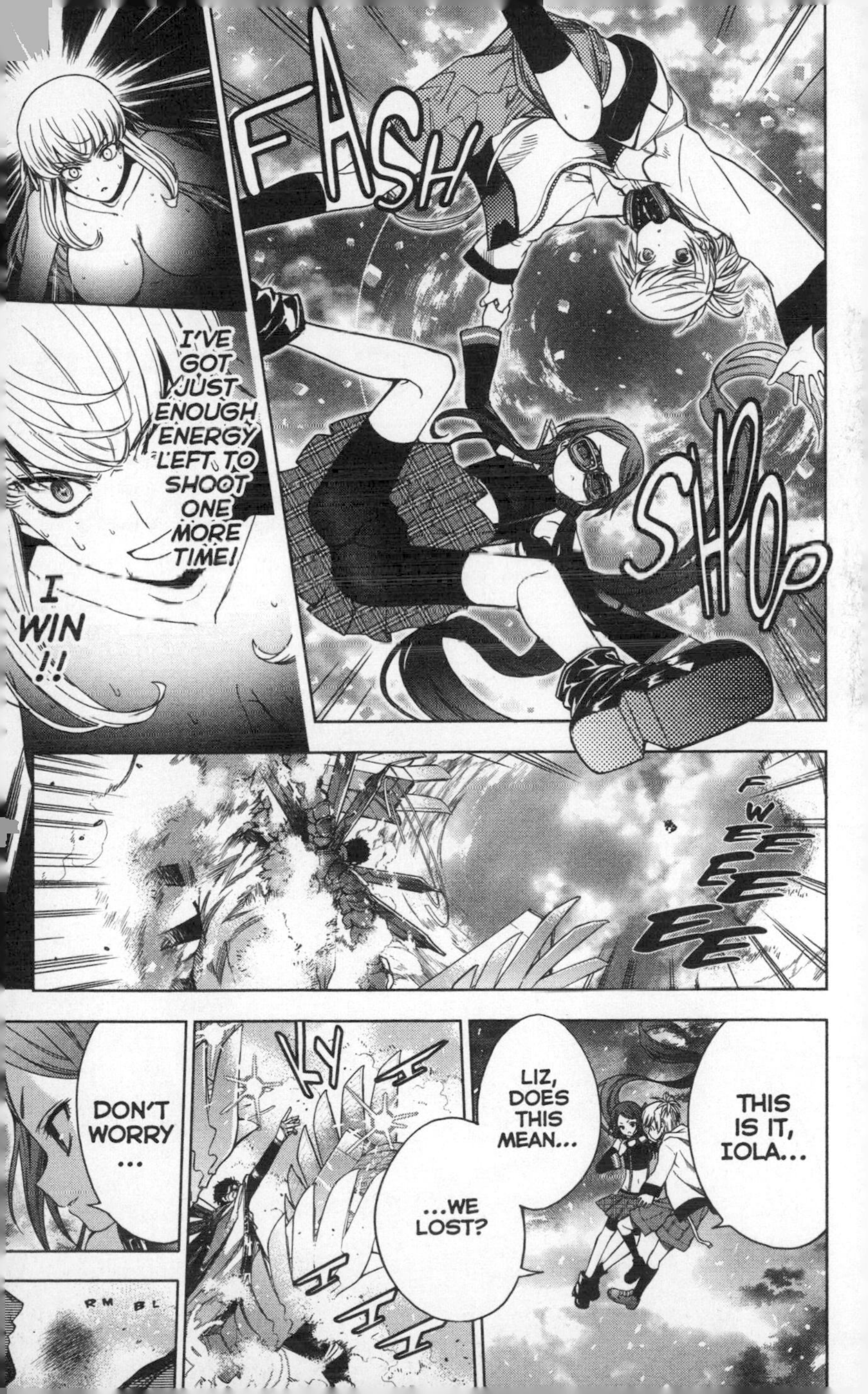
FASH
SHOOP
I'VE GOT JUST ENOUGH ENERGY LEFT TO SHOOT ONE MORE TIME!
I WIN!!
FWEEEEEE
THIS IS IT, IOLA...
LIZ, DOES THIS MEAN...
...WE LOST?
KLY
DON'T WORRY...
RM BL

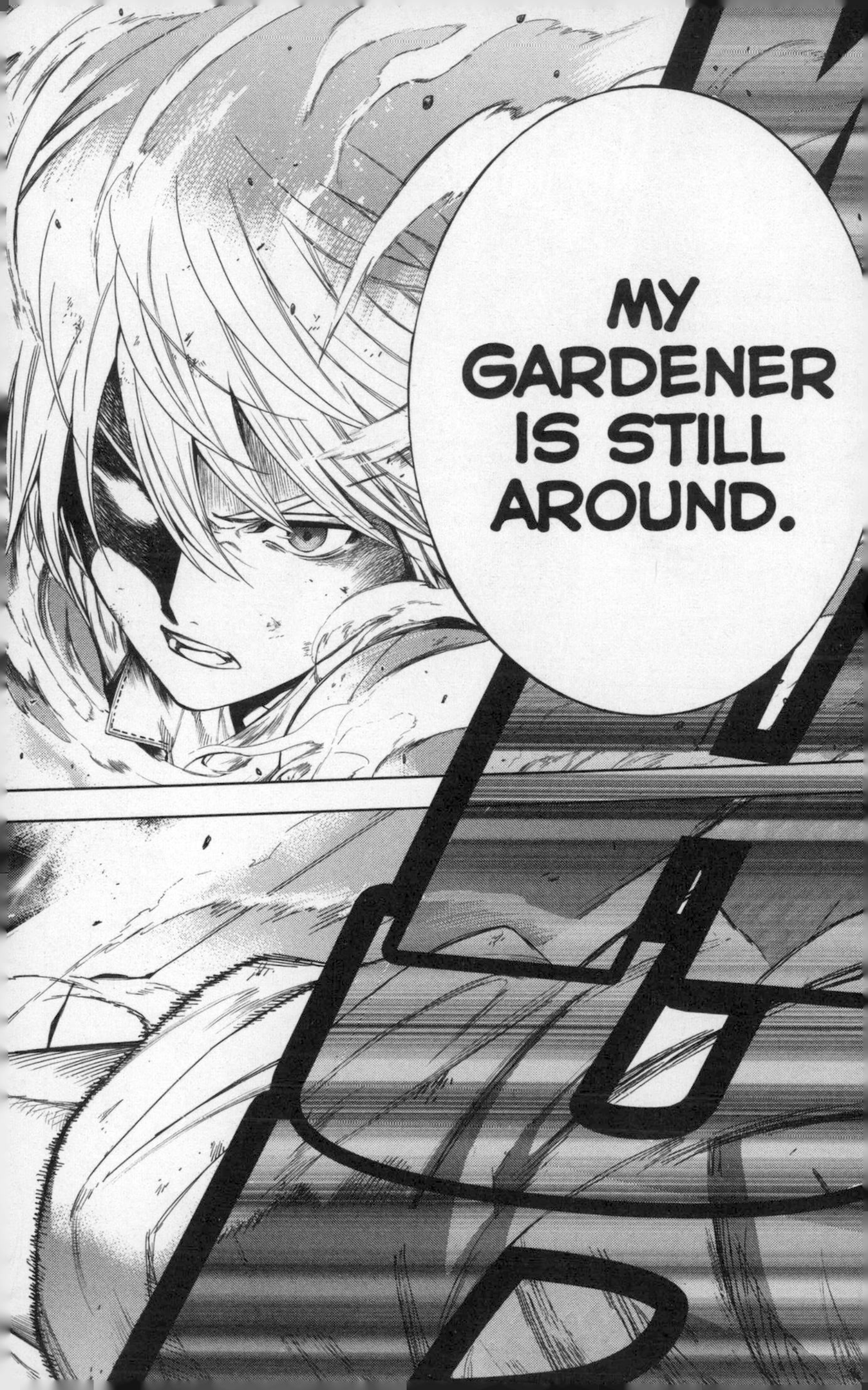
MY GARDENER IS STILL AROUND.

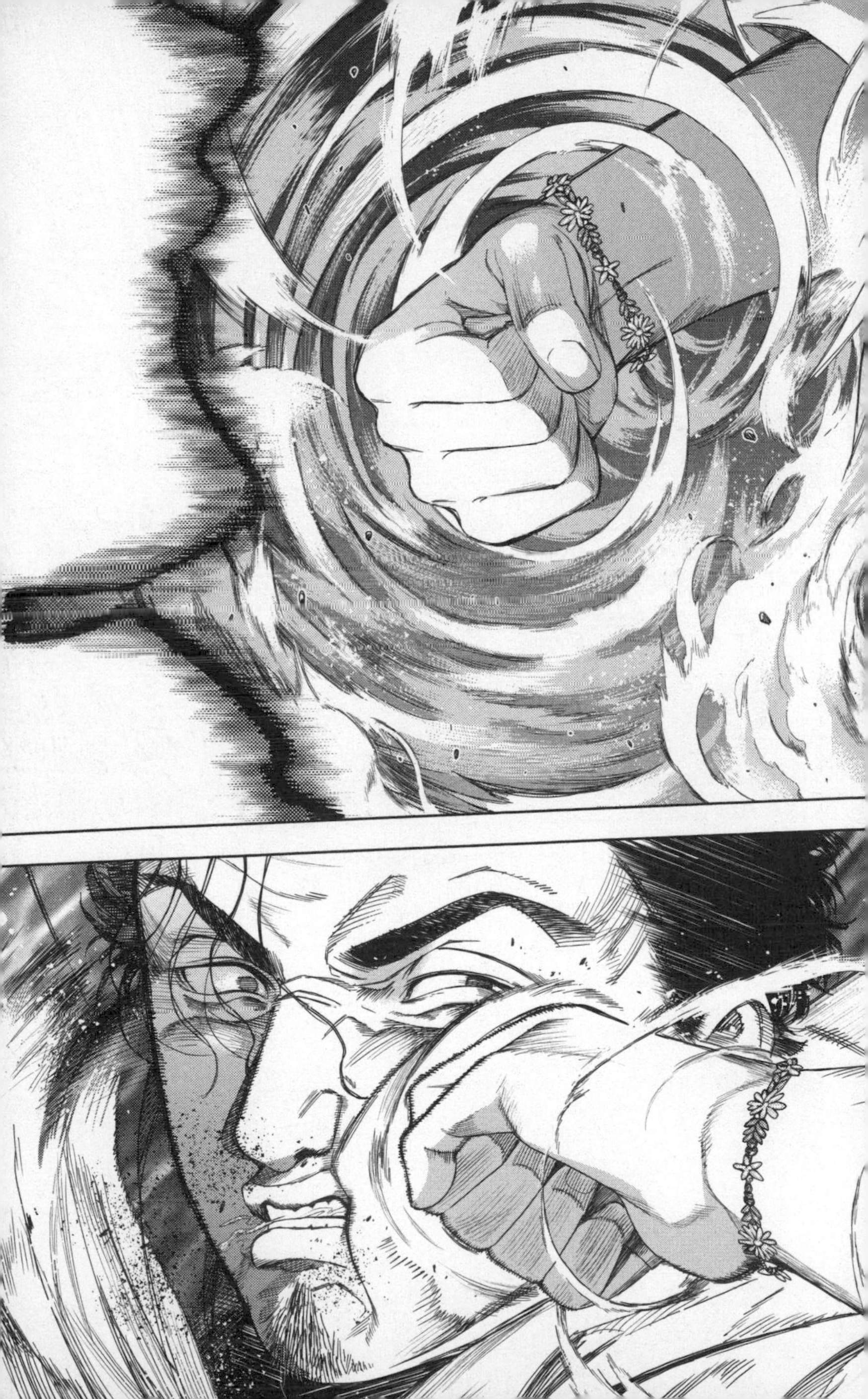

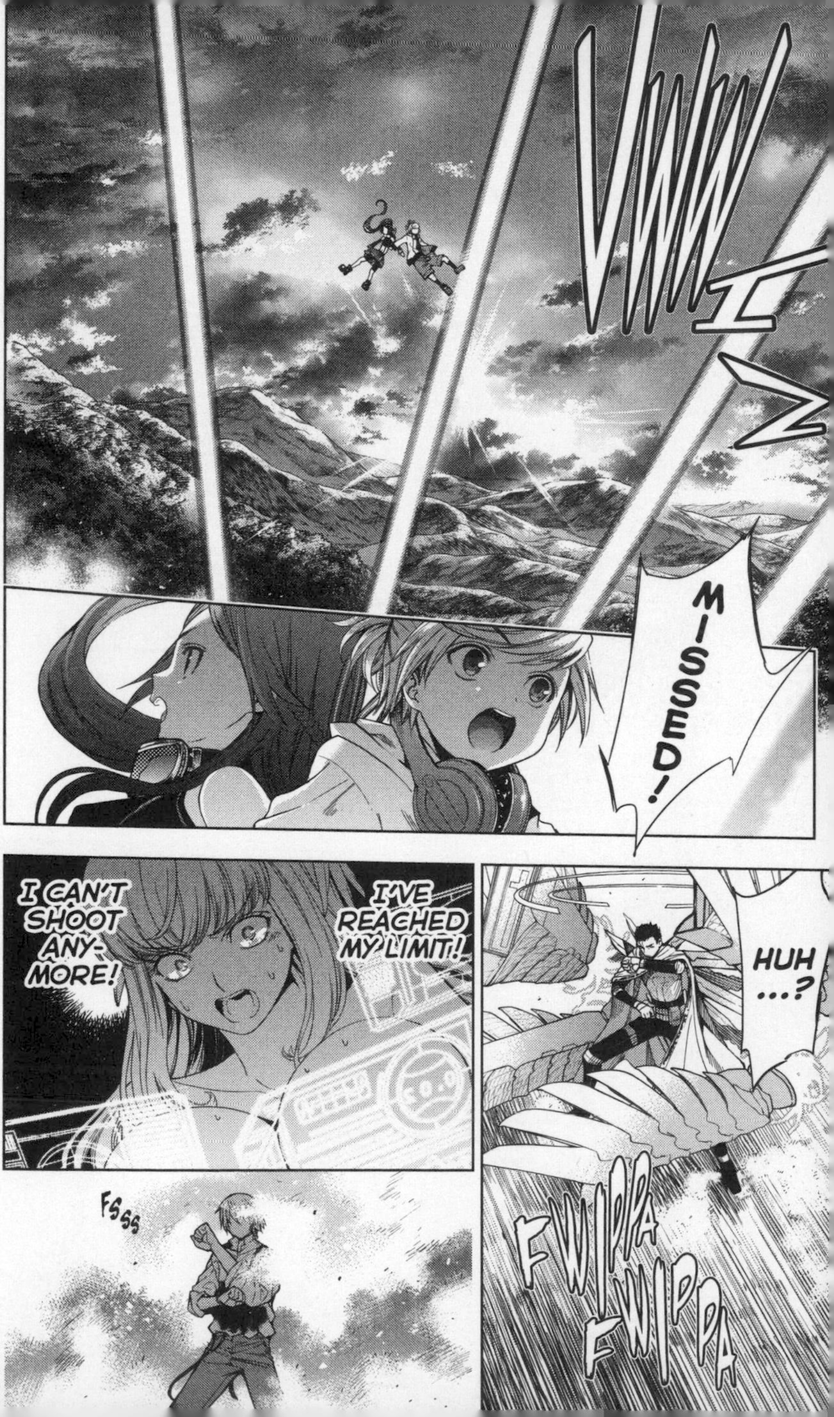
VWWW
I
N
MISSED!
HUH ...?
FWIPPA FWIPPA FWIPPA
I'VE REACHED MY LIMIT!
I CAN'T SHOOT ANY-MORE!
FSSS

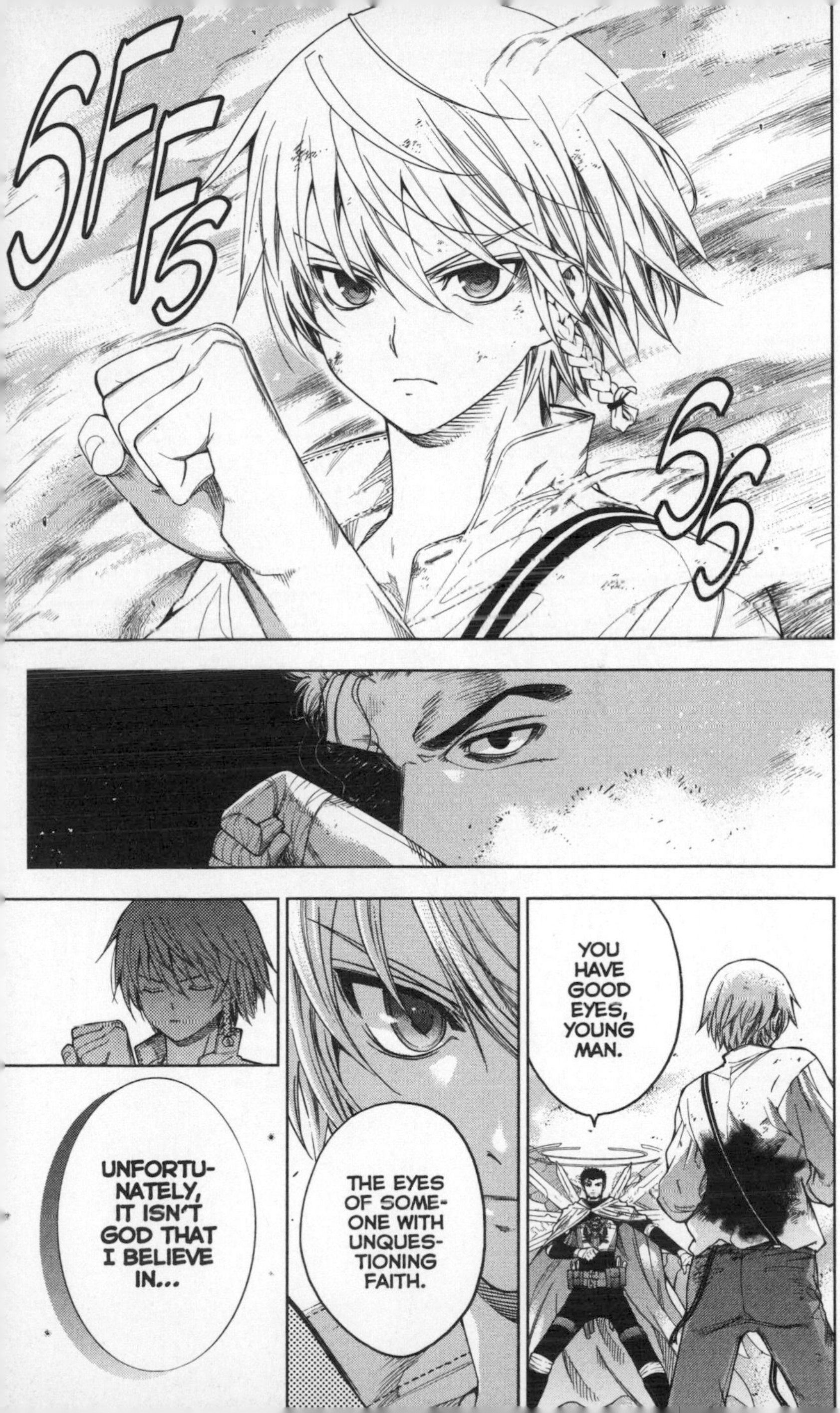
SFFS
SS
YOU HAVE GOOD EYES, YOUNG MAN.
THE EYES OF SOME-ONE WITH UNQUES-TIONING FAITH.
UNFORTU-NATELY, IT ISN'T GOD THAT I BELIEVE IN...

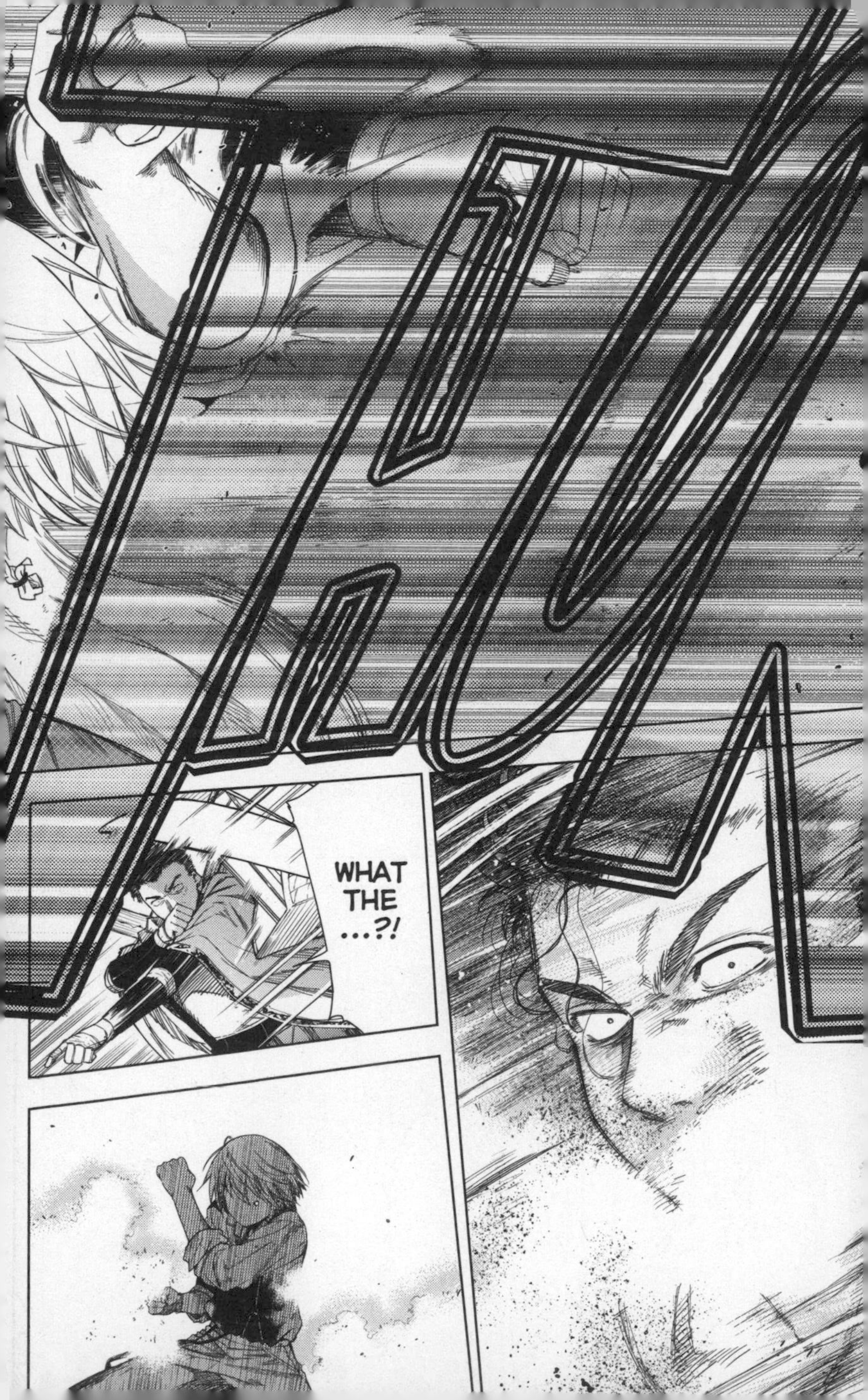
WHAT THE ...?!

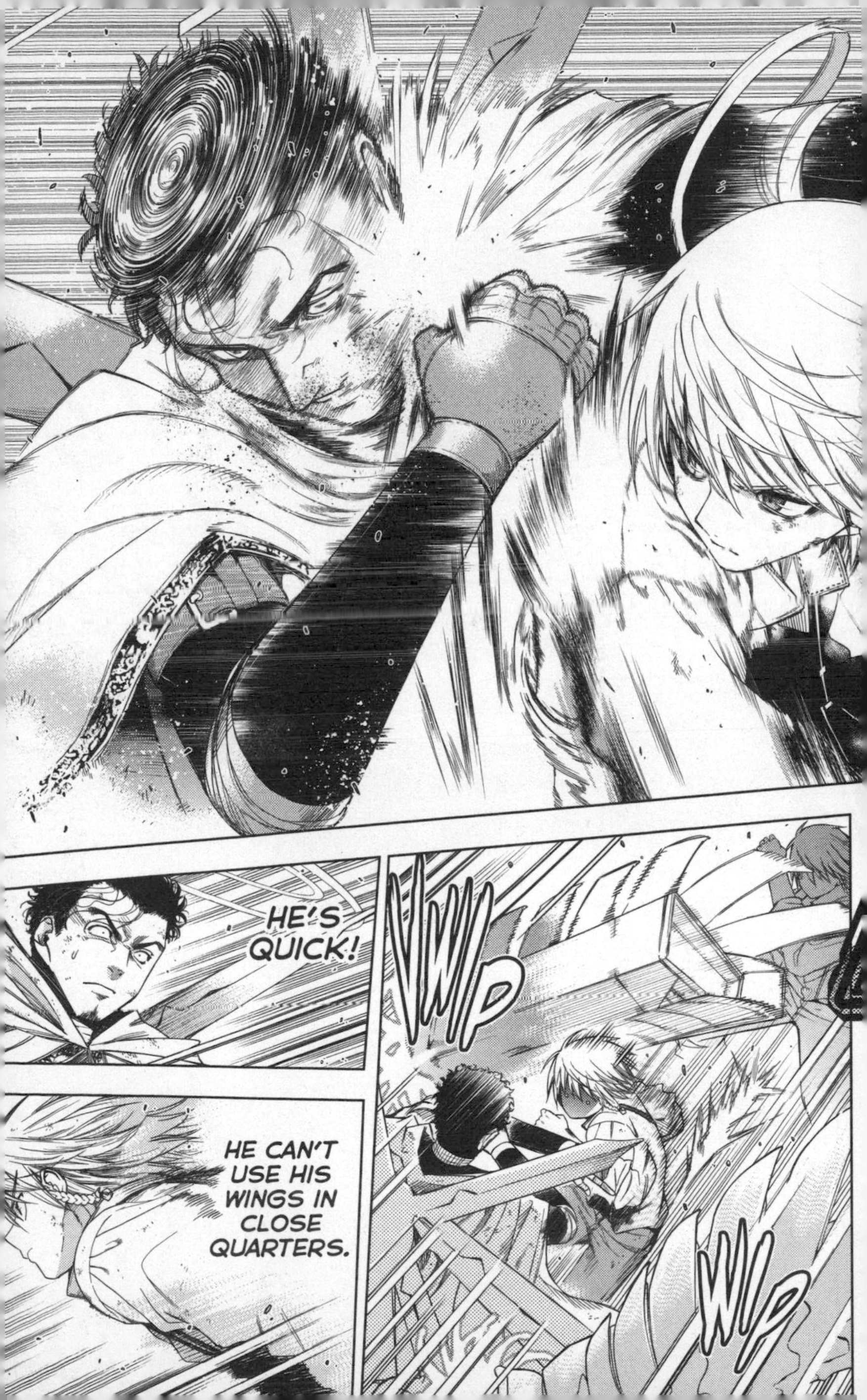
VWIP
WIP
HE'S QUICK!
HE CAN'T USE HIS WINGS IN CLOSE QUARTERS.

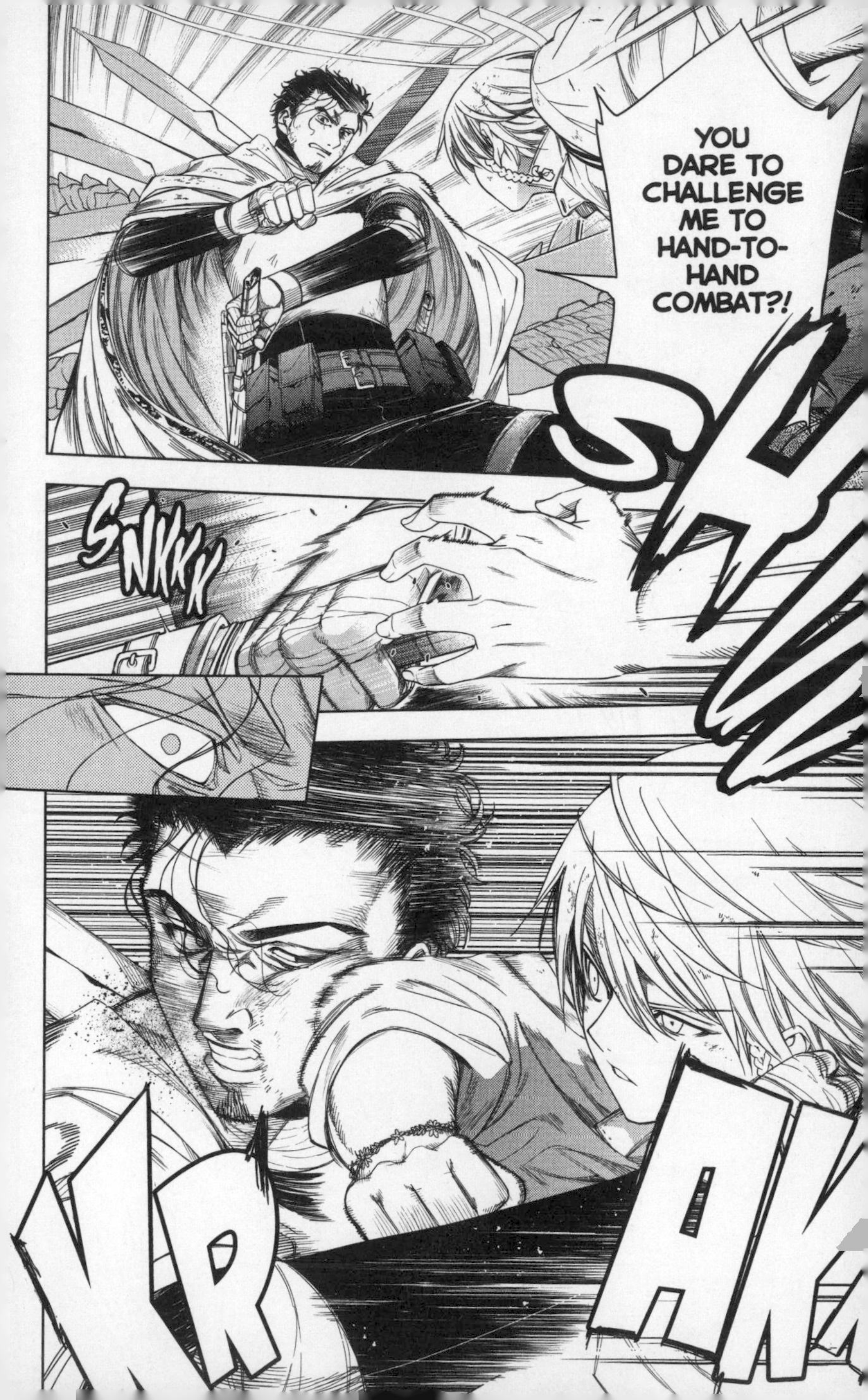
YOU DARE TO CHALLENGE ME TO HAND-TO-HAND COMBAT?!
SNKKK

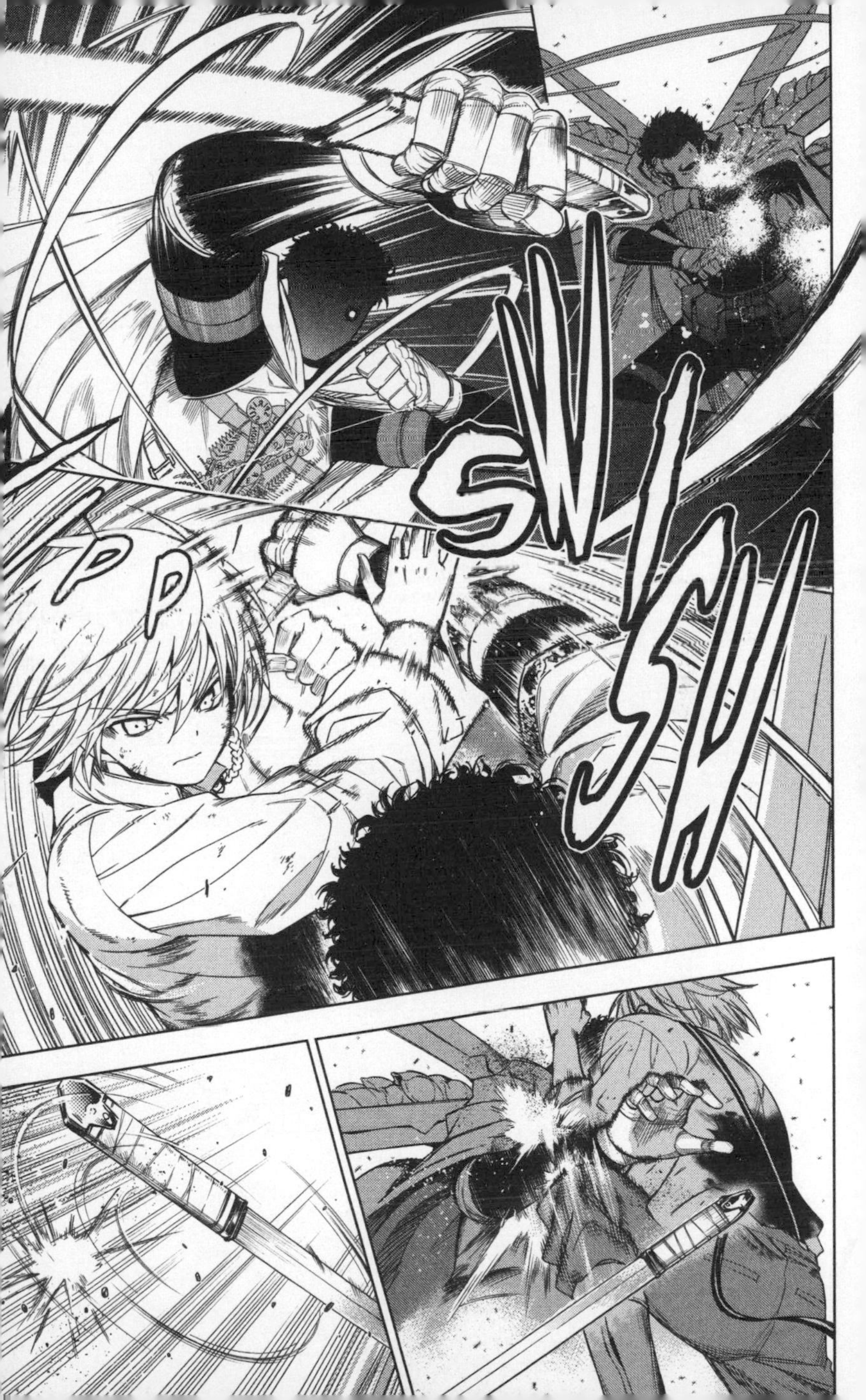
SWISH
PP

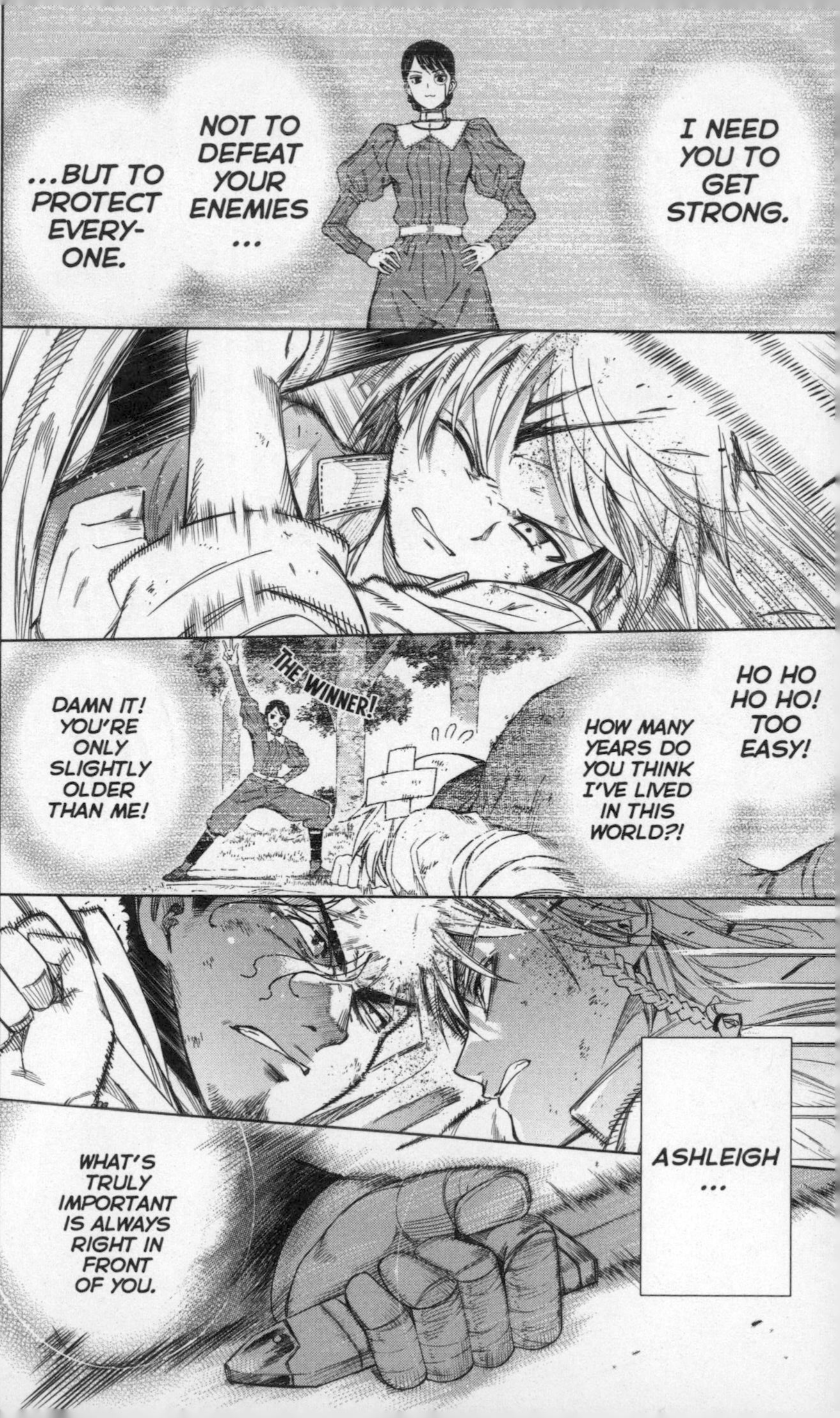
I NEED YOU TO GET STRONG.
NOT TO DEFEAT YOUR ENEMIES...
...BUT TO PROTECT EVERY-ONE.
HO HO HO HO! TOO EASY!
HOW MANY YEARS DO YOU THINK I'VE LIVED IN THIS WORLD?!
THE WINNER!
DAMN IT! YOU'RE ONLY SLIGHTLY OLDER THAN ME!
ASHLEIGH...
WHAT'S TRULY IMPORTANT IS ALWAYS RIGHT IN FRONT OF YOU.

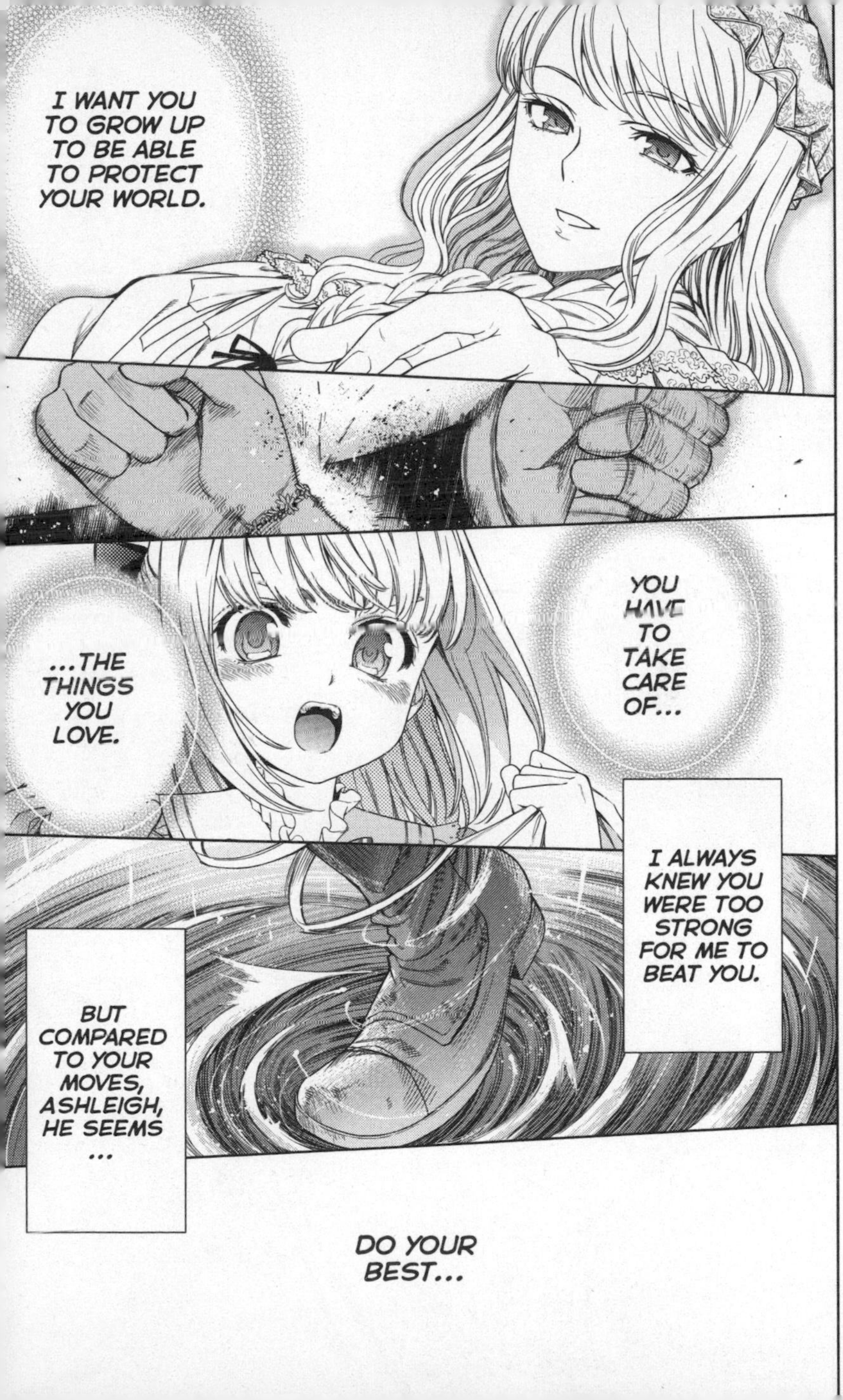
I WANT YOU TO GROW UP TO BE ABLE TO PROTECT YOUR WORLD.
YOU HAVE TO TAKE CARE OF...
...THE THINGS YOU LOVE.
I ALWAYS KNEW YOU WERE TOO STRONG FOR ME TO BEAT YOU.
BUT COMPARED TO YOUR MOVES, ASHLEIGH, HE SEEMS ...
DO YOUR BEST...

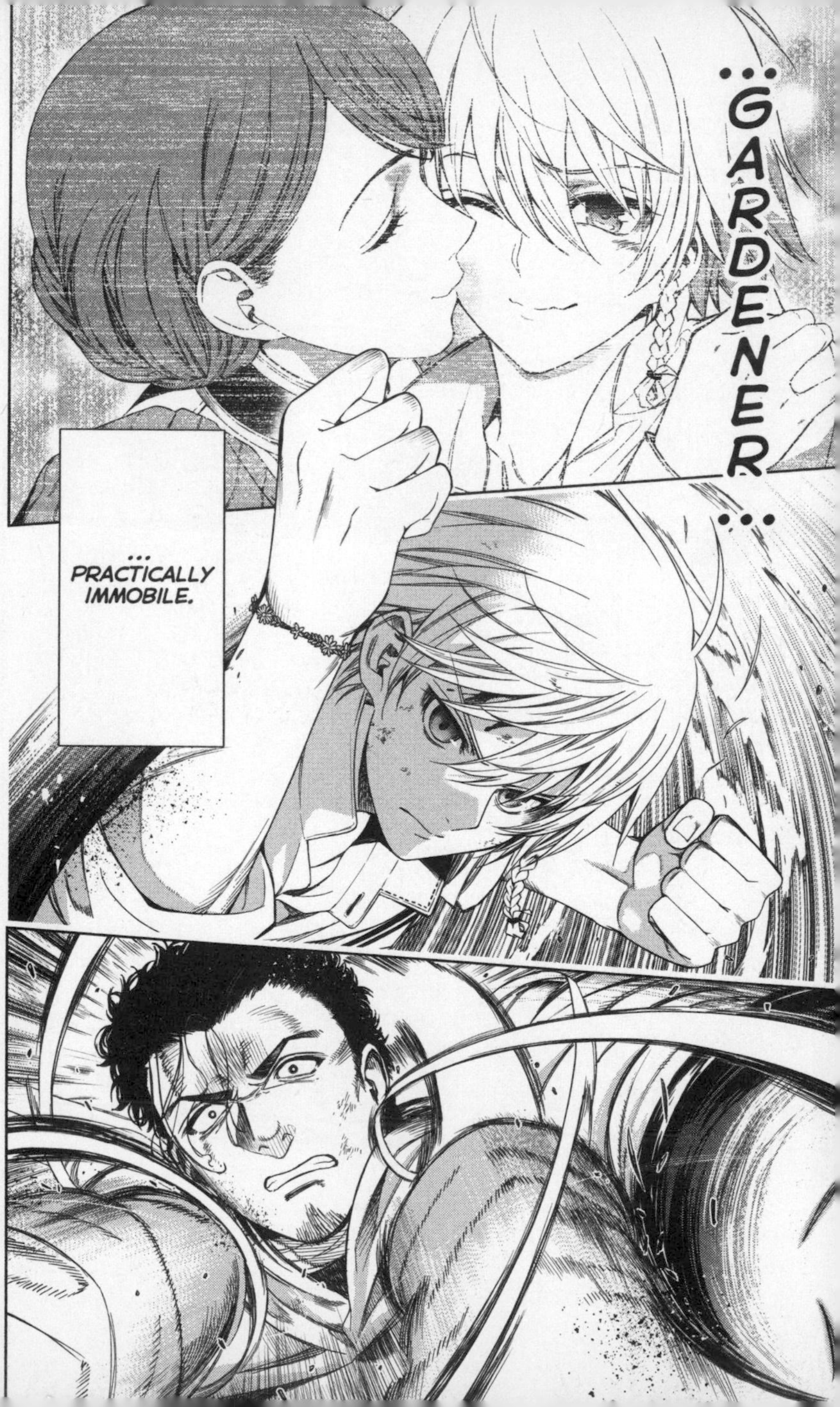
...GARDENER...
...PRACTICALLY IMMOBILE.

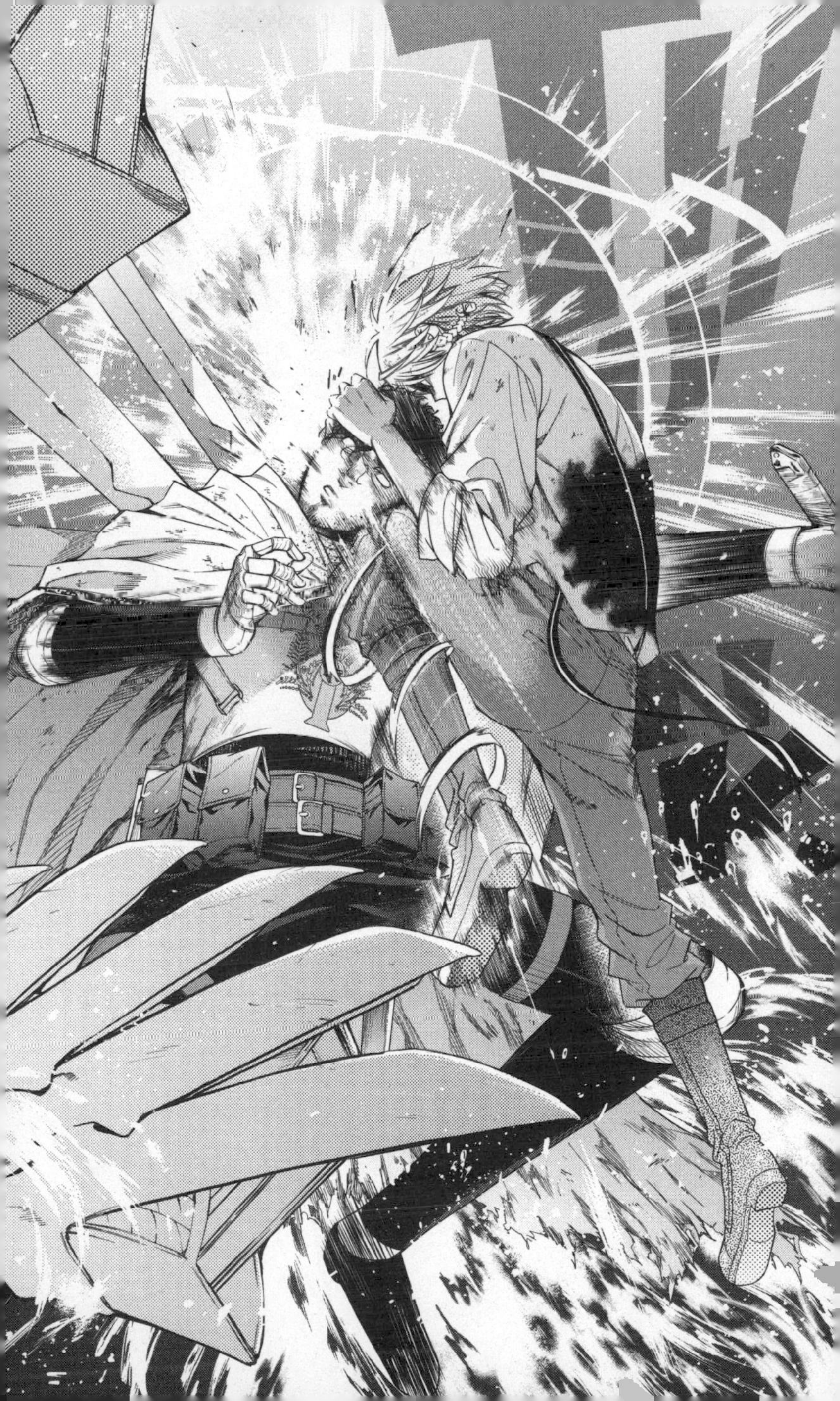

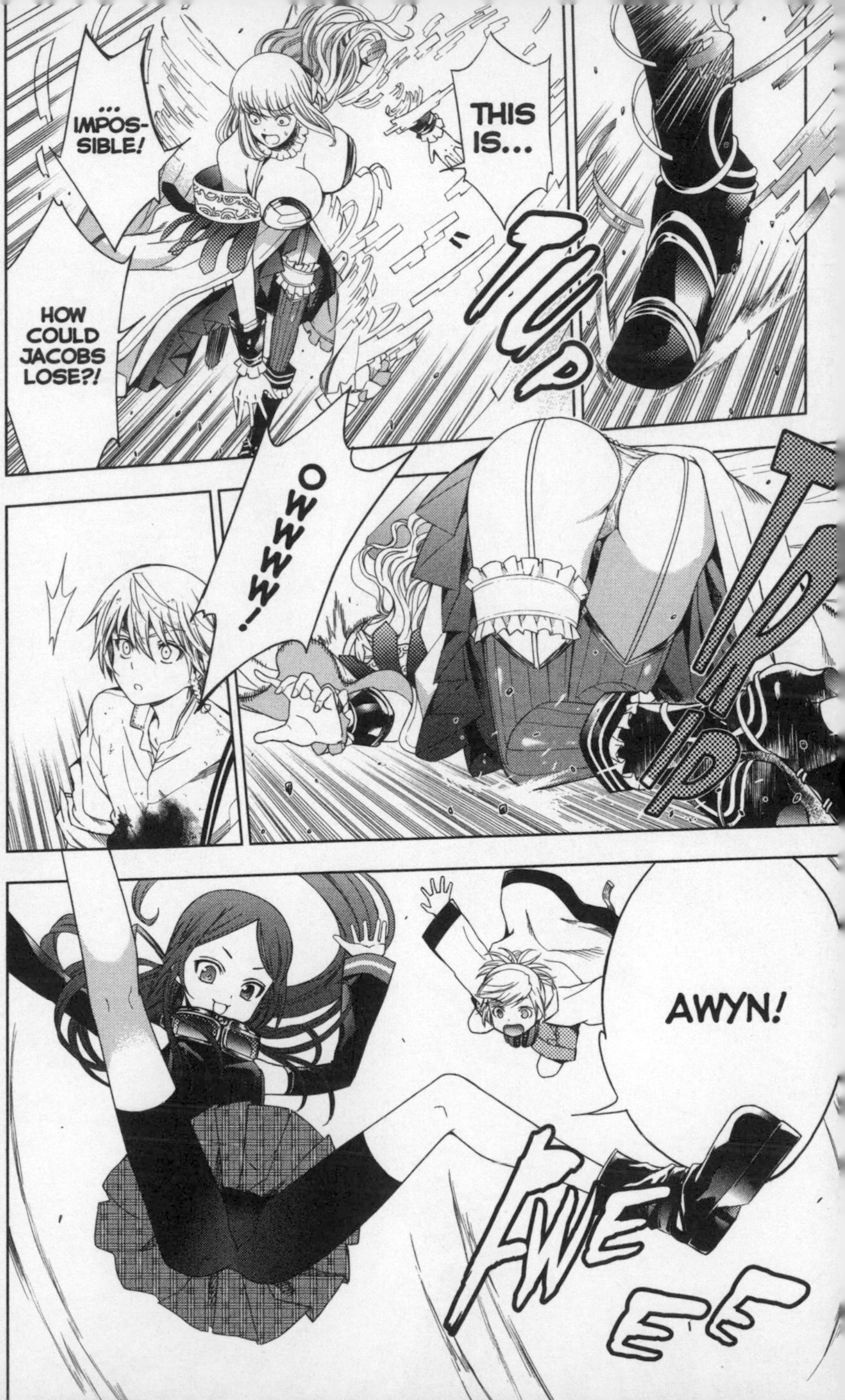
FLIP
THIS IS...
...IMPOSSIBLE!
HOW COULD JACOBS LOSE?!
TRIP
OWWWW!
AWYN!
FWEEE

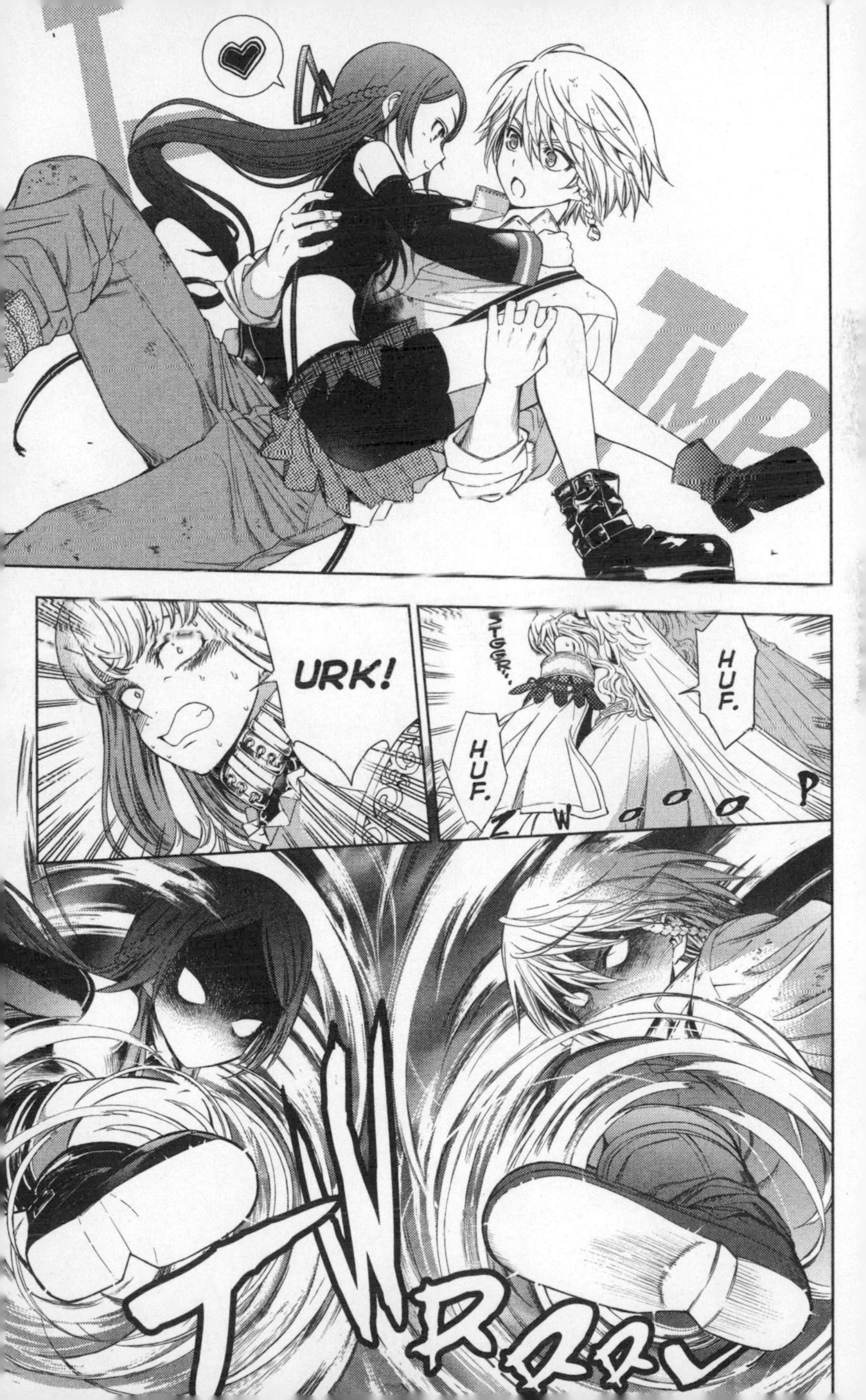
TMP
HUF. HUF.
STGGR...
ZWOOOP
URK!

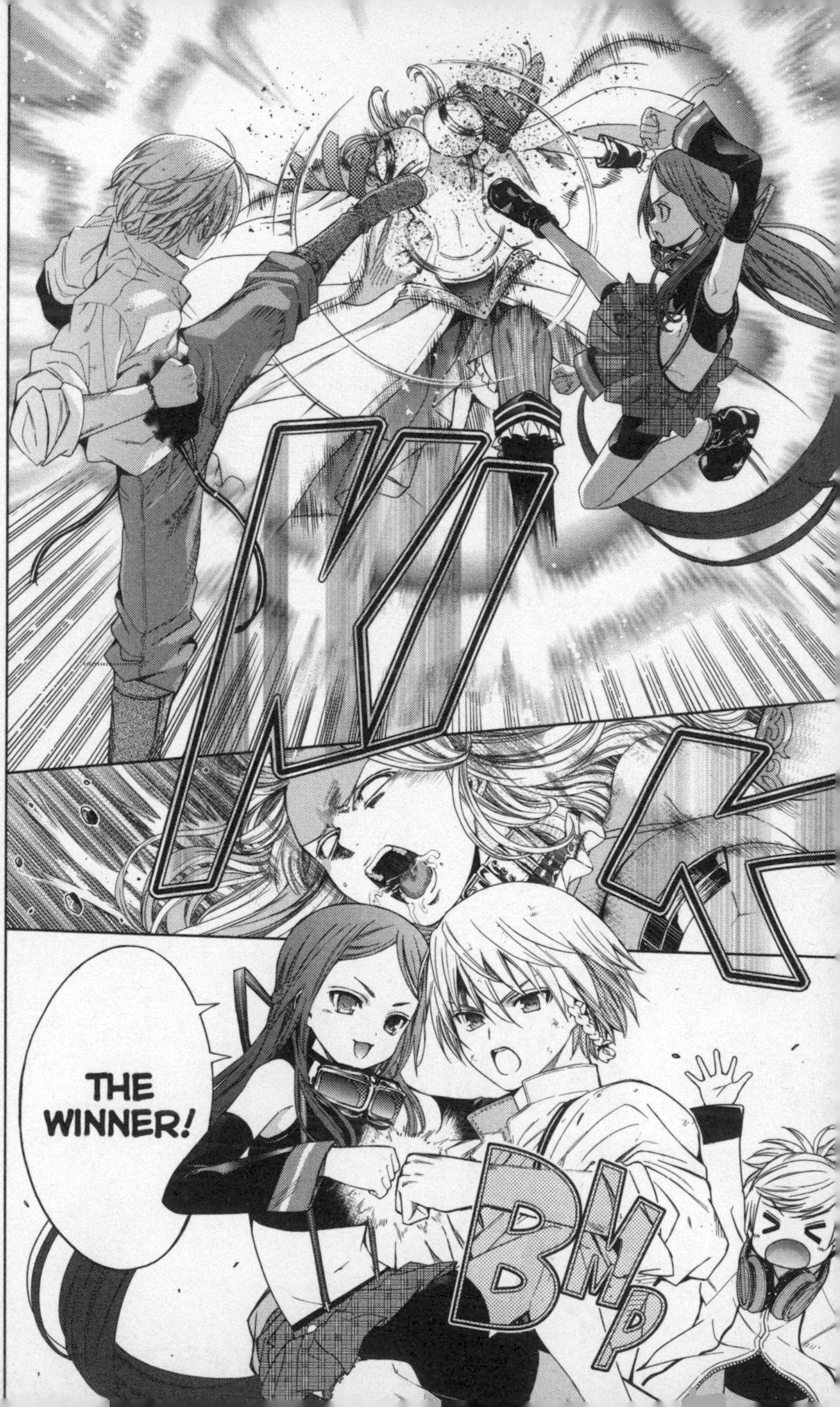
THE WINNER!
BMP

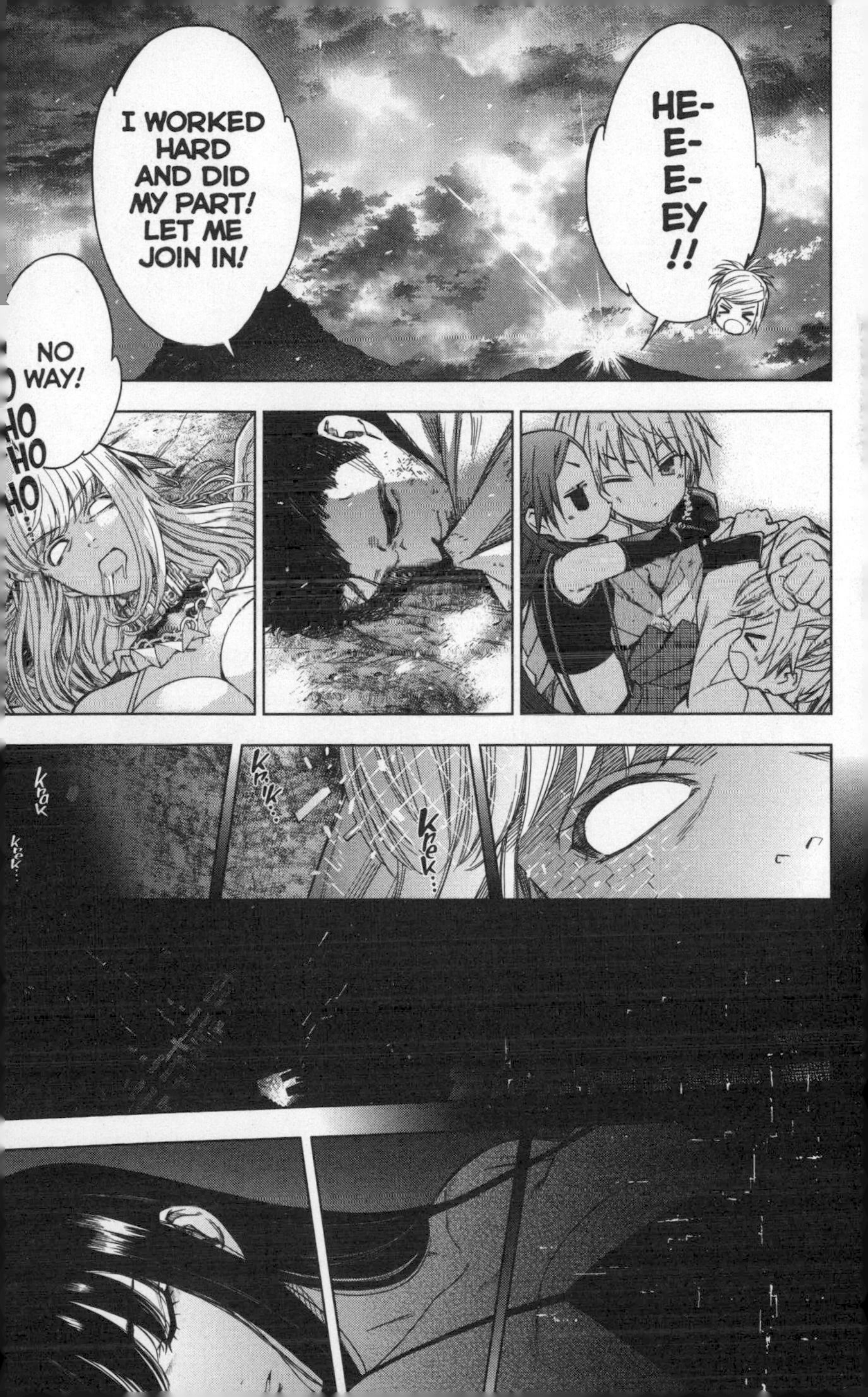
HE-E-E-EY!!
I WORKED HARD AND DID MY PART! LET ME JOIN IN!
NO WAY!
HO HO HO...
krik...
krek...
krak
krek...

OWW
...

SHHF

HUF
...

JRITY BREACH
INTREDRE

HUF
...

HUF
...

SECURITY BREACH
FACILITY CODES REPORTED STOLEN

INTRUDER

INTRUDER

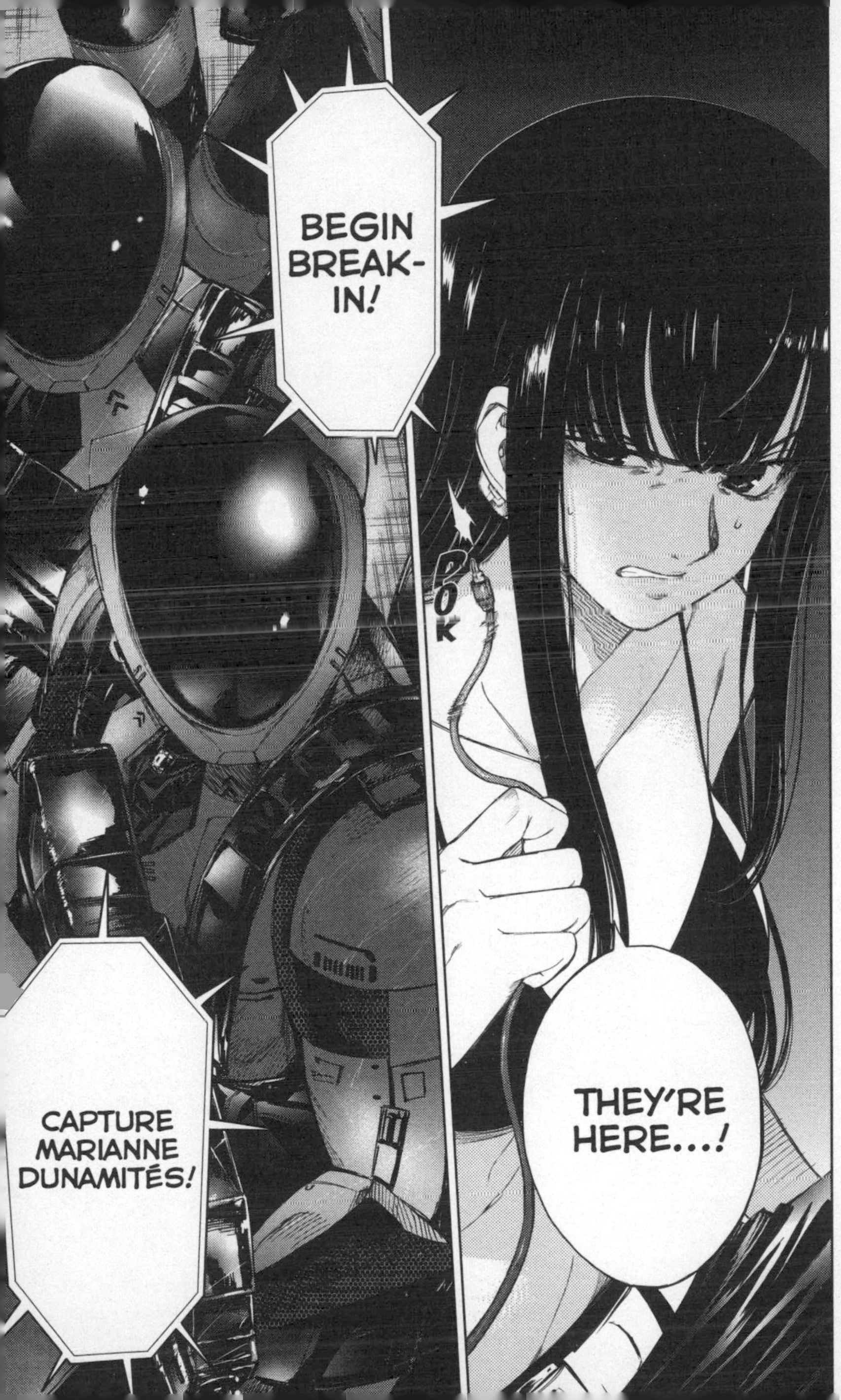
POK
THEY'RE HERE...!
BEGIN BREAK-IN!
CAPTURE MARIANNE DUNAMITÉS!

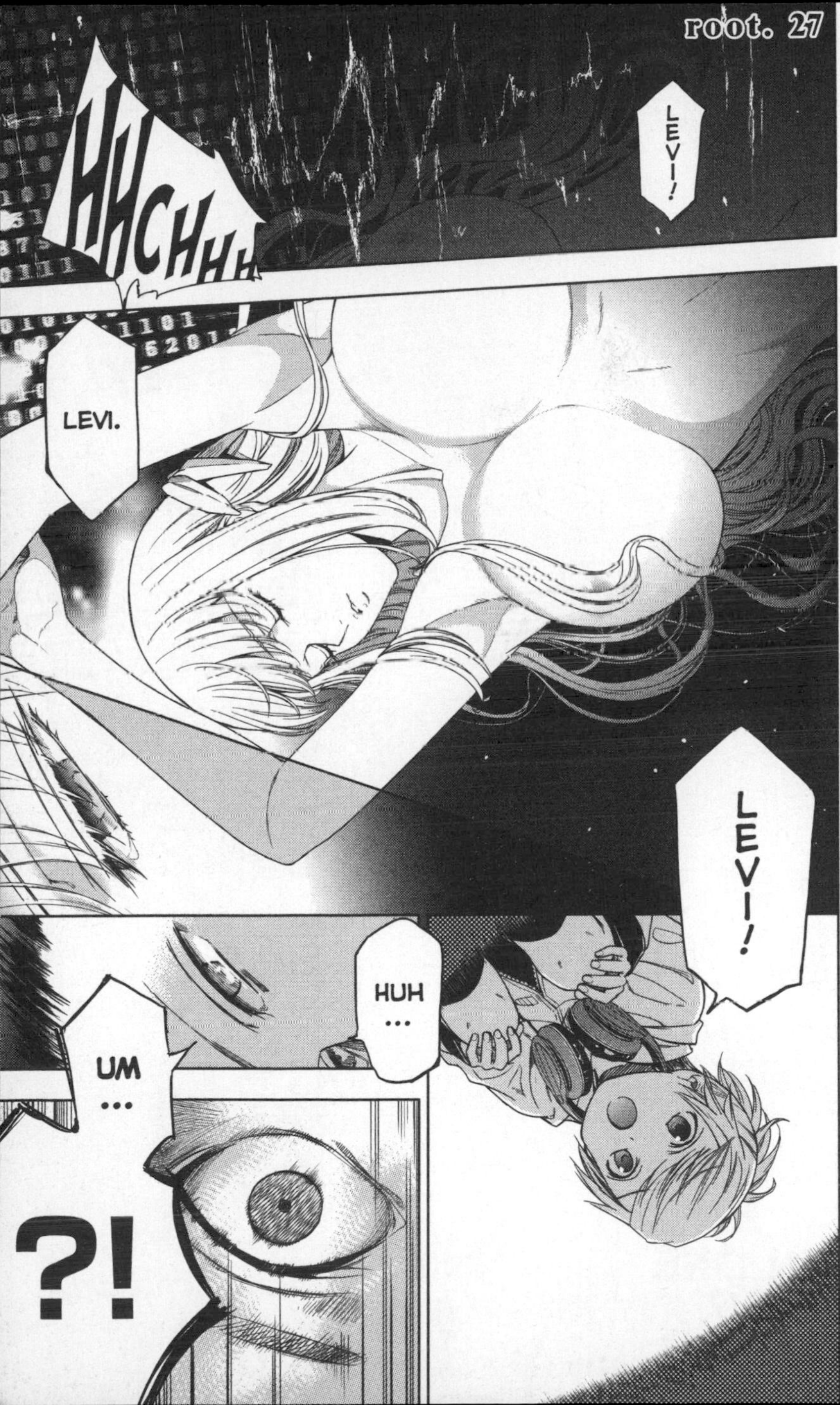
LEVI!
HHCHHH
LEVI.
LEVI!
HUH ...
UM ...
?!

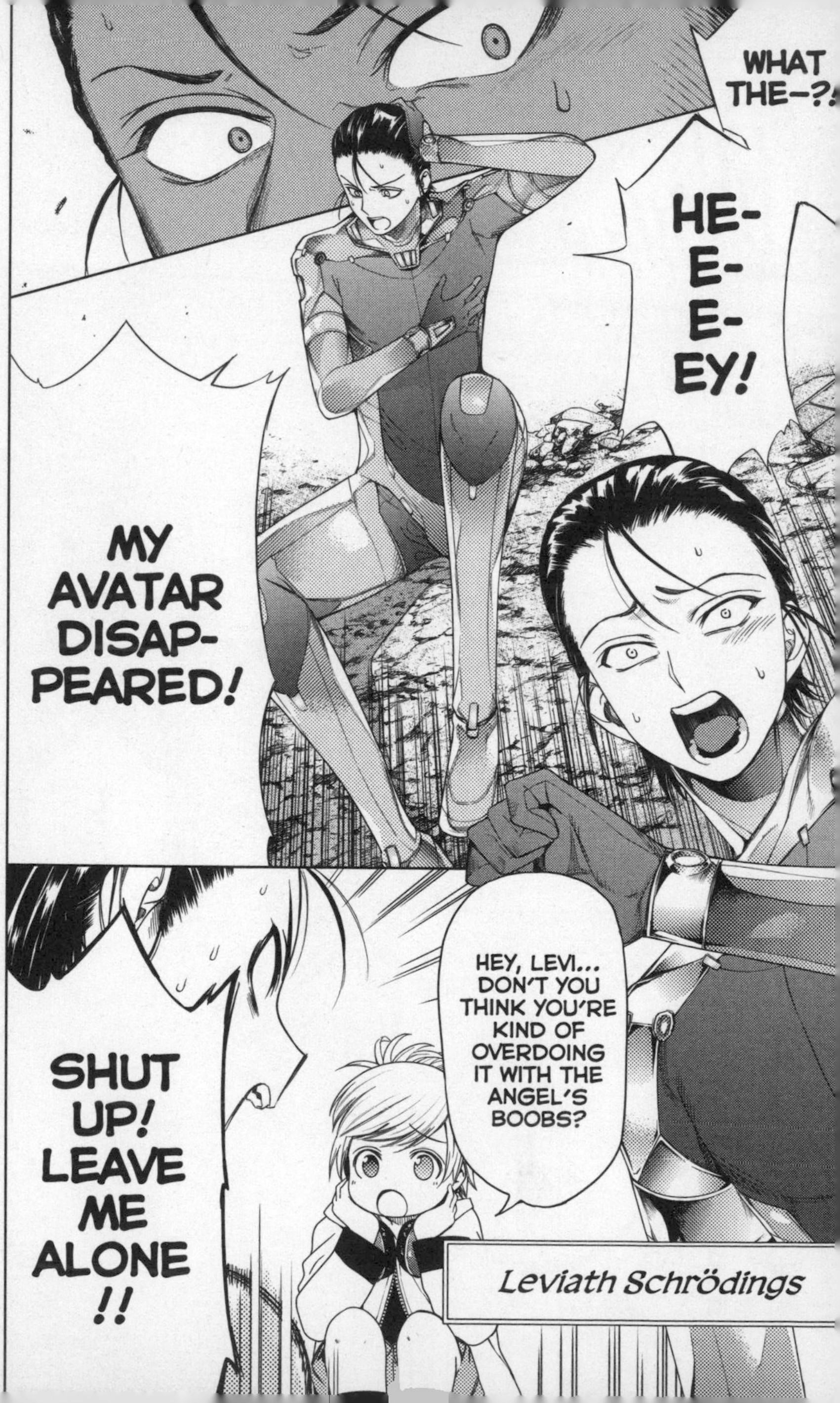
WHAT THE–?!
HE-E-E-EY!
MY AVATAR DISAPPEARED!
HEY, LEVI... DON'T YOU THINK YOU'RE KIND OF OVERDOING IT WITH THE ANGEL'S BOOBS?
SHUT UP! LEAVE ME ALONE!!
Leviath Schrödings

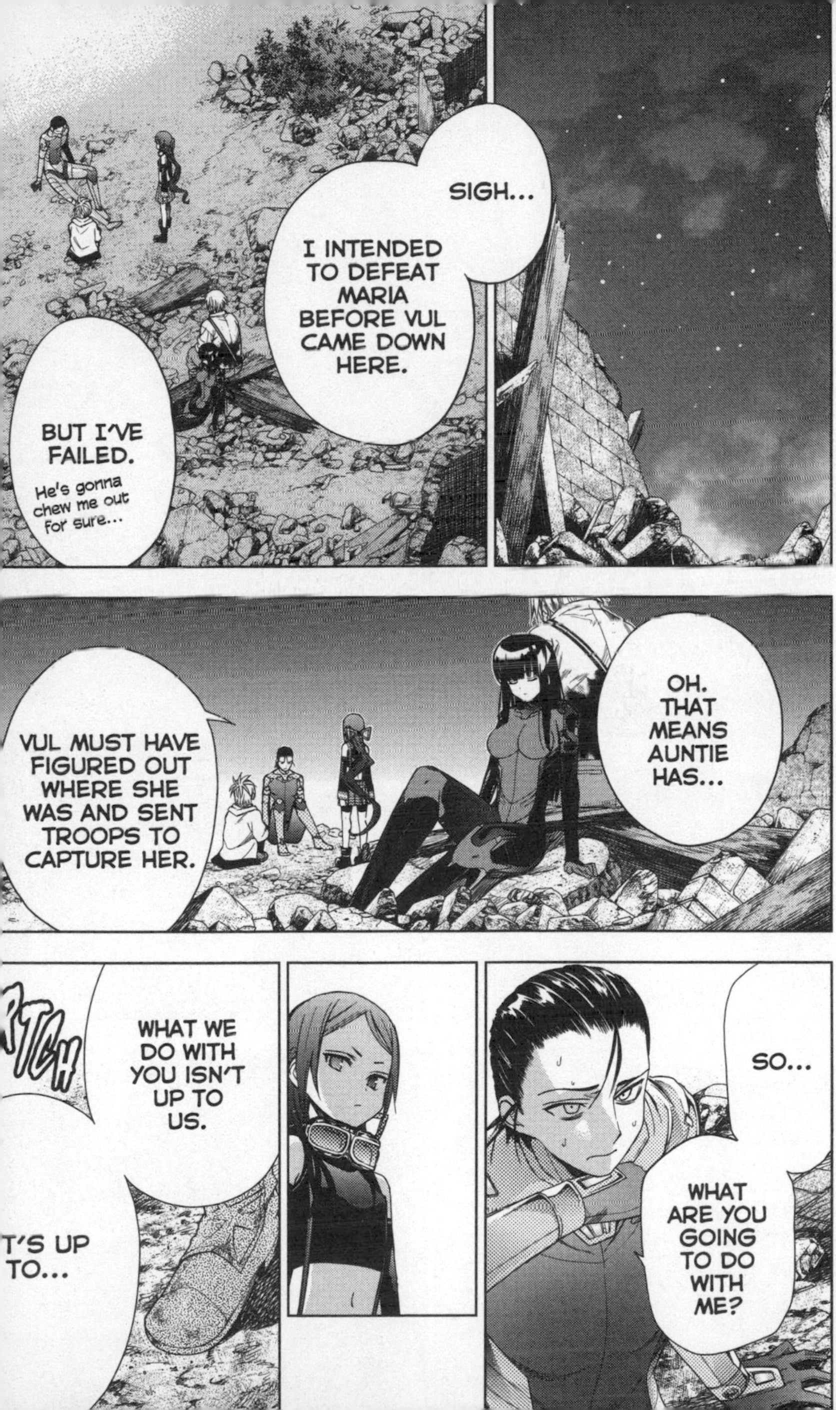
SIGH...
I INTENDED TO DEFEAT MARIA BEFORE VUL CAME DOWN HERE.
BUT I'VE FAILED.
He's gonna chew me out for sure...
OH. THAT MEANS AUNTIE HAS...
VUL MUST HAVE FIGURED OUT WHERE SHE WAS AND SENT TROOPS TO CAPTURE HER.
SO...
WHAT ARE YOU GOING TO DO WITH ME?
WHAT WE DO WITH YOU ISN'T UP TO US.
T'S UP TO...

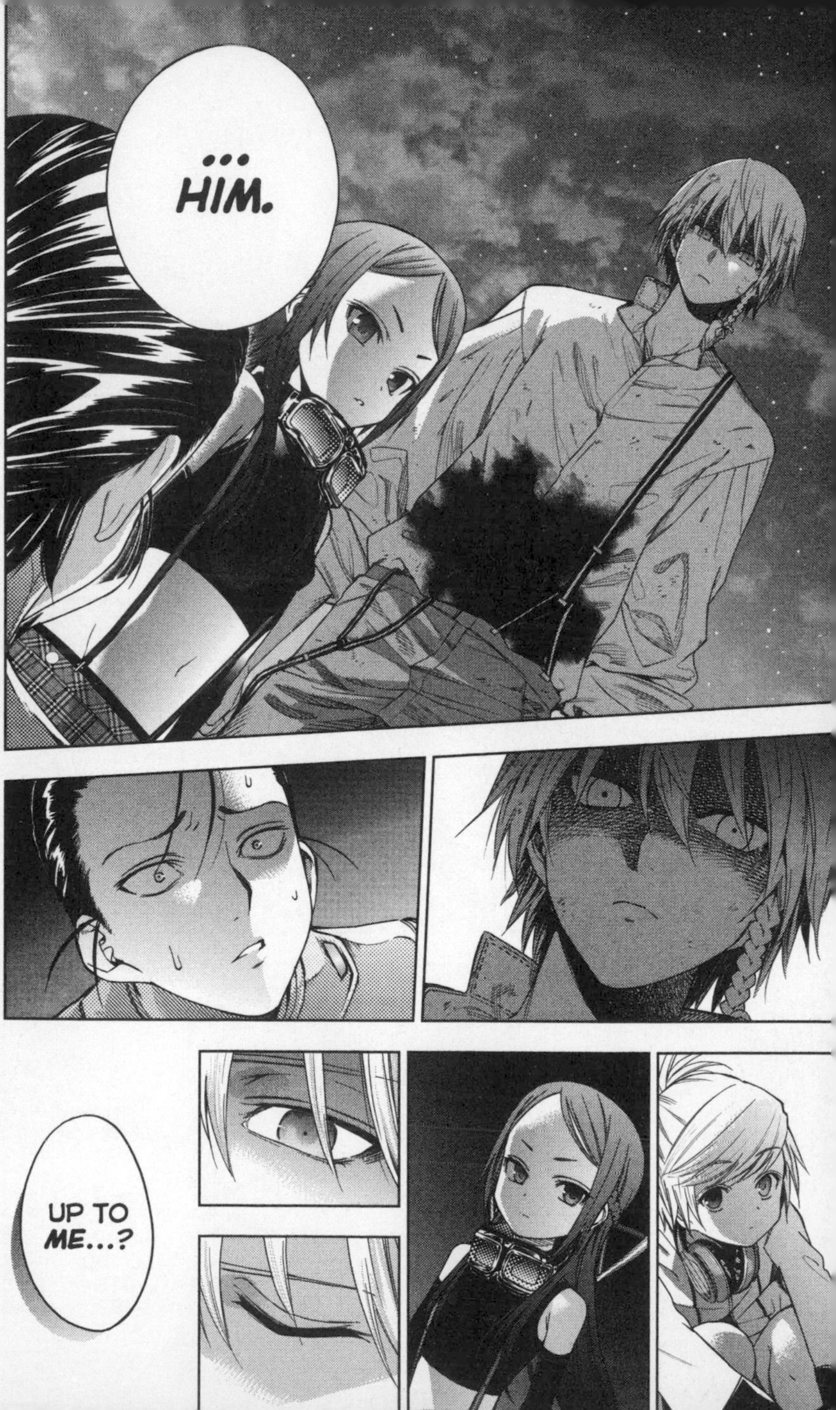
...HIM.
UP TO ME...?

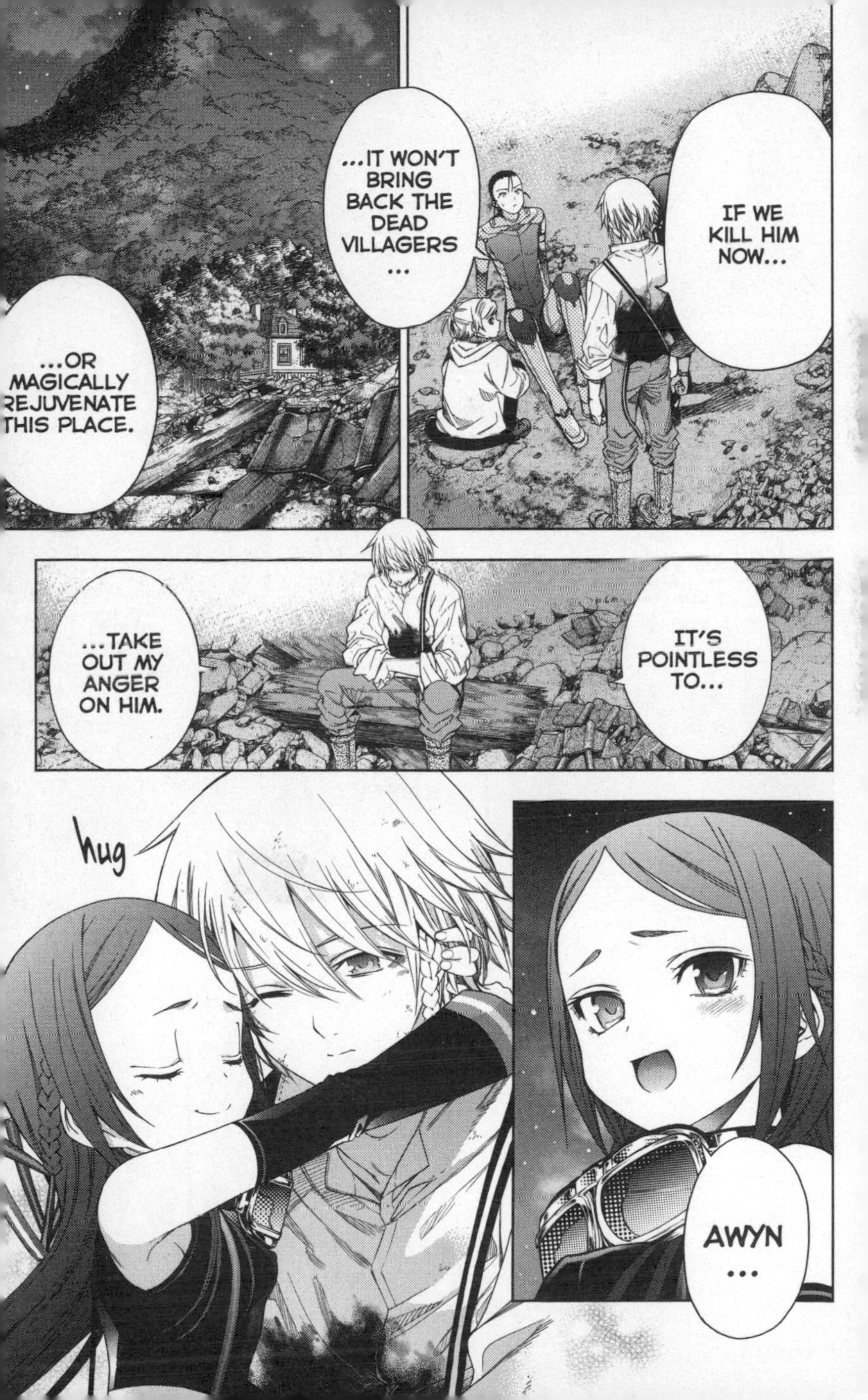
IF WE KILL HIM NOW...
...IT WON'T BRING BACK THE DEAD VILLAGERS ...
...OR MAGICALLY REJUVENATE THIS PLACE.
IT'S POINTLESS TO...
...TAKE OUT MY ANGER ON HIM.
AWYN ...
hug

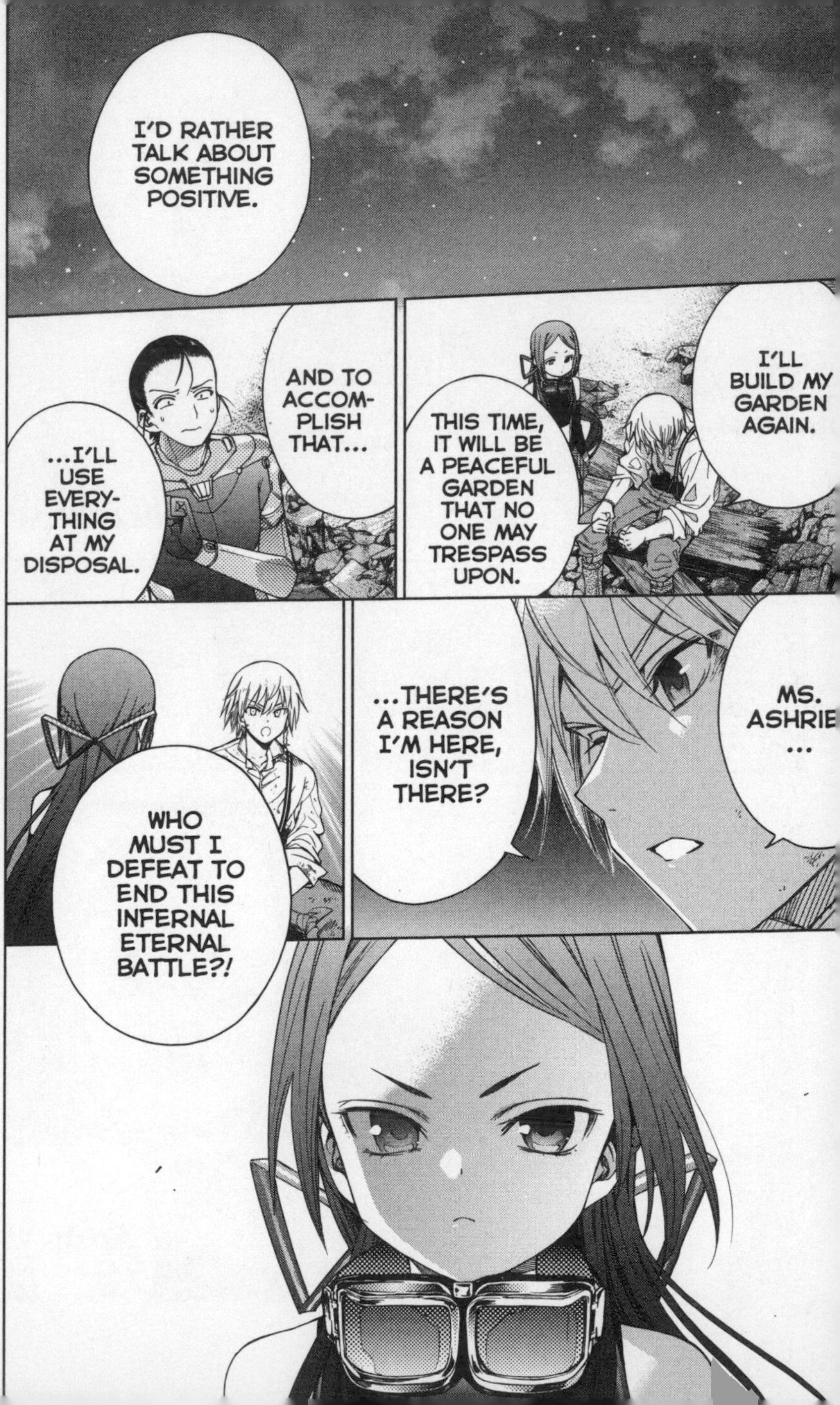
I'D RATHER TALK ABOUT SOMETHING POSITIVE.
I'LL BUILD MY GARDEN AGAIN.
THIS TIME, IT WILL BE A PEACEFUL GARDEN THAT NO ONE MAY TRESPASS UPON.
AND TO ACCOMPLISH THAT...
...I'LL USE EVERYTHING AT MY DISPOSAL.
MS. ASHRIE...
...THERE'S A REASON I'M HERE, ISN'T THERE?
WHO MUST I DEFEAT TO END THIS INFERNAL ETERNAL BATTLE?!

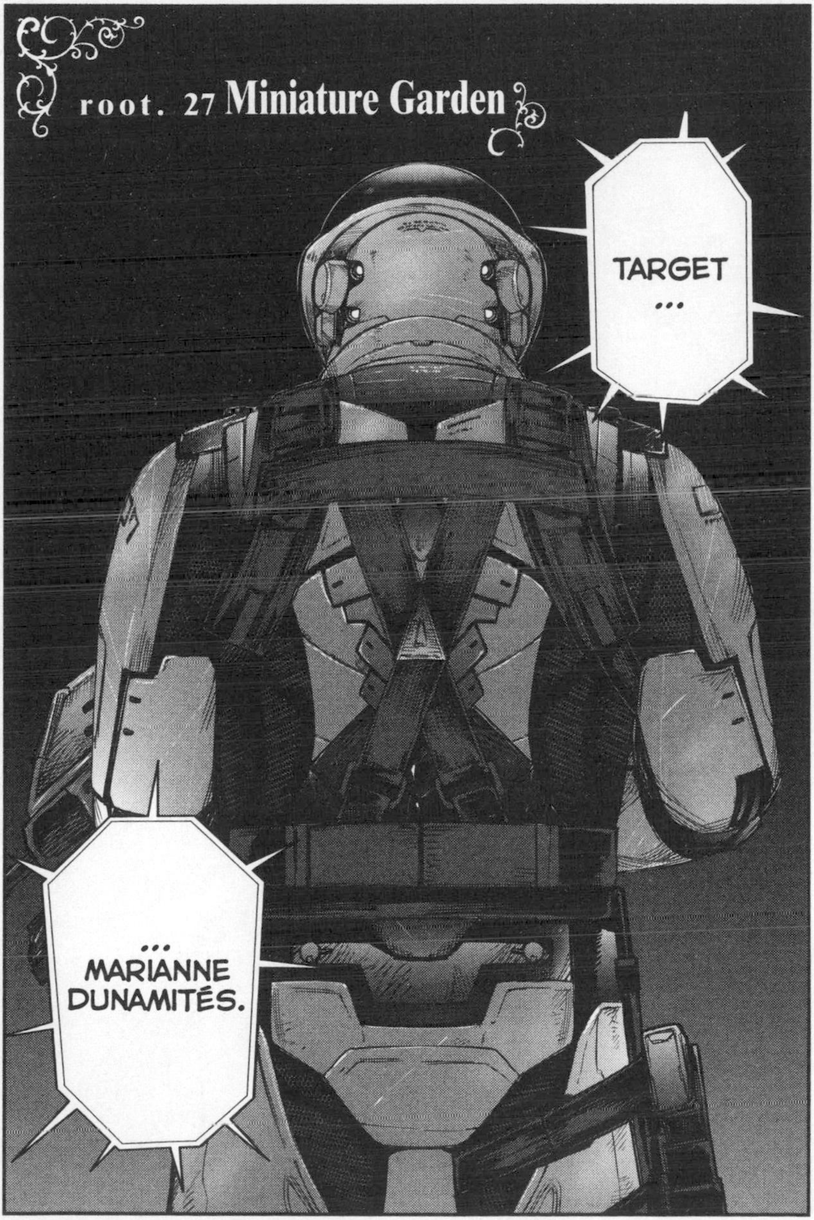
root. 27 Miniature Garden
TARGET ...
... MARIANNE DUNAMITÉS.

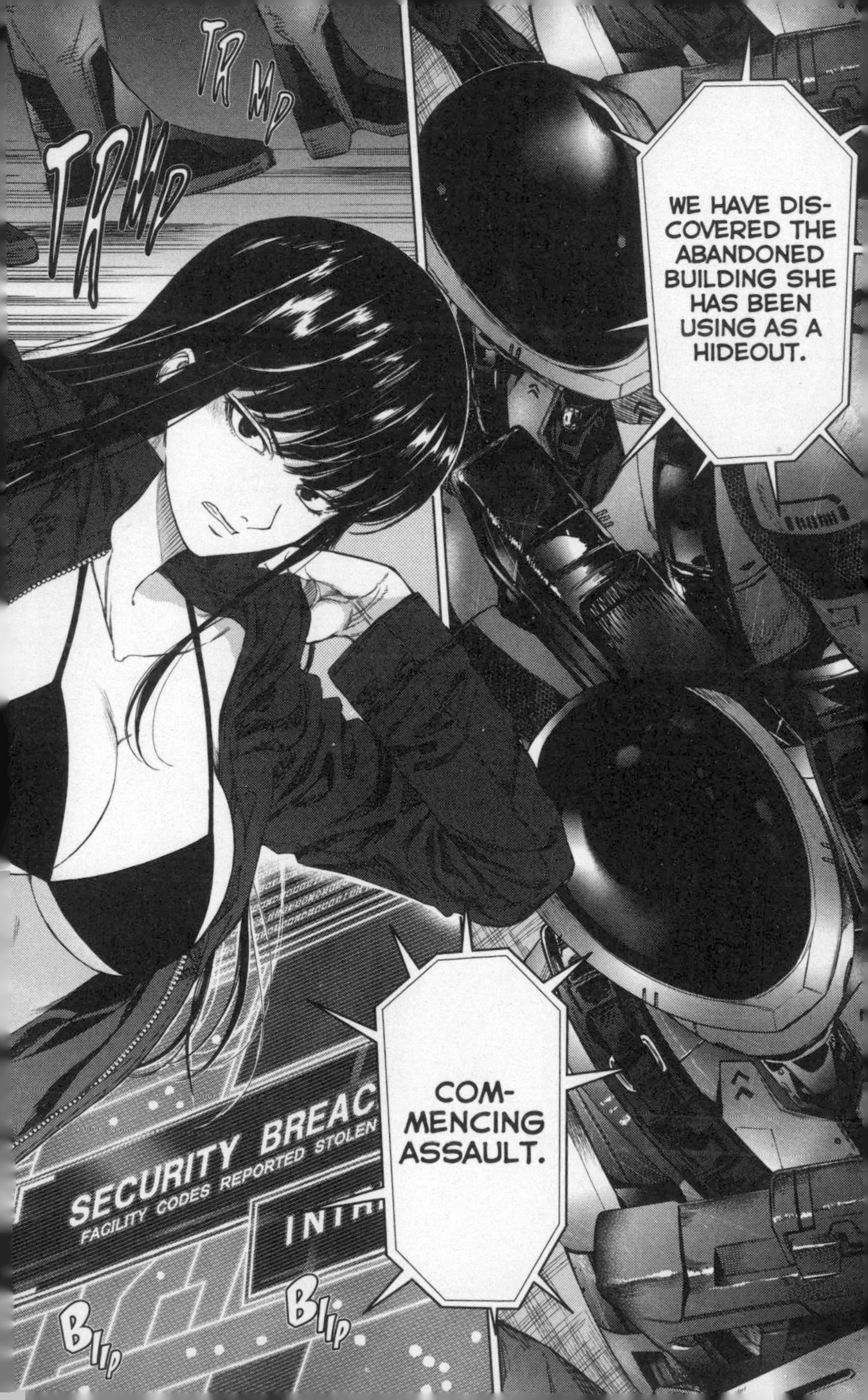

WE HAVE DIS-COVERED THE ABANDONED BUILDING SHE HAS BEEN USING AS A HIDEOUT.
TRMP
THMP
SECURITY BREAC
FACILITY CODES REPORTED STOLEN
INIT
COM-MENCING ASSAULT.
BLIP
BLIP

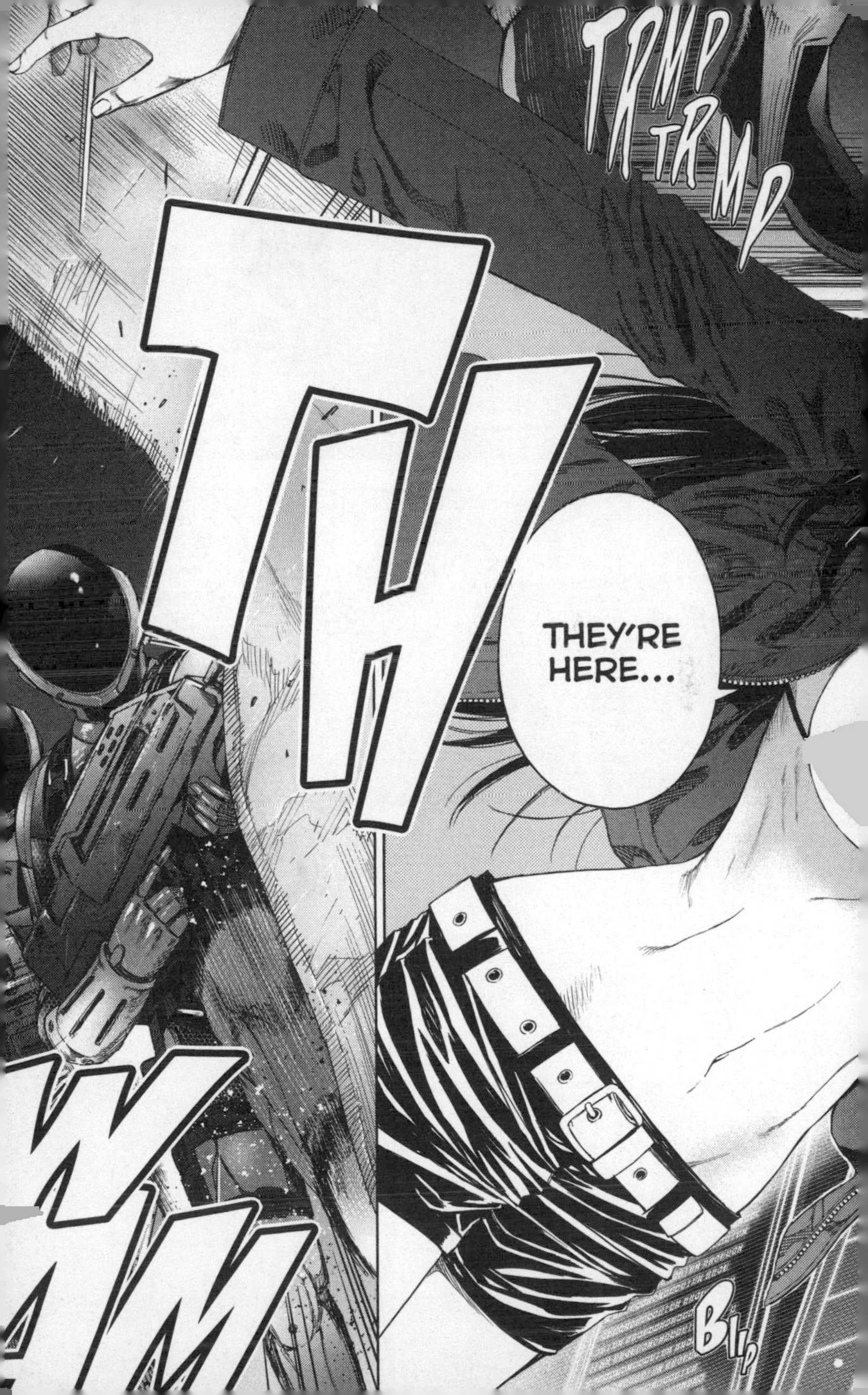
TRMP TRMP
THEY'RE HERE...
THWM
BLIP

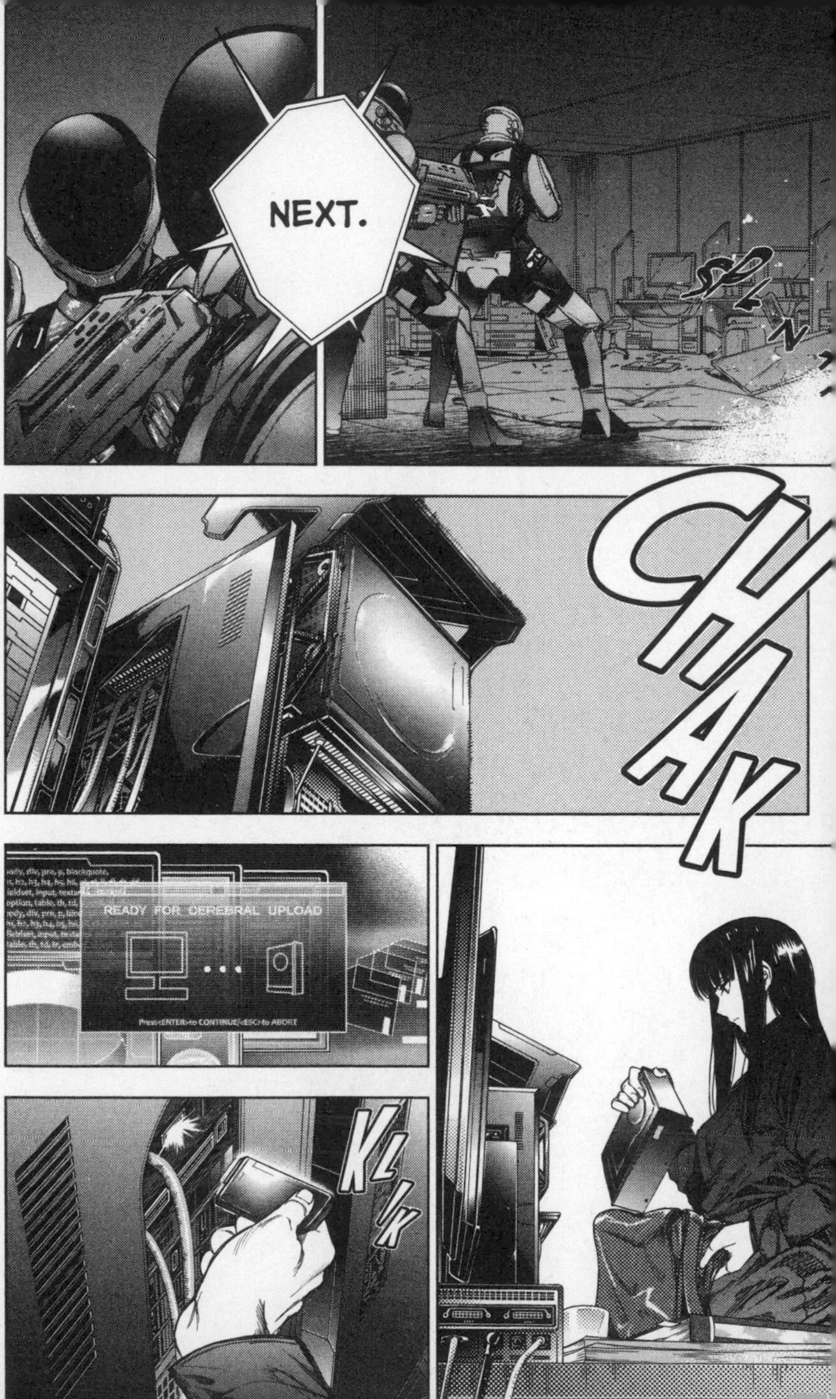
SPLN
NEXT.
CHAK
READY FOR CEREBRAL UPLOAD
Press<ENTER>to CONTINUE/<ESC>to ABORT
KLIK

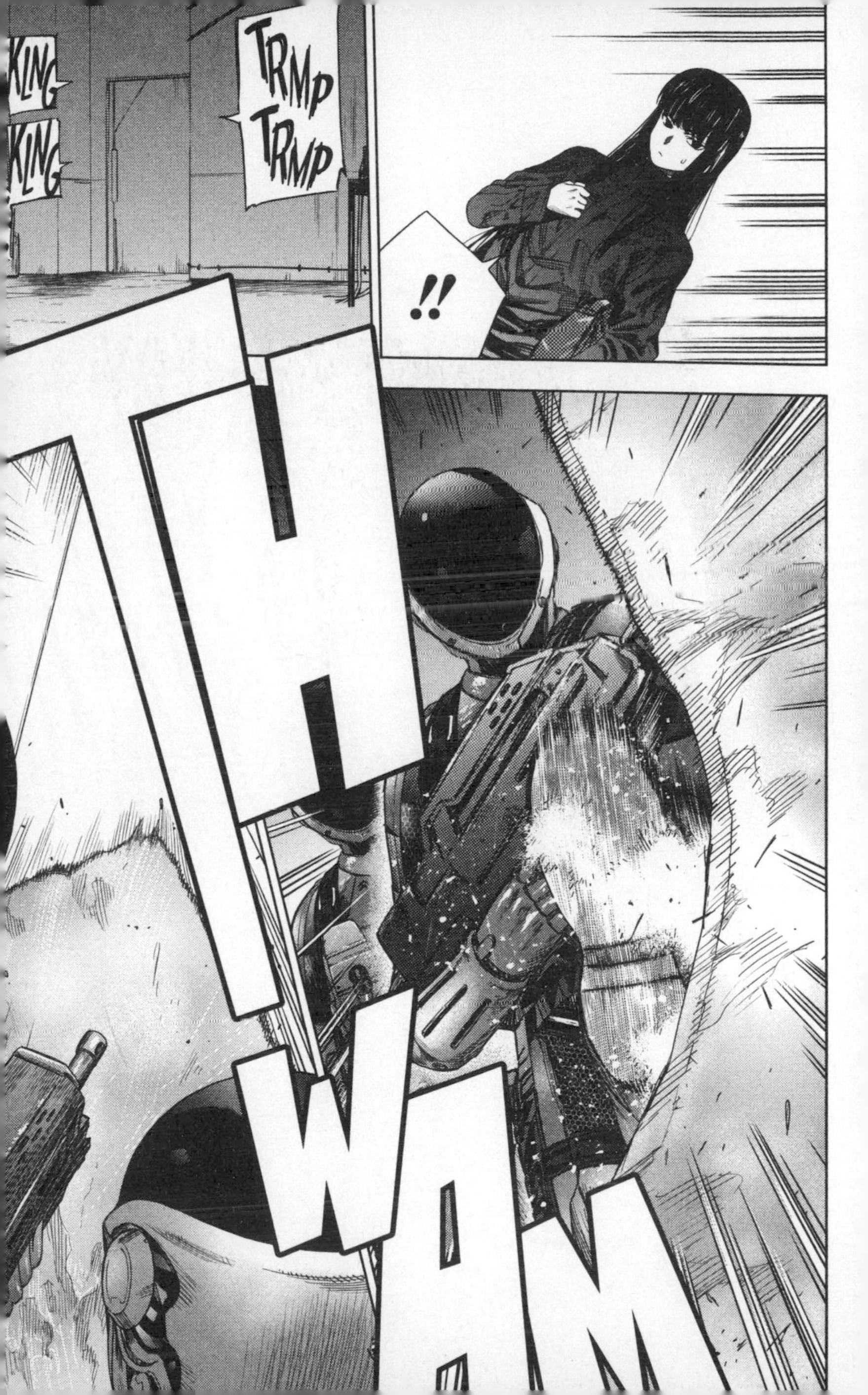
!!
TRMP TRMP
KLING KLING
HWAM

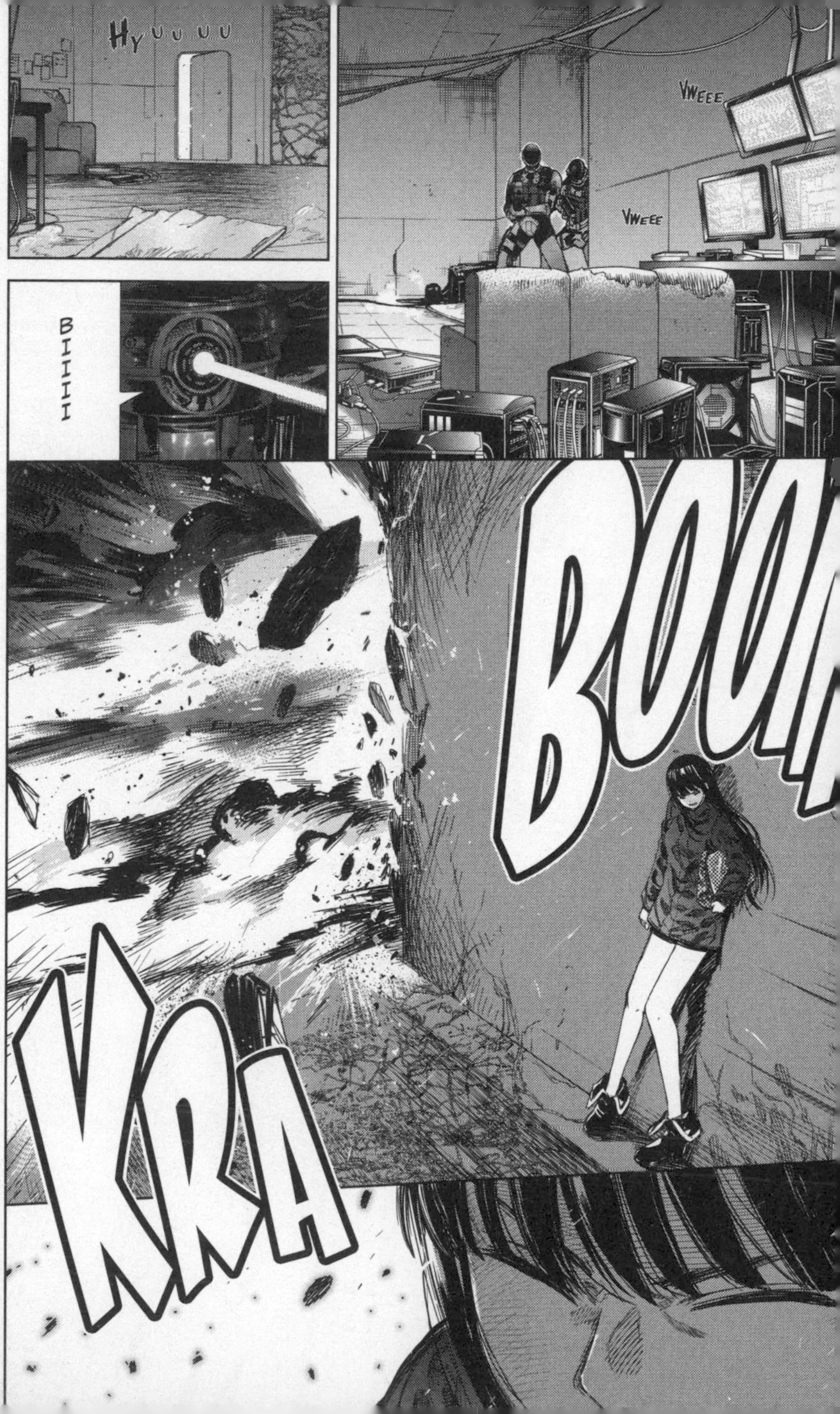
VWEEE
VWEEE
HYUUUU
BIIIII
BOOM
KRA

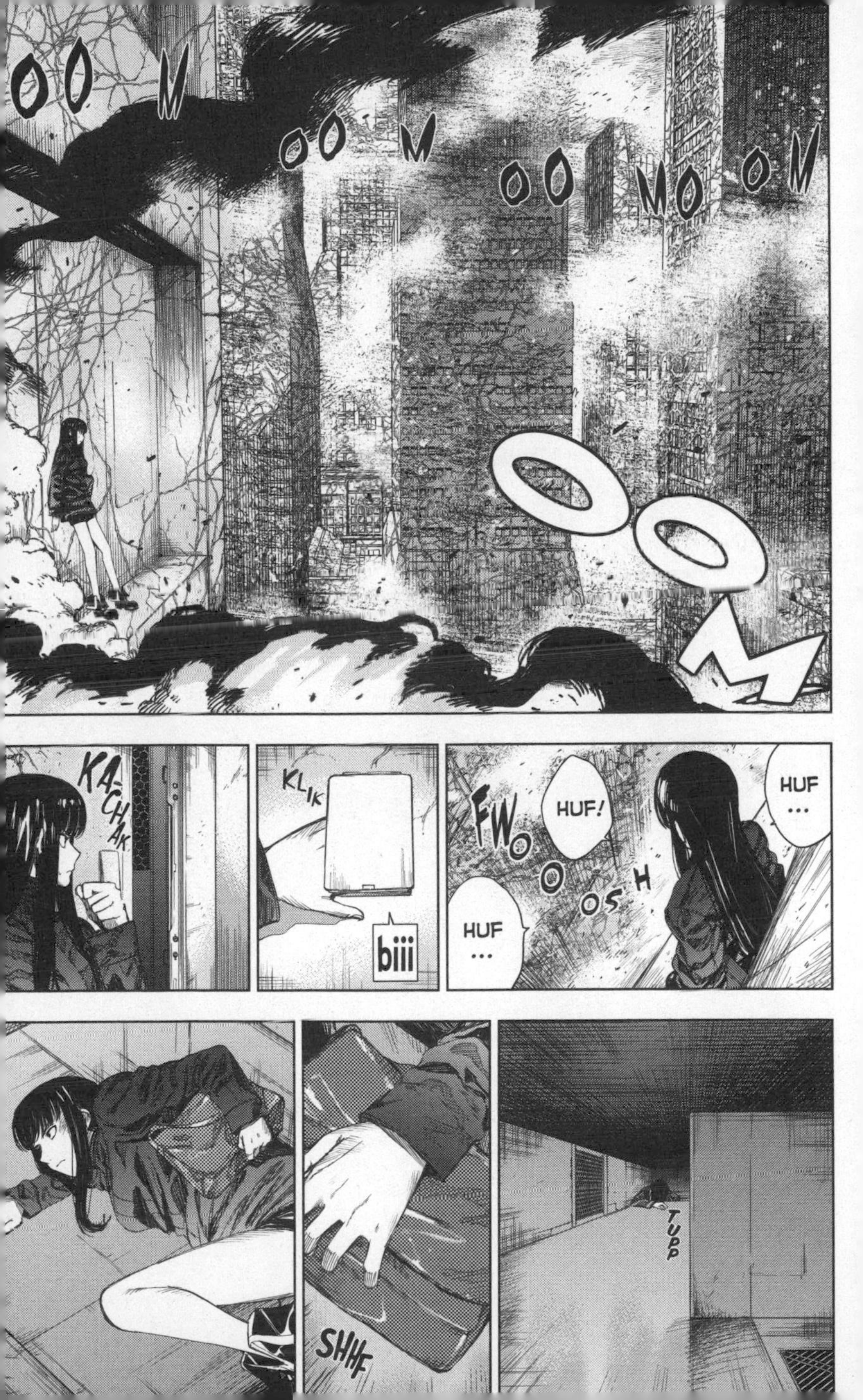
OOM
OOM
OOM
OOM
OOOM
HUF ...
FWOOOOSH
HUF!
HUF ...
KLIK
biii
KA-CHAK
TUPP
SHHF

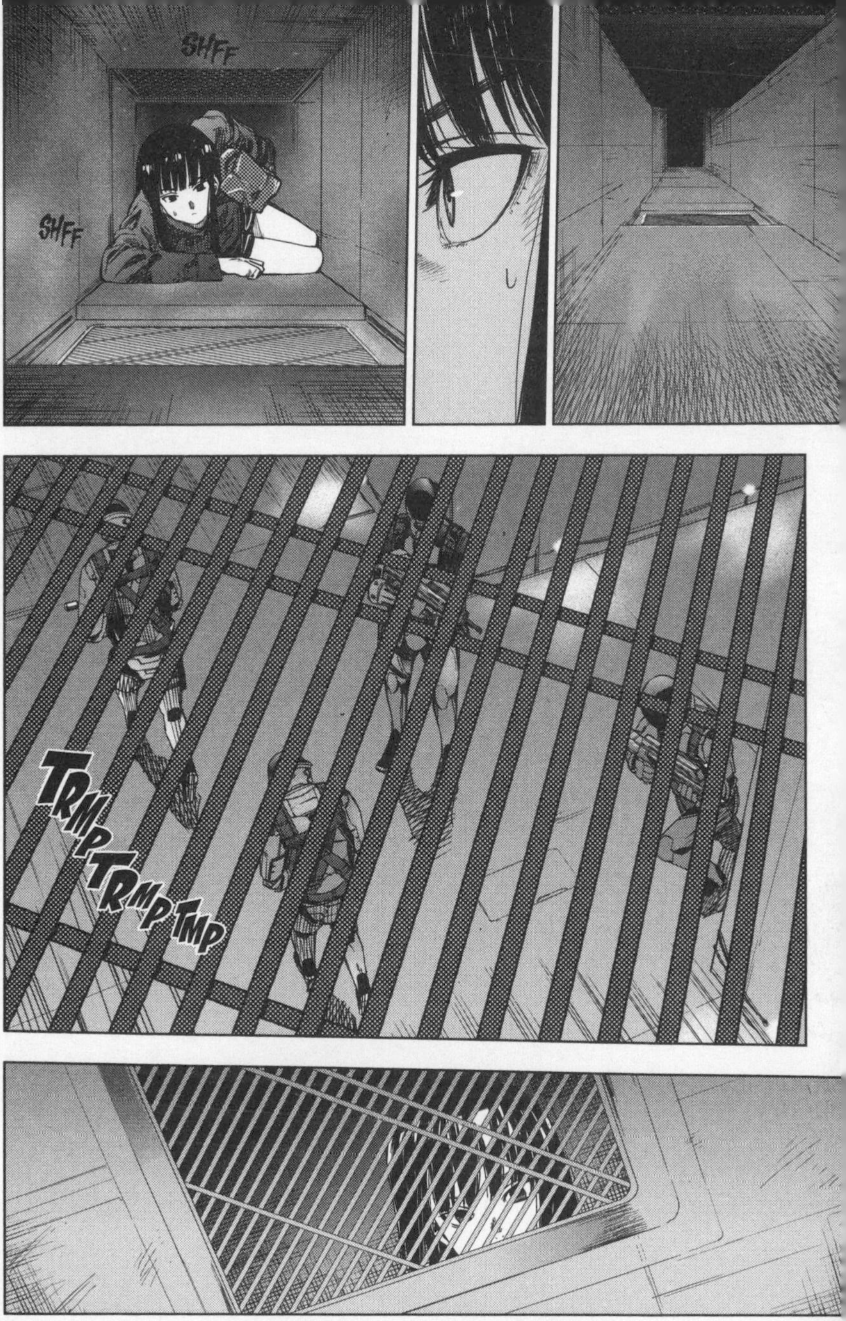
SHFF
SHFF
TRMP TRMP TMP

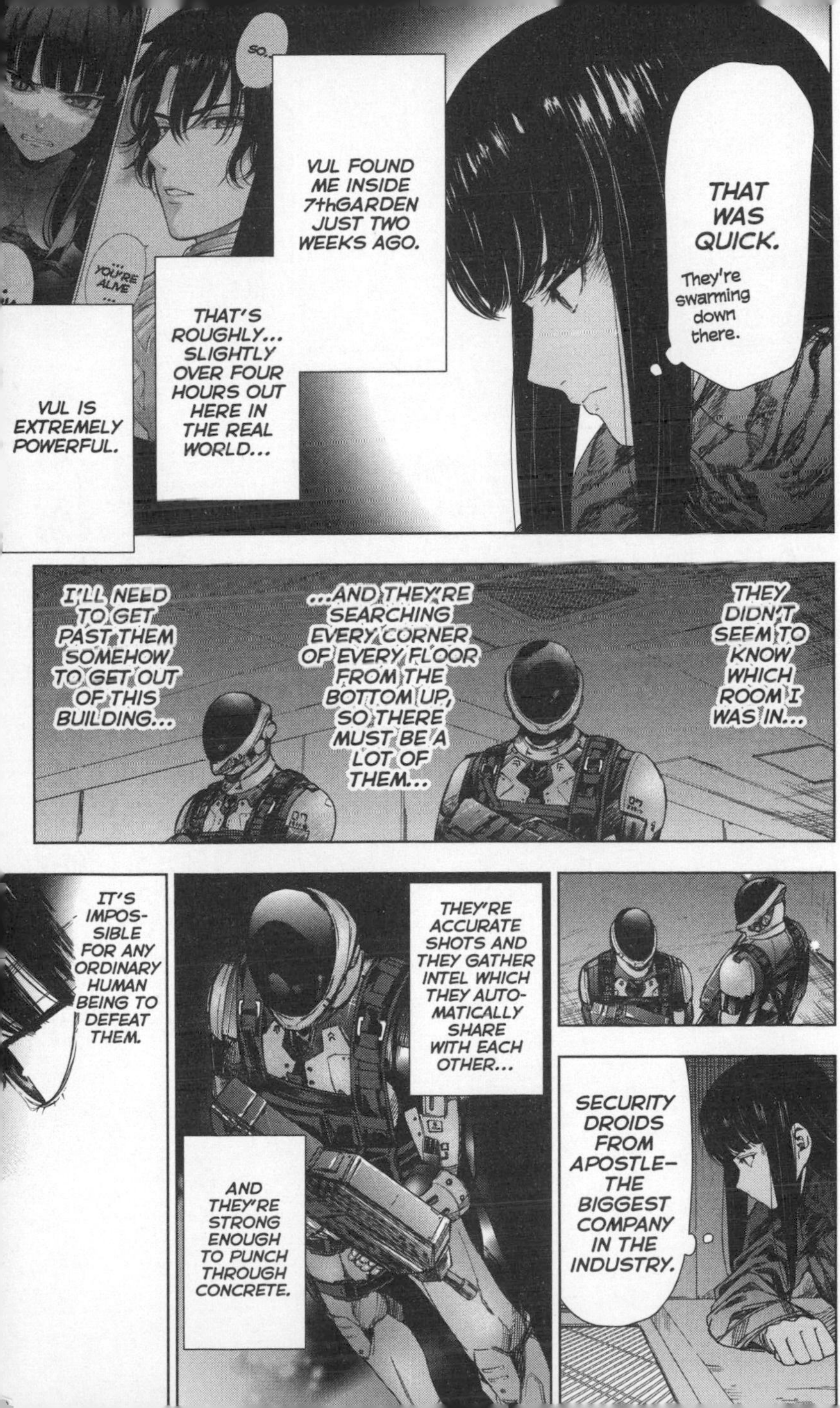
THAT WAS QUICK.
They're swarming down there.
SO...
VUL FOUND ME INSIDE 7thGARDEN JUST TWO WEEKS AGO.
THAT'S ROUGHLY... SLIGHTLY OVER FOUR HOURS OUT HERE IN THE REAL WORLD...
...YOU'RE ALIVE...
VUL IS EXTREMELY POWERFUL.
THEY DIDN'T SEEM TO KNOW WHICH ROOM I WAS IN...
...AND THEY'RE SEARCHING EVERY CORNER OF EVERY FLOOR FROM THE BOTTOM UP, SO THERE MUST BE A LOT OF THEM...
I'LL NEED TO GET PAST THEM SOMEHOW TO GET OUT OF THIS BUILDING...
SECURITY DROIDS FROM APOSTLE— THE BIGGEST COMPANY IN THE INDUSTRY.
THEY'RE ACCURATE SHOTS AND THEY GATHER INTEL WHICH THEY AUTO-MATICALLY SHARE WITH EACH OTHER...
AND THEY'RE STRONG ENOUGH TO PUNCH THROUGH CONCRETE.
IT'S IMPOS-SIBLE FOR ANY ORDINARY HUMAN BEING TO DEFEAT THEM.

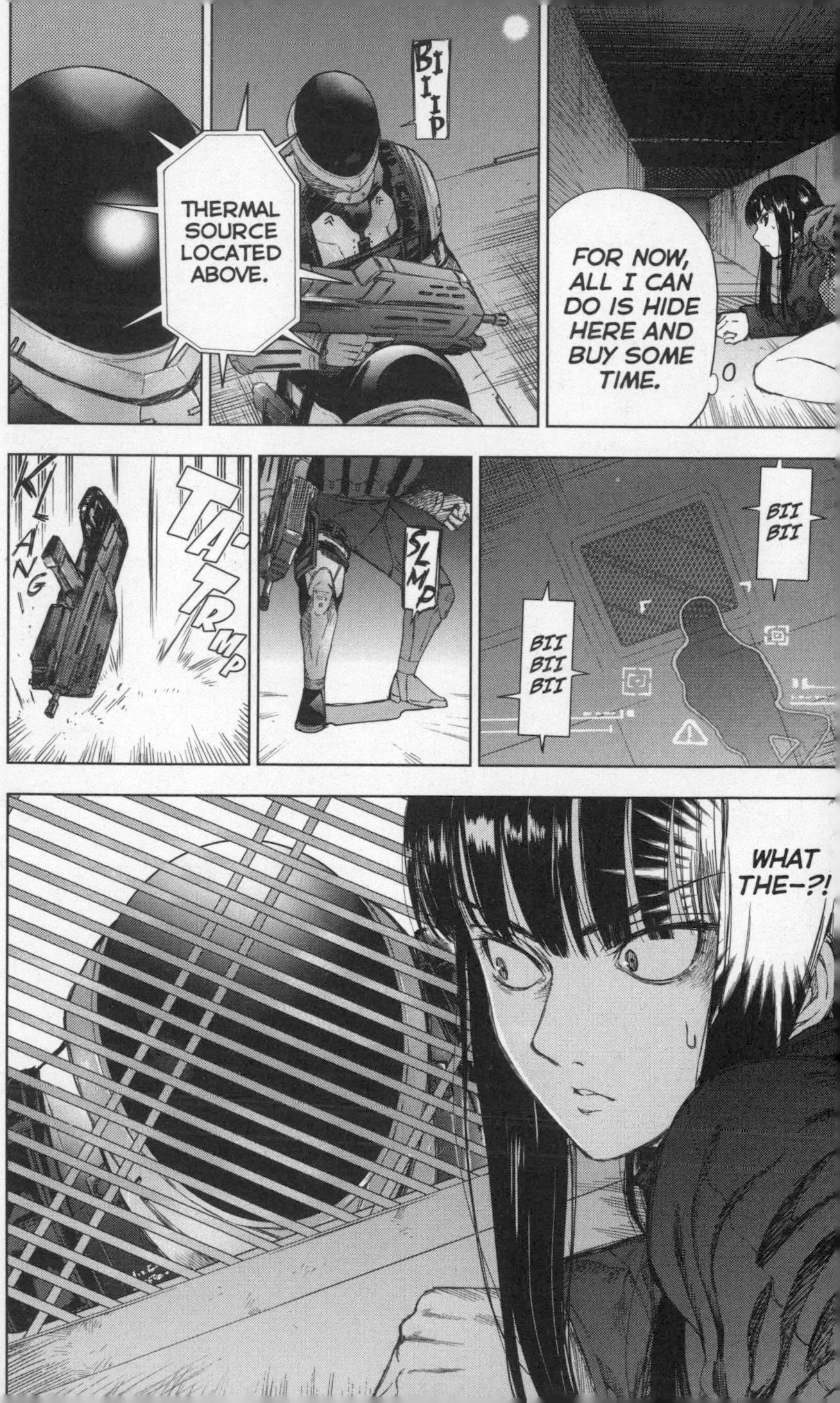
FOR NOW, ALL I CAN DO IS HIDE HERE AND BUY SOME TIME.
BIIIP
THERMAL SOURCE LOCATED ABOVE.
BII BII
BII BII BII
SLMP
KLANG
TA-TRMP
WHAT THE–?!

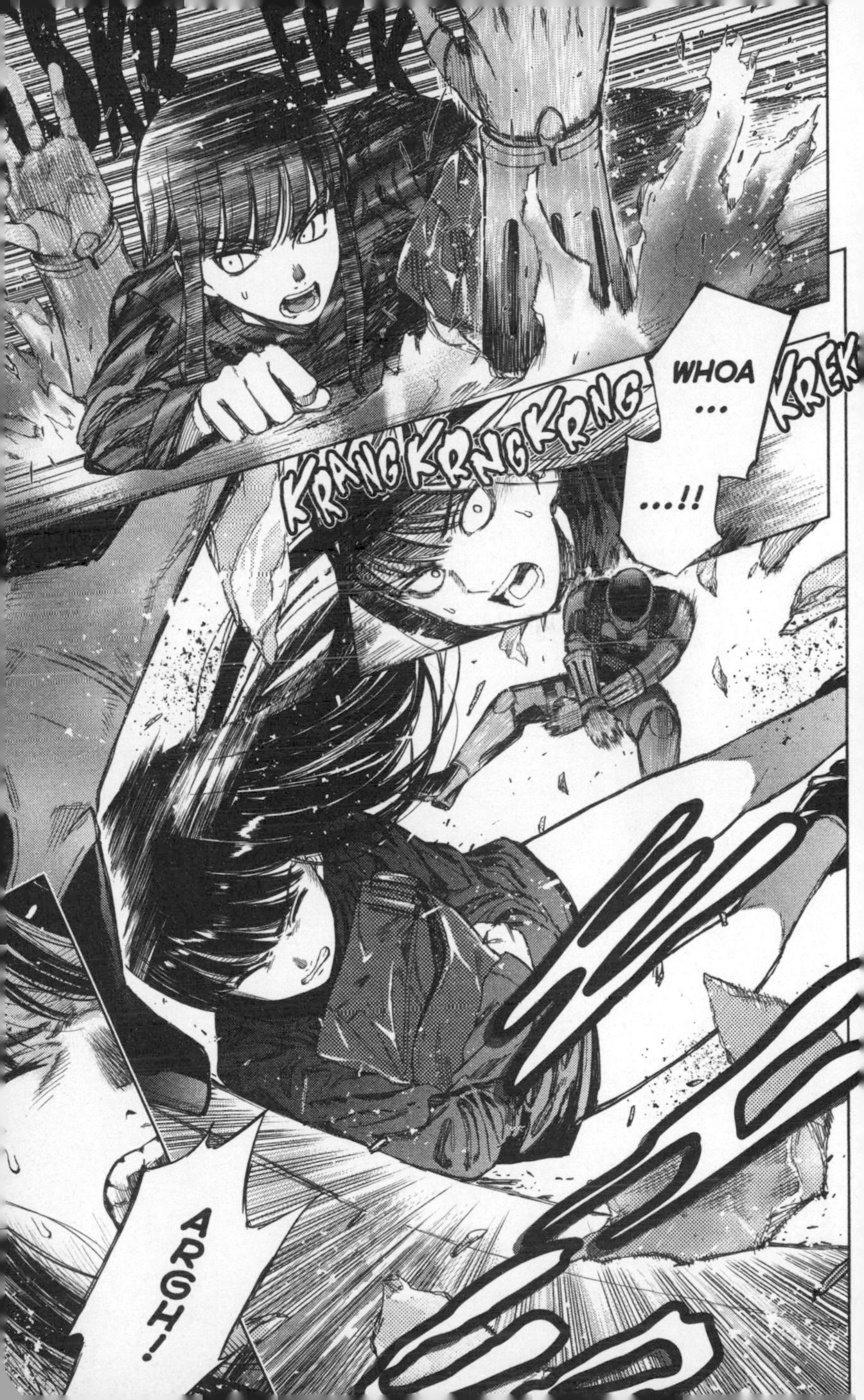
KREK
WHOA ...
KRANGKRNGKRNG
...!!
ARGH!

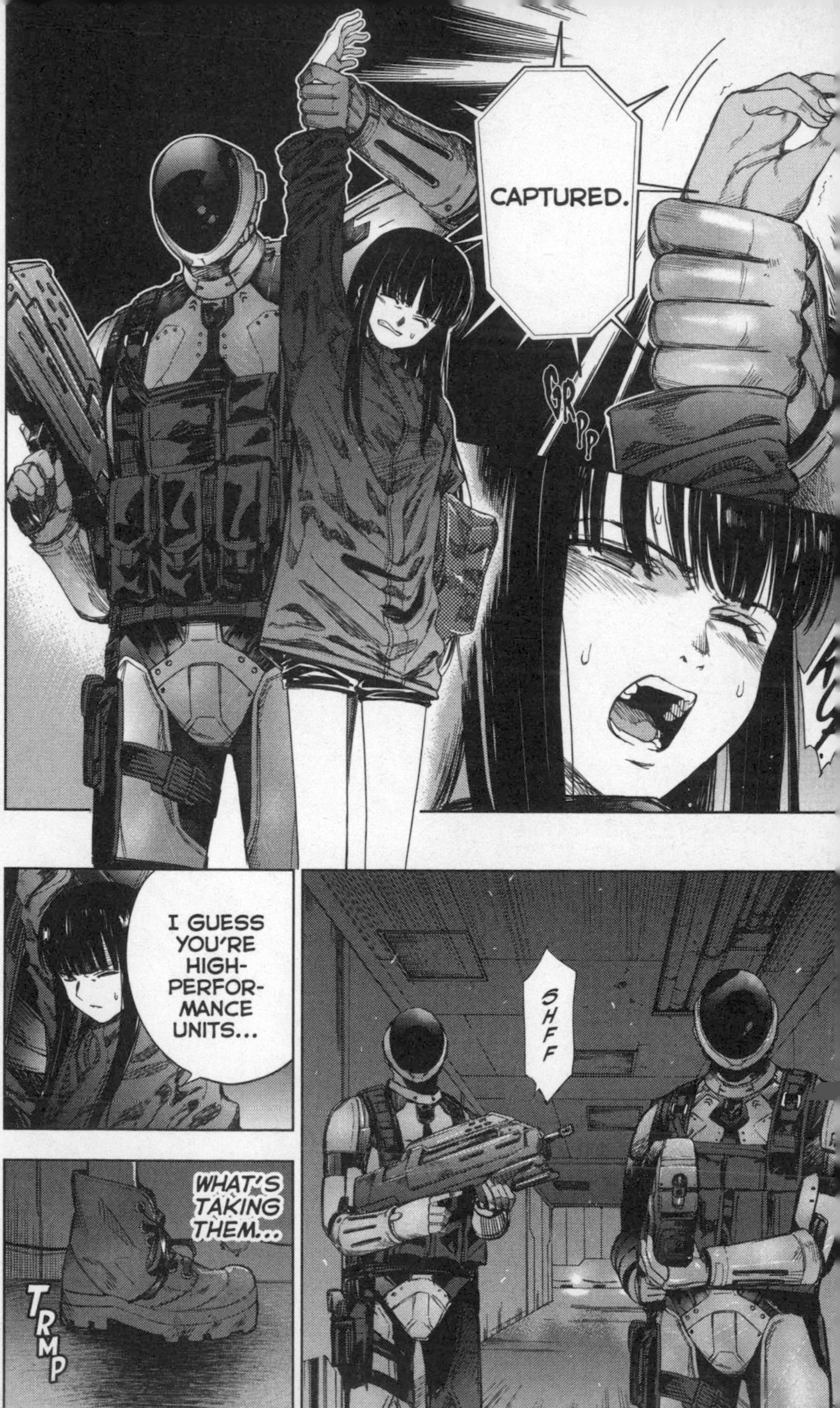
CAPTURED.
GRPP
SHFF
I GUESS YOU'RE HIGH-PERFORMANCE UNITS...
WHAT'S TAKING THEM...
TRMP

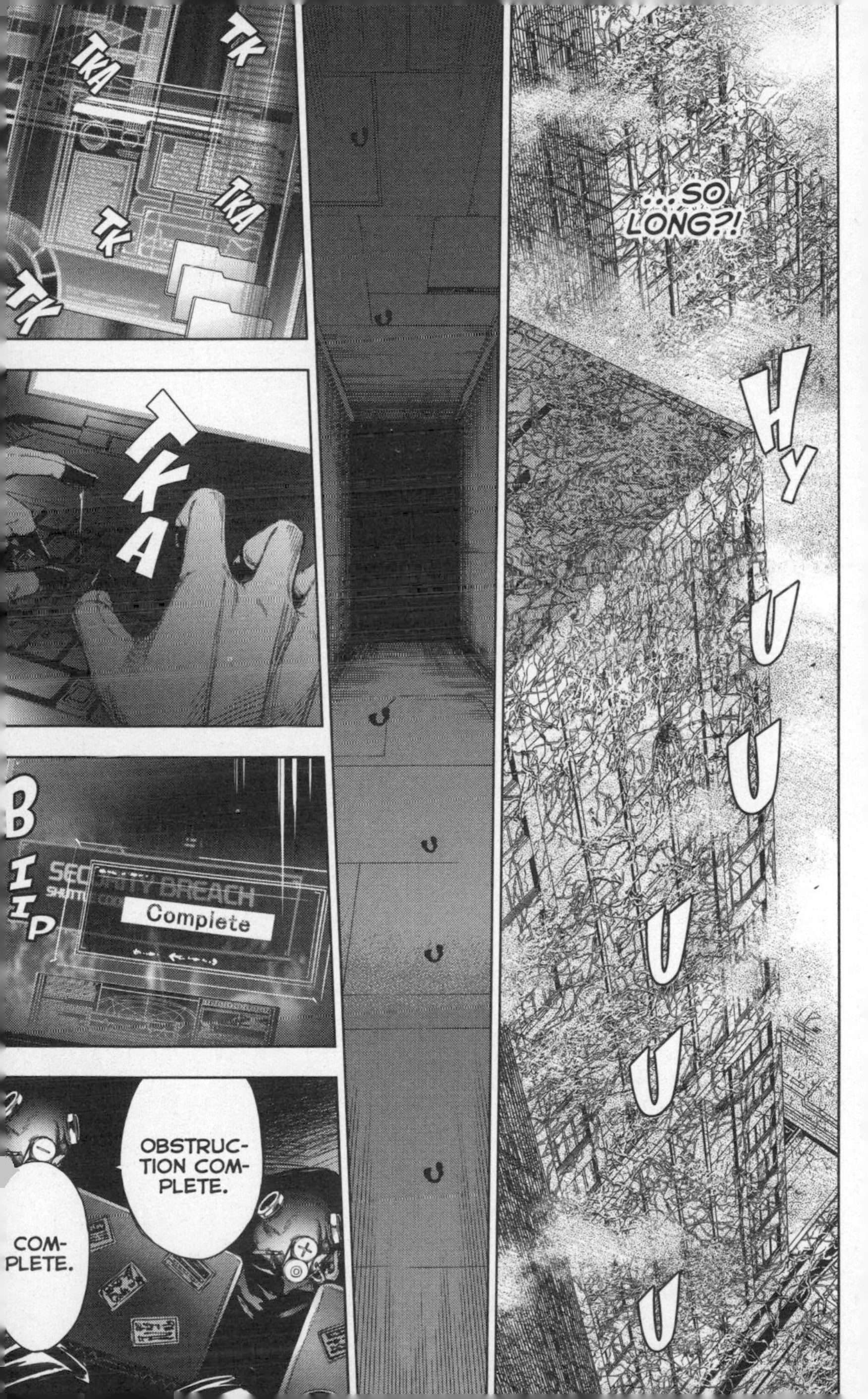
...SO LONG?!
HYUUUUUU
TK
TKA
TKA
TK
TK
TKA
BIIIP
Complete
OBSTRUCTION COMPLETE.
COMPLETE.

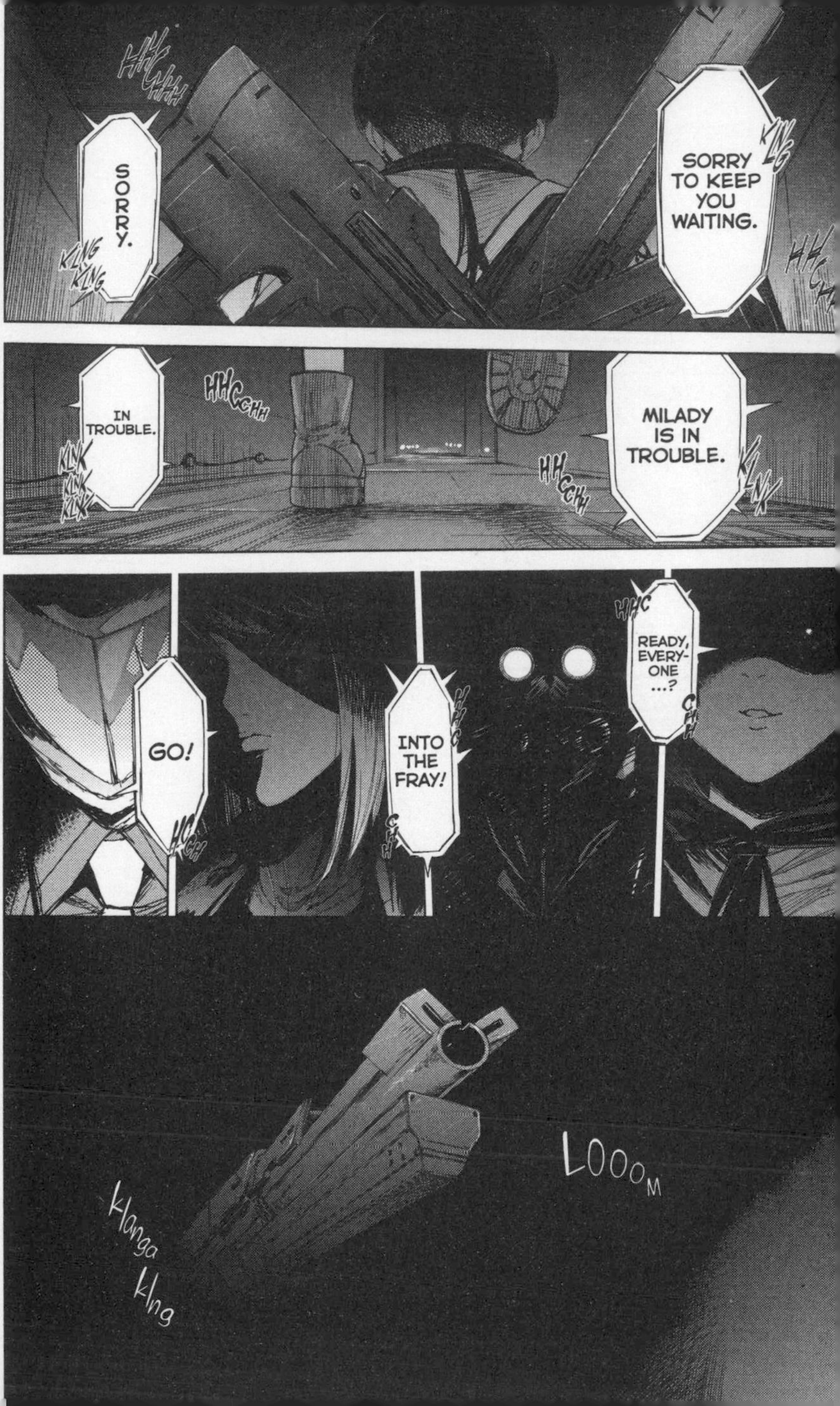
KLNG
SORRY TO KEEP YOU WAITING.
HHCH
HHCHH
SORRY.
KLNG KLNG
MILADY IS IN TROUBLE.
KLNK
HHCCHH
HHGCHH
IN TROUBLE.
KLNK KLNK KLNK
HHC
READY, EVERY-ONE ...?
CHH
HHC
INTO THE FRAY!
CHH
GO!
HCHH
LOOOM
klanga klng

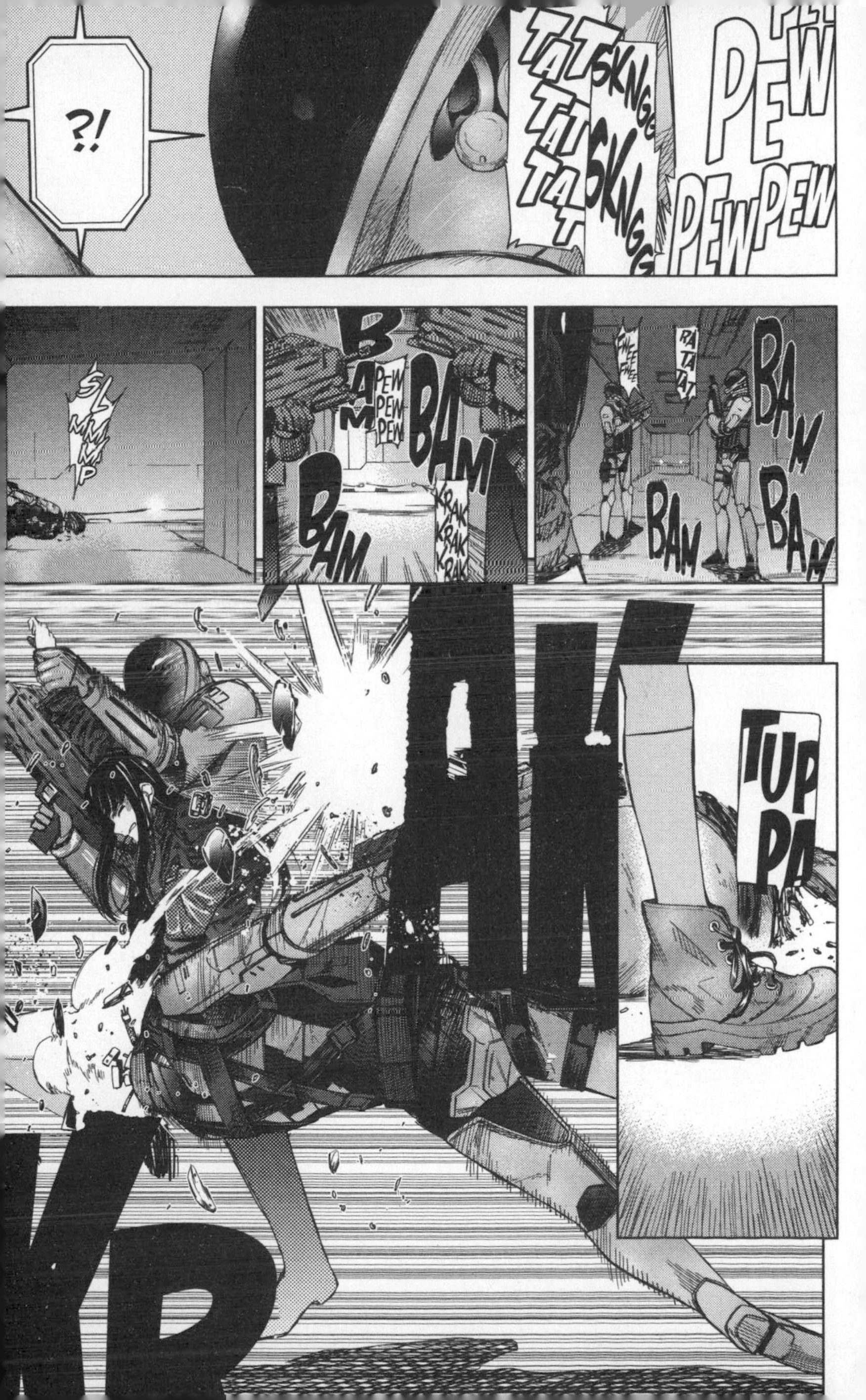
PEW PEW PEW PEW
SKNGG SKNGG
TATATAT
?!
BAM BAM BAM BAM
RATATAT
BAM
BAM
PEW PEW PEW
BAM
KRAK KRAK KRAK
BAM
SLMMMP
TUP PA

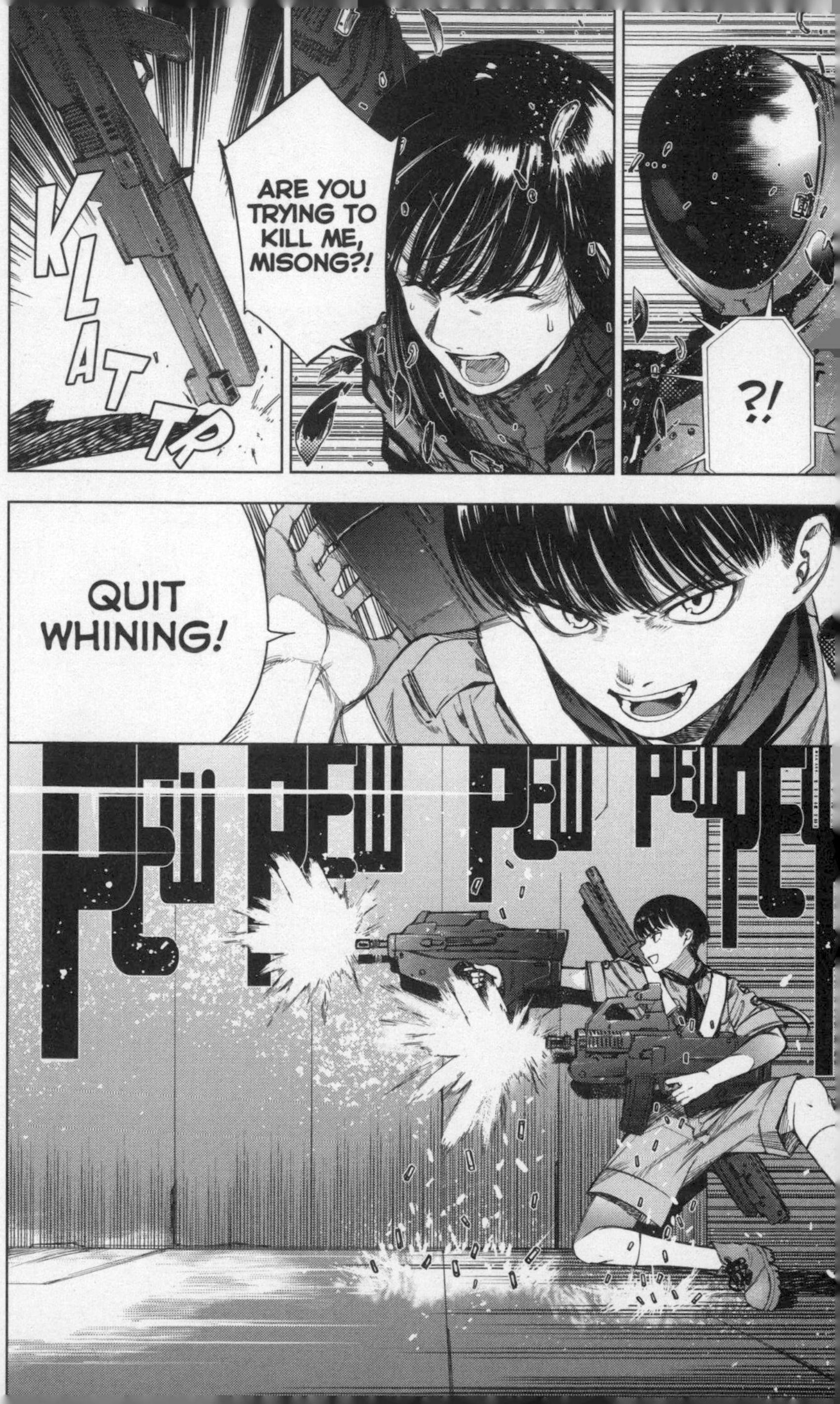
?!
ARE YOU TRYING TO KILL ME, MISONG?!
KLATTR
QUIT WHINING!
PEWPEW
PEW
PEW
PEW

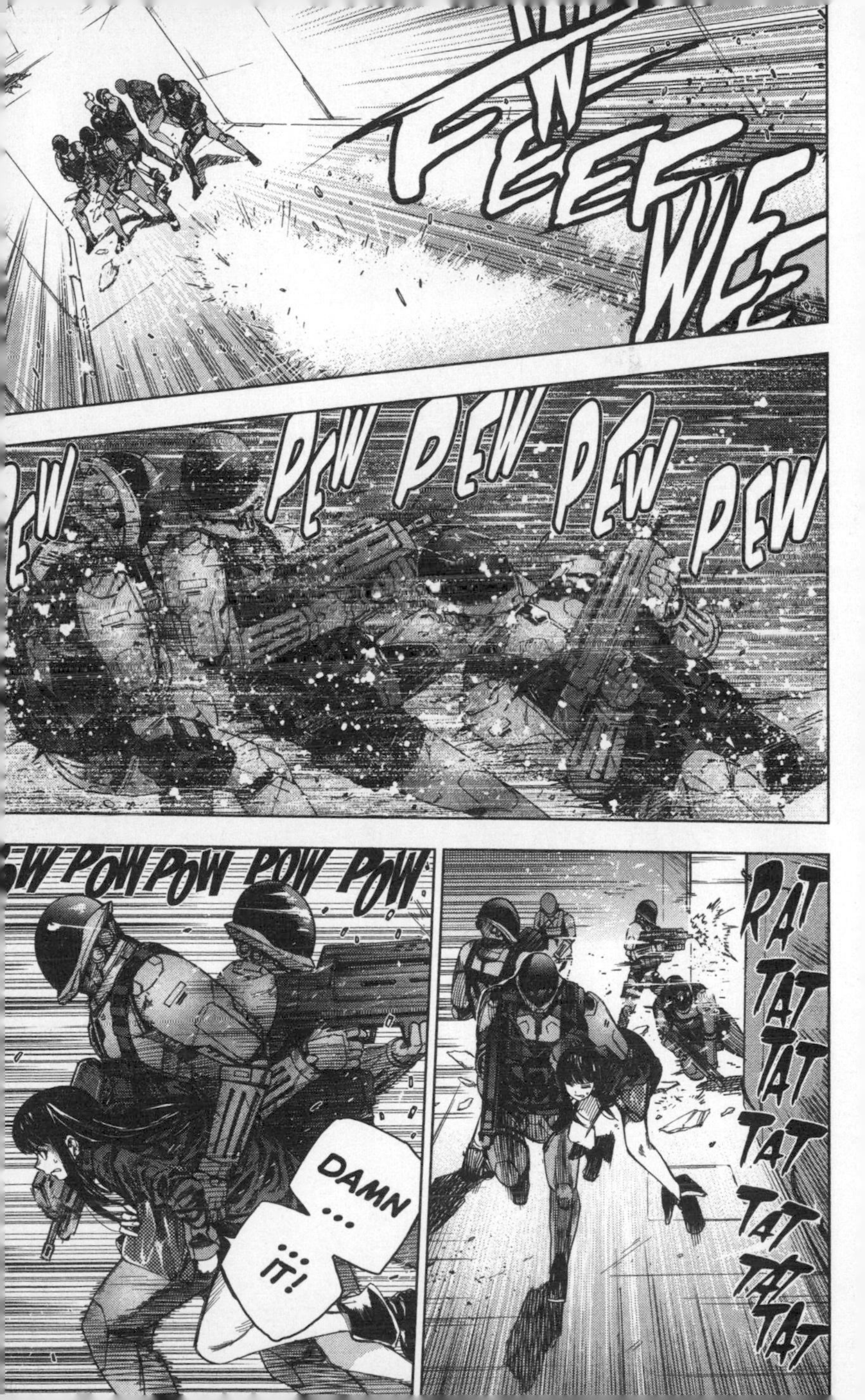
PEW PEW PEW PEW
RAT TAT TAT TAT TAT TAT TAT
POW POW POW POW
DAMN...
...IT!

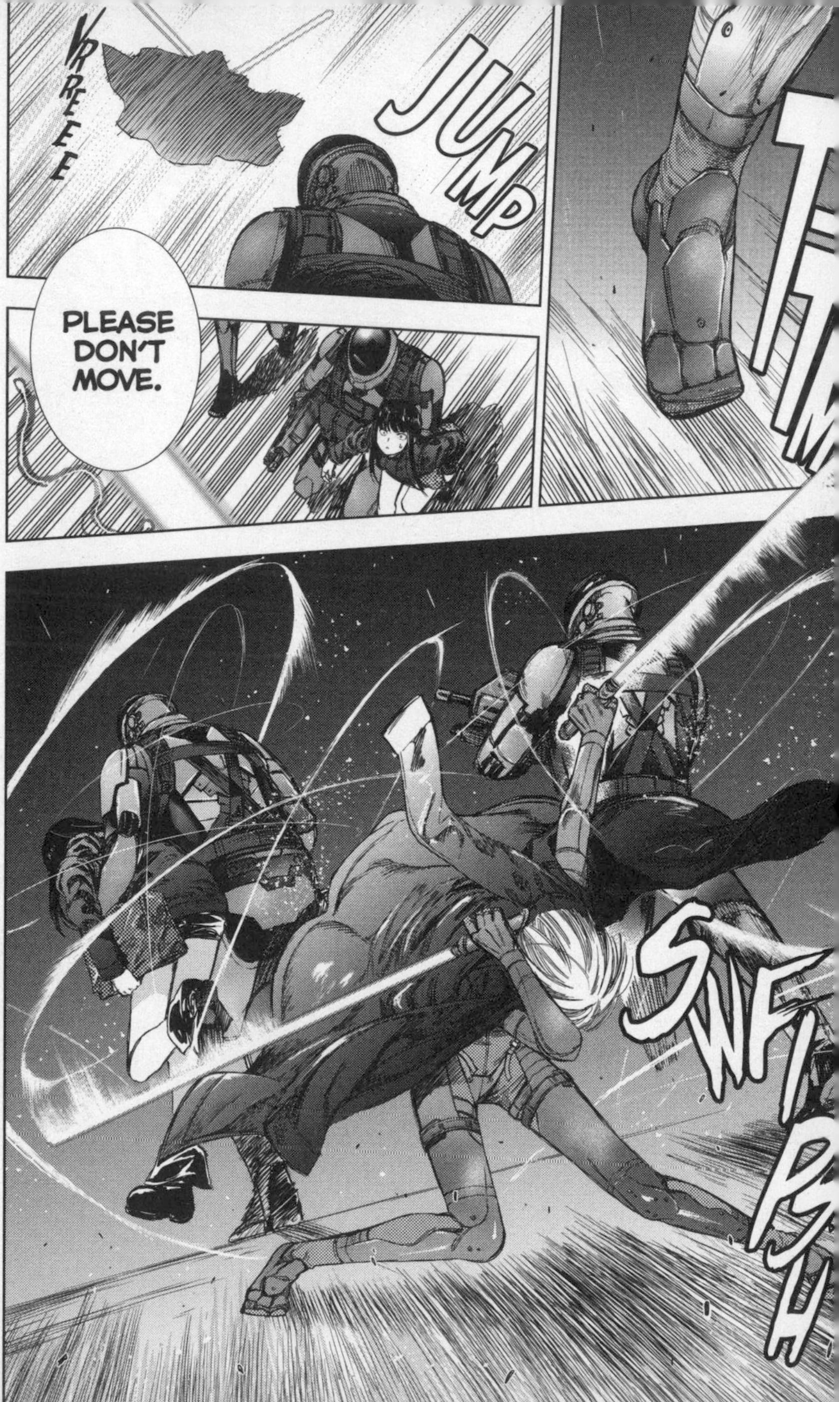
VRREEEE
JUMP
PLEASE DON'T MOVE.

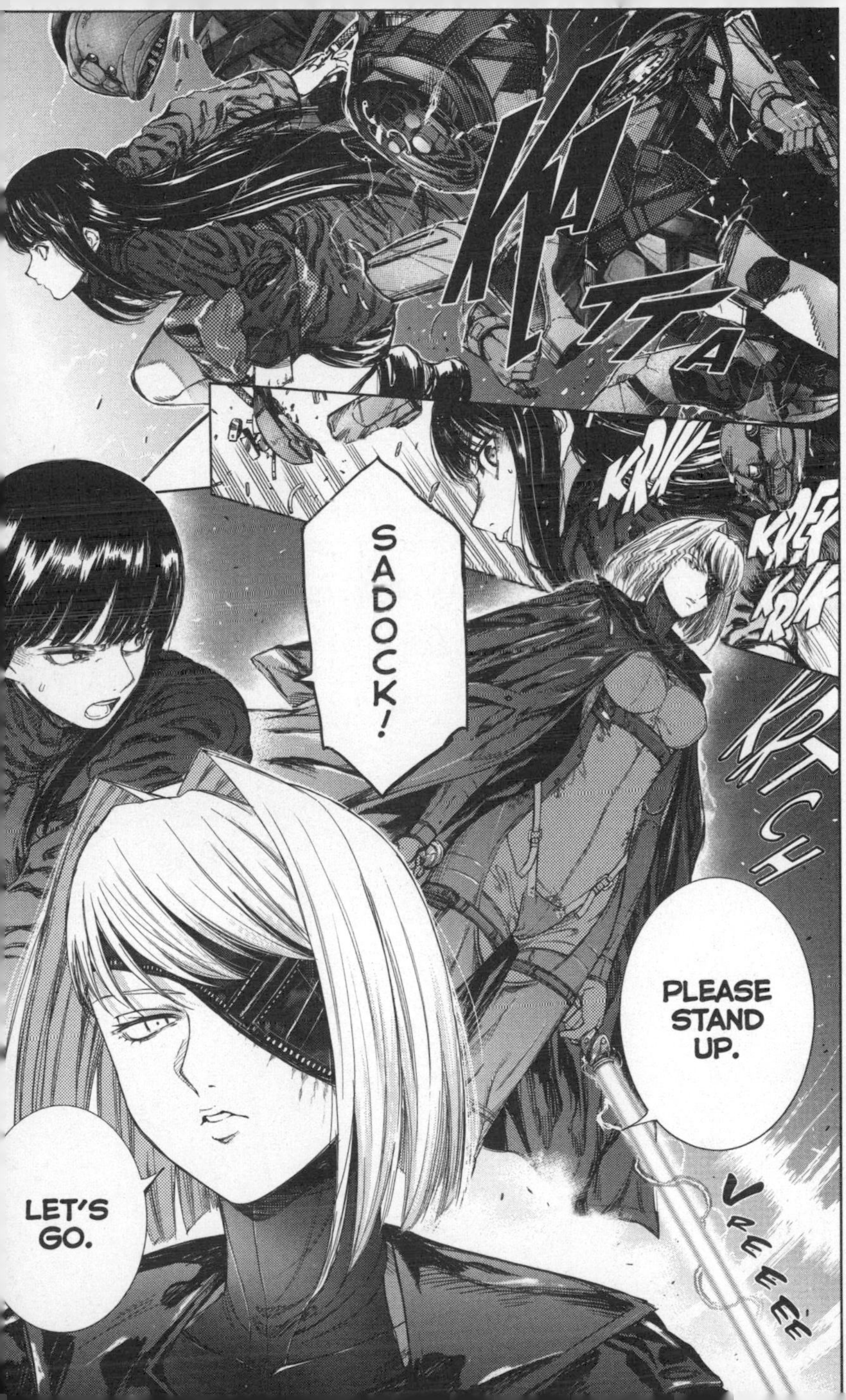
KATTA
KRIK
KRIK
KRTCH
SADOCK!
PLEASE STAND UP.
VREEEE
LET'S GO.

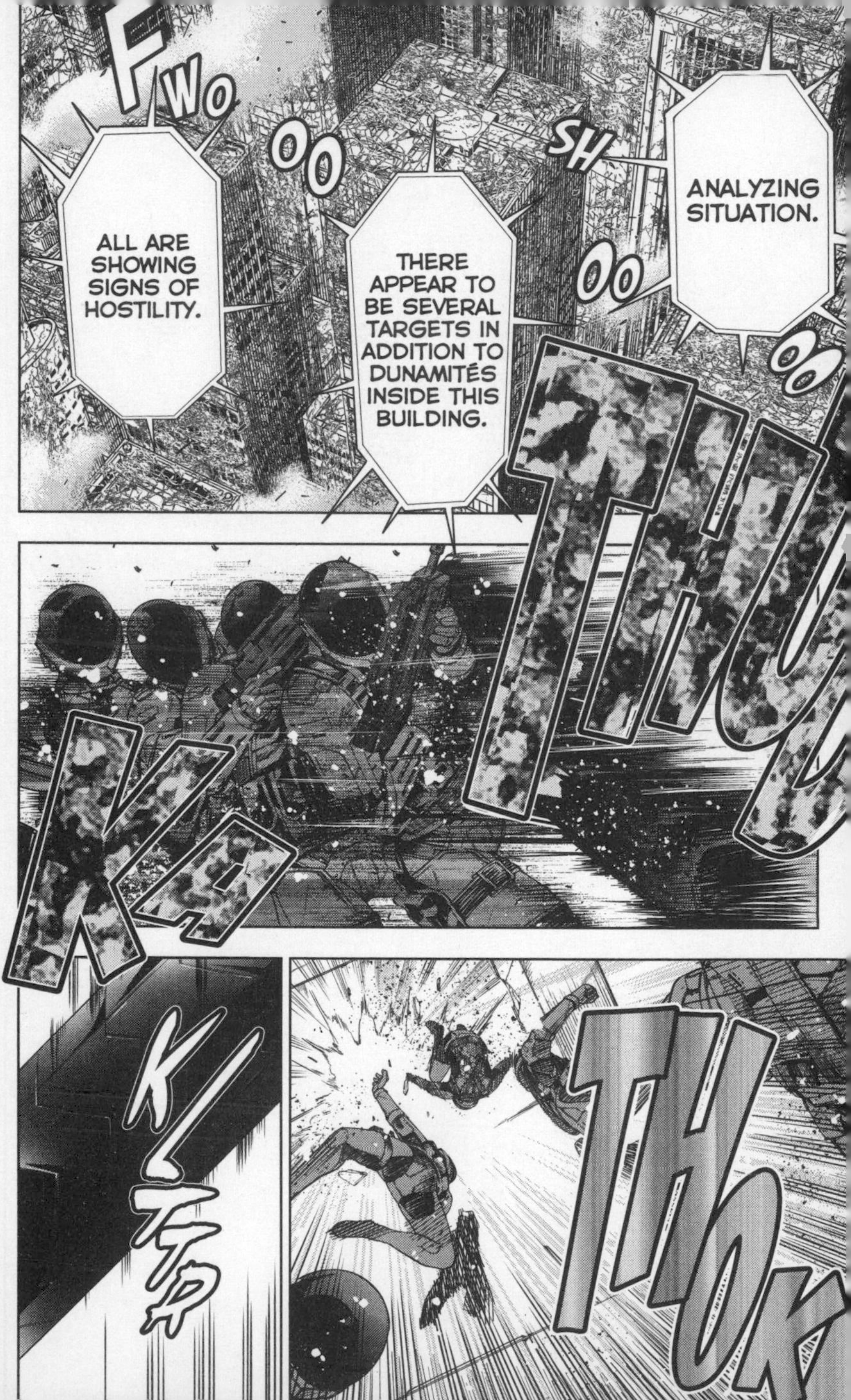
ANALYZING SITUATION.
THERE APPEAR TO BE SEVERAL TARGETS IN ADDITION TO DUNAMITÉS INSIDE THIS BUILDING.
ALL ARE SHOWING SIGNS OF HOSTILITY.
FWOOOOOOSH
THU
KA
THOK
KLTTR

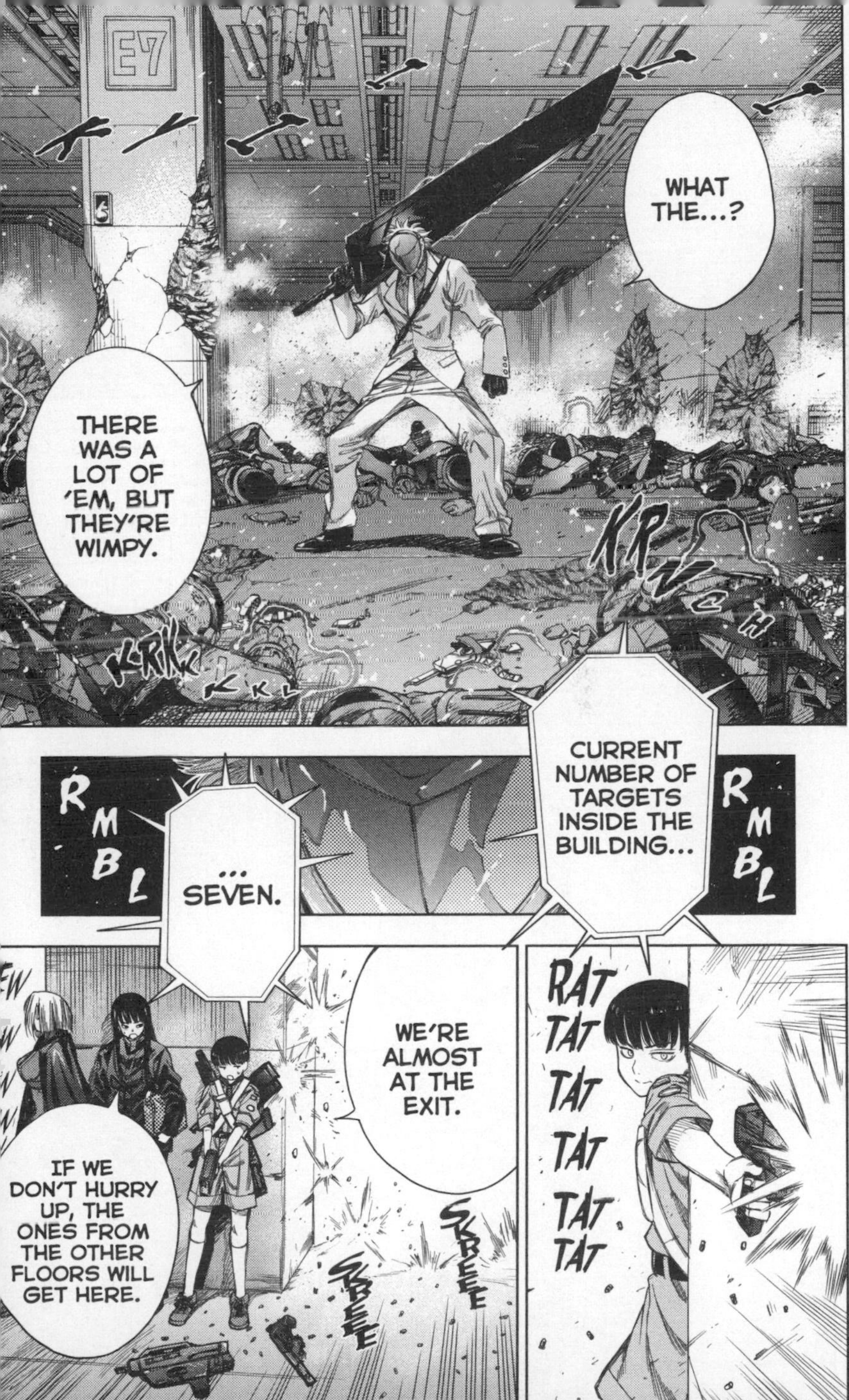
WHAT THE...?
THERE WAS A LOT OF 'EM, BUT THEY'RE WIMPY.
KRNCH
RMBL
CURRENT NUMBER OF TARGETS INSIDE THE BUILDING...
...SEVEN.
RMBL
RAT TAT TAT TAT TAT TAT
WE'RE ALMOST AT THE EXIT.
IF WE DON'T HURRY UP, THE ONES FROM THE OTHER FLOORS WILL GET HERE.
SKREEE
SKREEE

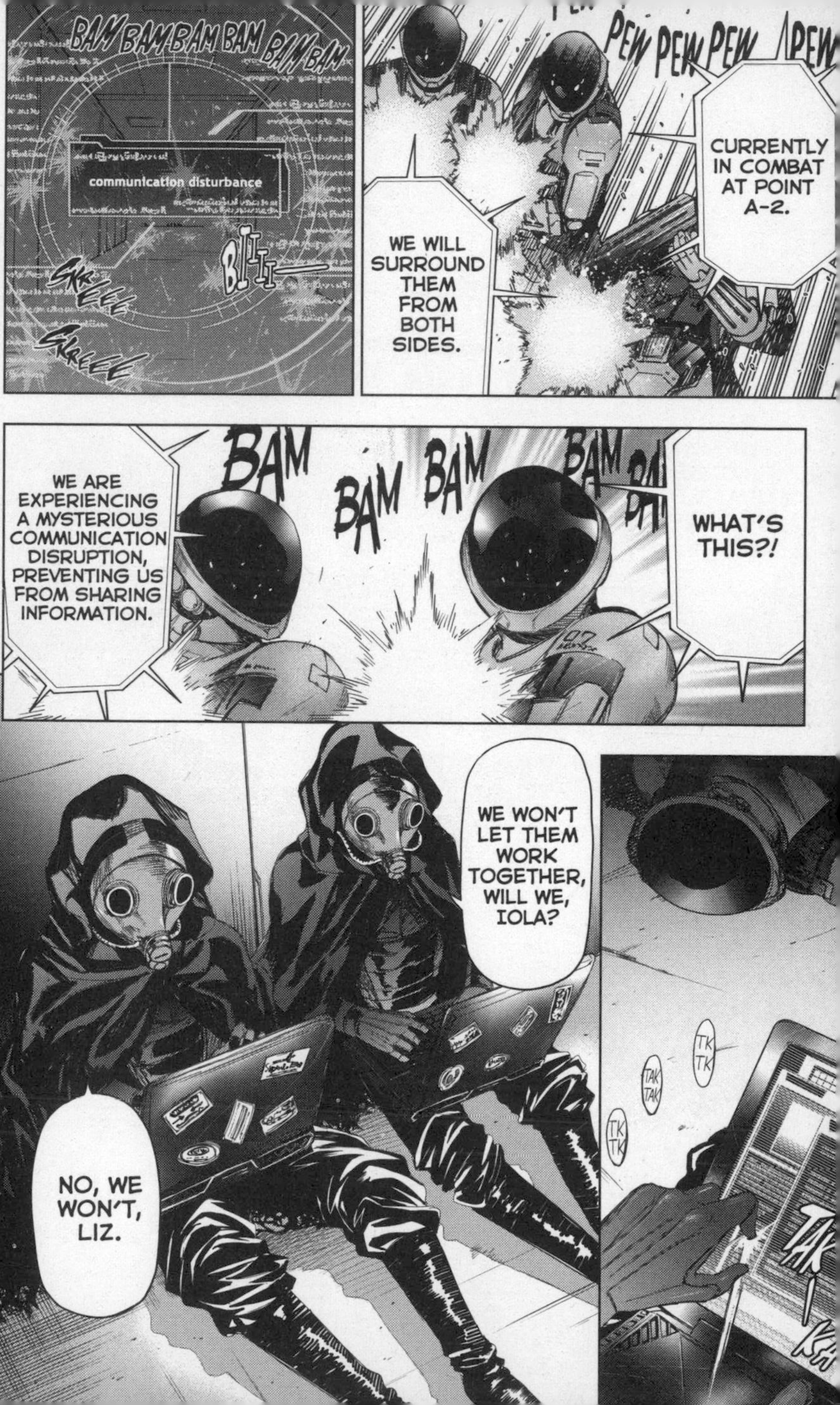
PEW PEW PEW PEW
CURRENTLY IN COMBAT AT POINT A-2.
WE WILL SURROUND THEM FROM BOTH SIDES.
BAM BAM BAM BAM BAM BAM
communication disturbance
BIIII—
SKREEE
SKREEE
WHAT'S THIS?!
BAM BAM BAM BAM
WE ARE EXPERIENCING A MYSTERIOUS COMMUNICATION DISRUPTION, PREVENTING US FROM SHARING INFORMATION.
TK TK
TAK TAK
TK TK
TAK
WE WON'T LET THEM WORK TOGETHER, WILL WE, IOLA?
NO, WE WON'T, LIZ.

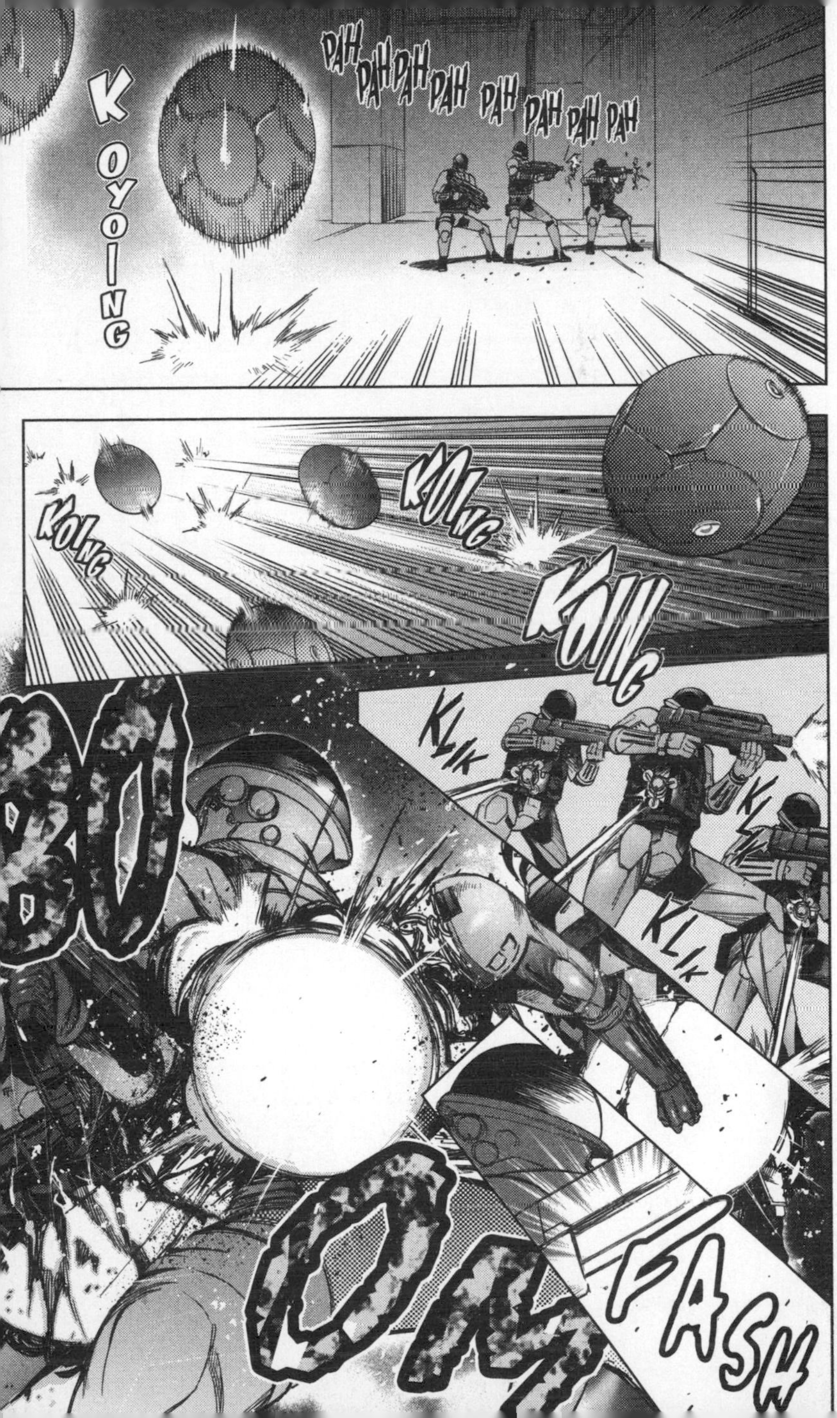
PAH PAH PAH PAH PAH PAH PAH PAH
KOYOING
KOING
KOING
KOING
KLIK
KLIK
KLIK
FASH

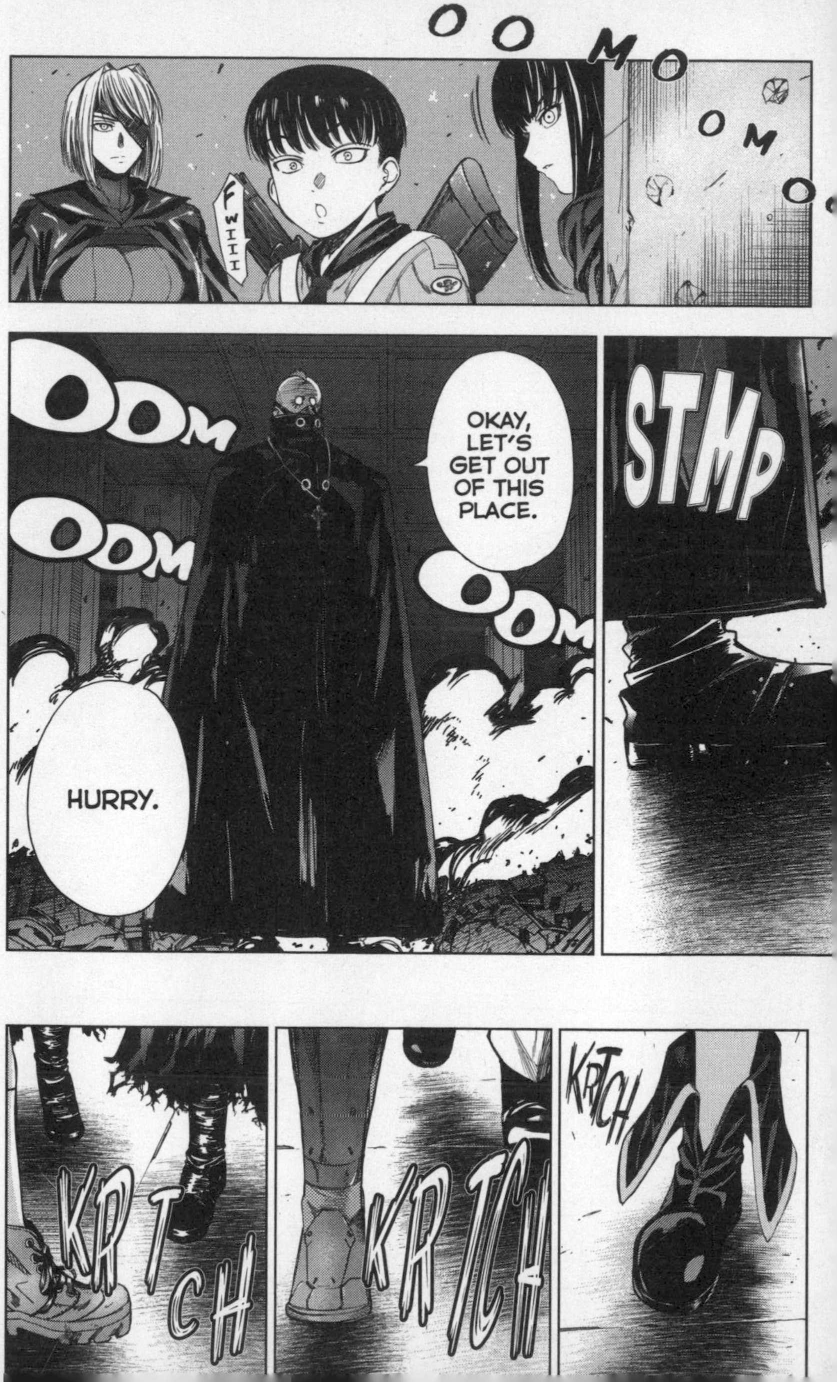
OOMOOMOO
FWIII
STMP
OKAY, LET'S GET OUT OF THIS PLACE.
OOM
OOM
OOM
HURRY.
KRTCH
KRTCH
KRTCH

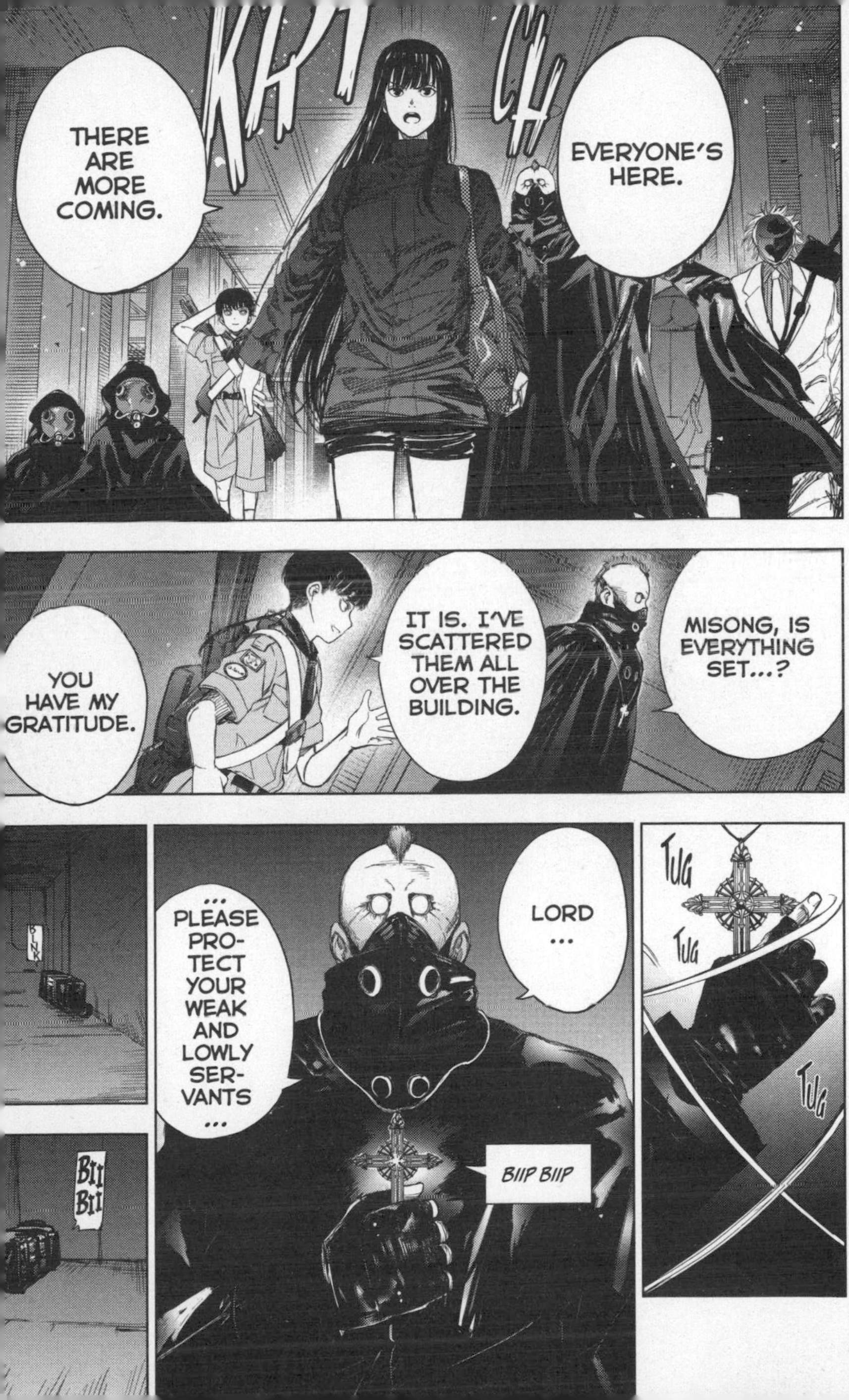
EVERYONE'S HERE.
THERE ARE MORE COMING.
MISONG, IS EVERYTHING SET...?
IT IS. I'VE SCATTERED THEM ALL OVER THE BUILDING.
YOU HAVE MY GRATITUDE.
TUG
TUG
TUG
LORD ...
... PLEASE PROTECT YOUR WEAK AND LOWLY SERVANTS ...
BIIP BIIP
BLINK
BII BII

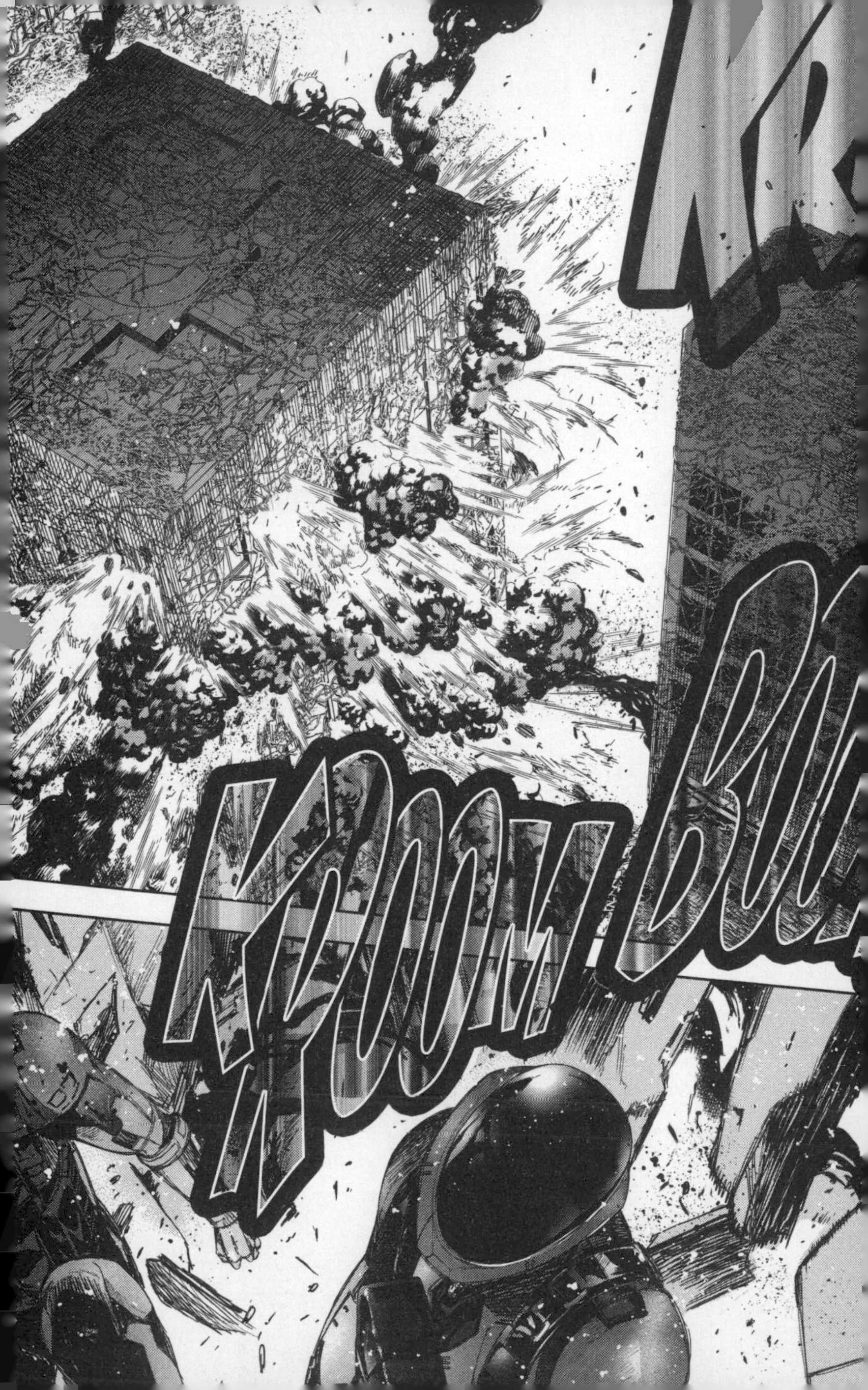

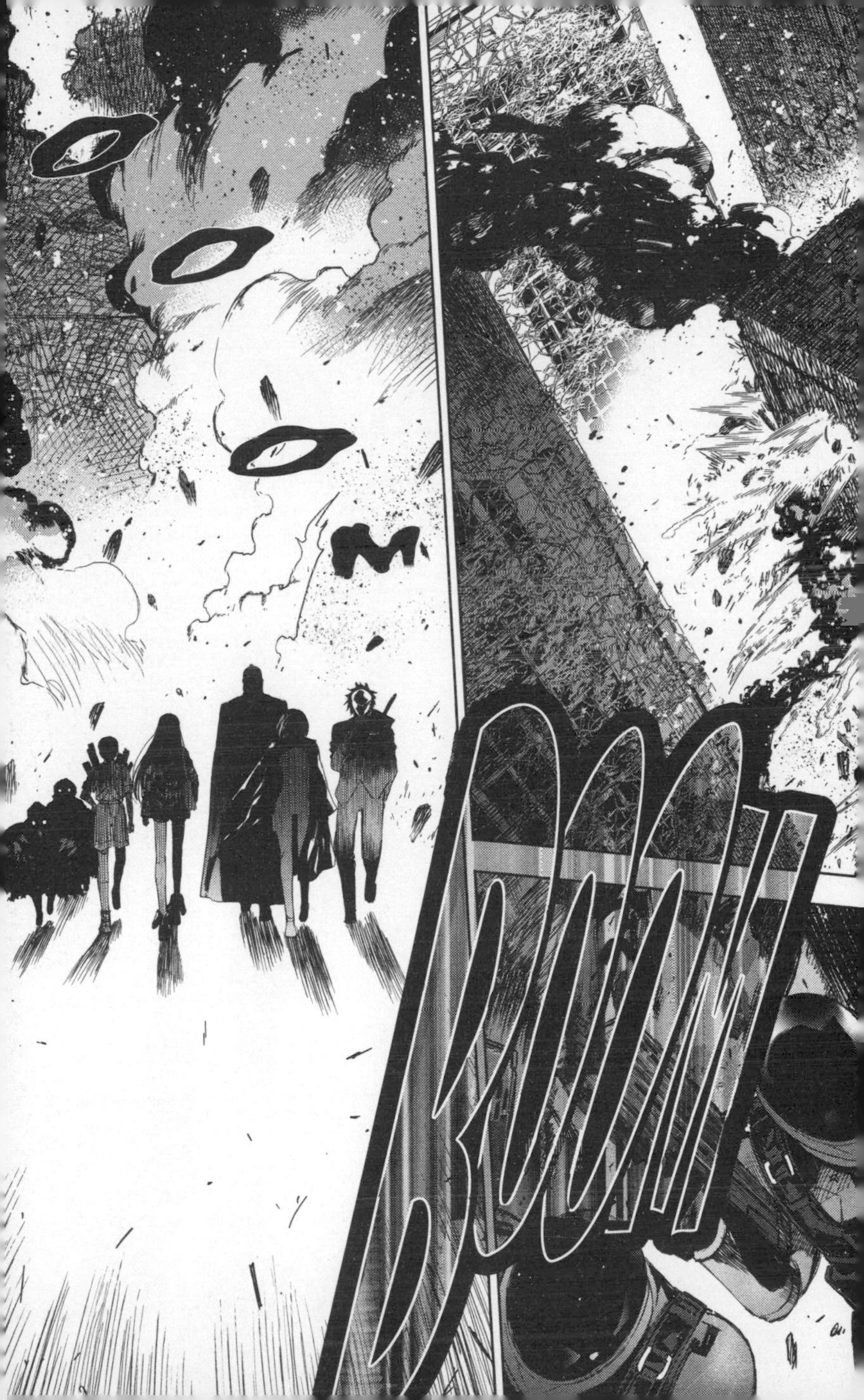
BOOOM
OOOM

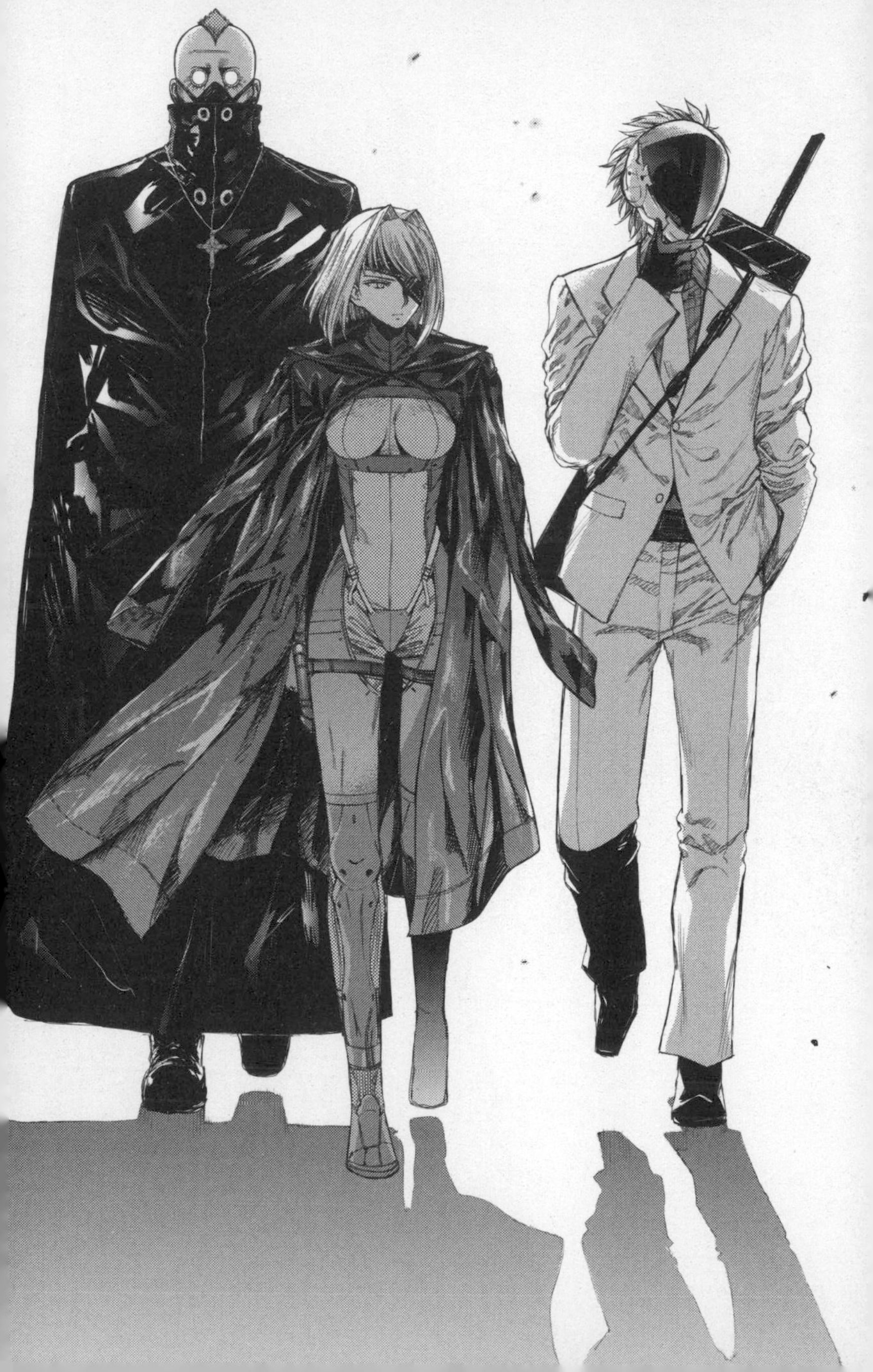

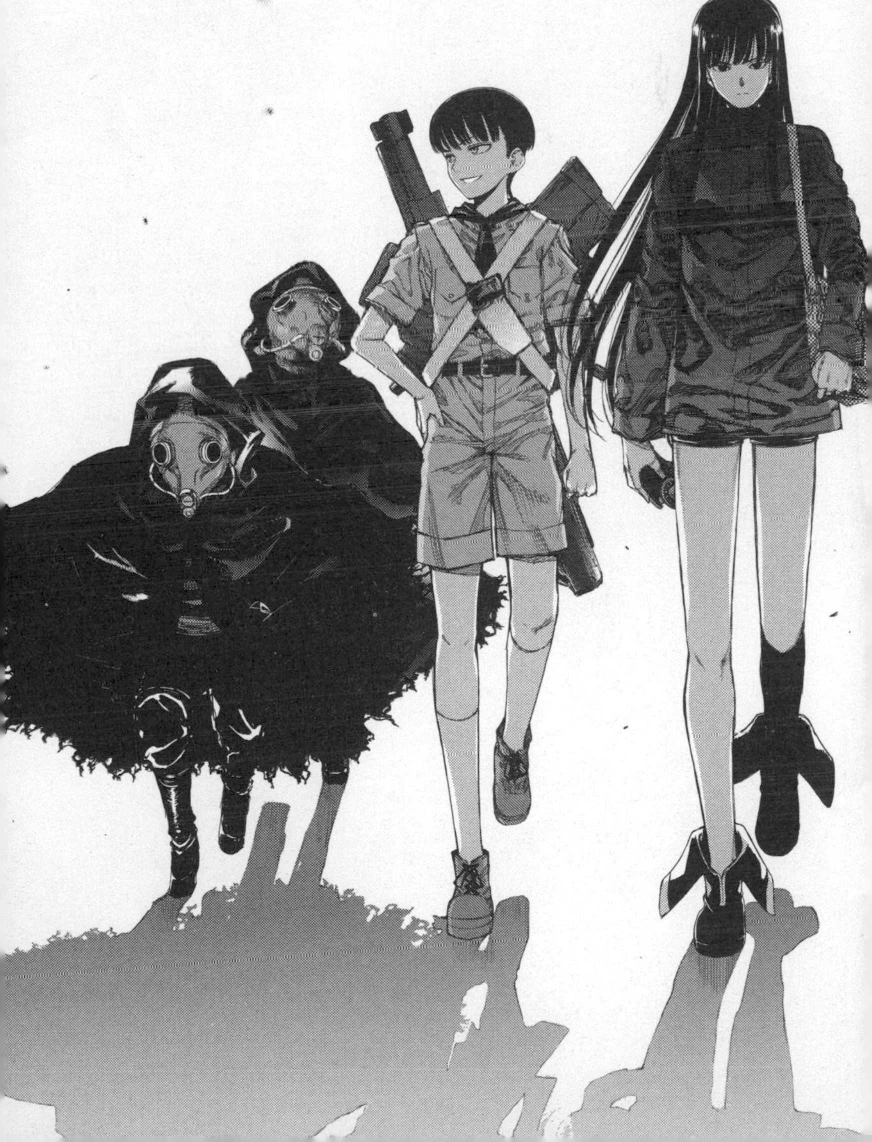

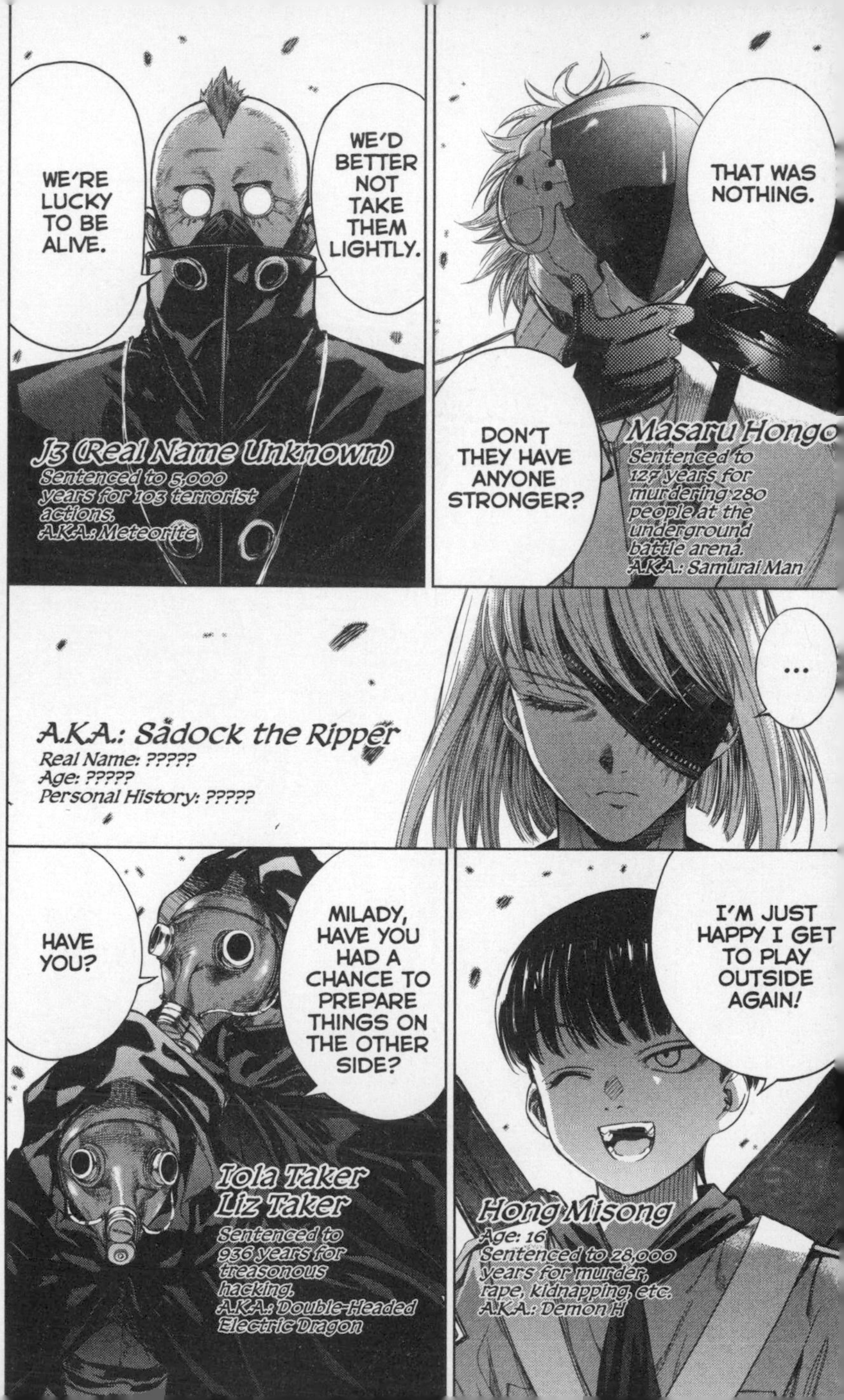
THAT WAS NOTHING.
DON'T THEY HAVE ANYONE STRONGER?
Masaru Hongo
Sentenced to 127 years for murdering 280 people at the underground battle arena.
A.K.A.: Samurai Man
WE'D BETTER NOT TAKE THEM LIGHTLY.
WE'RE LUCKY TO BE ALIVE.
J3 (Real Name Unknown)
Sentenced to 5,000 years for 103 terrorist actions.
A.K.A.: Meteorite
...
A.K.A.: Sădock the Ripper
Real Name: ?????
Age: ?????
Personal History: ?????
I'M JUST HAPPY I GET TO PLAY OUTSIDE AGAIN!
Hong Misong
Age: 16
Sentenced to 28,000 years for murder, rape, kidnapping, etc.
A.K.A.: Demon H
MILADY, HAVE YOU HAD A CHANCE TO PREPARE THINGS ON THE OTHER SIDE?
HAVE YOU?
Iola Taker
Liz Taker
Sentenced to 936 years for treasonous hacking.
A.K.A.: Double-Headed Electric Dragon

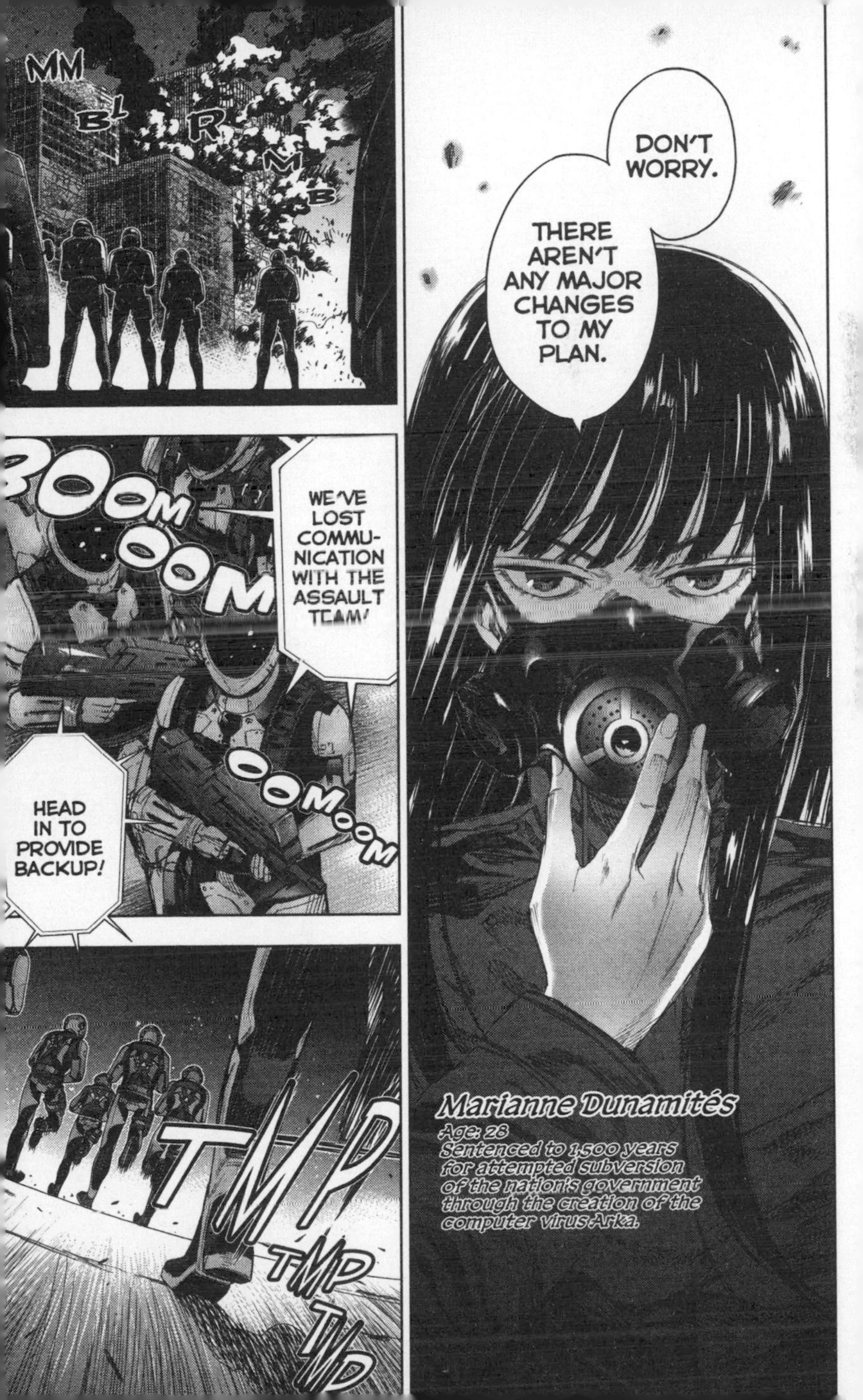
DON'T WORRY.
THERE AREN'T ANY MAJOR CHANGES TO MY PLAN.
Marianne Dunamités
Age: 28
Sentenced to 1,500 years for attempted subversion of the nation's government through the creation of the computer virus Arka.
MM BLRMMB
BOOOOM BOOOOM
WE'VE LOST COMMUNICATION WITH THE ASSAULT TEAM!
HEAD IN TO PROVIDE BACKUP!
OOMOOM
TMP
TMP
TMP

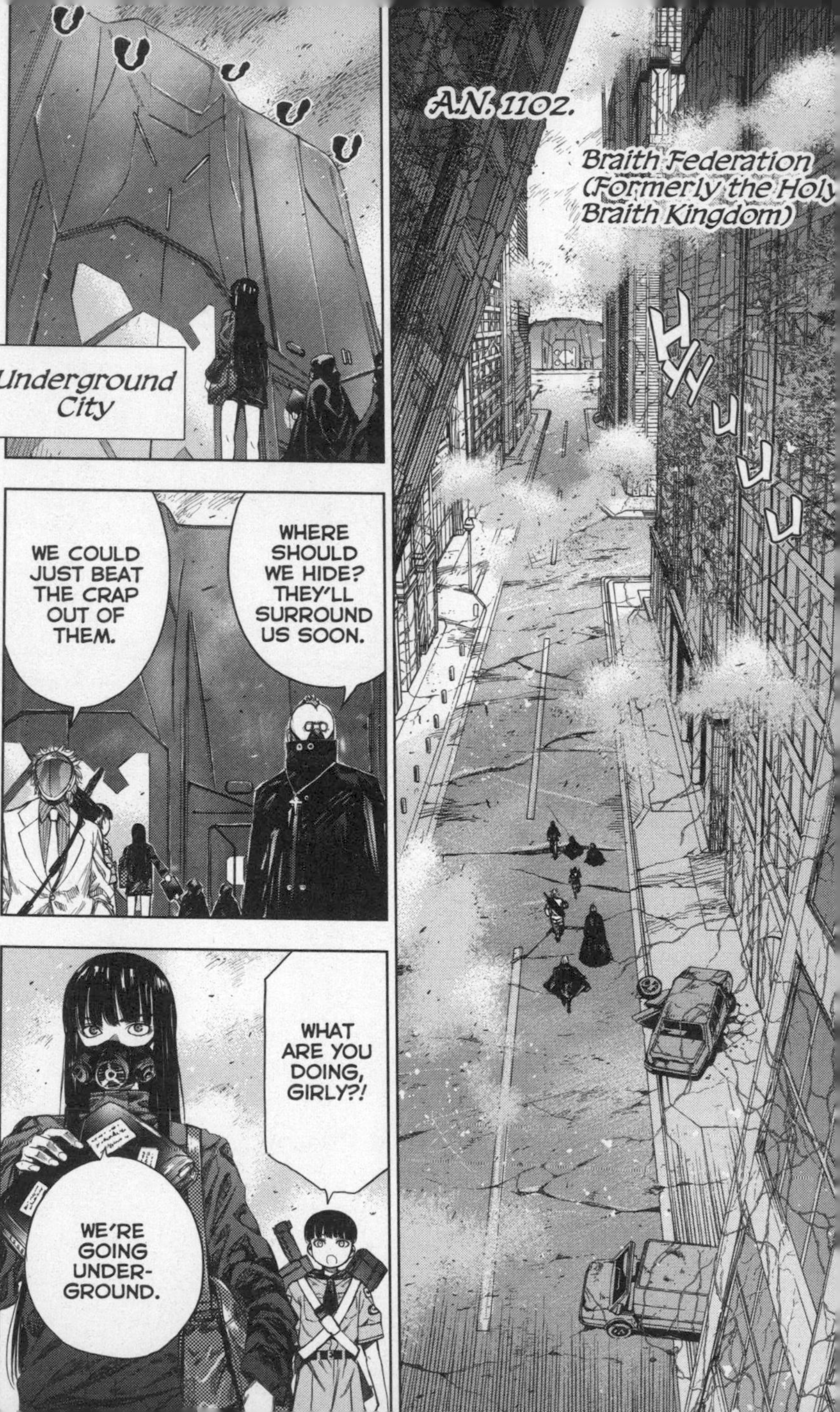
A.N. 1102.
Braith Federation (Formerly the Holy Braith Kingdom)
Underground City
WHERE SHOULD WE HIDE? THEY'LL SURROUND US SOON.
WE COULD JUST BEAT THE CRAP OUT OF THEM.
WHAT ARE YOU DOING, GIRLY?!
WE'RE GOING UNDER-GROUND.

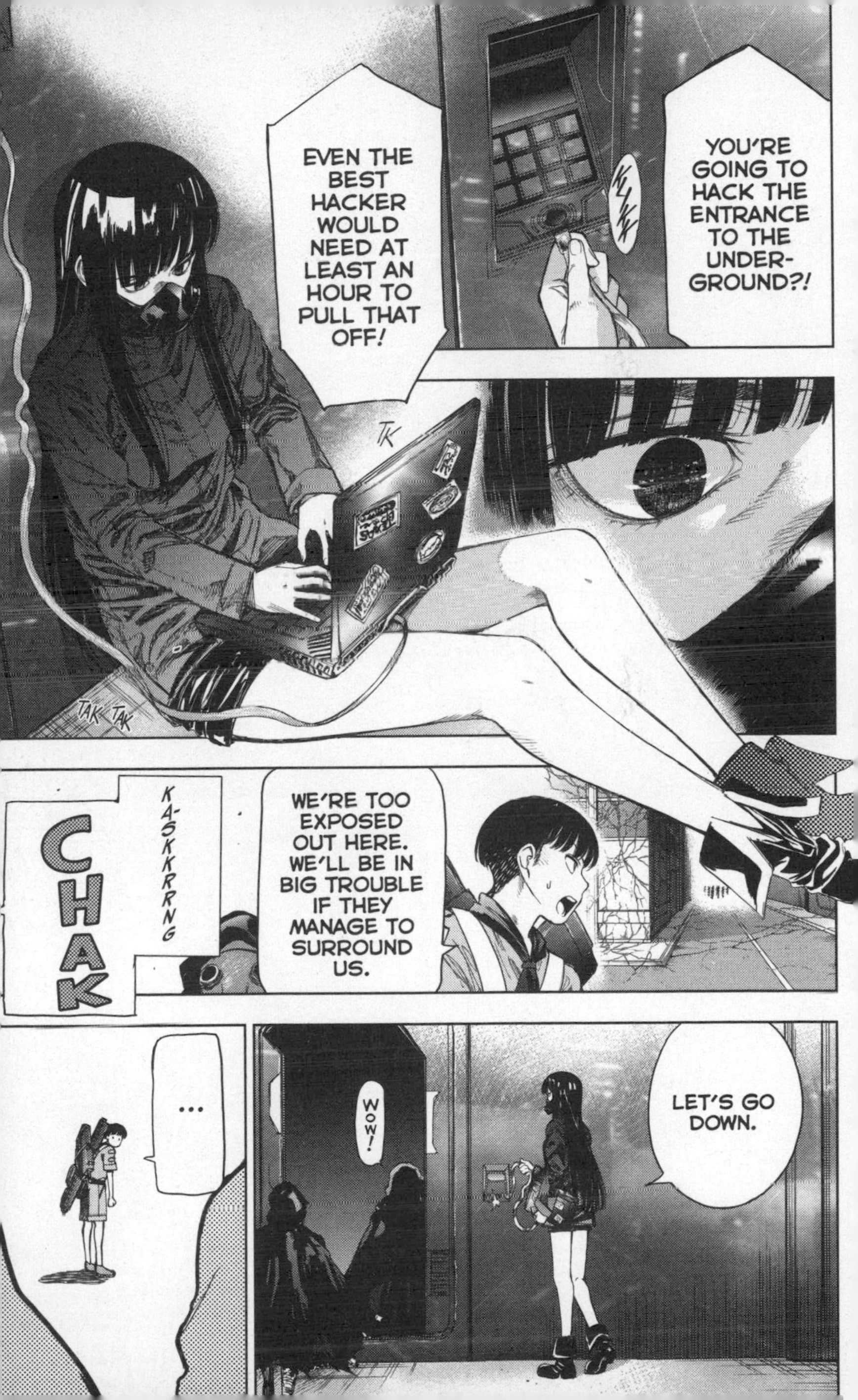
YOU'RE GOING TO HACK THE ENTRANCE TO THE UNDER-GROUND?!
KLIKK
EVEN THE BEST HACKER WOULD NEED AT LEAST AN HOUR TO PULL THAT OFF!
TK
TAK TAK
WE'RE TOO EXPOSED OUT HERE. WE'LL BE IN BIG TROUBLE IF THEY MANAGE TO SURROUND US.
KA-SKKRRNG
CHAK
LET'S GO DOWN.
WOW!
...

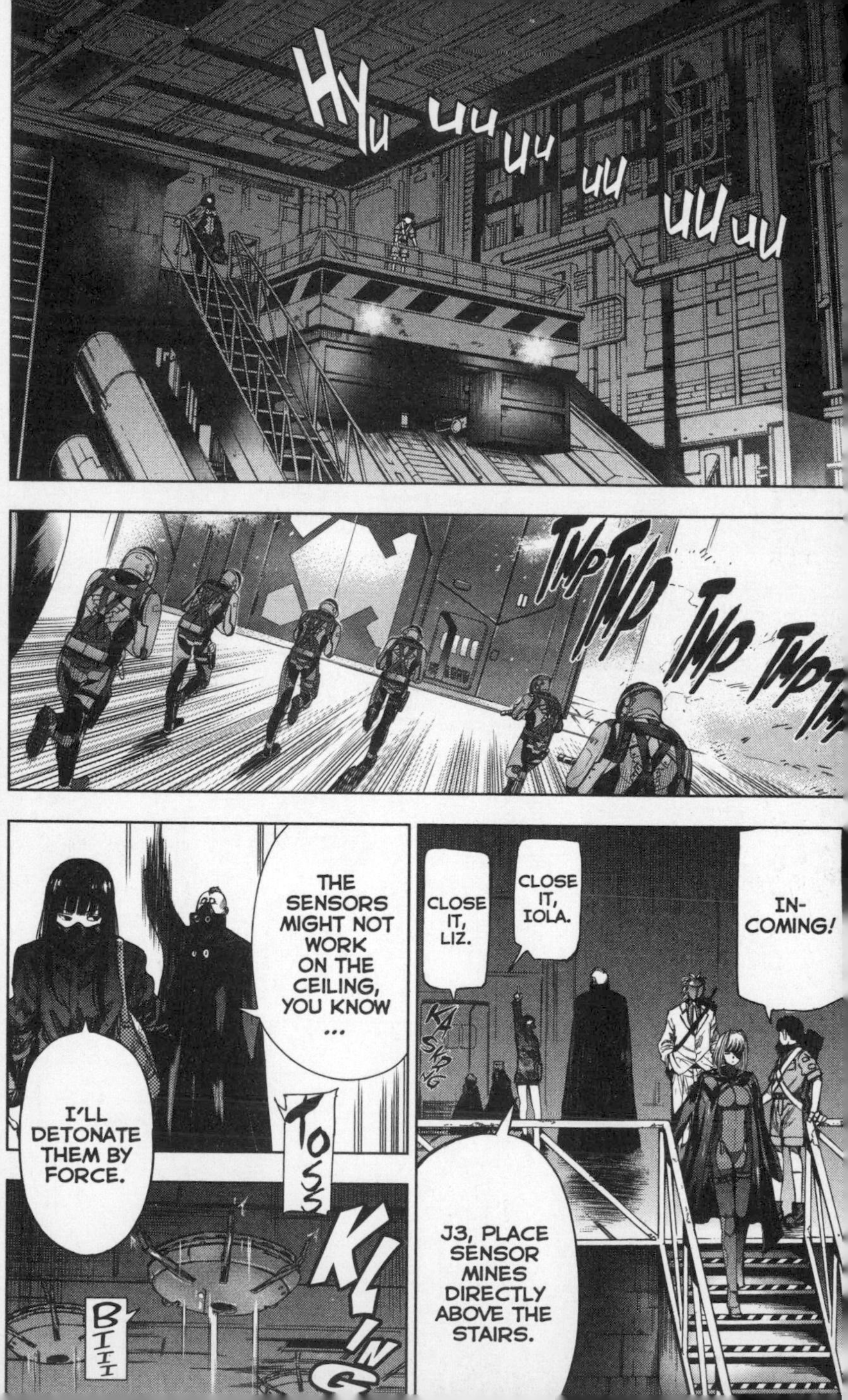
HYu uu uu uu uu uu uu
TMP TMP TMP TMP TMP TMP
IN-COMING!
CLOSE IT, IOLA.
CLOSE IT, LIZ.
J3, PLACE SENSOR MINES DIRECTLY ABOVE THE STAIRS.
THE SENSORS MIGHT NOT WORK ON THE CEILING, YOU KNOW...
I'LL DETONATE THEM BY FORCE.
TOSS
KLING
BIIII

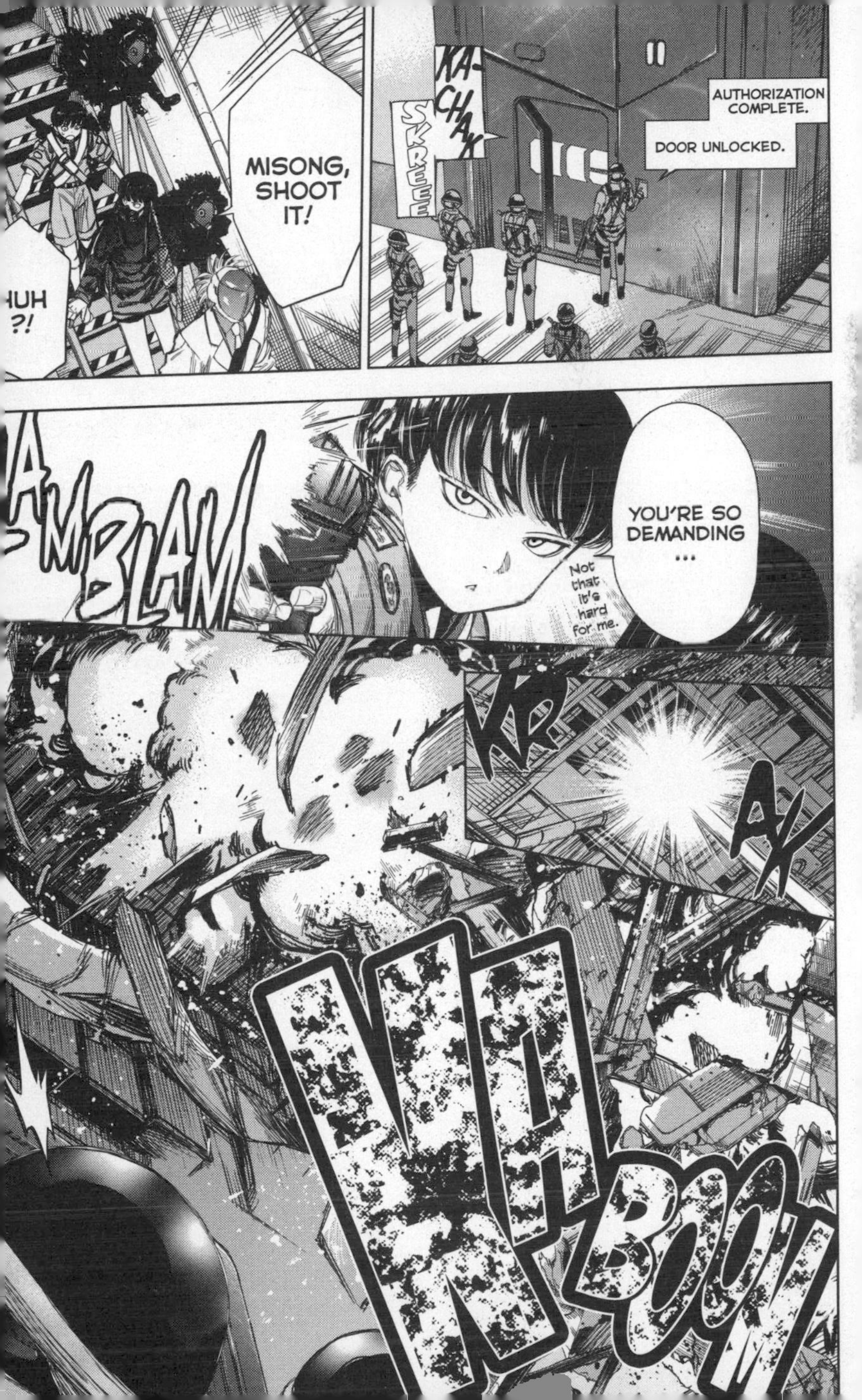
AUTHORIZATION COMPLETE.
DOOR UNLOCKED.
KA-CHAK
SKREEE
MISONG, SHOOT IT!
HUH ?!
YOU'RE SO DEMANDING ...
Not that it's hard for me.
AM BLAM
KR AK
KA-BOOM

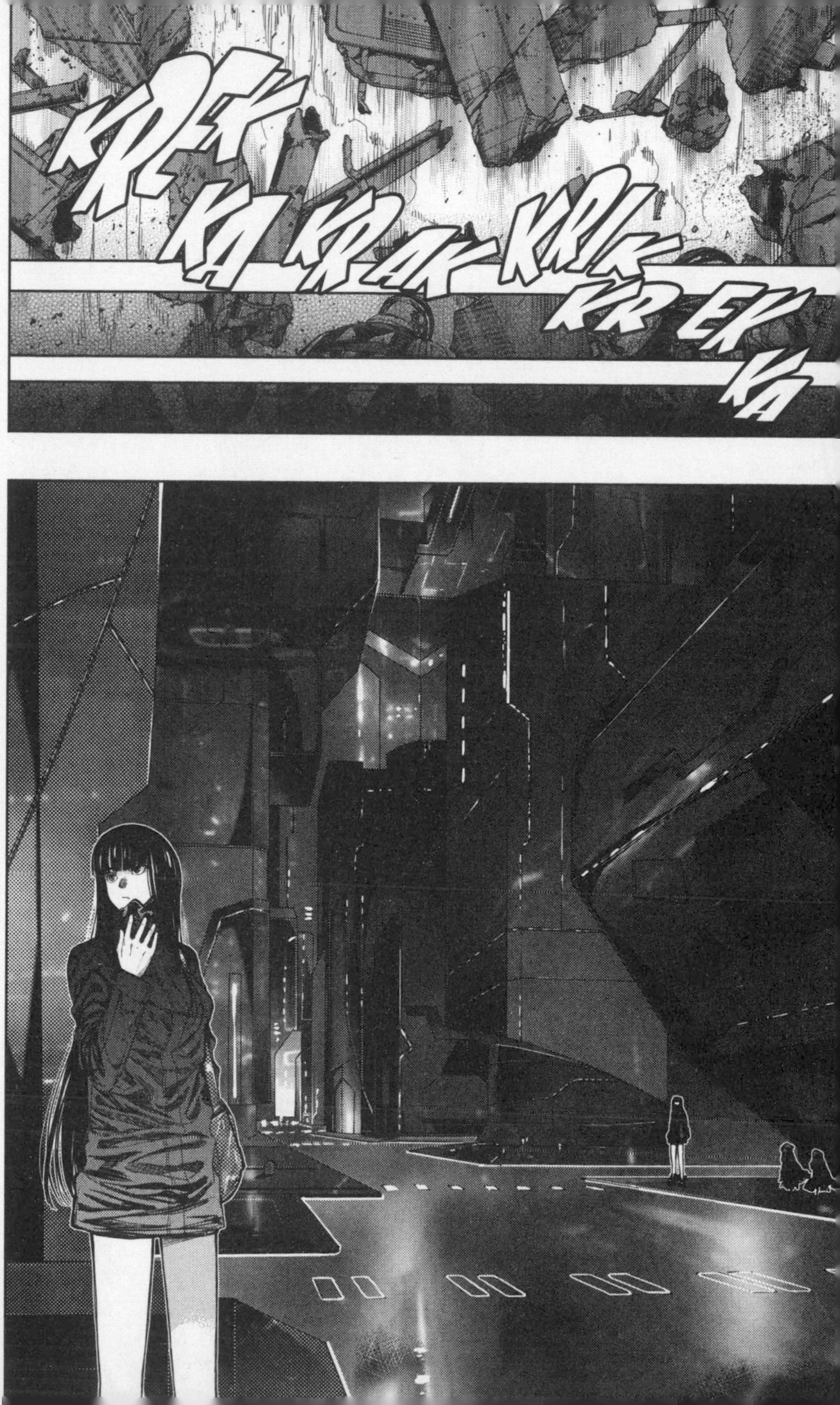
KREK
KA
KRAK
KRIK
KR
EK
KA

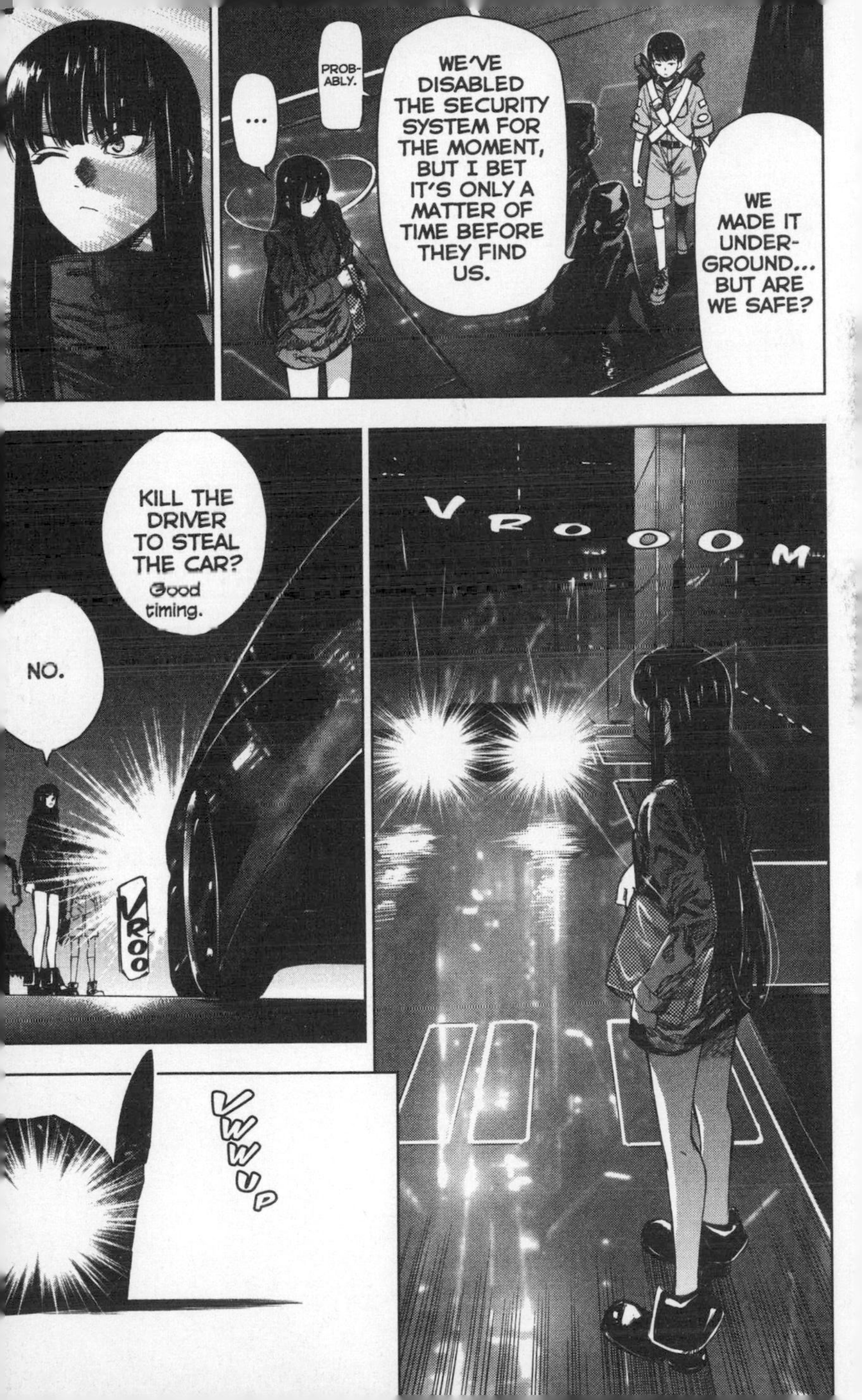
WE MADE IT UNDER-GROUND... BUT ARE WE SAFE?
WE'VE DISABLED THE SECURITY SYSTEM FOR THE MOMENT, BUT I BET IT'S ONLY A MATTER OF TIME BEFORE THEY FIND US.
PROB-ABLY.
...
VROOOOM
KILL THE DRIVER TO STEAL THE CAR? Good timing.
NO.
VROO
VWWUP

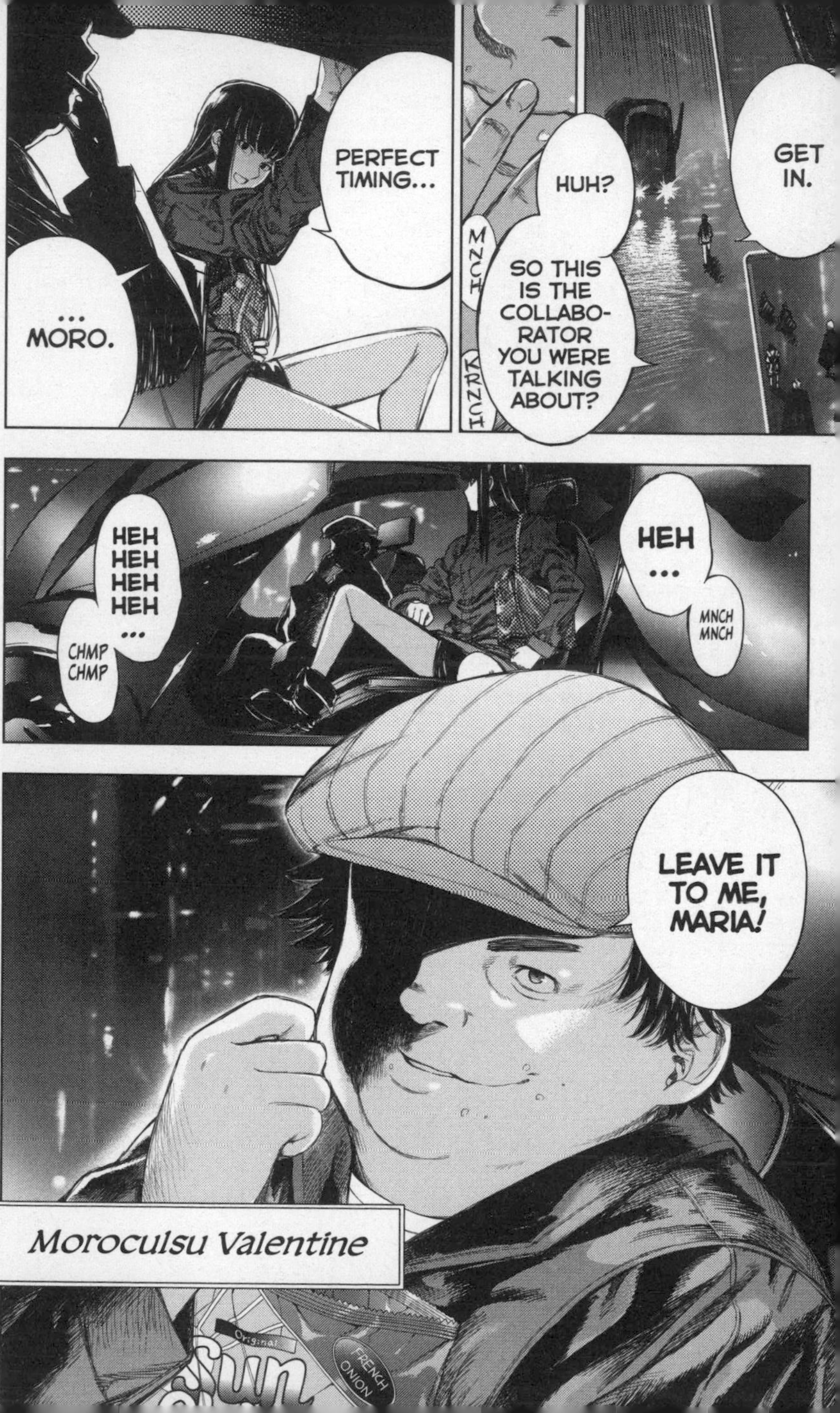
GET IN.
HUH?
MNCH
SO THIS IS THE COLLABORATOR YOU WERE TALKING ABOUT?
KRNCH
PERFECT TIMING...
... MORO.
HEH ...
MNCH MNCH
HEH HEH HEH HEH ...
CHMP CHMP
LEAVE IT TO ME, MARIA!
Moroculsu Valentine
Original
FRENCH ONION

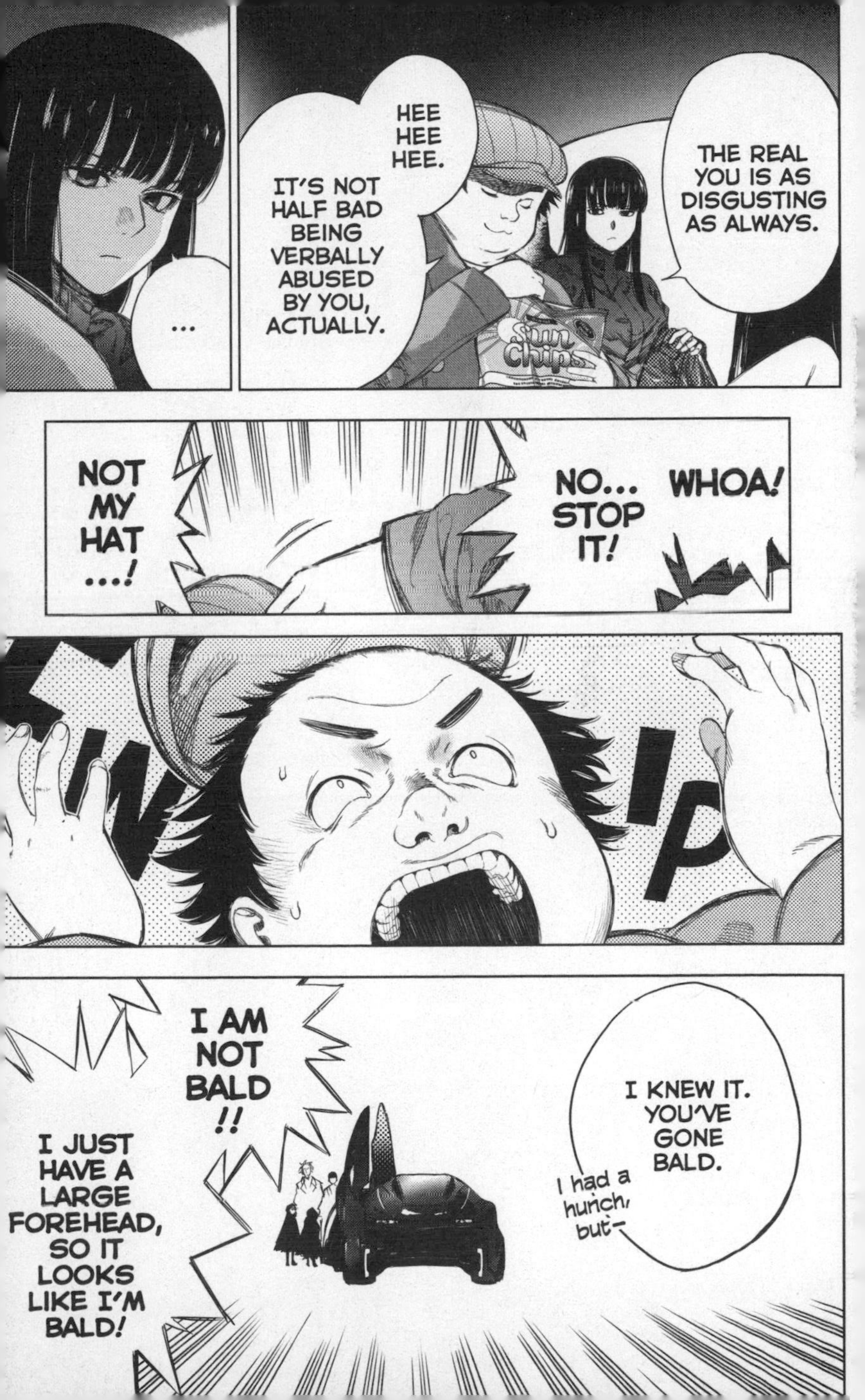
THE REAL YOU IS AS DISGUSTING AS ALWAYS.
HEE HEE HEE.
IT'S NOT HALF BAD BEING VERBALLY ABUSED BY YOU, ACTUALLY.
Sun Chips
...
WHOA!
NO... STOP IT!
NOT MY HAT ...!
I KNEW IT. YOU'VE GONE BALD.
I had a hunch, but—
I AM NOT BALD!!
I JUST HAVE A LARGE FOREHEAD, SO IT LOOKS LIKE I'M BALD!

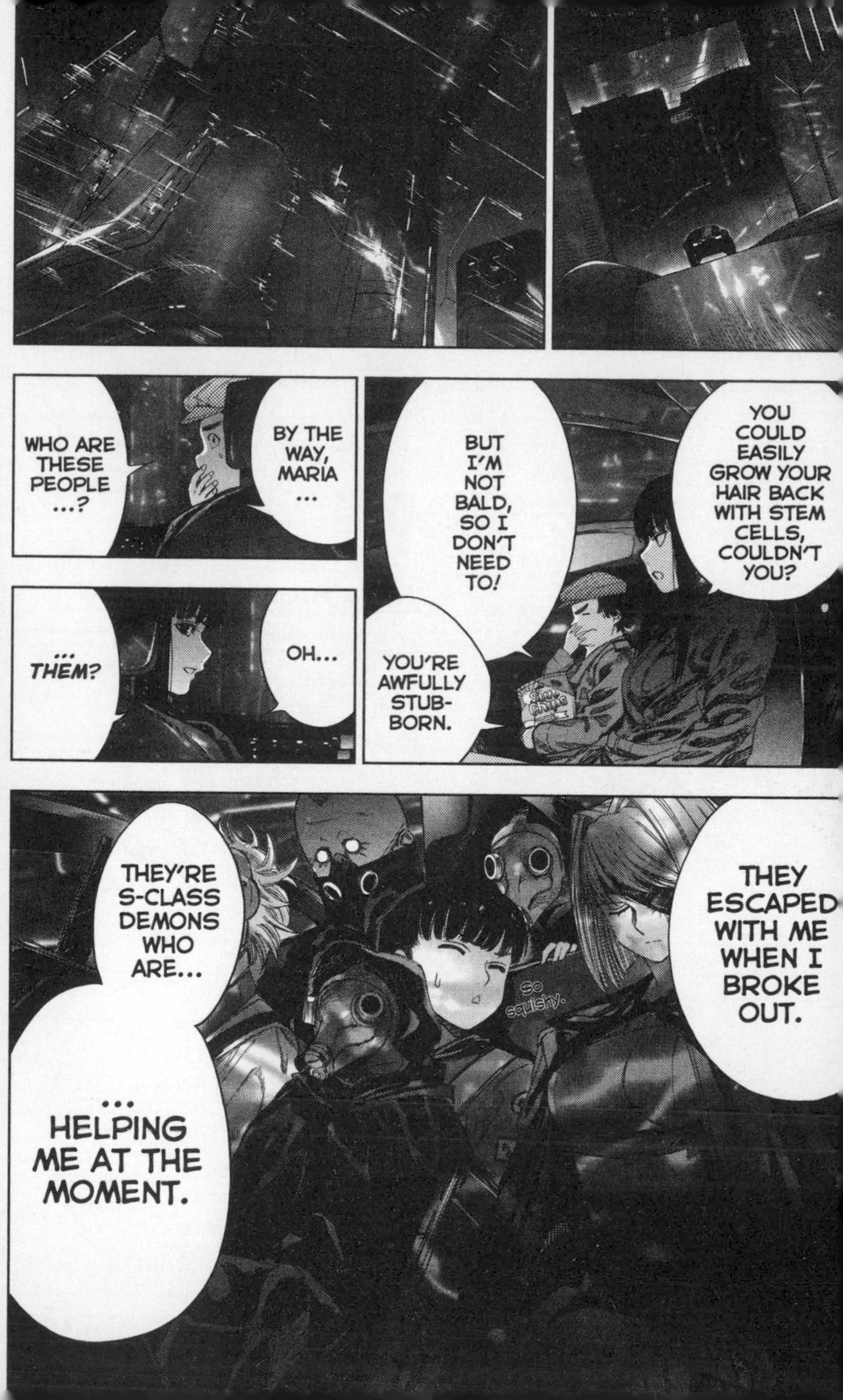
YOU COULD EASILY GROW YOUR HAIR BACK WITH STEM CELLS, COULDN'T YOU?
BUT I'M NOT BALD, SO I DON'T NEED TO!
YOU'RE AWFULLY STUB-BORN.
BY THE WAY, MARIA...
WHO ARE THESE PEOPLE...?
OH...
...THEM?
THEY ESCAPED WITH ME WHEN I BROKE OUT.
So squishy.
THEY'RE S-CLASS DEMONS WHO ARE...
...HELPING ME AT THE MOMENT.

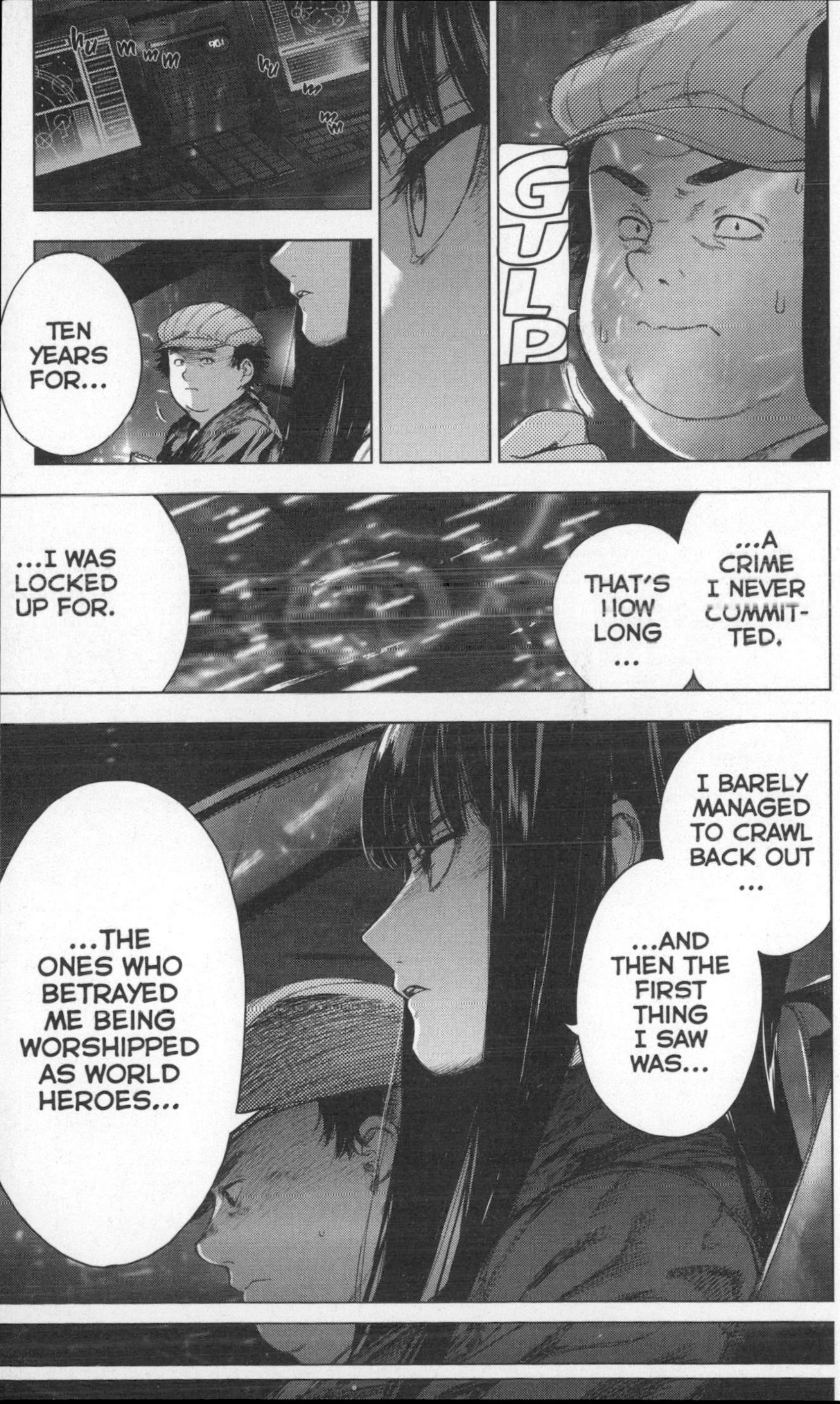
GULP
TEN YEARS FOR...
...A CRIME I NEVER COMMIT-TED.
THAT'S HOW LONG ...
...I WAS LOCKED UP FOR.
I BARELY MANAGED TO CRAWL BACK OUT ...
...AND THEN THE FIRST THING I SAW WAS...
...THE ONES WHO BETRAYED ME BEING WORSHIPPED AS WORLD HEROES...

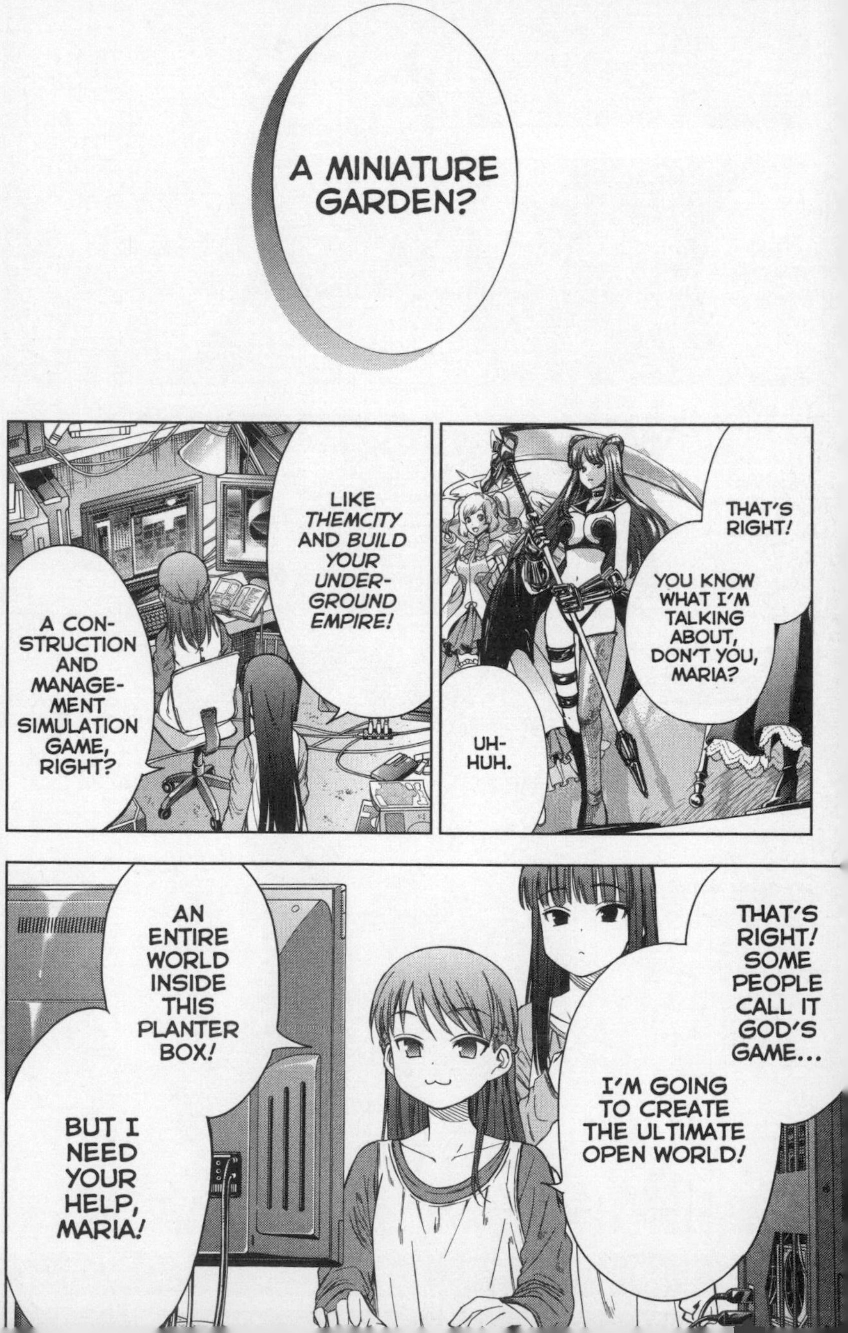
A MINIATURE GARDEN?
THAT'S RIGHT!
YOU KNOW WHAT I'M TALKING ABOUT, DON'T YOU, MARIA?
UH-HUH.
LIKE *THEMCITY* AND BUILD YOUR UNDERGROUND EMPIRE!
A CONSTRUCTION AND MANAGEMENT SIMULATION GAME, RIGHT?
THAT'S RIGHT! SOME PEOPLE CALL IT GOD'S GAME...
I'M GOING TO CREATE THE ULTIMATE OPEN WORLD!
AN ENTIRE WORLD INSIDE THIS PLANTER BOX!
BUT I NEED YOUR HELP, MARIA!

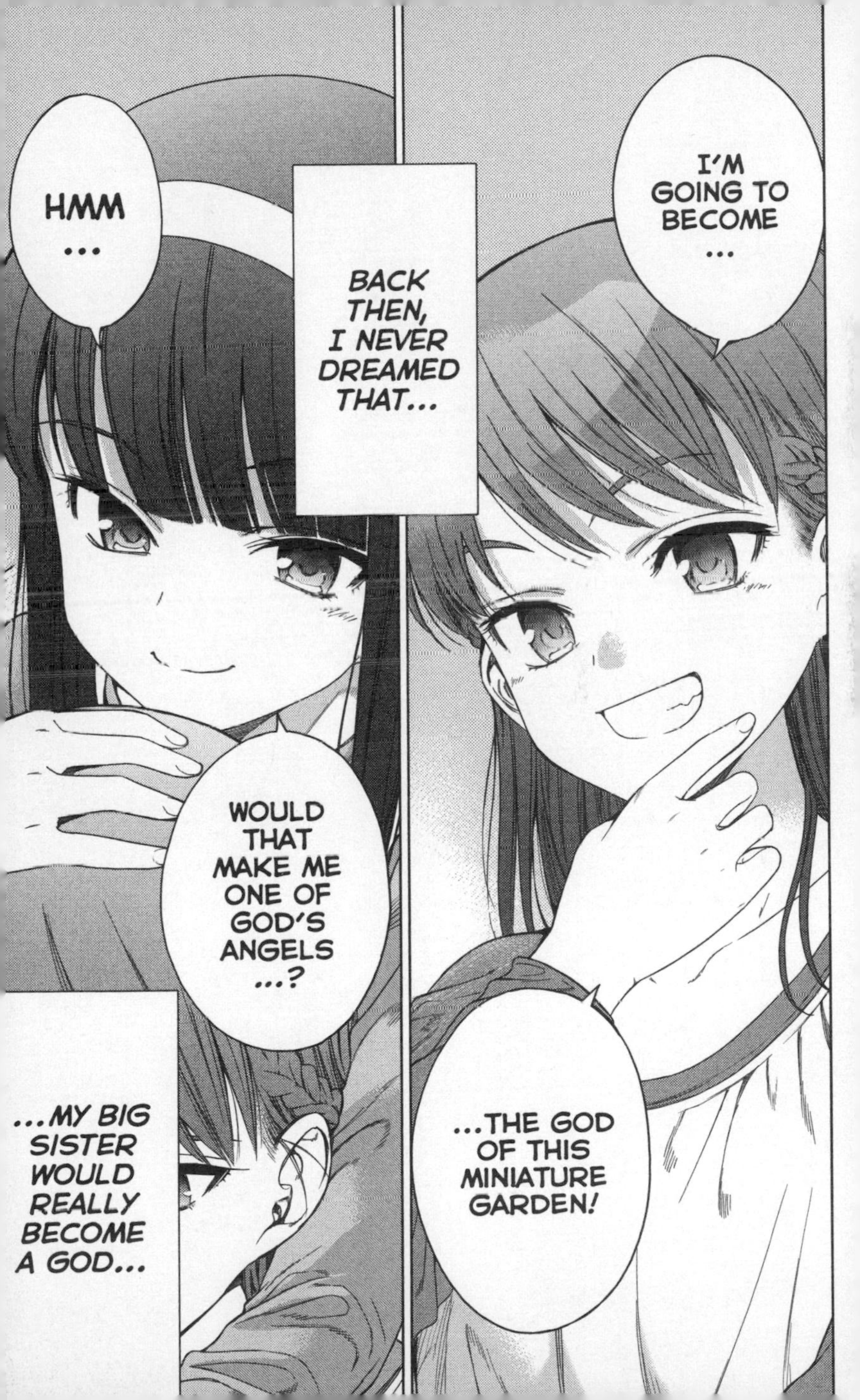
I'M GOING TO BECOME ...
...THE GOD OF THIS MINIATURE GARDEN!
HMM ...
WOULD THAT MAKE ME ONE OF GOD'S ANGELS ...?
BACK THEN, I NEVER DREAMED THAT...
...MY BIG SISTER WOULD REALLY BECOME A GOD...

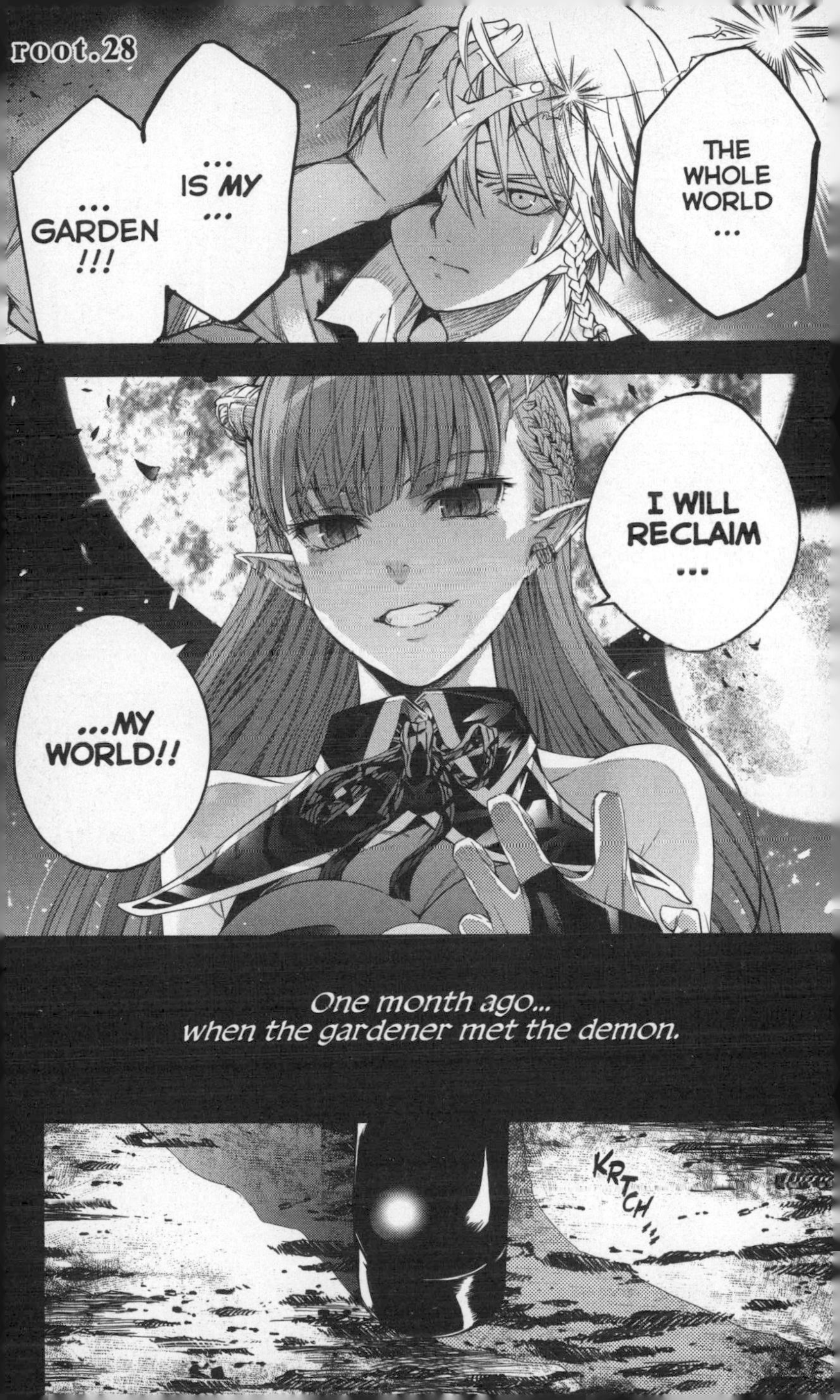
root.28
THE WHOLE WORLD ...
... IS MY ...
... GARDEN !!!
I WILL RECLAIM ...
...MY WORLD!!
One month ago... when the gardener met the demon.
KRTCH

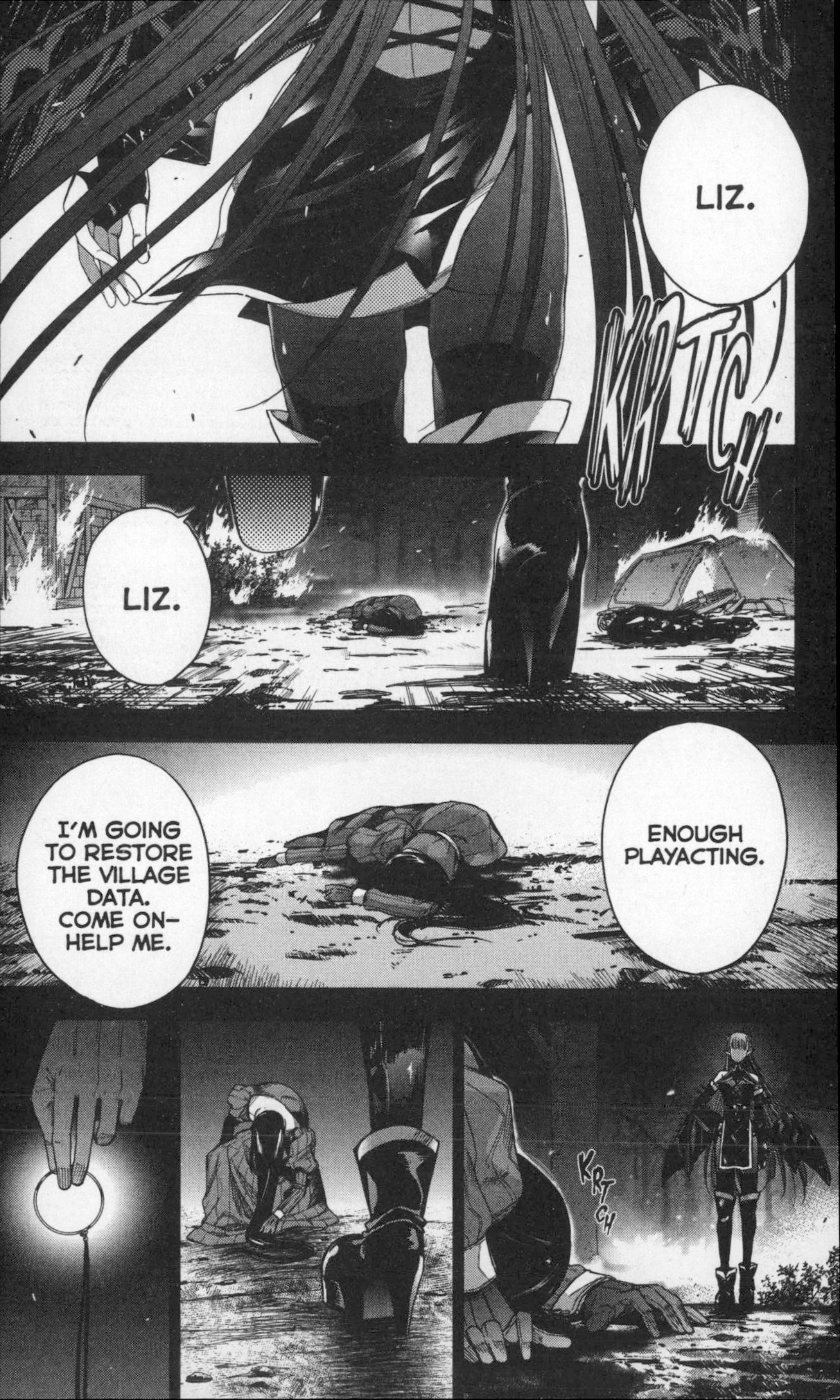
LIZ.
KATCH
LIZ.
ENOUGH PLAYACTING.
I'M GOING TO RESTORE THE VILLAGE DATA. COME ON— HELP ME.
KRTCH

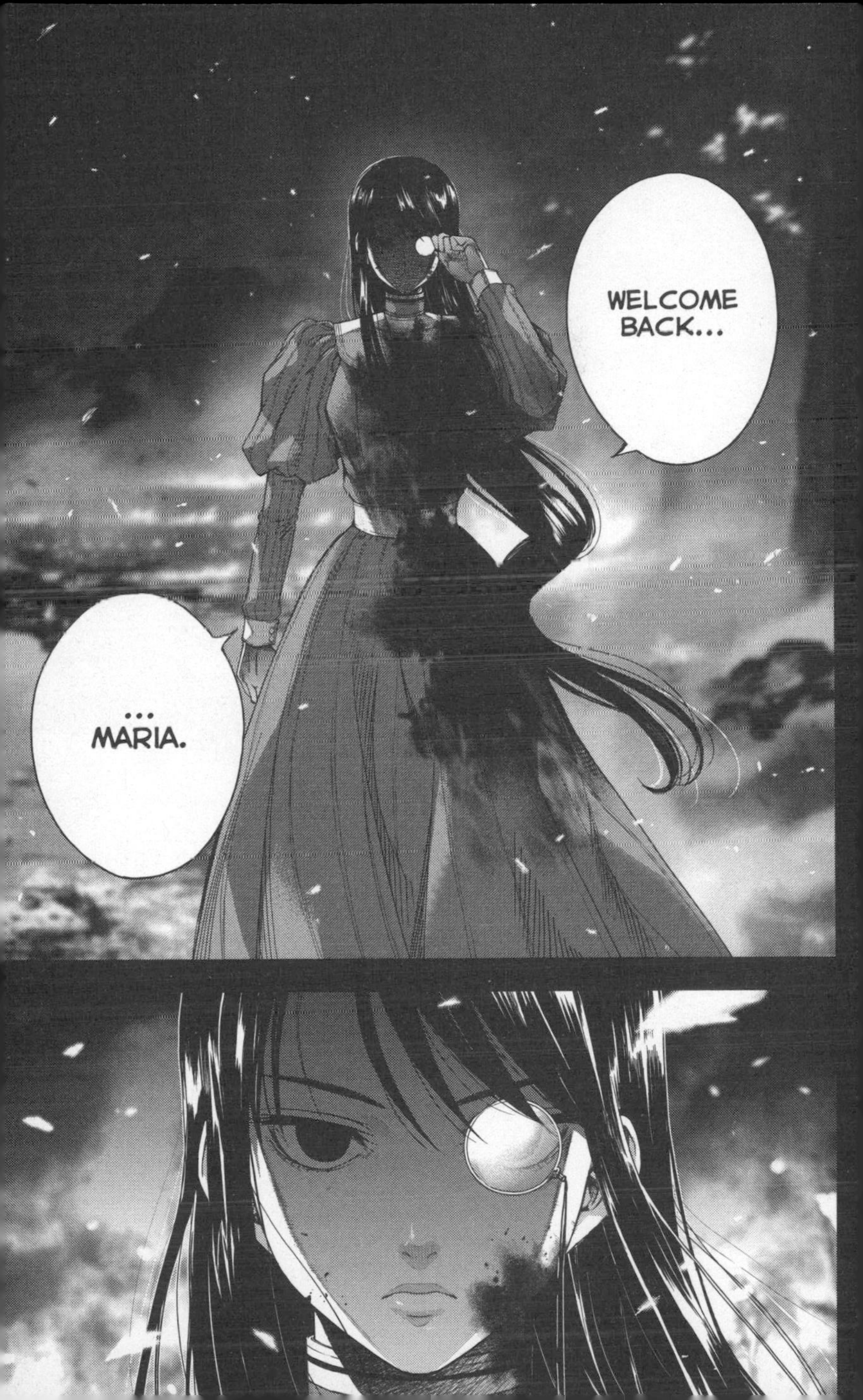
WELCOME BACK...
...MARIA.

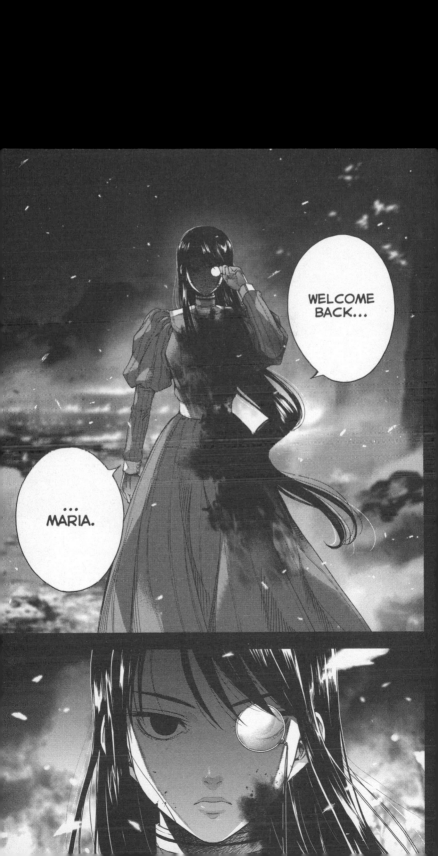

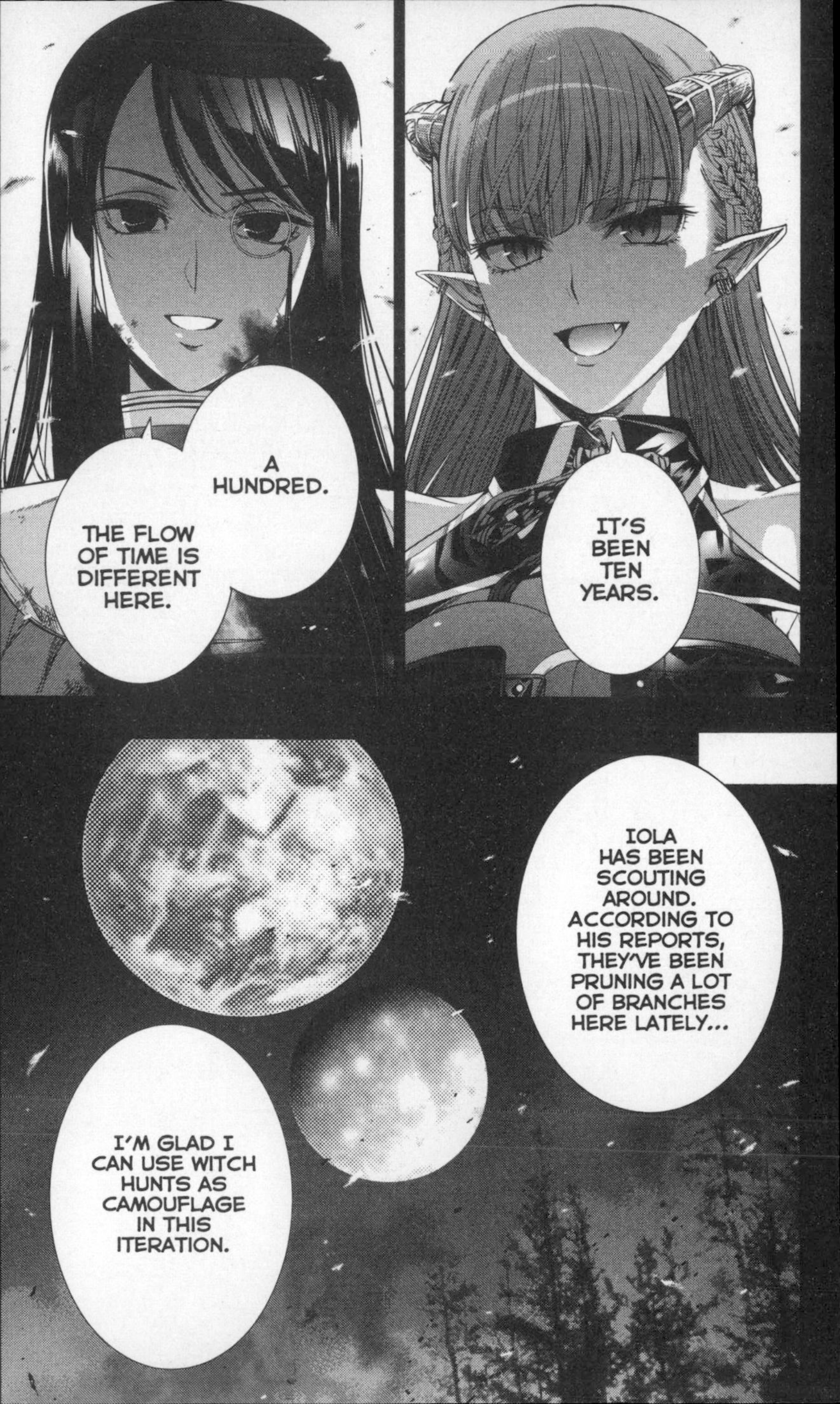
IT'S BEEN TEN YEARS.
A HUNDRED.
THE FLOW OF TIME IS DIFFERENT HERE.
IOLA HAS BEEN SCOUTING AROUND. ACCORDING TO HIS REPORTS, THEY'VE BEEN PRUNING A LOT OF BRANCHES HERE LATELY...
I'M GLAD I CAN USE WITCH HUNTS AS CAMOUFLAGE IN THIS ITERATION.

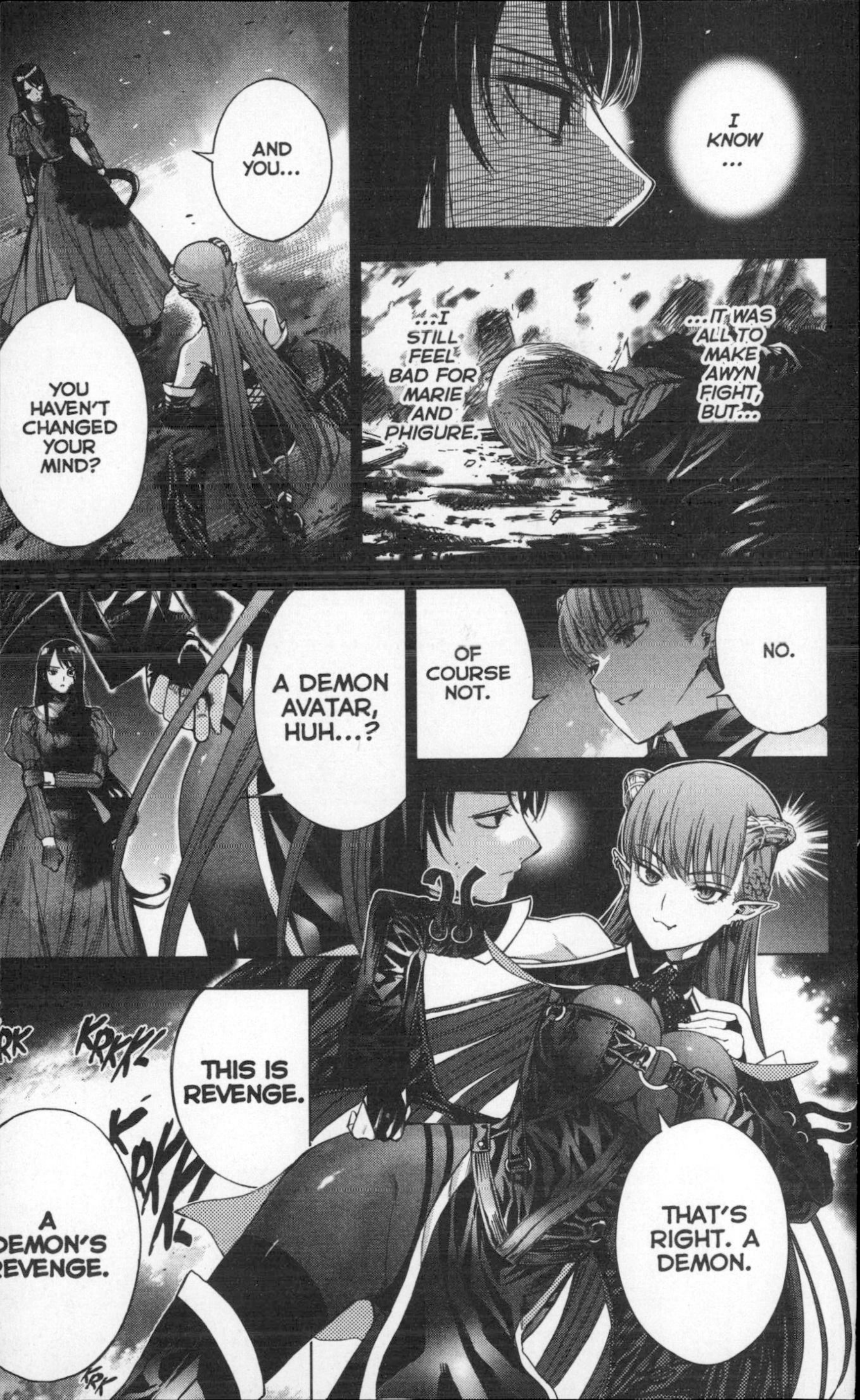
I KNOW...
...IT WAS ALL TO MAKE AWYN FIGHT, BUT...
...I STILL FEEL BAD FOR MARIE AND PHIGURE.
AND YOU...
YOU HAVEN'T CHANGED YOUR MIND?
NO.
OF COURSE NOT.
A DEMON AVATAR, HUH...?
THAT'S RIGHT. A DEMON.
THIS IS REVENGE.
KRKKL
KRK
KRKKL
A DEMON'S EVENGE.
KRK

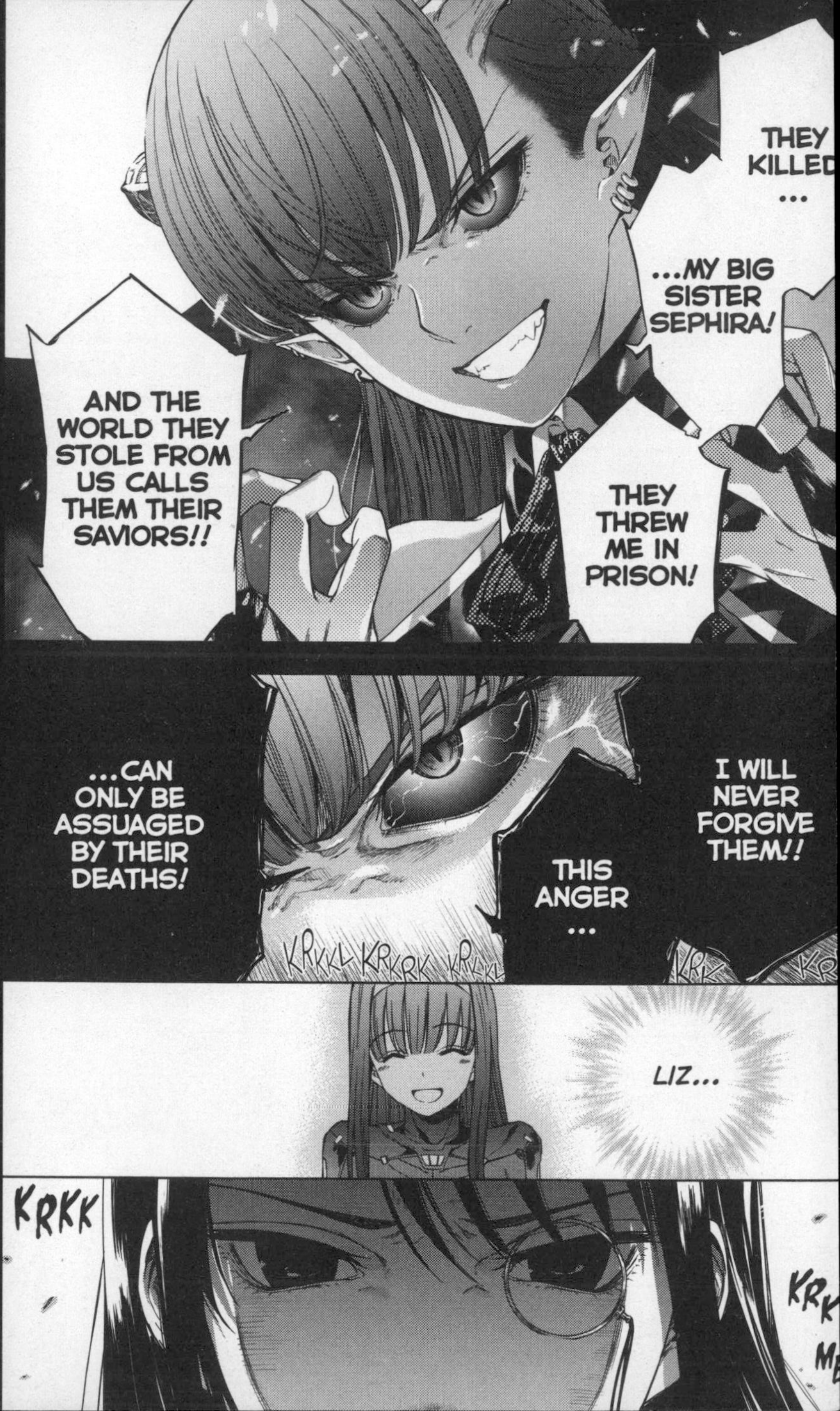
THEY KILLED...
...MY BIG SISTER SEPHIRA!
THEY THREW ME IN PRISON!
AND THE WORLD THEY STOLE FROM US CALLS THEM THEIR SAVIORS!!
I WILL NEVER FORGIVE THEM!!
THIS ANGER...
...CAN ONLY BE ASSUAGED BY THEIR DEATHS!
KRKKL KRKRK KRKKL
LIZ...
KRKK

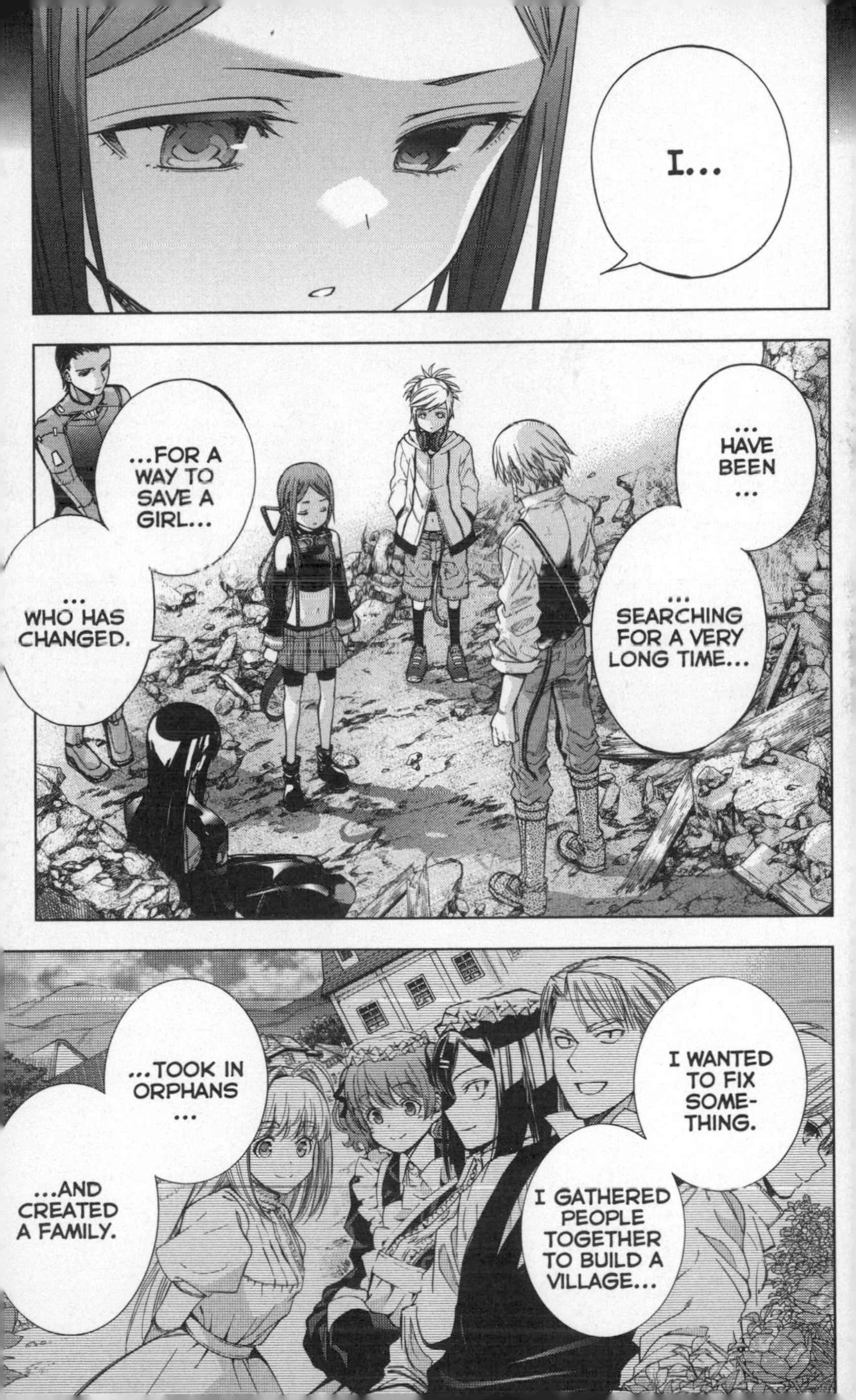
I...
...HAVE BEEN...
...SEARCHING FOR A VERY LONG TIME...
...FOR A WAY TO SAVE A GIRL...
...WHO HAS CHANGED.
I WANTED TO FIX SOME-THING.
I GATHERED PEOPLE TOGETHER TO BUILD A VILLAGE...
...TOOK IN ORPHANS...
...AND CREATED A FAMILY.

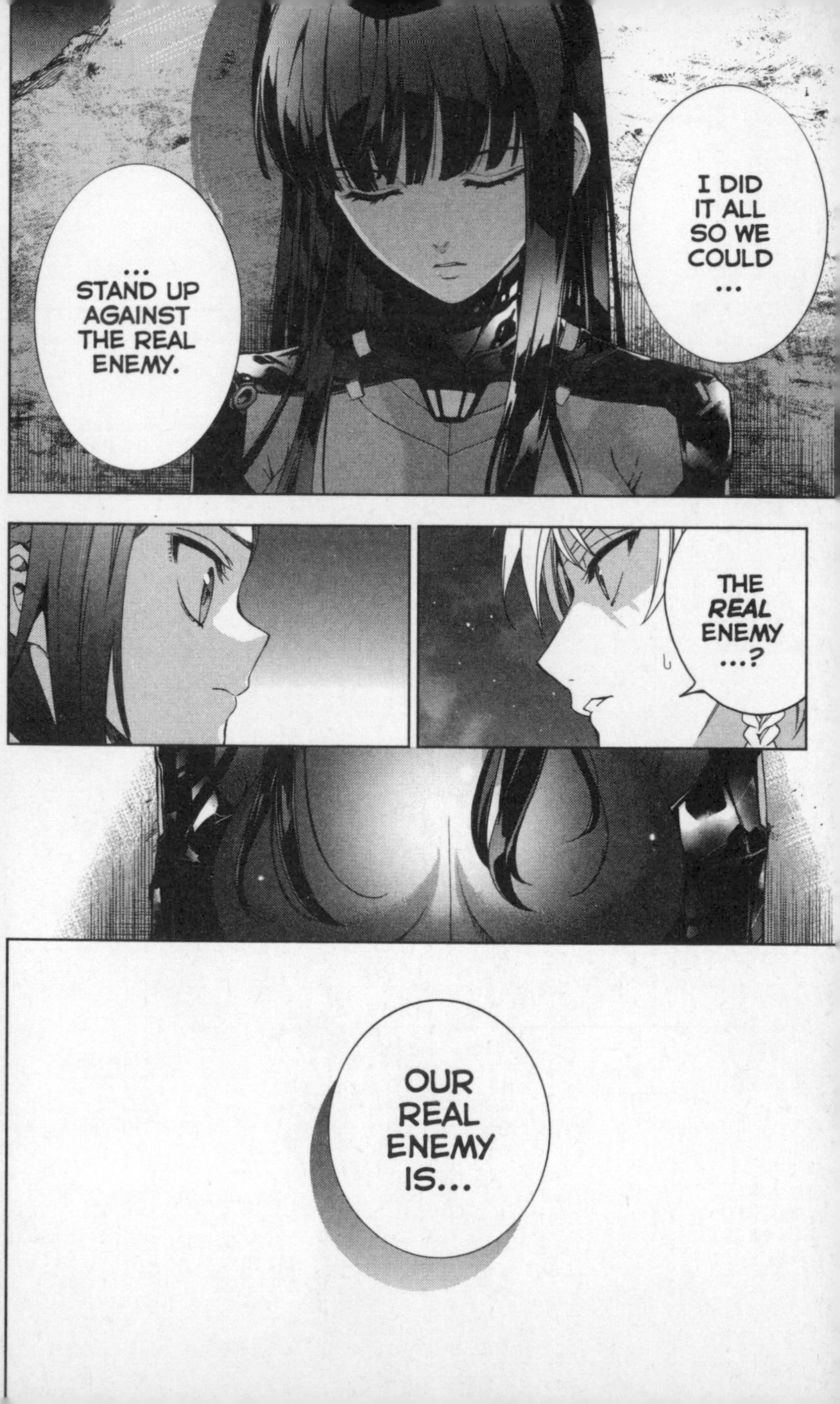
I DID IT ALL SO WE COULD ...
... STAND UP AGAINST THE REAL ENEMY.
THE *REAL* ENEMY ...?
OUR REAL ENEMY IS...

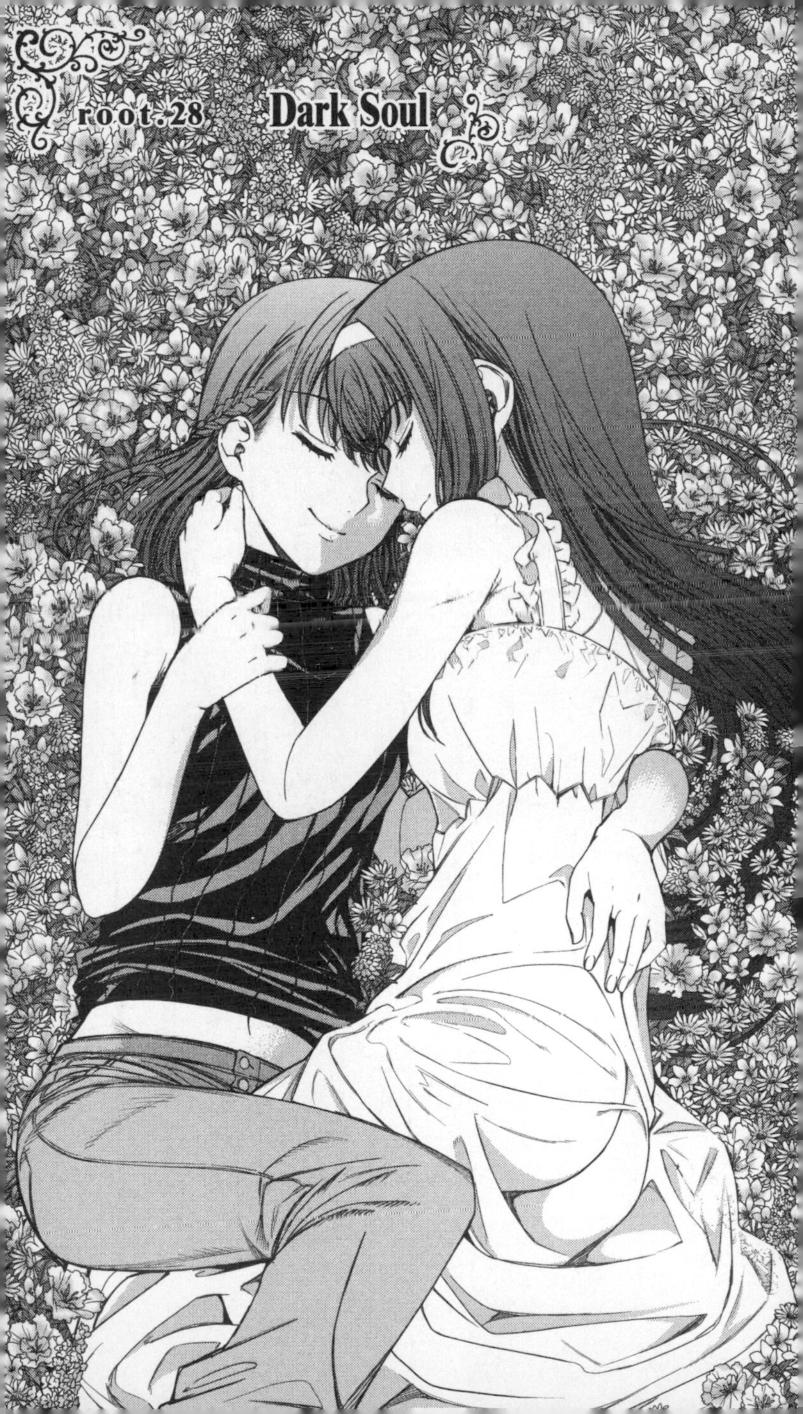
root.28
Dark Soul

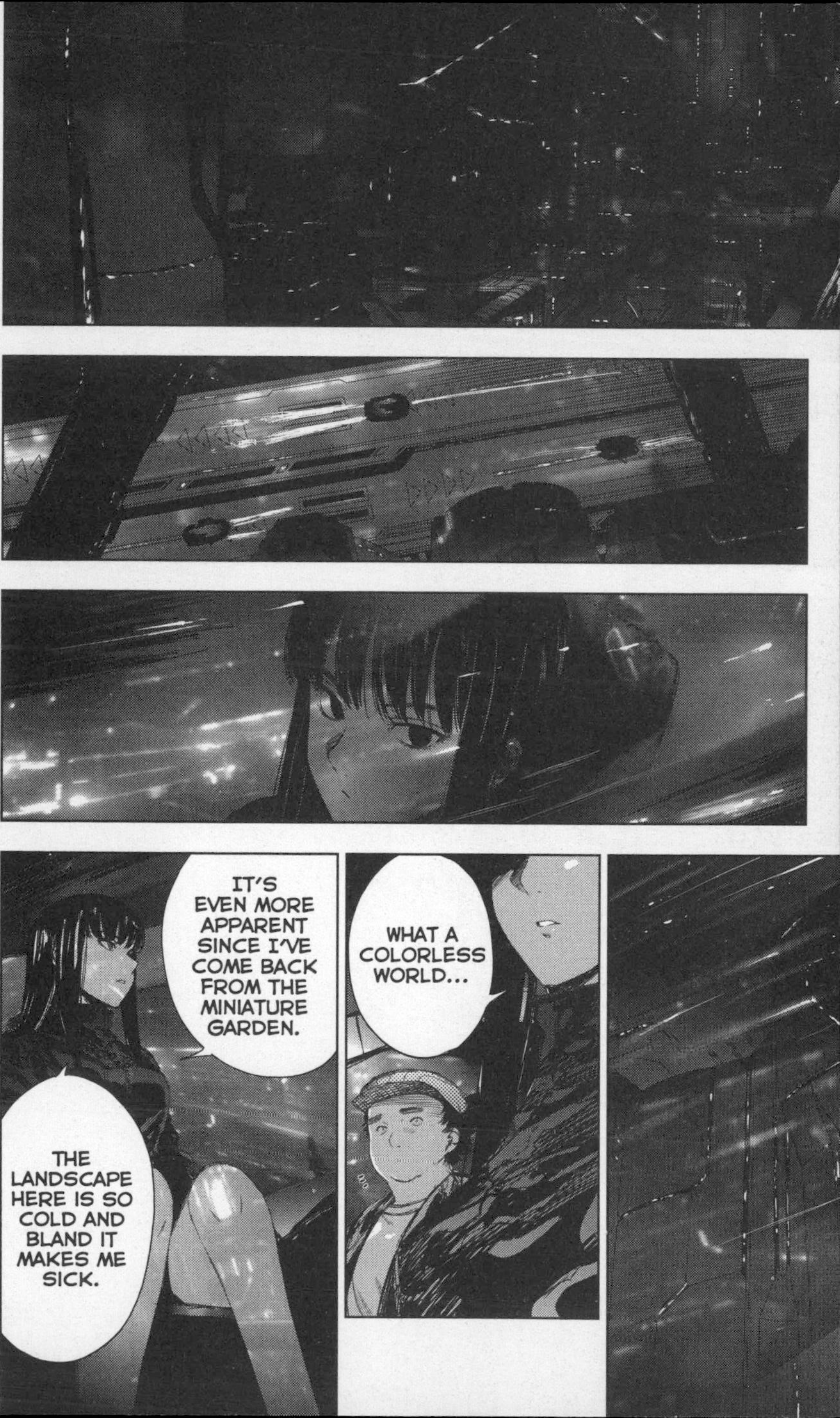
WHAT A COLORLESS WORLD...
IT'S EVEN MORE APPARENT SINCE I'VE COME BACK FROM THE MINIATURE GARDEN.
THE LANDSCAPE HERE IS SO COLD AND BLAND IT MAKES ME SICK.

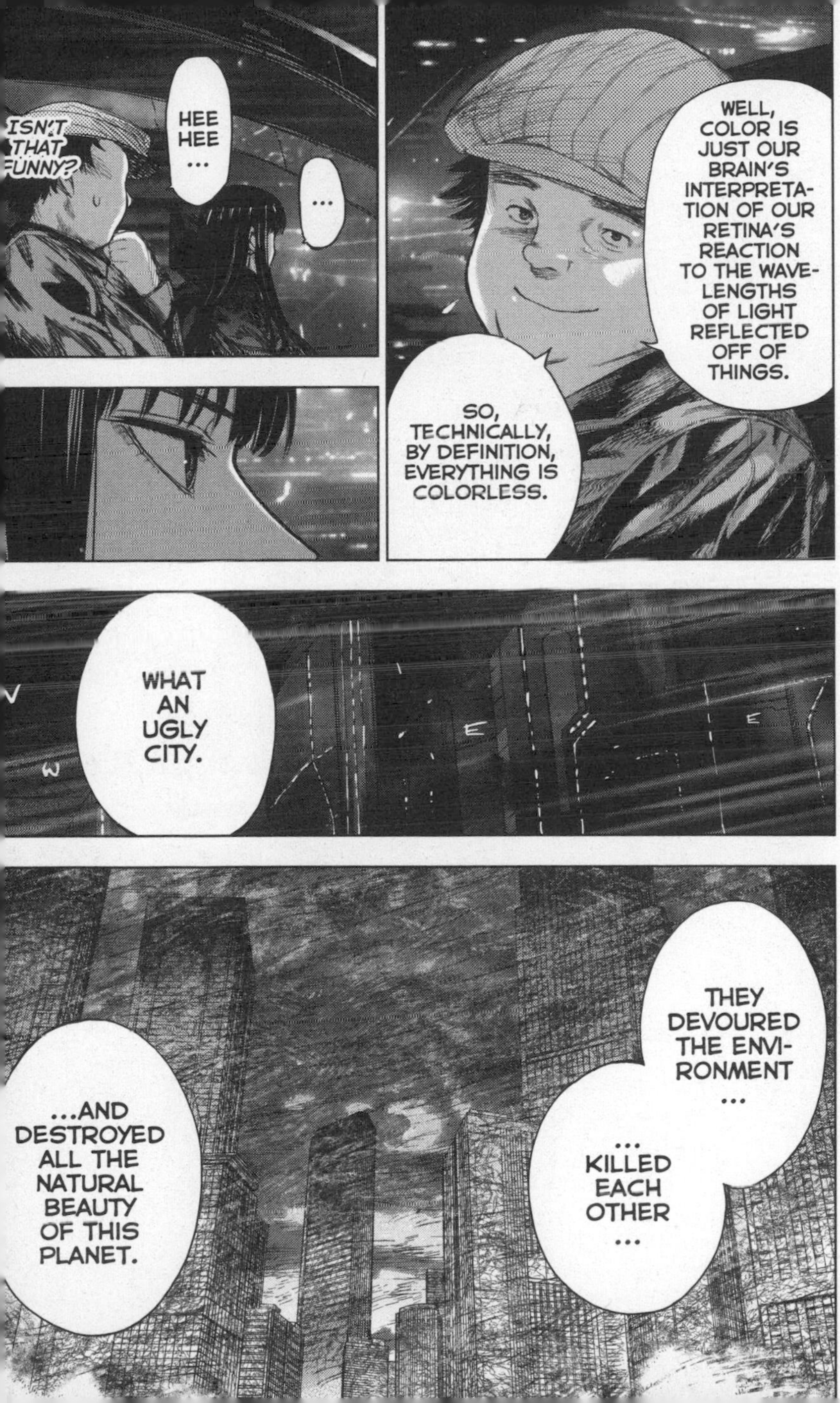
WELL, COLOR IS JUST OUR BRAIN'S INTERPRETATION OF OUR RETINA'S REACTION TO THE WAVELENGTHS OF LIGHT REFLECTED OFF OF THINGS.
SO, TECHNICALLY, BY DEFINITION, EVERYTHING IS COLORLESS.
HEE HEE ...
...
ISN'T THAT FUNNY?
WHAT AN UGLY CITY.
THEY DEVOURED THE ENVIRONMENT ...
... KILLED EACH OTHER ...
...AND DESTROYED ALL THE NATURAL BEAUTY OF THIS PLANET.

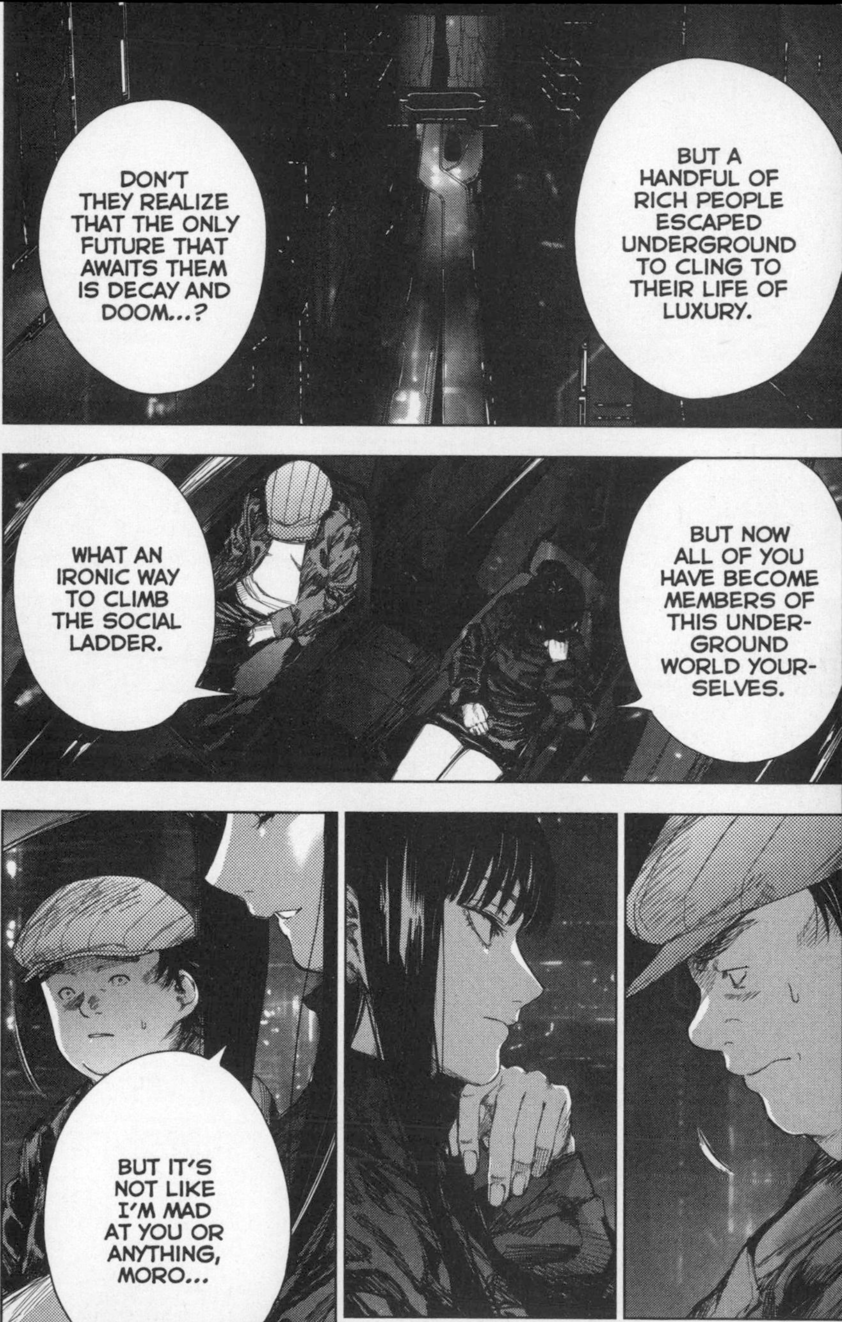

BUT A HANDFUL OF RICH PEOPLE ESCAPED UNDERGROUND TO CLING TO THEIR LIFE OF LUXURY.
DON'T THEY REALIZE THAT THE ONLY FUTURE THAT AWAITS THEM IS DECAY AND DOOM...?
BUT NOW ALL OF YOU HAVE BECOME MEMBERS OF THIS UNDER-GROUND WORLD YOUR-SELVES.
WHAT AN IRONIC WAY TO CLIMB THE SOCIAL LADDER.
BUT IT'S NOT LIKE I'M MAD AT YOU OR ANYTHING, MORO...

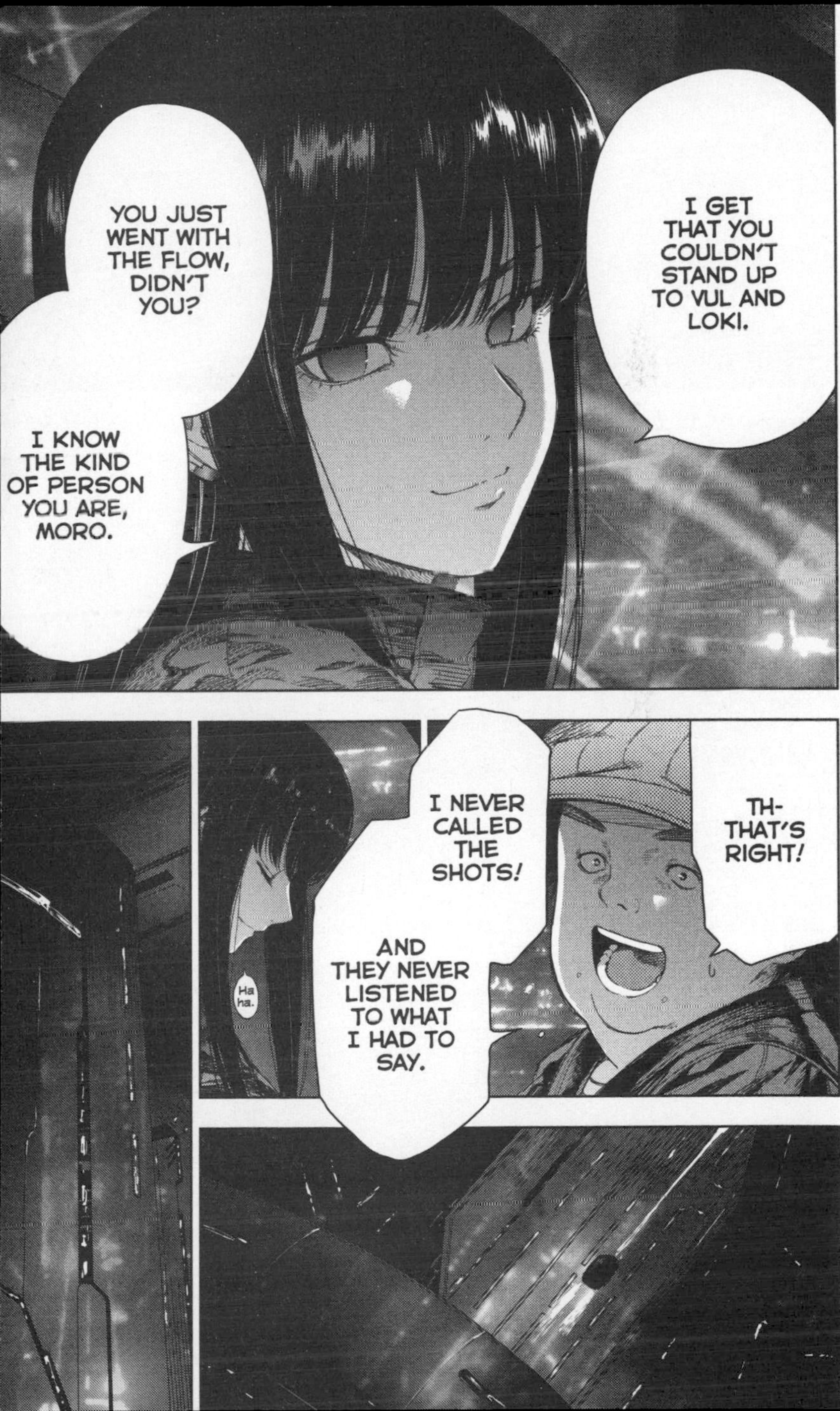
I GET THAT YOU COULDN'T STAND UP TO VUL AND LOKI.
YOU JUST WENT WITH THE FLOW, DIDN'T YOU?
I KNOW THE KIND OF PERSON YOU ARE, MORO.
TH- THAT'S RIGHT!
I NEVER CALLED THE SHOTS!
AND THEY NEVER LISTENED TO WHAT I HAD TO SAY.
Ha ha.

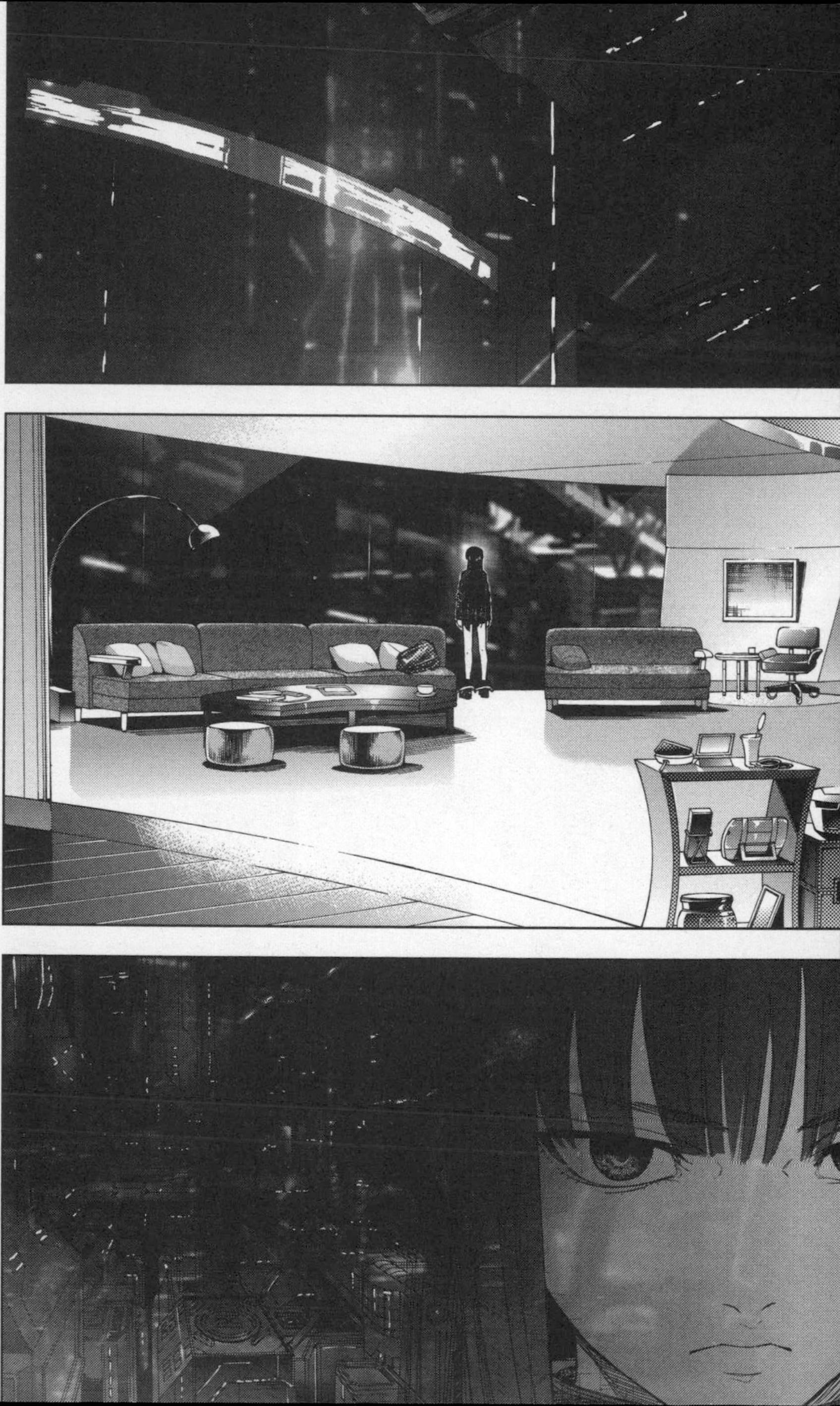

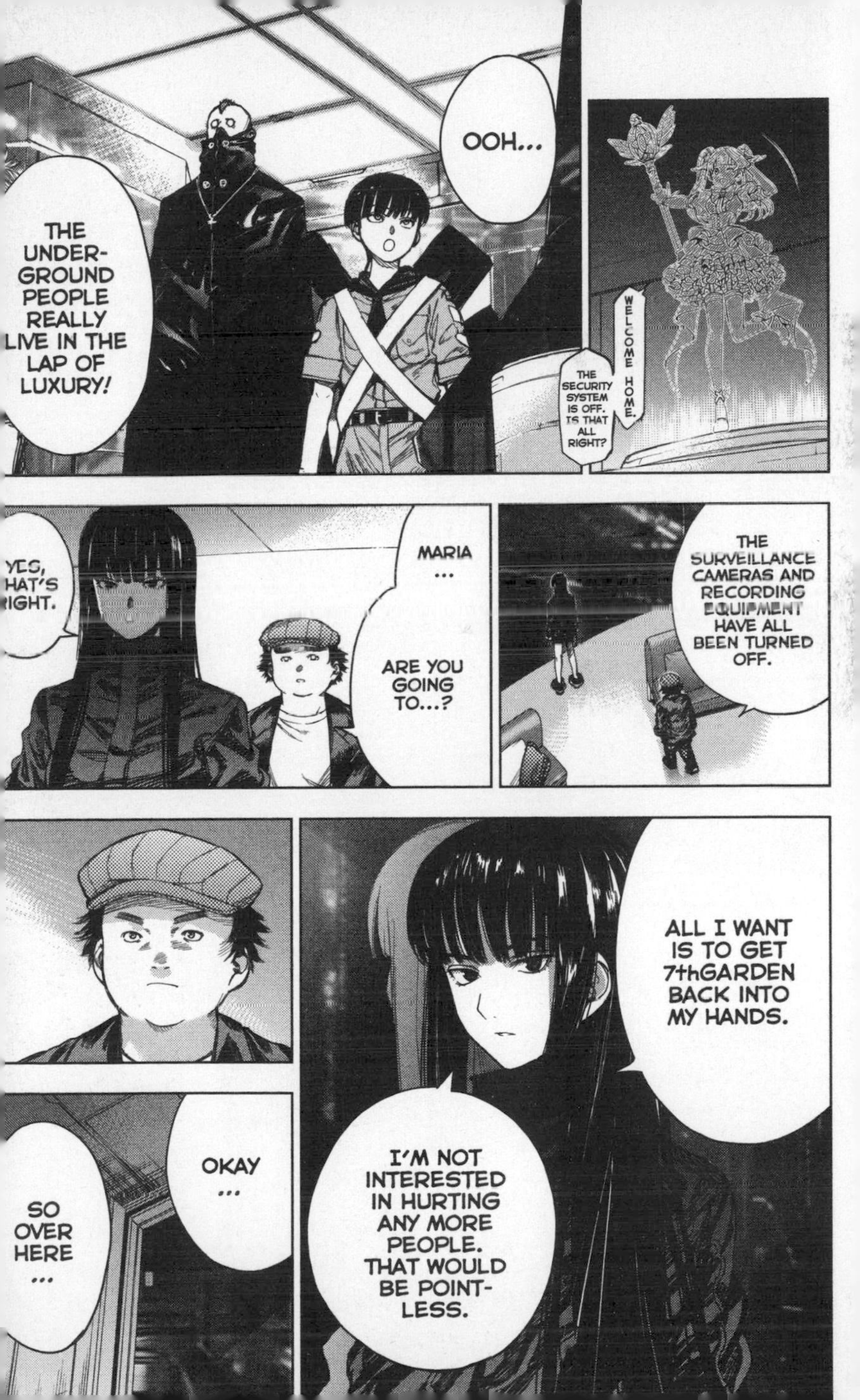
WELCOME HOME.
THE SECURITY SYSTEM IS OFF. IS THAT ALL RIGHT?
OOH...
THE UNDERGROUND PEOPLE REALLY LIVE IN THE LAP OF LUXURY!
THE SURVEILLANCE CAMERAS AND RECORDING EQUIPMENT HAVE ALL BEEN TURNED OFF.
MARIA ...
ARE YOU GOING TO...?
YES, HAT'S IGHT.
ALL I WANT IS TO GET 7thGARDEN BACK INTO MY HANDS.
I'M NOT INTERESTED IN HURTING ANY MORE PEOPLE. THAT WOULD BE POINTLESS.
OKAY ...
SO OVER HERE ...

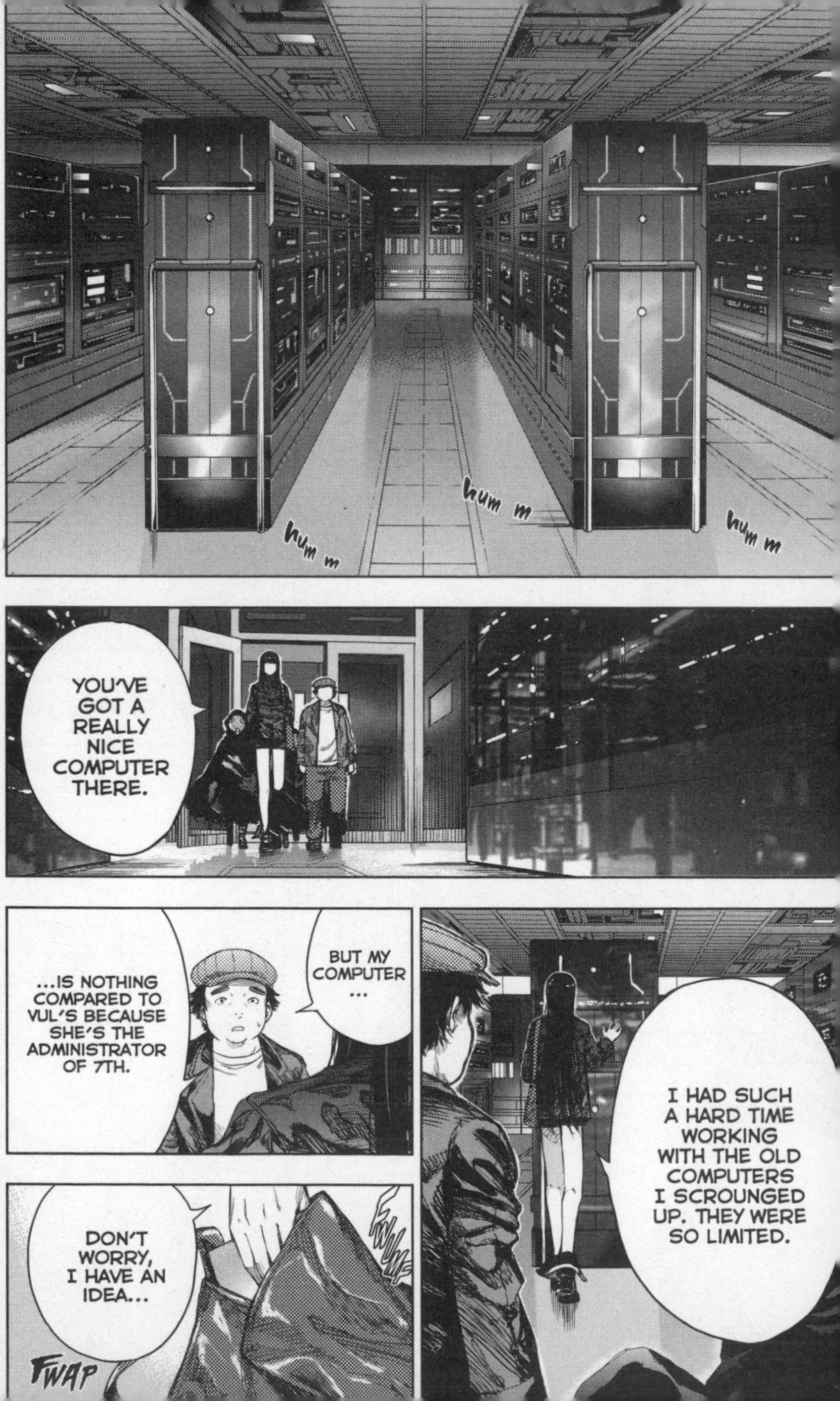
hum m
hum m
hum m
YOU'VE GOT A REALLY NICE COMPUTER THERE.
I HAD SUCH A HARD TIME WORKING WITH THE OLD COMPUTERS I SCROUNGED UP. THEY WERE SO LIMITED.
BUT MY COMPUTER ...
...IS NOTHING COMPARED TO VUL'S BECAUSE SHE'S THE ADMINISTRATOR OF 7TH.
DON'T WORRY, I HAVE AN IDEA...
FWAP

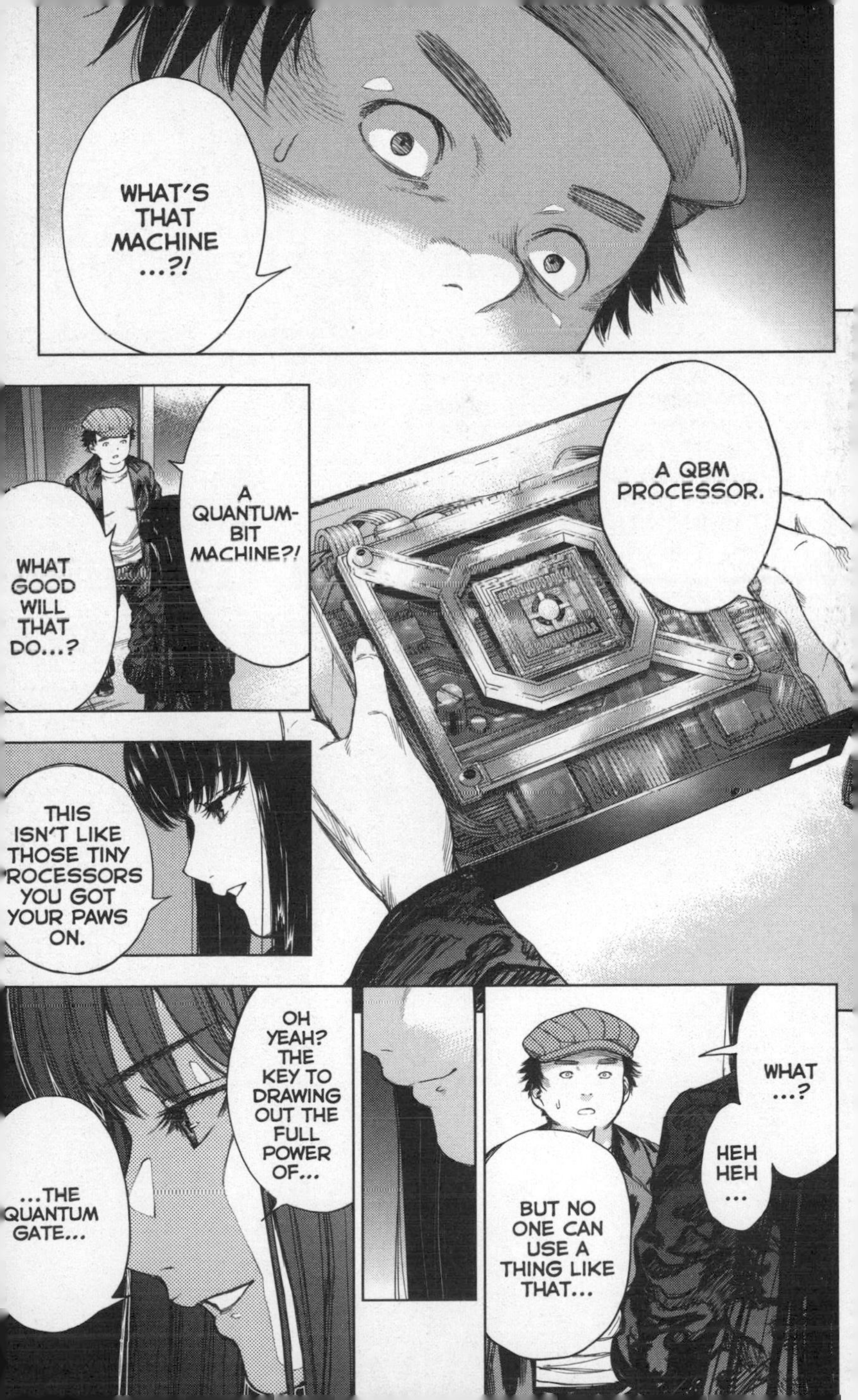
WHAT'S THAT MACHINE ...?!
A QBM PROCESSOR.
A QUANTUM-BIT MACHINE?!
WHAT GOOD WILL THAT DO...?
THIS ISN'T LIKE THOSE TINY ROCESSORS YOU GOT YOUR PAWS ON.
WHAT ...?
HEH HEH ...
BUT NO ONE CAN USE A THING LIKE THAT...
OH YEAH? THE KEY TO DRAWING OUT THE FULL POWER OF...
...THE QUANTUM GATE...

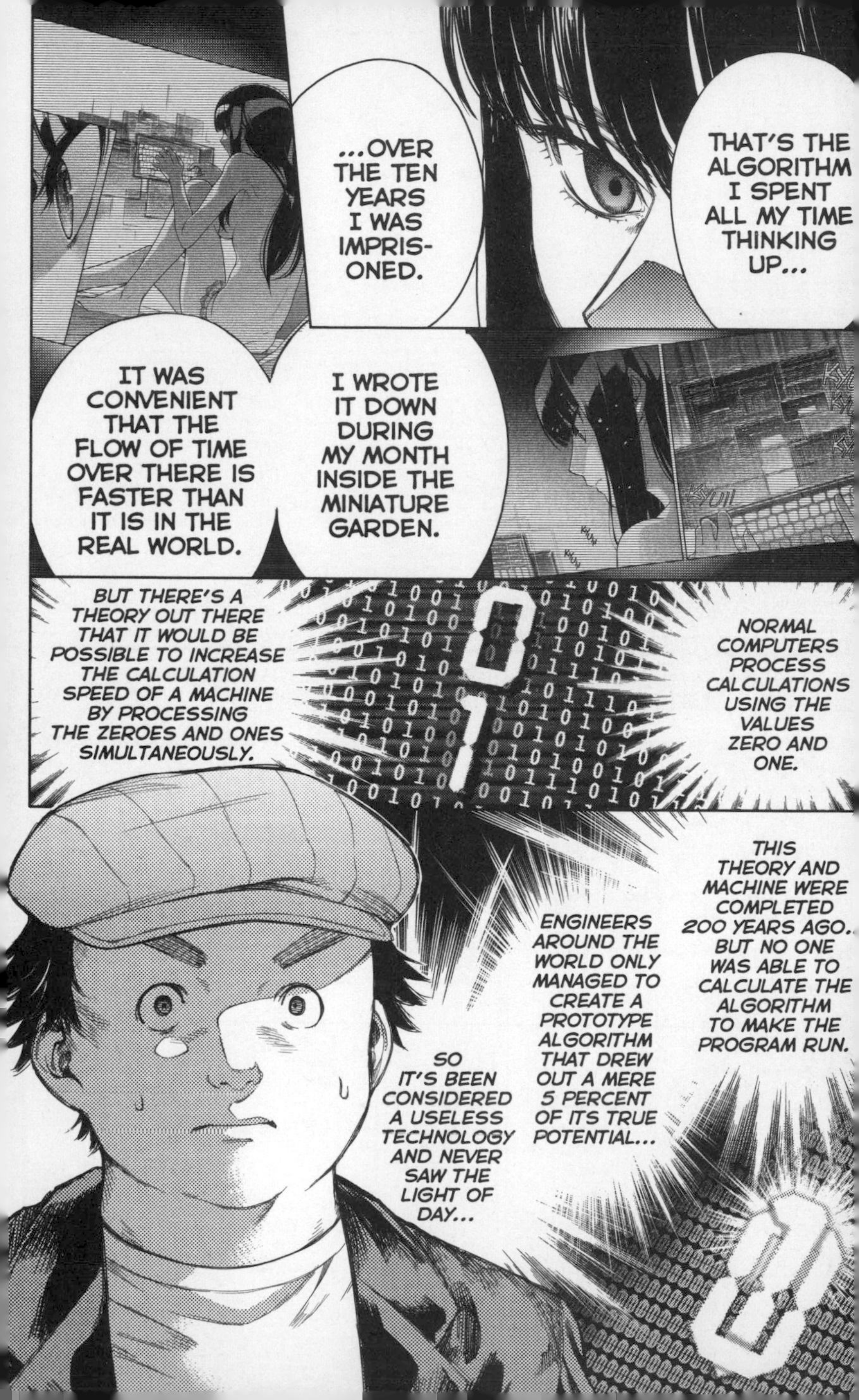
THAT'S THE ALGORITHM I SPENT ALL MY TIME THINKING UP...
...OVER THE TEN YEARS I WAS IMPRIS-ONED.
I WROTE IT DOWN DURING MY MONTH INSIDE THE MINIATURE GARDEN.
IT WAS CONVENIENT THAT THE FLOW OF TIME OVER THERE IS FASTER THAN IT IS IN THE REAL WORLD.
NORMAL COMPUTERS PROCESS CALCULATIONS USING THE VALUES ZERO AND ONE.
BUT THERE'S A THEORY OUT THERE THAT IT WOULD BE POSSIBLE TO INCREASE THE CALCULATION SPEED OF A MACHINE BY PROCESSING THE ZEROES AND ONES SIMULTANEOUSLY.
THIS THEORY AND MACHINE WERE COMPLETED 200 YEARS AGO... BUT NO ONE WAS ABLE TO CALCULATE THE ALGORITHM TO MAKE THE PROGRAM RUN.
ENGINEERS AROUND THE WORLD ONLY MANAGED TO CREATE A PROTOTYPE ALGORITHM THAT DREW OUT A MERE 5 PERCENT OF ITS TRUE POTENTIAL...
SO IT'S BEEN CONSIDERED A USELESS TECHNOLOGY AND NEVER SAW THE LIGHT OF DAY...

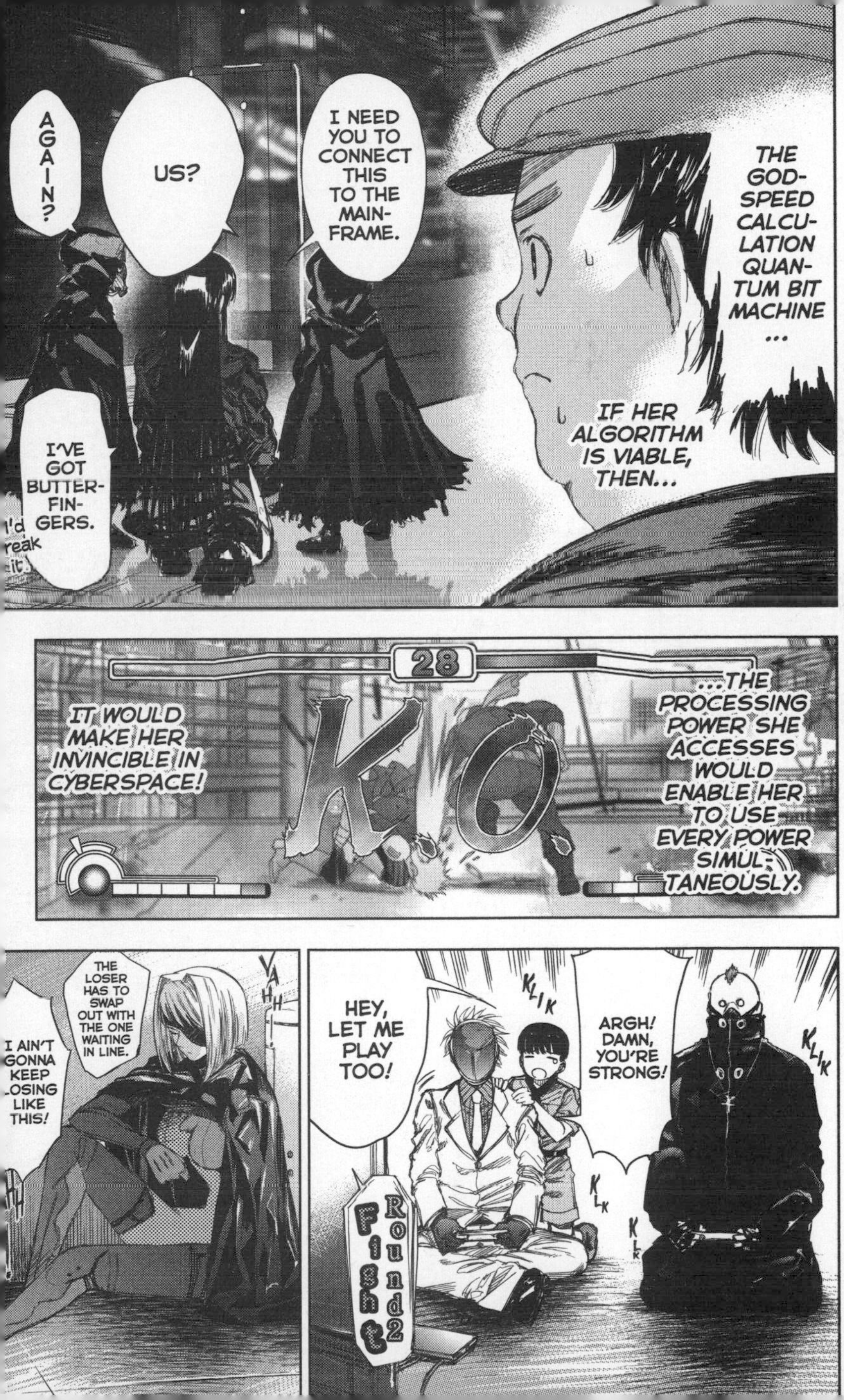

THE GOD-SPEED CALCULATION QUANTUM BIT MACHINE...
IF HER ALGORITHM IS VIABLE, THEN...
I NEED YOU TO CONNECT THIS TO THE MAINFRAME.
US?
AGAIN?
I'VE GOT BUTTERFINGERS.
28
...THE PROCESSING POWER SHE ACCESSES WOULD ENABLE HER TO USE EVERY POWER SIMULTANEOUSLY.
KO
IT WOULD MAKE HER INVINCIBLE IN CYBERSPACE!
KLIK
KLIK
ARGH! DAMN, YOU'RE STRONG!
HEY, LET ME PLAY TOO!
KLK
KLK
Round2
Fight
VAHH
THE LOSER HAS TO SWAP OUT WITH THE ONE WAITING IN LINE.
I AIN'T GONNA KEEP LOSING LIKE THIS!

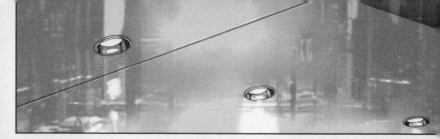

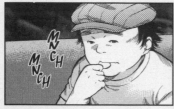

MNCH MNCH
THERE'S JUST ONE THING I DON'T UNDER-STAND...
I SEE WHY YOU'RE TRYING TO MAKE 7thGARDEN THE NEXT NEW WORLD FOR HUMANITY.
...
IF YOU CAN TRANSFORM PEOPLE INTO BITS OF DATA, LAND, FOOD, ENERGY... ALL OUR PROBLEMS WOULD BE SOLVED.

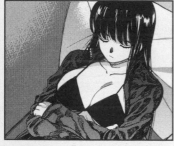

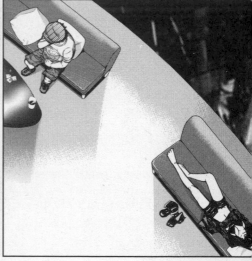

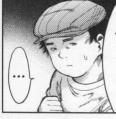

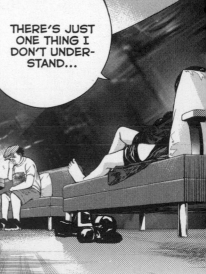

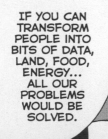

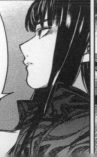

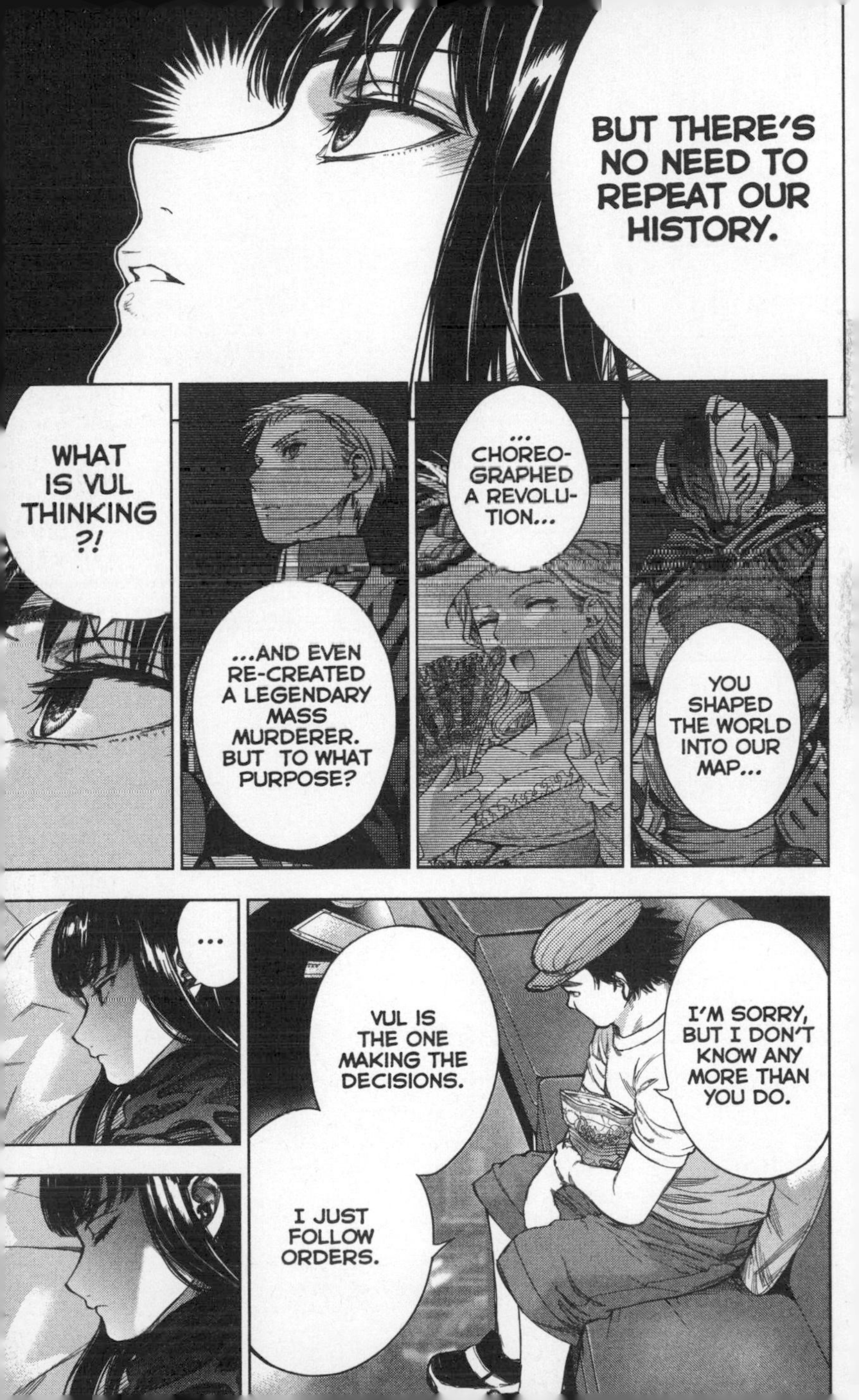
BUT THERE'S NO NEED TO REPEAT OUR HISTORY.
YOU SHAPED THE WORLD INTO OUR MAP...
...CHOREOGRAPHED A REVOLUTION...
...AND EVEN RE-CREATED A LEGENDARY MASS MURDERER. BUT TO WHAT PURPOSE?
WHAT IS VUL THINKING?!
I'M SORRY, BUT I DON'T KNOW ANY MORE THAN YOU DO.
VUL IS THE ONE MAKING THE DECISIONS.
I JUST FOLLOW ORDERS.
...

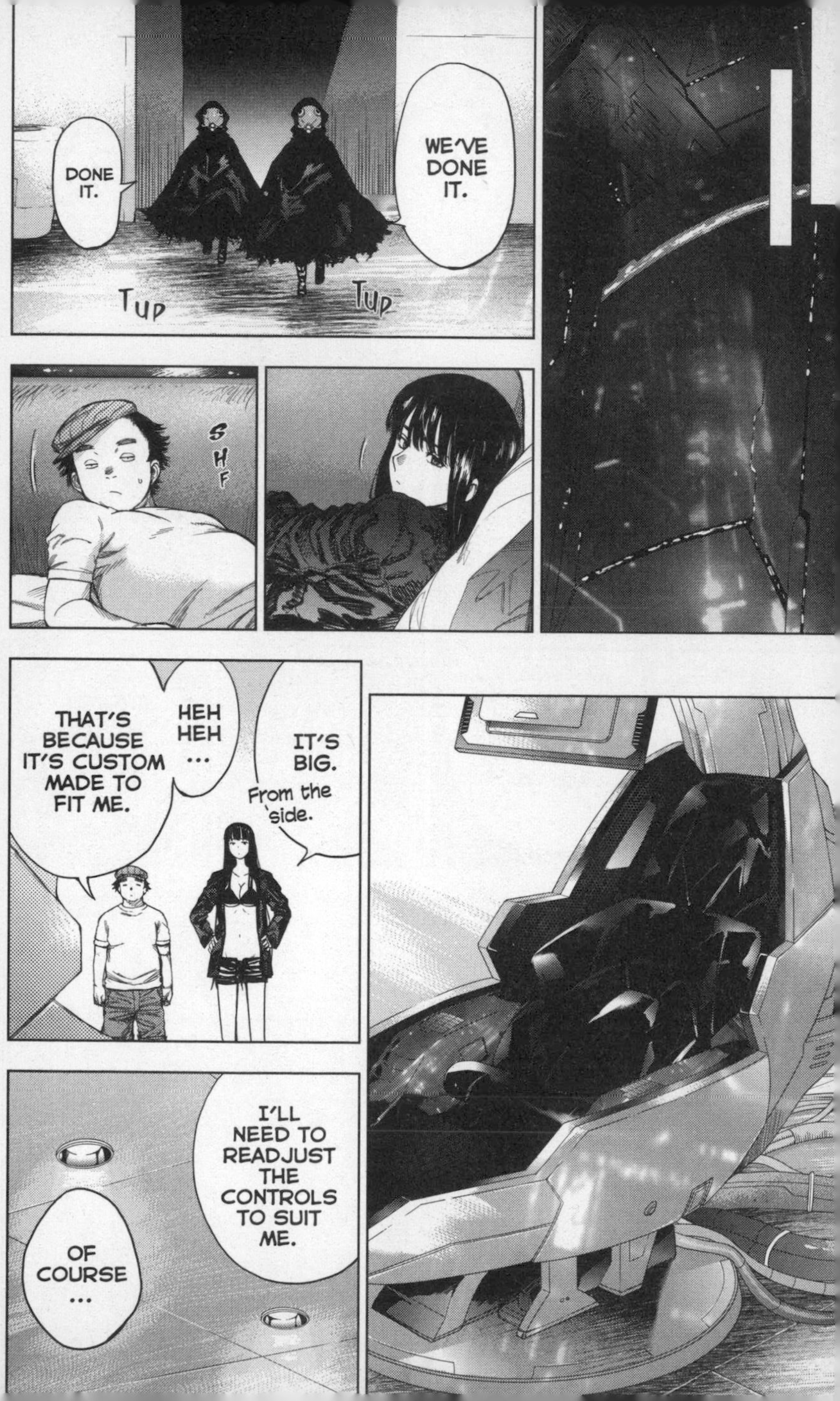
WE'VE DONE IT.
DONE IT.
TUP
TUP
SHF
IT'S BIG.
From the side.
HEH HEH ...
THAT'S BECAUSE IT'S CUSTOM MADE TO FIT ME.
I'LL NEED TO READJUST THE CONTROLS TO SUIT ME.
OF COURSE ...

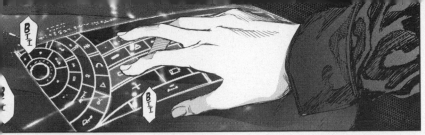

BII

BII

WORK-
ING TO-
GETHER
LIKE THIS...

...BRINGS
BACK
MEMORIES
...

...TO THE
GNOMES
THROUGH
DREAMS AND
CLERICAL
SERMONS...

...SO AS TO
MAKE THEIR
HISTORY
MATCH AS
CLOSELY AS
POSSIBLE
TO OURS.

I GIVE
ORDERS
...

BII

BII

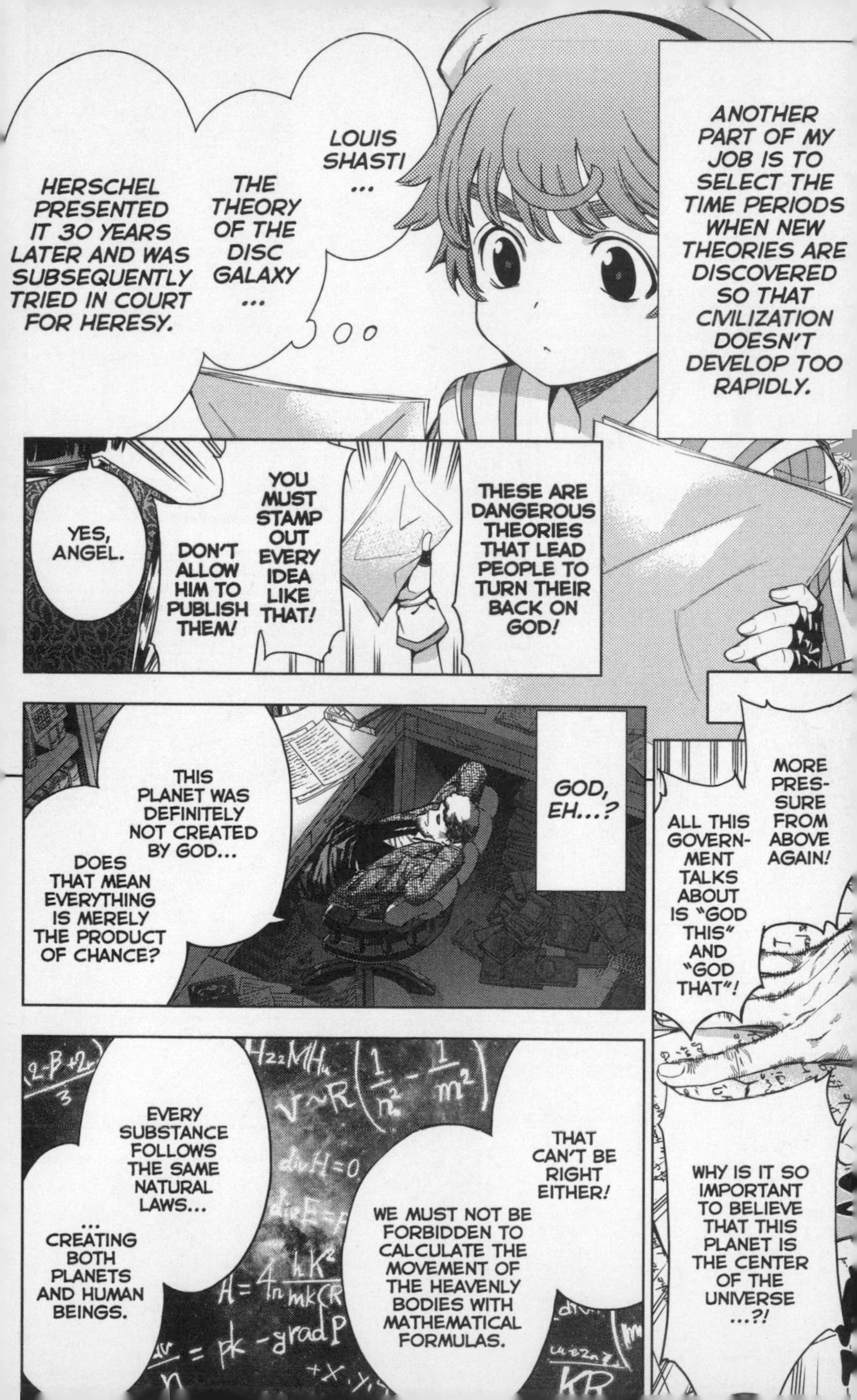
ANOTHER PART OF MY JOB IS TO SELECT THE TIME PERIODS WHEN NEW THEORIES ARE DISCOVERED SO THAT CIVILIZATION DOESN'T DEVELOP TOO RAPIDLY.
LOUIS SHASTI ...
THE THEORY OF THE DISC GALAXY ...
HERSCHEL PRESENTED IT 30 YEARS LATER AND WAS SUBSEQUENTLY TRIED IN COURT FOR HERESY.
THESE ARE DANGEROUS THEORIES THAT LEAD PEOPLE TO TURN THEIR BACK ON GOD!
YOU MUST STAMP OUT EVERY IDEA LIKE THAT!
DON'T ALLOW HIM TO PUBLISH THEM!
YES, ANGEL.
MORE PRES-SURE FROM ABOVE AGAIN!
ALL THIS GOVERN-MENT TALKS ABOUT IS "GOD THIS" AND "GOD THAT"!
WHY IS IT SO IMPORTANT TO BELIEVE THAT THIS PLANET IS THE CENTER OF THE UNIVERSE ...?!
GOD, EH...?
THIS PLANET WAS DEFINITELY NOT CREATED BY GOD...
DOES THAT MEAN EVERYTHING IS MERELY THE PRODUCT OF CHANCE?
THAT CAN'T BE RIGHT EITHER!
WE MUST NOT BE FORBIDDEN TO CALCULATE THE MOVEMENT OF THE HEAVENLY BODIES WITH MATHEMATICAL FORMULAS.
EVERY SUBSTANCE FOLLOWS THE SAME NATURAL LAWS...
... CREATING BOTH PLANETS AND HUMAN BEINGS.

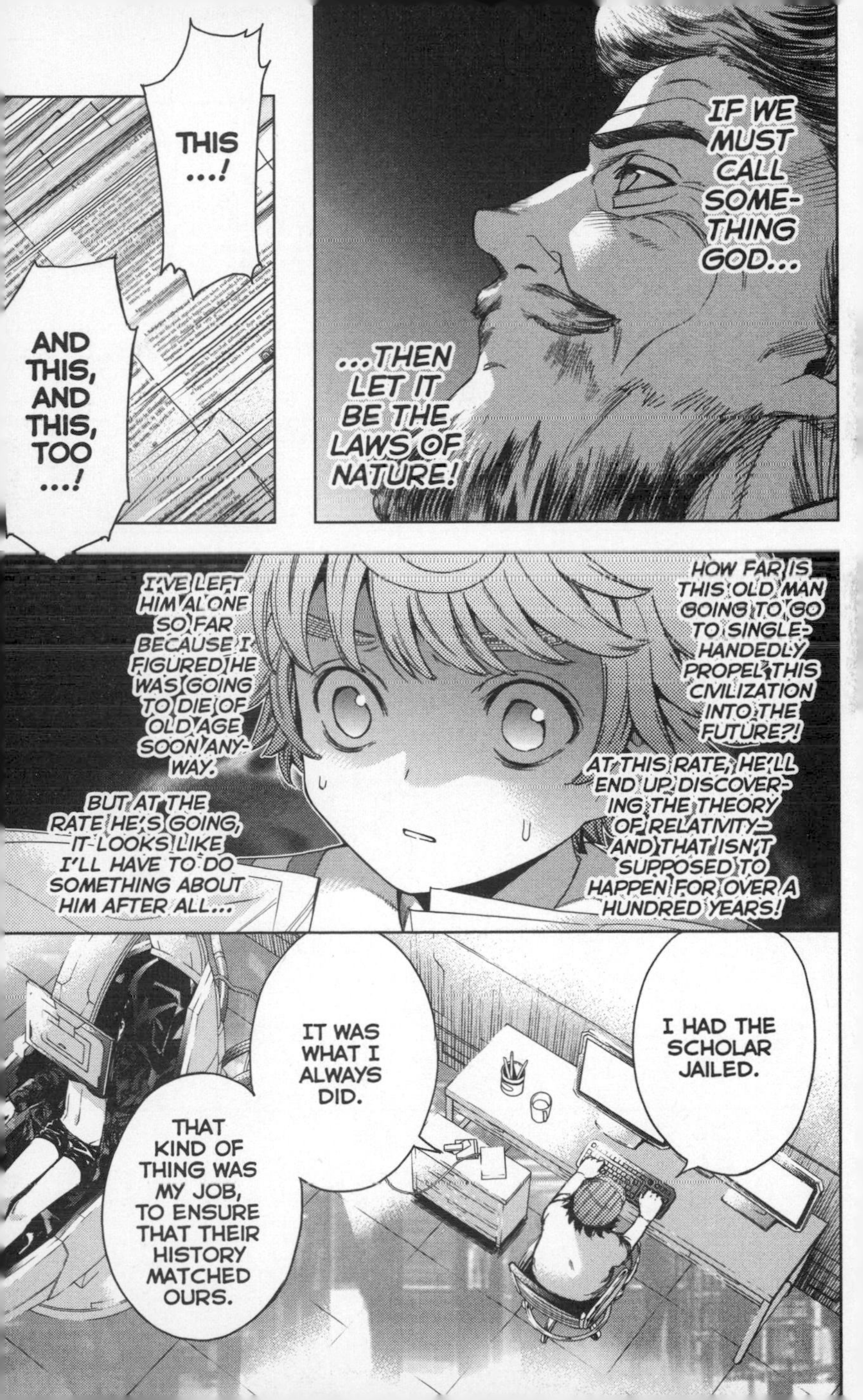
IF WE MUST CALL SOMETHING GOD...
...THEN LET IT BE THE LAWS OF NATURE!
THIS ...!
AND THIS, AND THIS, TOO ...!
HOW FAR IS THIS OLD MAN GOING TO GO TO SINGLE-HANDEDLY PROPEL THIS CIVILIZATION INTO THE FUTURE?!
AT THIS RATE, HE'LL END UP DISCOVERING THE THEORY OF RELATIVITY—AND THAT ISN'T SUPPOSED TO HAPPEN FOR OVER A HUNDRED YEARS!
I'VE LEFT HIM ALONE SO FAR BECAUSE I FIGURED HE WAS GOING TO DIE OF OLD AGE SOON ANYWAY.
BUT AT THE RATE HE'S GOING, IT LOOKS LIKE I'LL HAVE TO DO SOMETHING ABOUT HIM AFTER ALL...
I HAD THE SCHOLAR JAILED.
IT WAS WHAT I ALWAYS DID.
THAT KIND OF THING WAS MY JOB, TO ENSURE THAT THEIR HISTORY MATCHED OURS.

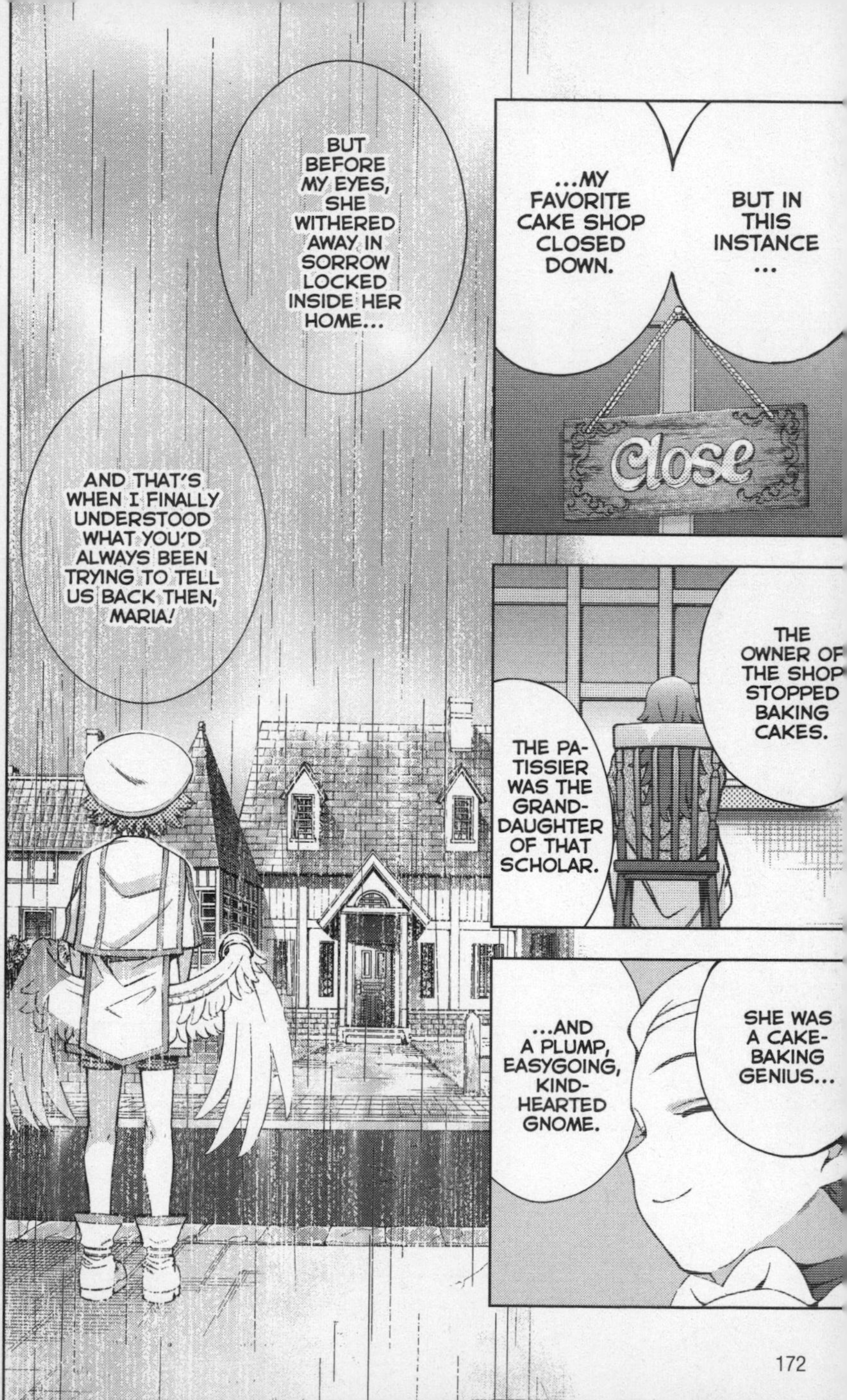
BUT IN THIS INSTANCE...
...MY FAVORITE CAKE SHOP CLOSED DOWN.
Close
THE OWNER OF THE SHOP STOPPED BAKING CAKES.
THE PATISSIER WAS THE GRANDDAUGHTER OF THAT SCHOLAR.
SHE WAS A CAKE-BAKING GENIUS...
...AND A PLUMP, EASYGOING, KIND-HEARTED GNOME.
BUT BEFORE MY EYES, SHE WITHERED AWAY IN SORROW LOCKED INSIDE HER HOME...
AND THAT'S WHEN I FINALLY UNDERSTOOD WHAT YOU'D ALWAYS BEEN TRYING TO TELL US BACK THEN, MARIA!

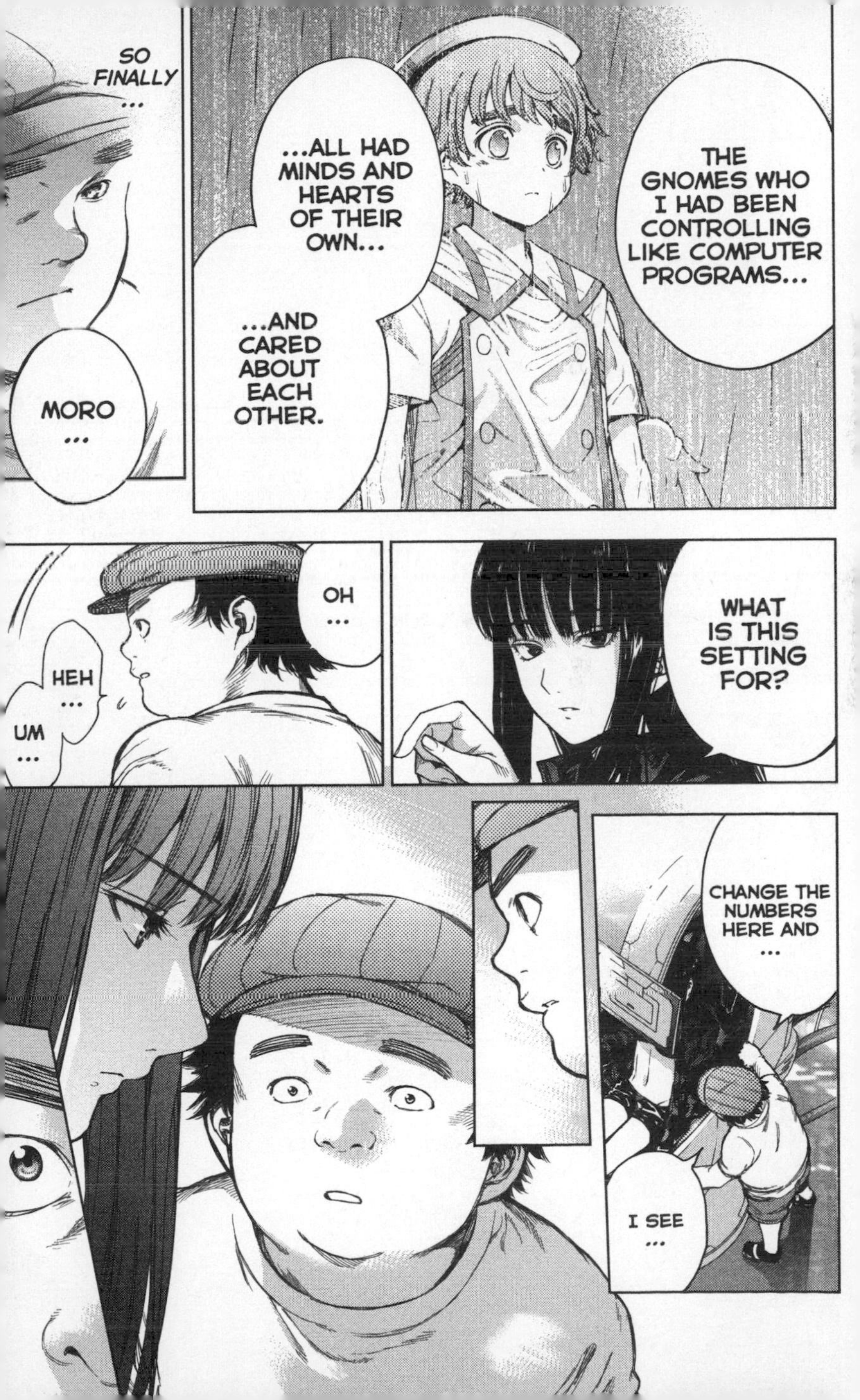
THE GNOMES WHO I HAD BEEN CONTROLLING LIKE COMPUTER PROGRAMS...
...ALL HAD MINDS AND HEARTS OF THEIR OWN...
...AND CARED ABOUT EACH OTHER.
SO FINALLY ...
MORO ...
WHAT IS THIS SETTING FOR?
OH ...
HEH ...
UM ...
CHANGE THE NUMBERS HERE AND ...
I SEE ...

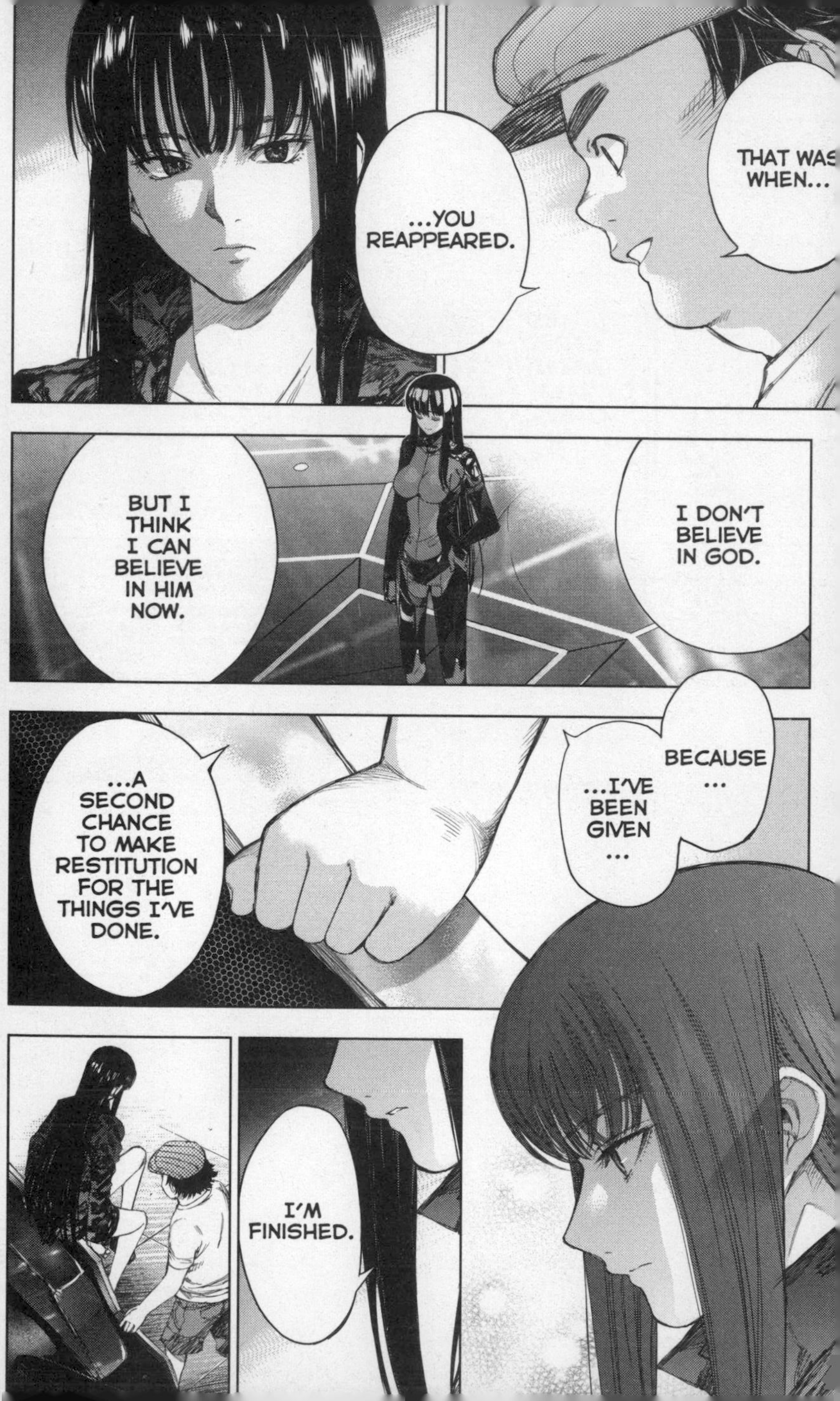
THAT WAS WHEN...
...YOU REAPPEARED.
I DON'T BELIEVE IN GOD.
BUT I THINK I CAN BELIEVE IN HIM NOW.
BECAUSE...
...I'VE BEEN GIVEN...
...A SECOND CHANCE TO MAKE RESTITUTION FOR THE THINGS I'VE DONE.
I'M FINISHED.

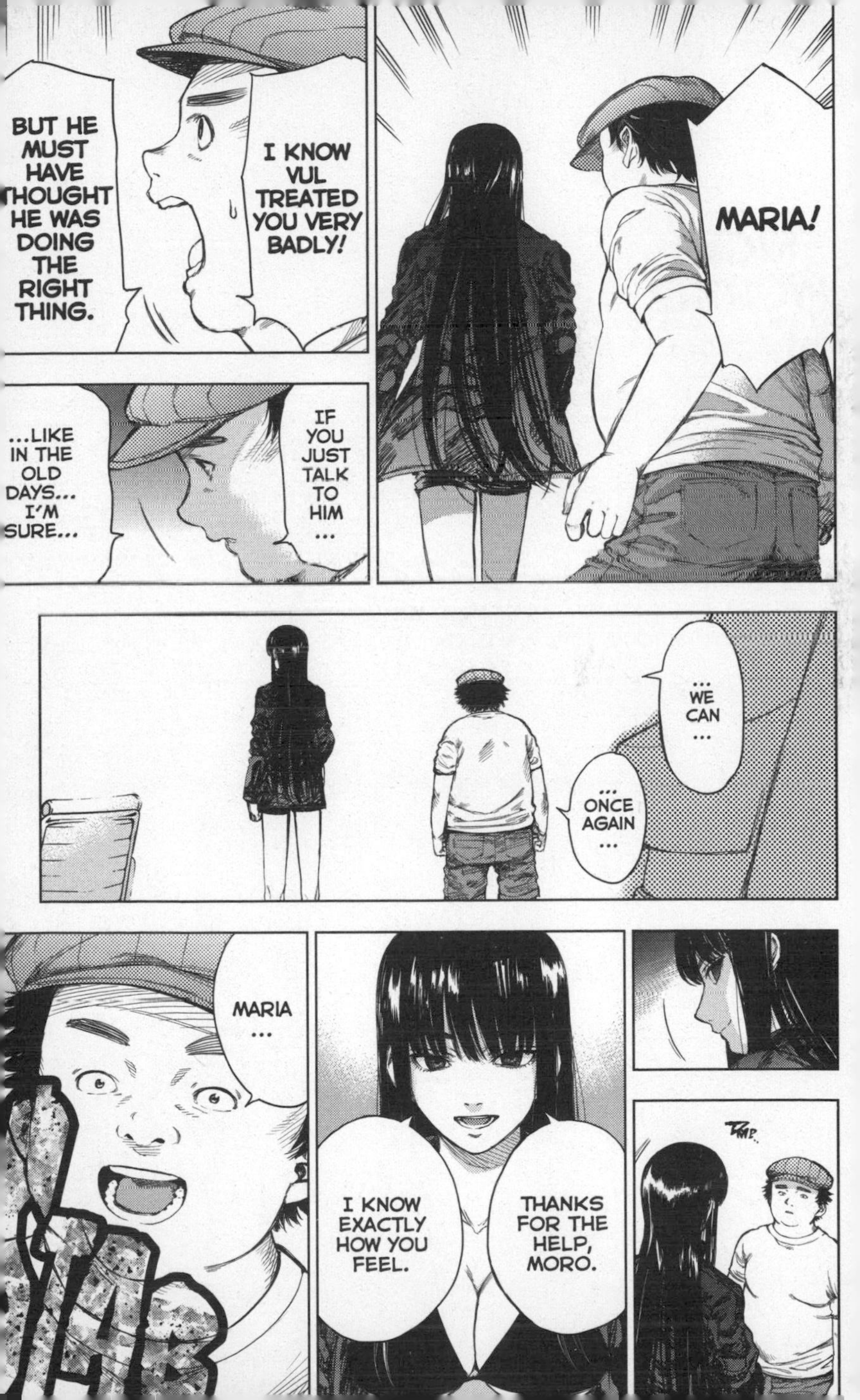
MARIA!
I KNOW VUL TREATED YOU VERY BADLY!
BUT HE MUST HAVE THOUGHT HE WAS DOING THE RIGHT THING.
IF YOU JUST TALK TO HIM ...
...LIKE IN THE OLD DAYS... I'M SURE...
... WE CAN ...
... ONCE AGAIN ...
THANKS FOR THE HELP, MORO.
I KNOW EXACTLY HOW YOU FEEL.
MARIA ...

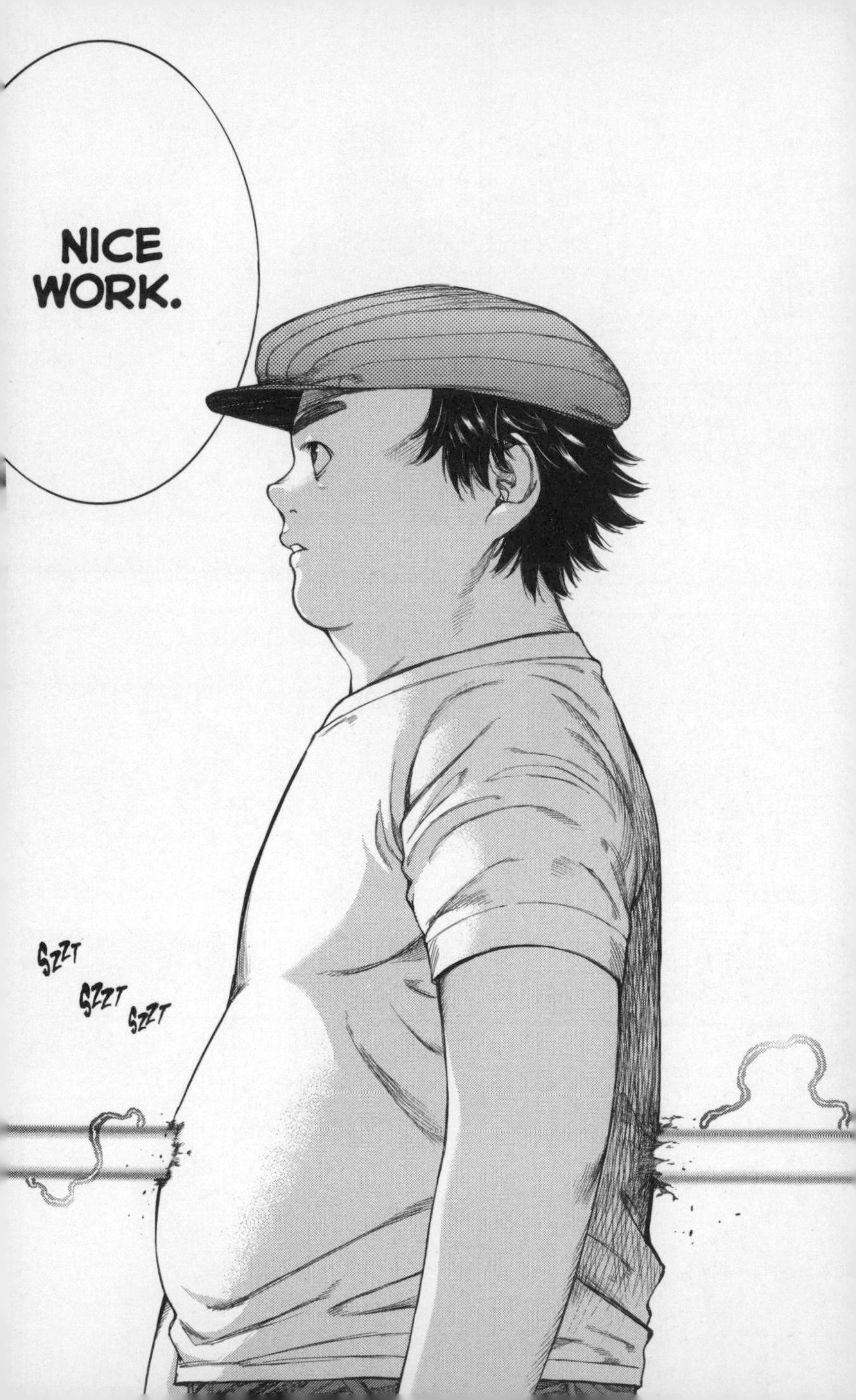
NICE WORK.
SZZT
SZZT
SZZT

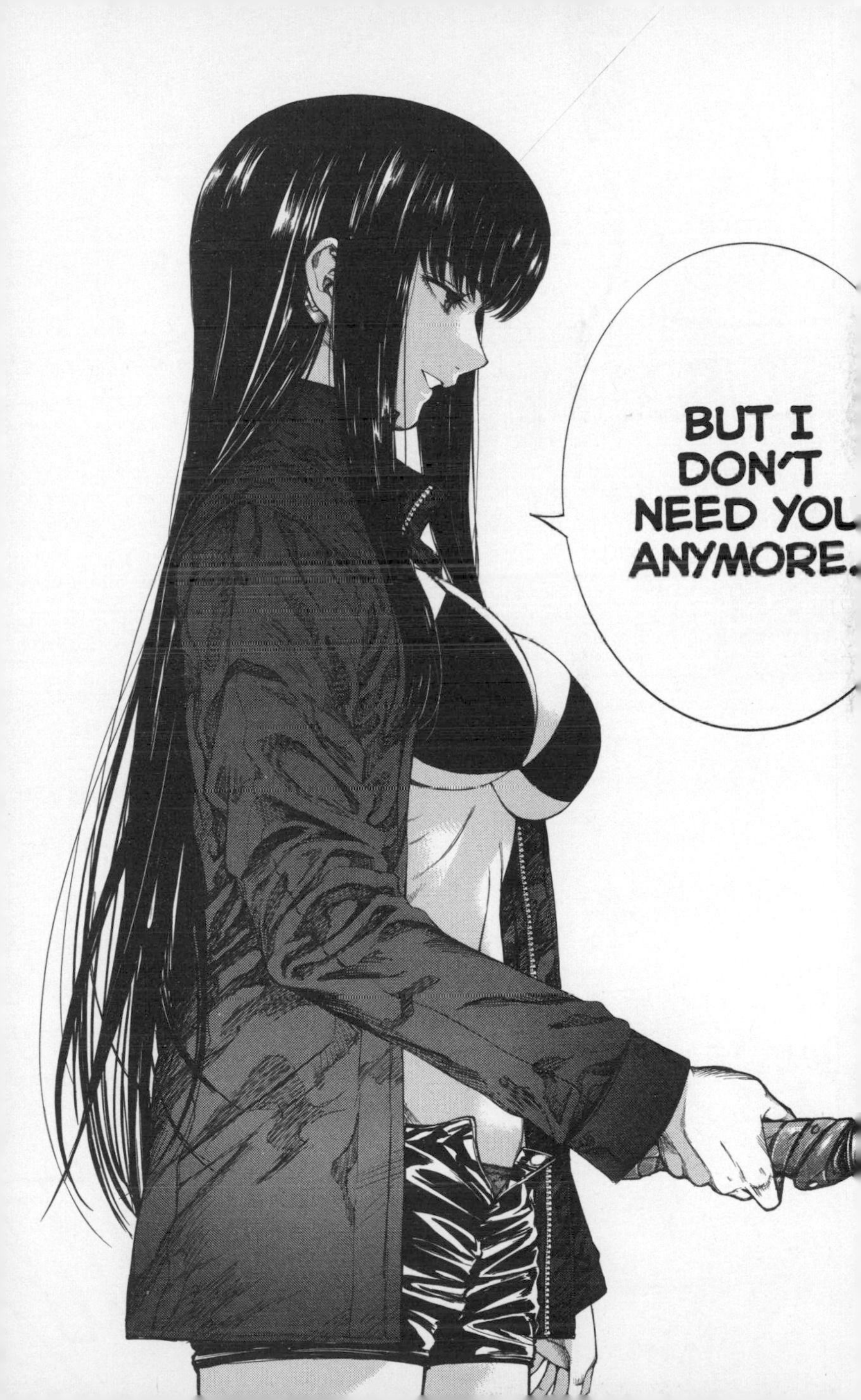
BUT I DON'T NEED YOU ANYMORE.

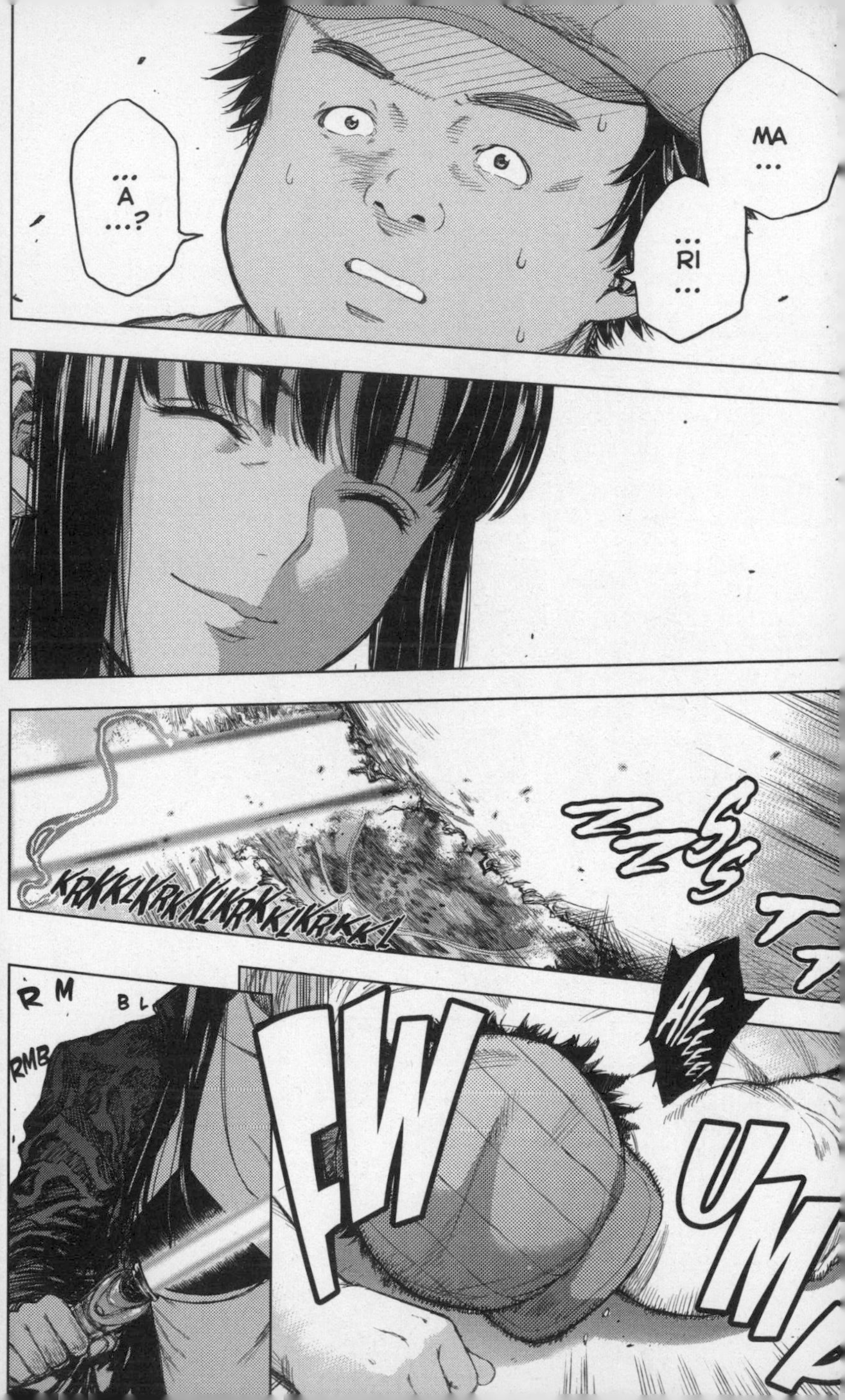
MA... ...RI...
...A...?
KRKKLKRKKLKRKKLKRKKK!
ZZSSTT
AEEEEE!

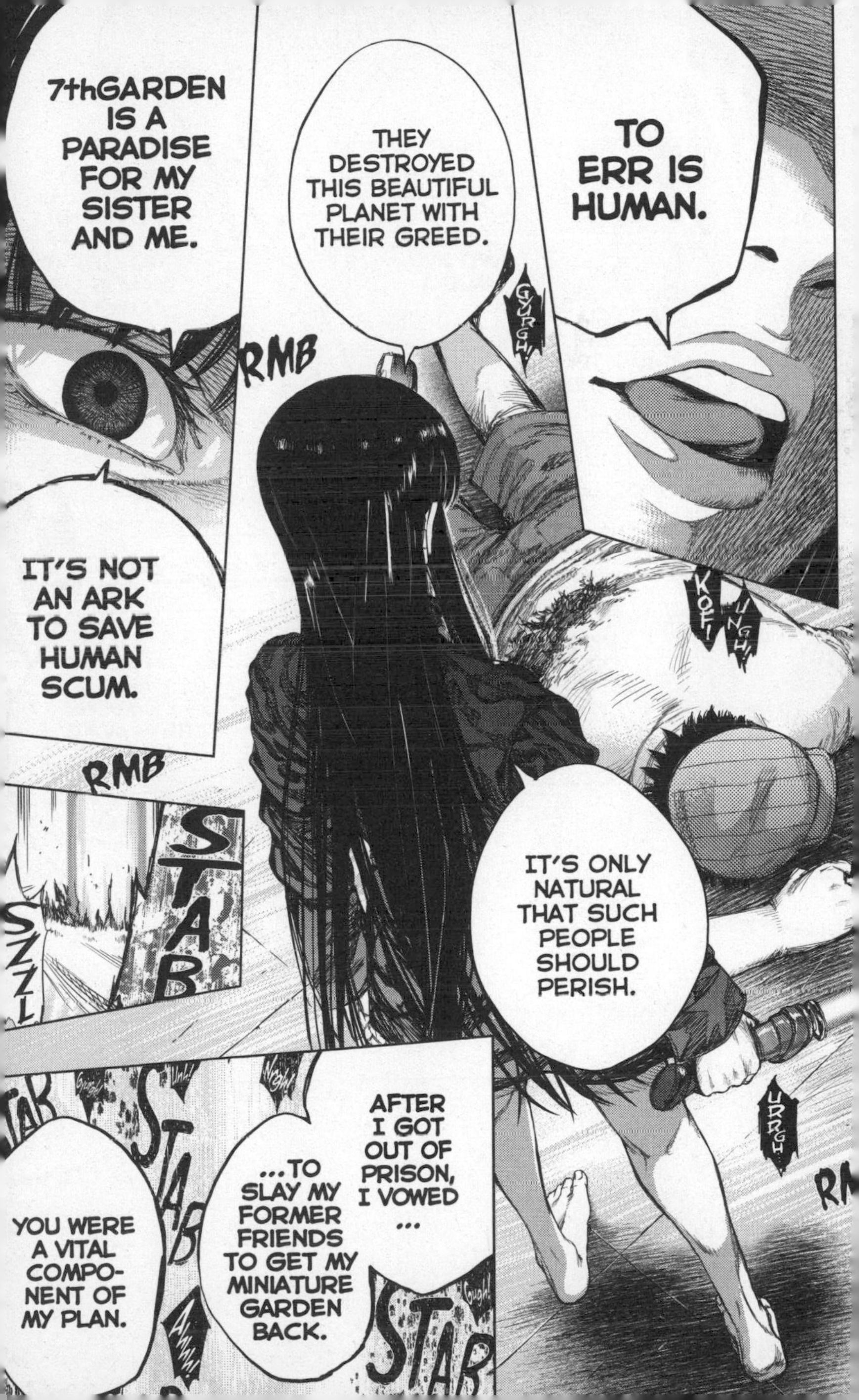
TO ERR IS HUMAN.
GYURGH!
THEY DESTROYED THIS BEAUTIFUL PLANET WITH THEIR GREED.
RMB
7thGARDEN IS A PARADISE FOR MY SISTER AND ME.
IT'S NOT AN ARK TO SAVE HUMAN SCUM.
RMB
KOF!
UNGH!
IT'S ONLY NATURAL THAT SUCH PEOPLE SHOULD PERISH.
URRGH
STAB
SZZL
AFTER I GOT OUT OF PRISON, I VOWED...
...TO SLAY MY FORMER FRIENDS TO GET MY MINIATURE GARDEN BACK.
YOU WERE A VITAL COMPONENT OF MY PLAN.
STAB
STAB
STAB

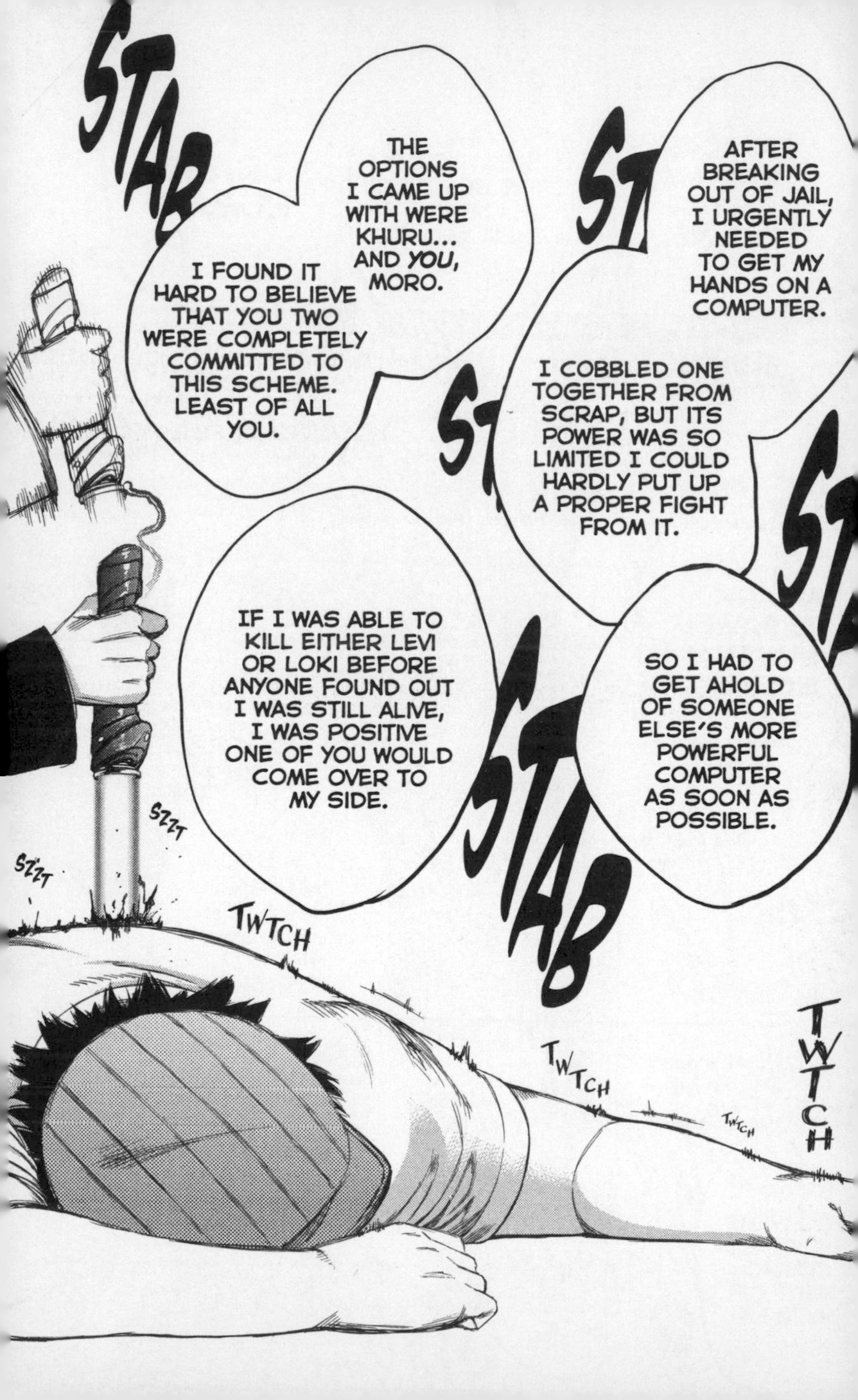
STAB
STAB
AFTER BREAKING OUT OF JAIL, I URGENTLY NEEDED TO GET MY HANDS ON A COMPUTER.
I COBBLED ONE TOGETHER FROM SCRAP, BUT ITS POWER WAS SO LIMITED I COULD HARDLY PUT UP A PROPER FIGHT FROM IT.
SO I HAD TO GET AHOLD OF SOMEONE ELSE'S MORE POWERFUL COMPUTER AS SOON AS POSSIBLE.
THE OPTIONS I CAME UP WITH WERE KHURU... AND *YOU*, MORO.
I FOUND IT HARD TO BELIEVE THAT YOU TWO WERE COMPLETELY COMMITTED TO THIS SCHEME. LEAST OF ALL YOU.
IF I WAS ABLE TO KILL EITHER LEVI OR LOKI BEFORE ANYONE FOUND OUT I WAS STILL ALIVE, I WAS POSITIVE ONE OF YOU WOULD COME OVER TO MY SIDE.
STAB
TWTCH
SZZT
SZZT
TWTCH
TWTCH
TWTCH

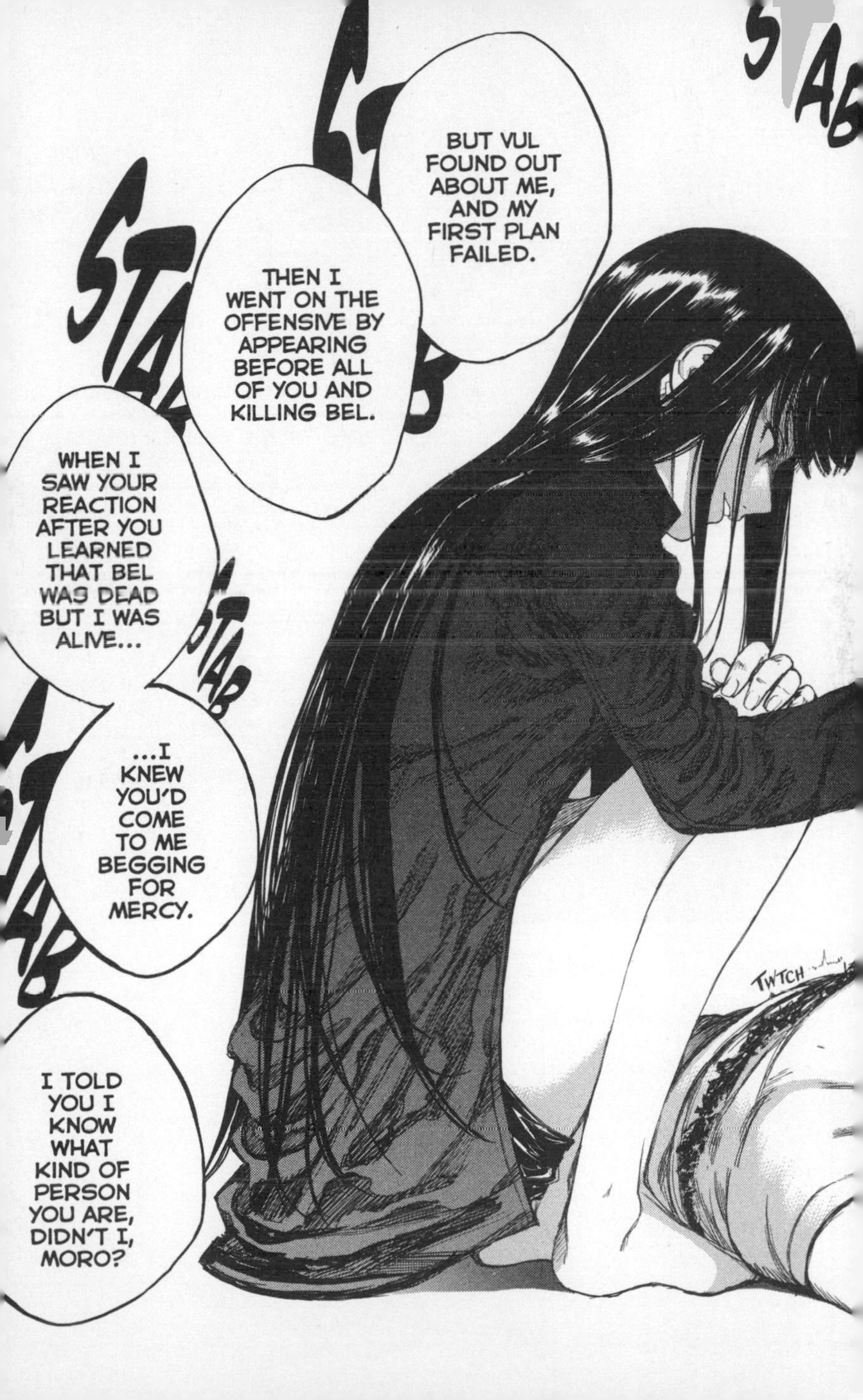
STAB
BUT VUL FOUND OUT ABOUT ME, AND MY FIRST PLAN FAILED.
STAB
THEN I WENT ON THE OFFENSIVE BY APPEARING BEFORE ALL OF YOU AND KILLING BEL.
STAB
WHEN I SAW YOUR REACTION AFTER YOU LEARNED THAT BEL WAS DEAD BUT I WAS ALIVE...
STAB
...I KNEW YOU'D COME TO ME BEGGING FOR MERCY.
TWTCH
I TOLD YOU I KNOW WHAT KIND OF PERSON YOU ARE, DIDN'T I, MORO?

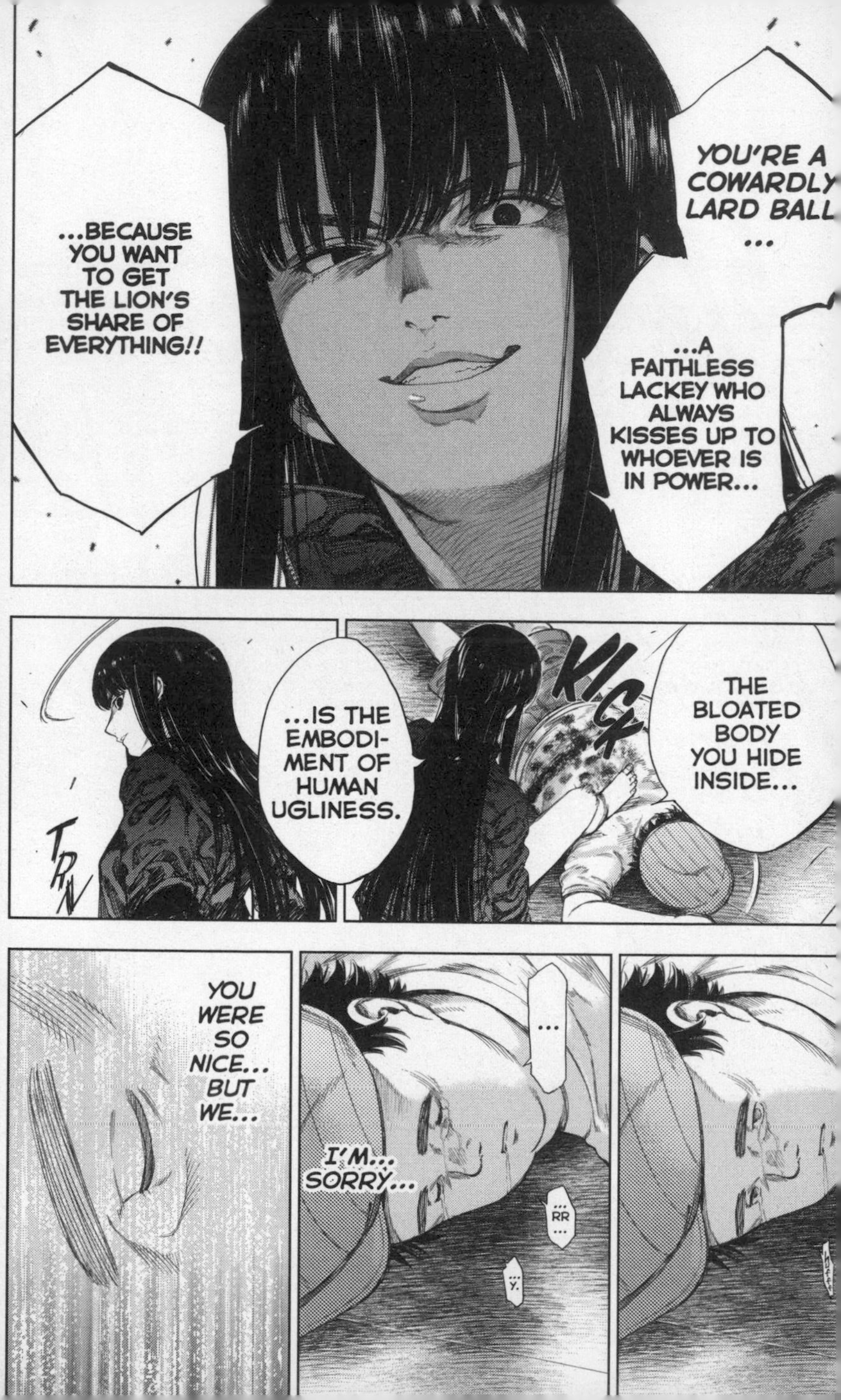
YOU'RE A COWARDLY LARD BALL...
...A FAITHLESS LACKEY WHO ALWAYS KISSES UP TO WHOEVER IS IN POWER...
...BECAUSE YOU WANT TO GET THE LION'S SHARE OF EVERYTHING!!
THE BLOATED BODY YOU HIDE INSIDE...
KICK
...IS THE EMBODI-MENT OF HUMAN UGLINESS.
TRN
...
I'M... SORRY...
...RR...
...Y.
YOU WERE SO NICE... BUT WE...

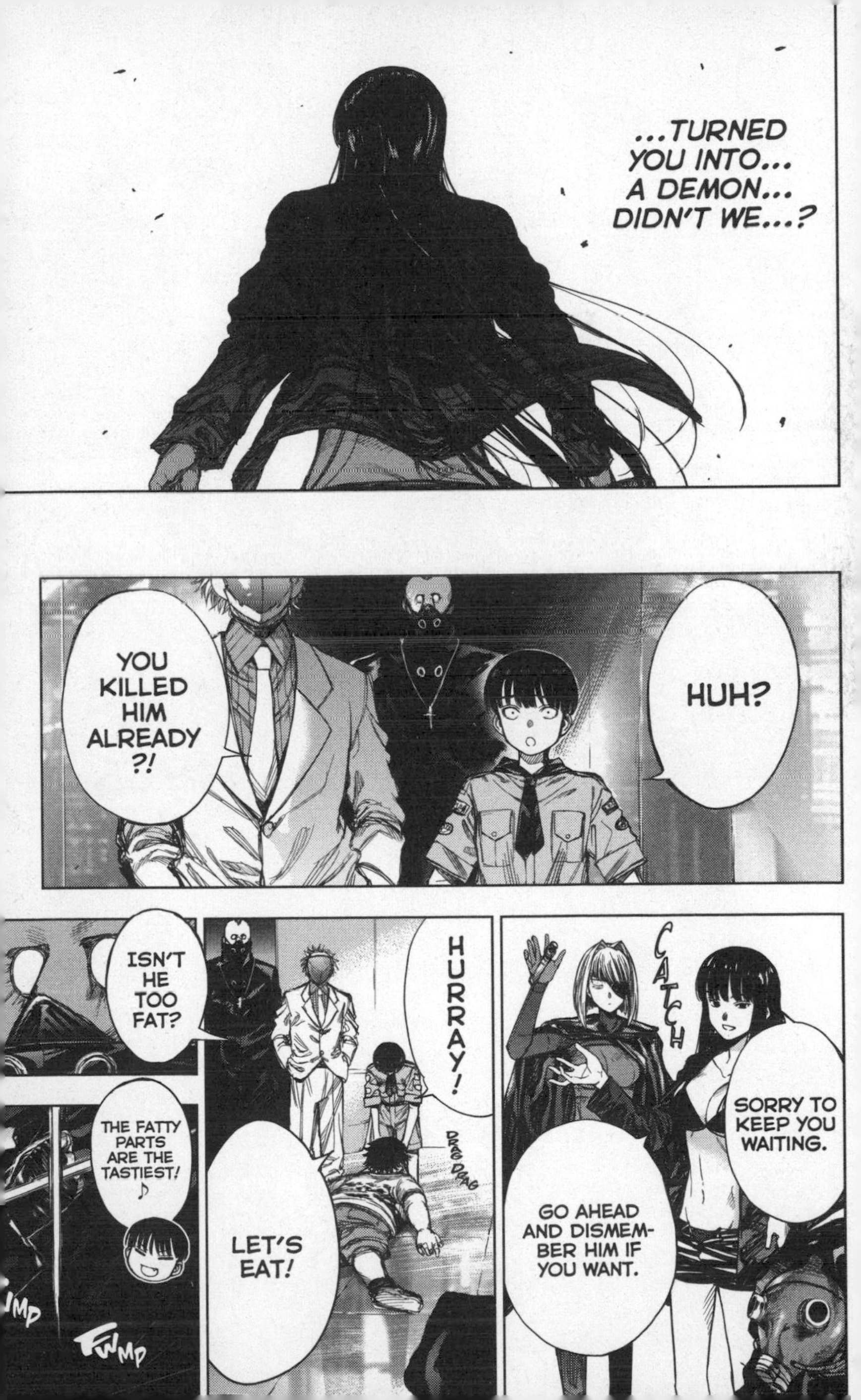
...TURNED YOU INTO... A DEMON... DIDN'T WE...?
HUH?
YOU KILLED HIM ALREADY?!
CATCH
SORRY TO KEEP YOU WAITING.
GO AHEAD AND DISMEM-BER HIM IF YOU WANT.
HURRAY!
DRAG DRAG
LET'S EAT!
ISN'T HE TOO FAT?
THE FATTY PARTS ARE THE TASTIEST! ♪
FWMP

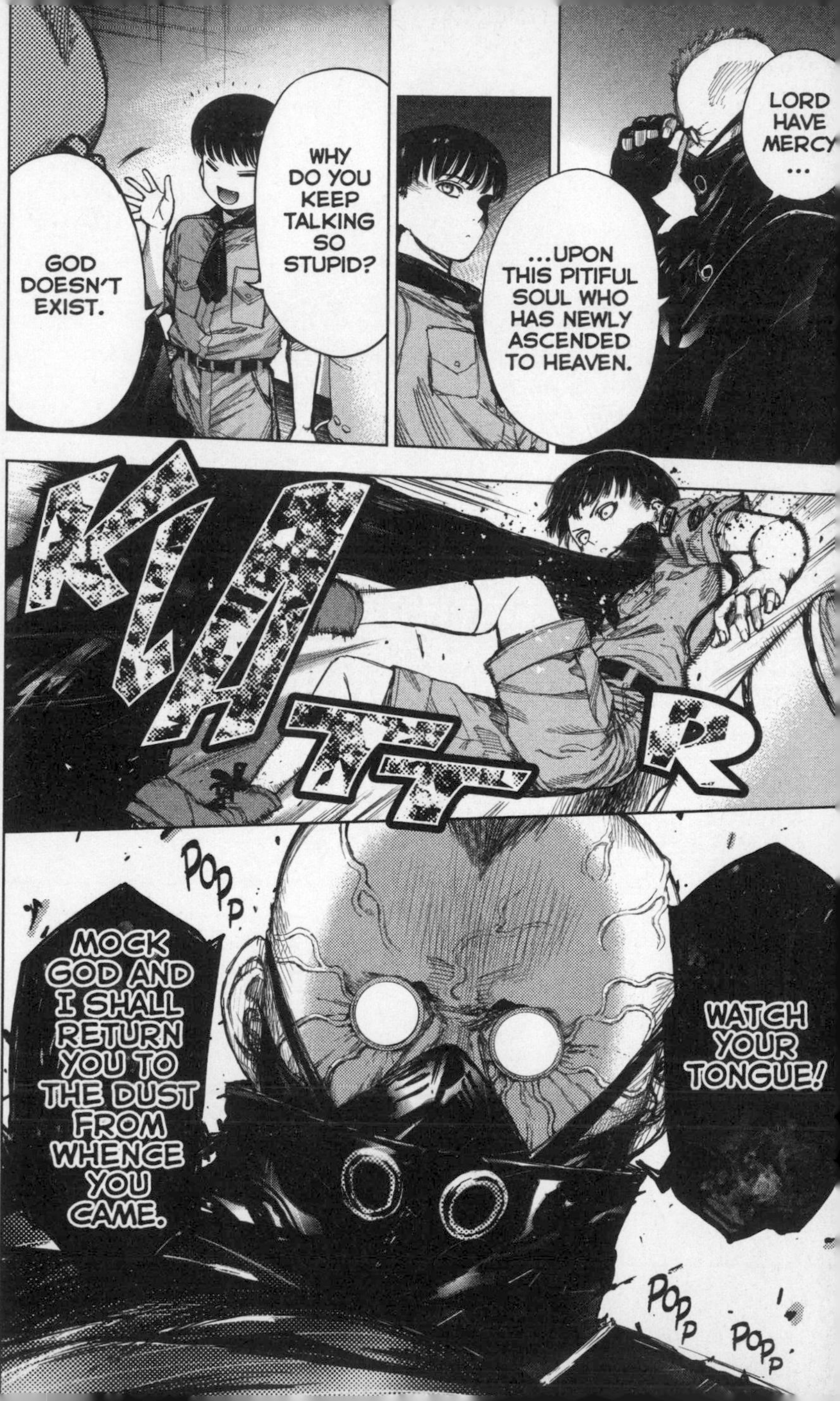
LORD HAVE MERCY ...
...UPON THIS PITIFUL SOUL WHO HAS NEWLY ASCENDED TO HEAVEN.
WHY DO YOU KEEP TALKING SO STUPID?
GOD DOESN'T EXIST.
KLATTER
POPP
WATCH YOUR TONGUE!
MOCK GOD AND I SHALL RETURN YOU TO THE DUST FROM WHENCE YOU CAME.
POPP
POPP

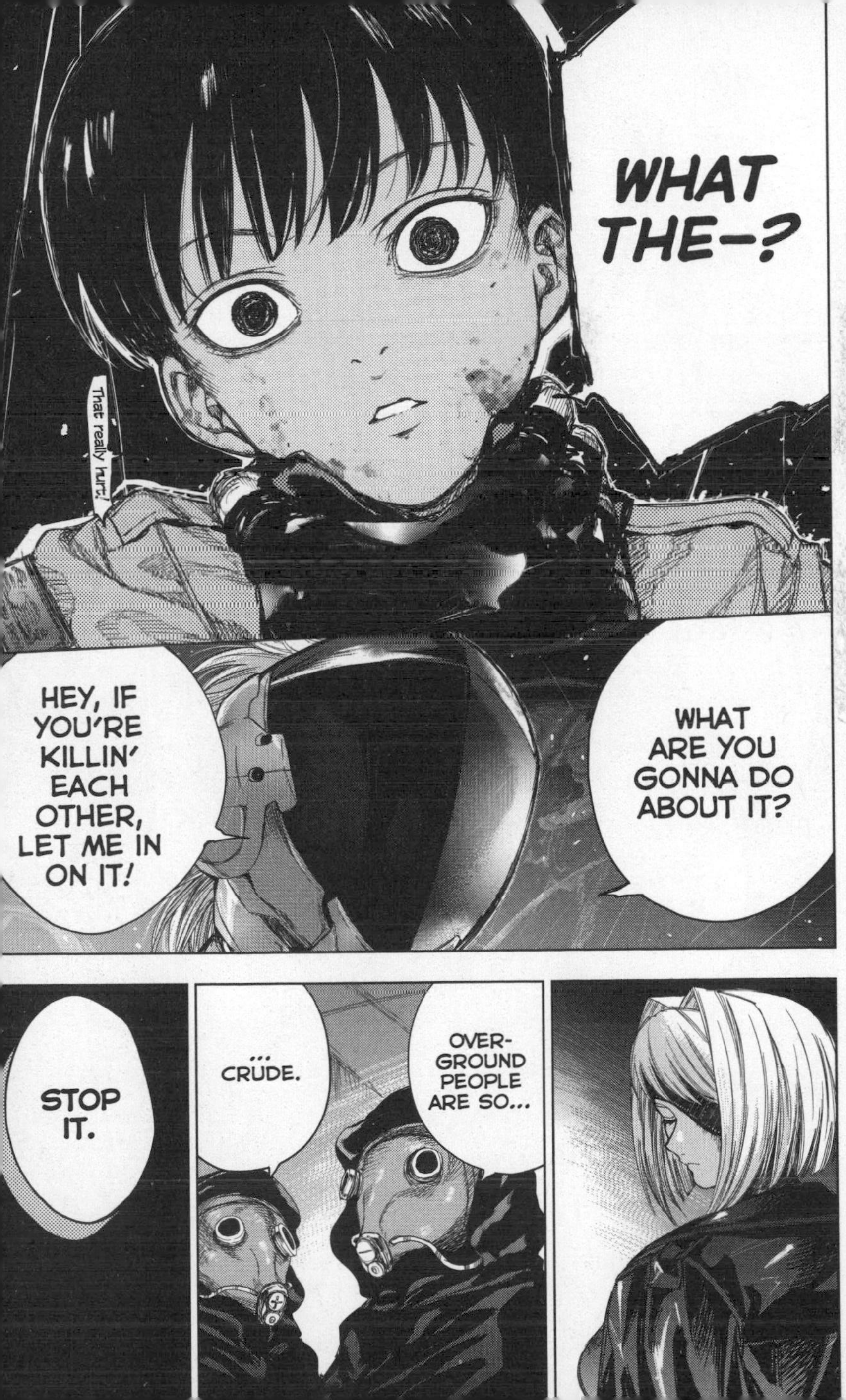
WHAT THE-?
That really hurt!
WHAT ARE YOU GONNA DO ABOUT IT?
HEY, IF YOU'RE KILLIN' EACH OTHER, LET ME IN ON IT!
OVER-GROUND PEOPLE ARE SO...
...CRUDE.
STOP IT.

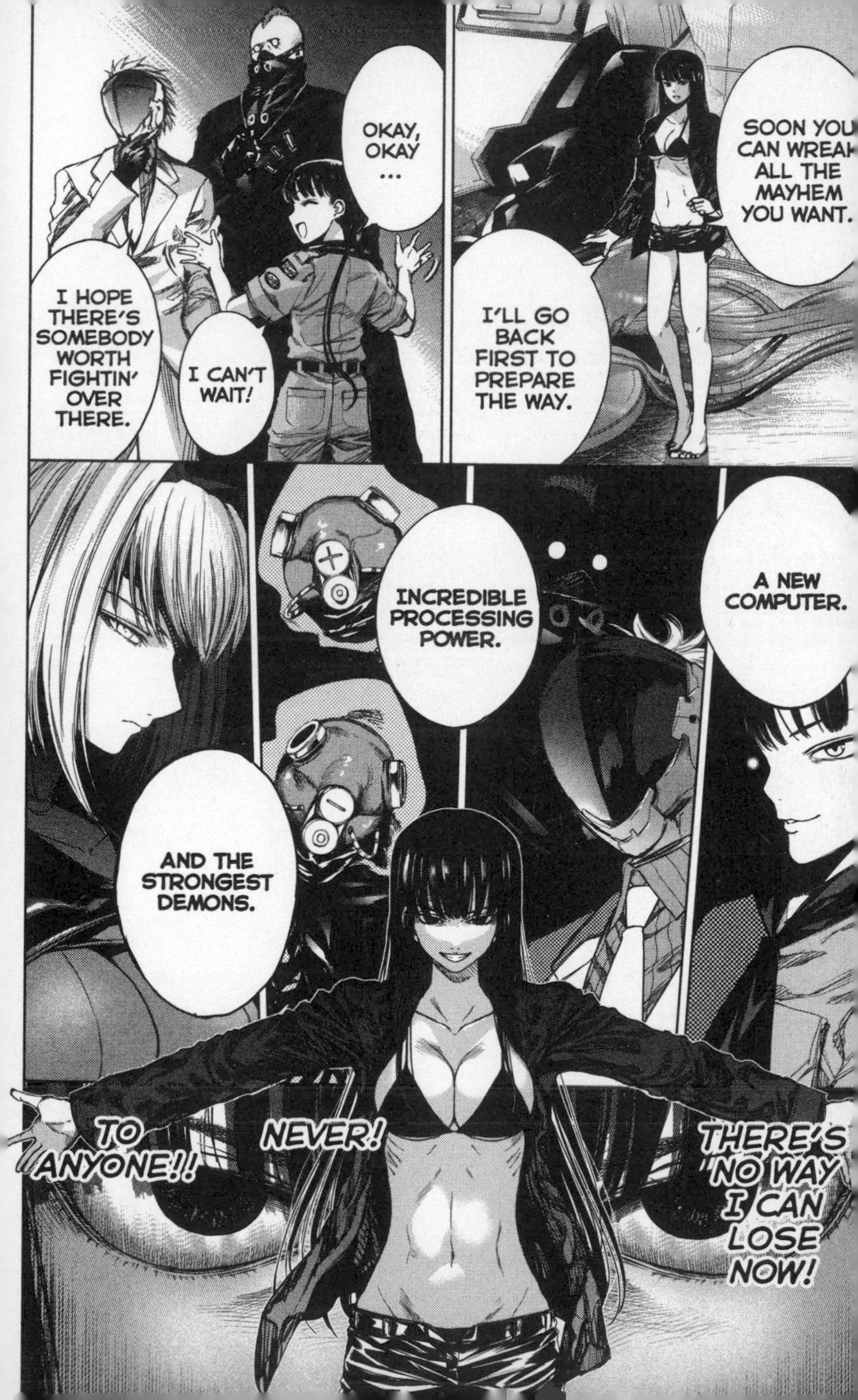
SOON YOU CAN WREAK ALL THE MAYHEM YOU WANT.
I'LL GO BACK FIRST TO PREPARE THE WAY.
OKAY, OKAY ...
I CAN'T WAIT!
I HOPE THERE'S SOMEBODY WORTH FIGHTIN' OVER THERE.
A NEW COMPUTER.
INCREDIBLE PROCESSING POWER.
AND THE STRONGEST DEMONS.
THERE'S NO WAY I CAN LOSE NOW!
NEVER!
TO ANYONE!!

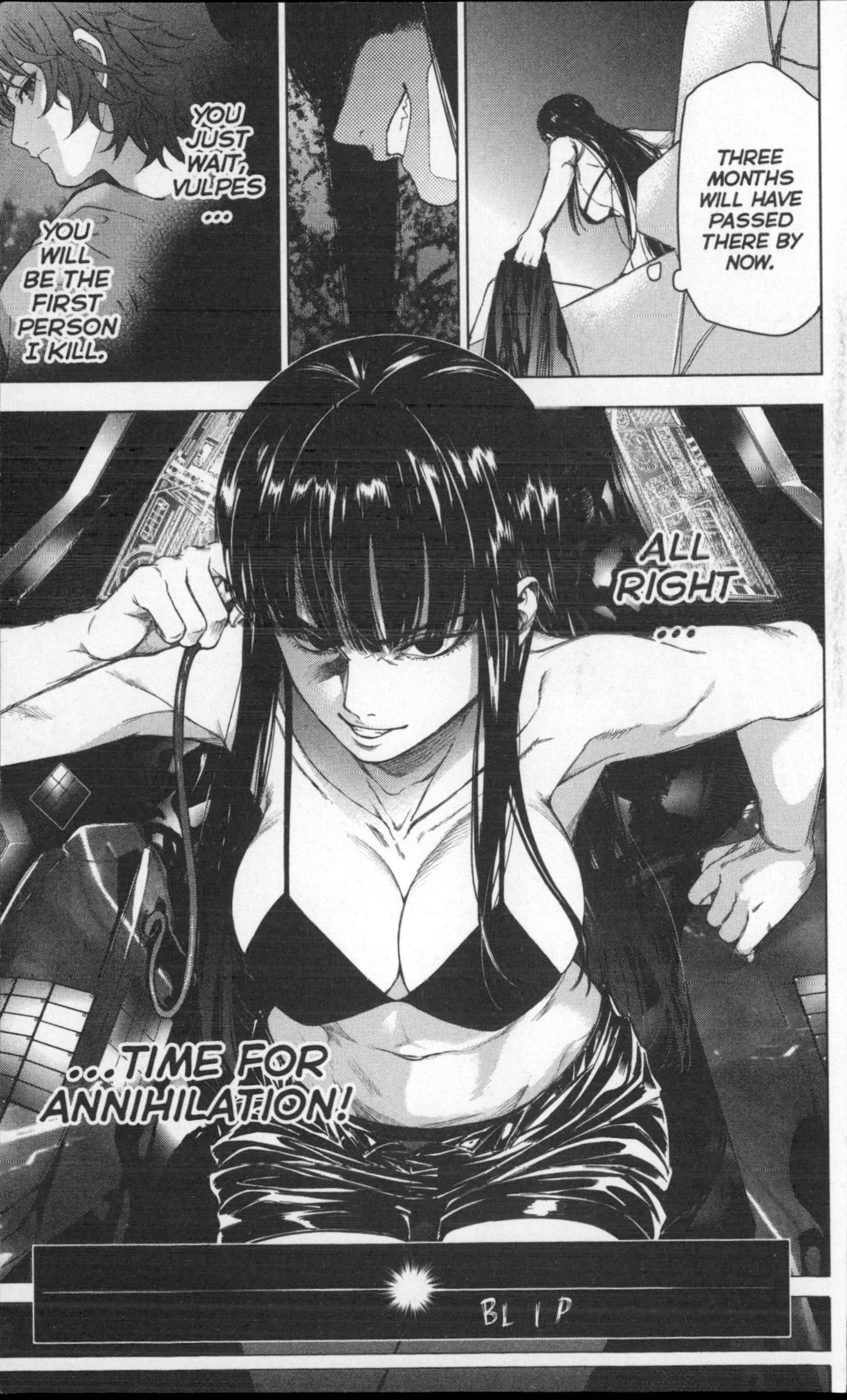
THREE MONTHS WILL HAVE PASSED THERE BY NOW.
YOU JUST WAIT, VULPES...
YOU WILL BE THE FIRST PERSON I KILL.
ALL RIGHT...
...TIME FOR ANNIHILATION!
BLIP

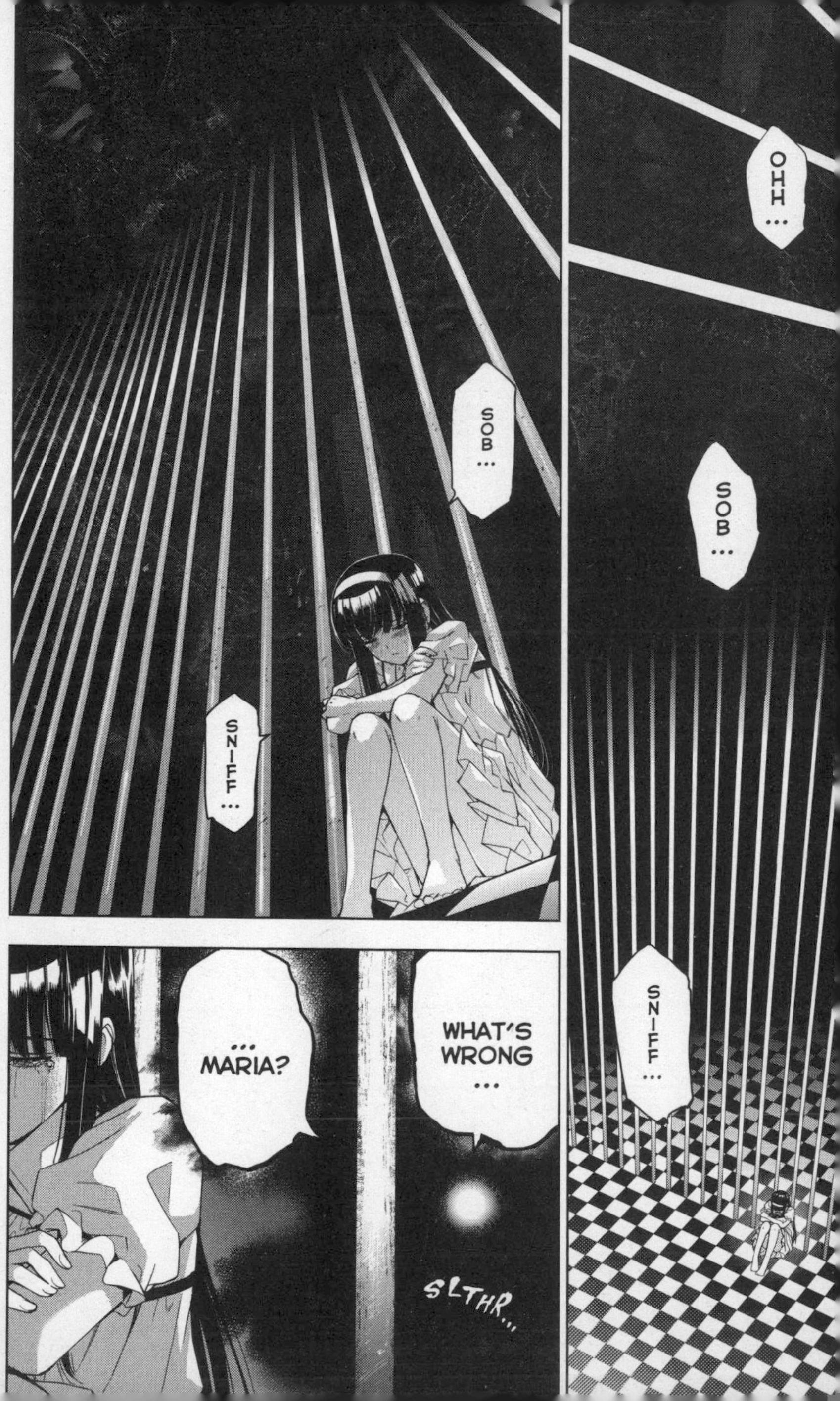
OHH ...
SOB ...
SNIFF ...
SOB ...
SNIFF ...
WHAT'S WRONG ...
... MARIA?
SLTHR...

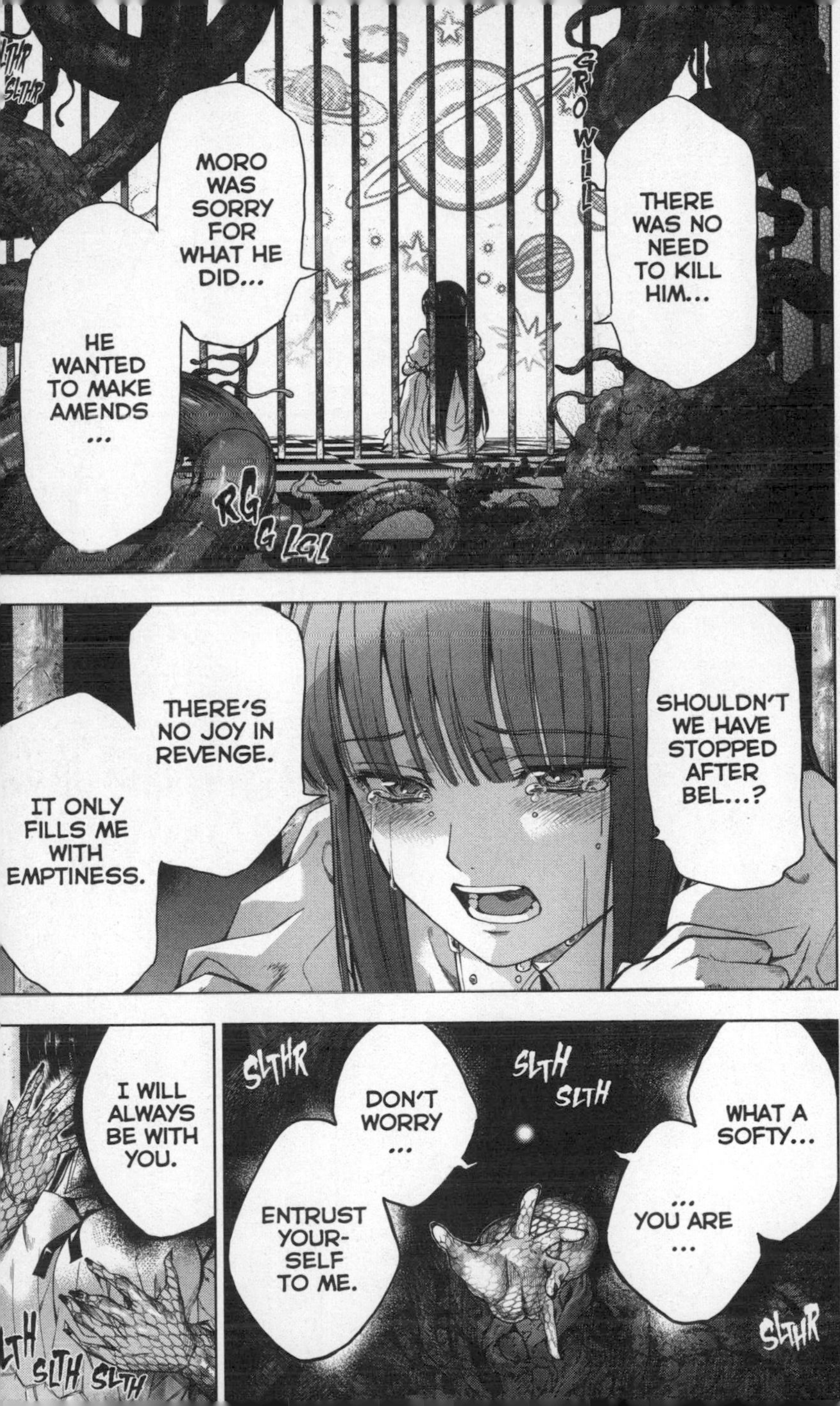
GROWLL
THERE WAS NO NEED TO KILL HIM...
MORO WAS SORRY FOR WHAT HE DID...
HE WANTED TO MAKE AMENDS ...
SLTHR SLTHR
RGG LGL
SHOULDN'T WE HAVE STOPPED AFTER BEL...?
THERE'S NO JOY IN REVENGE.
IT ONLY FILLS ME WITH EMPTINESS.
SLTH SLTH
WHAT A SOFTY...
... YOU ARE ...
SLTHR
DON'T WORRY ...
ENTRUST YOURSELF TO ME.
SLTHR
I WILL ALWAYS BE WITH YOU.
SLTH SLTH SLTH

I— YOUR RAGE— WILL ALWAYS BE BY YOUR SIDE.
SLTHR
SNAP
BND BND
SLTHR

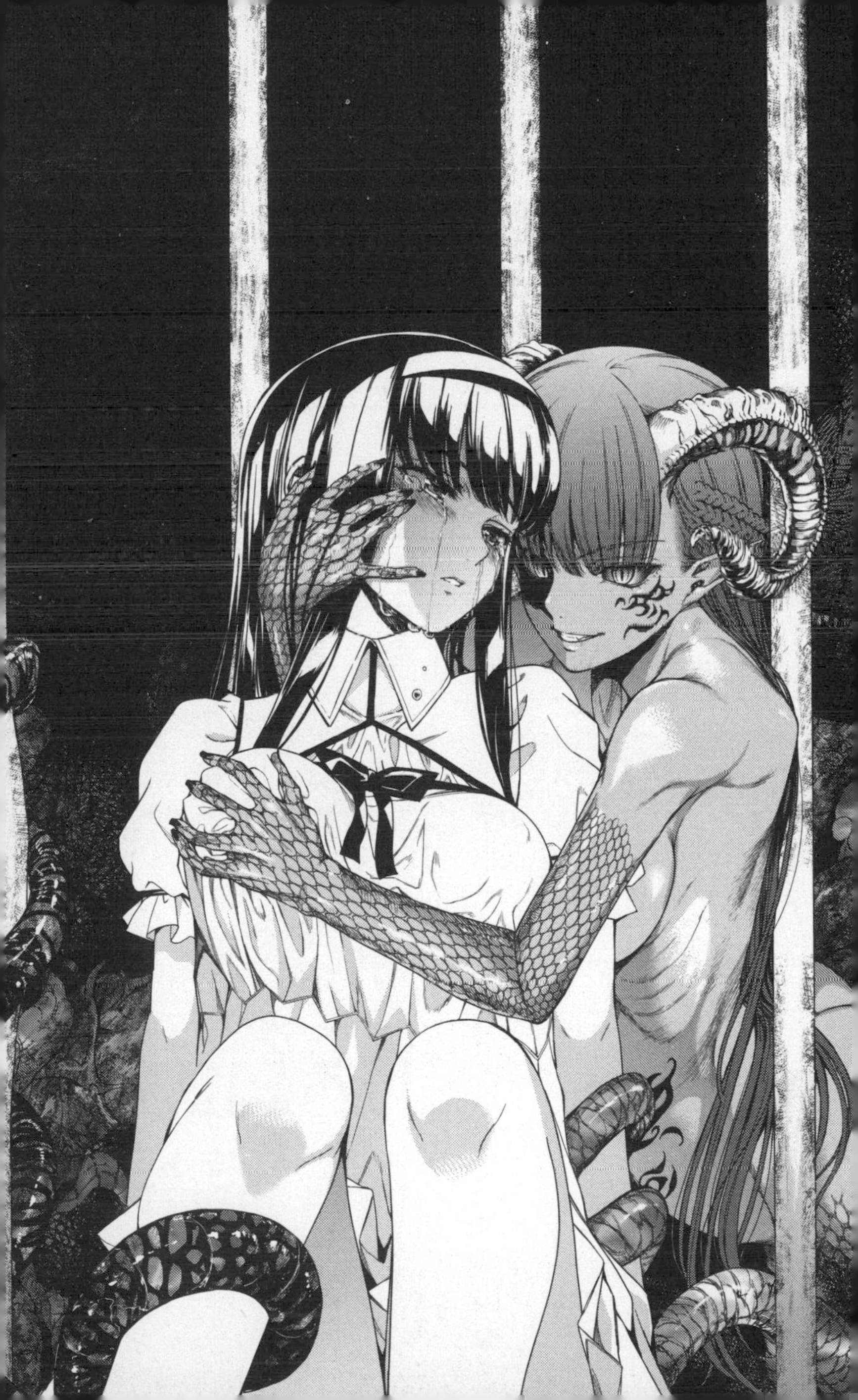

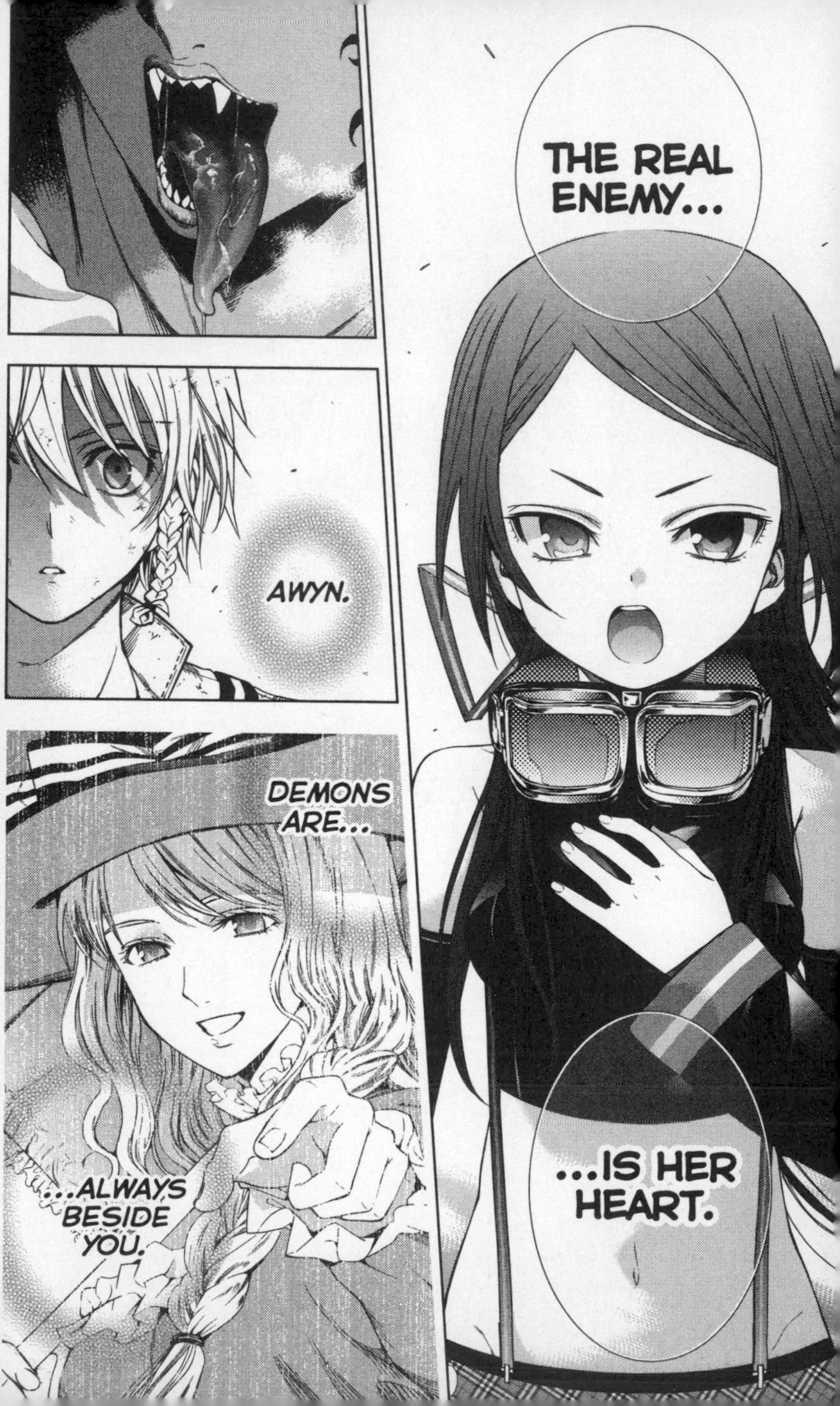
THE REAL ENEMY...
...IS HER HEART.
AWYN.
DEMONS ARE...
...ALWAYS BESIDE YOU.

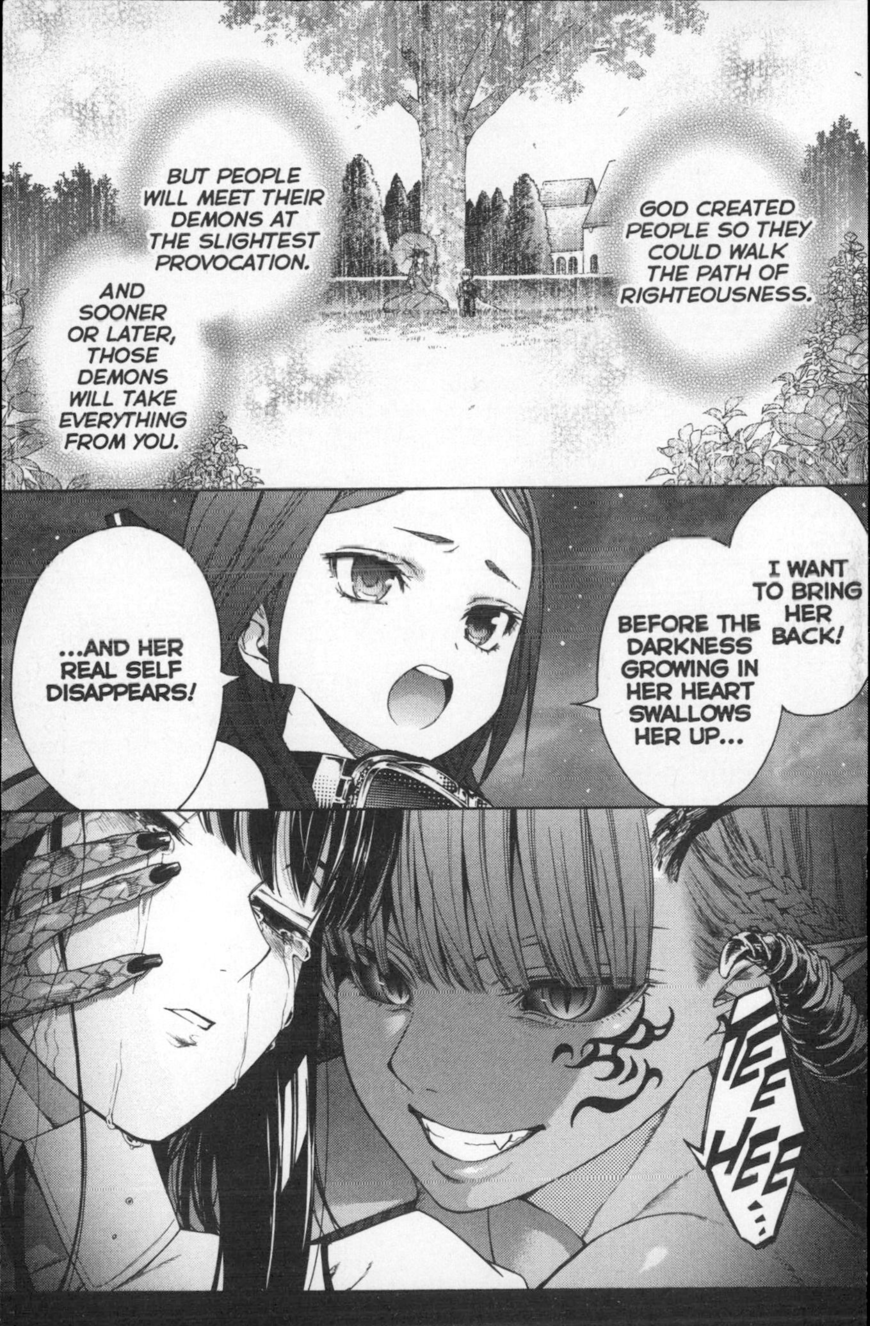
GOD CREATED PEOPLE SO THEY COULD WALK THE PATH OF RIGHTEOUSNESS.
BUT PEOPLE WILL MEET THEIR DEMONS AT THE SLIGHTEST PROVOCATION.
AND SOONER OR LATER, THOSE DEMONS WILL TAKE EVERYTHING FROM YOU.
I WANT TO BRING HER BACK!
BEFORE THE DARKNESS GROWING IN HER HEART SWALLOWS HER UP...
...AND HER REAL SELF DISAPPEARS!
HEE HEE...
YOU MUSTN'T GIVE IN.

To be continued...

Mitsu Izumi

Mysterious manga creator Mitsu Izumi was born on February 7 in Kanagawa Prefecture and is the creator of the manga adaptation of *Anohana: The Flower We Saw That Day*, originally serialized in *Jump SQ*.

To err is human...

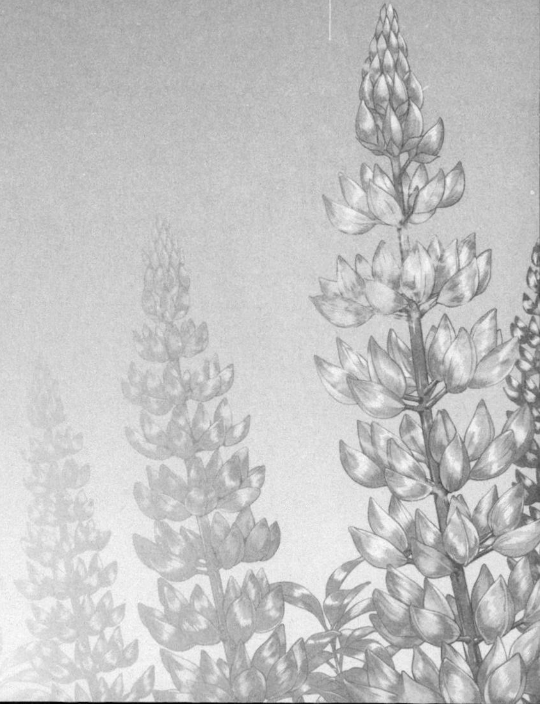

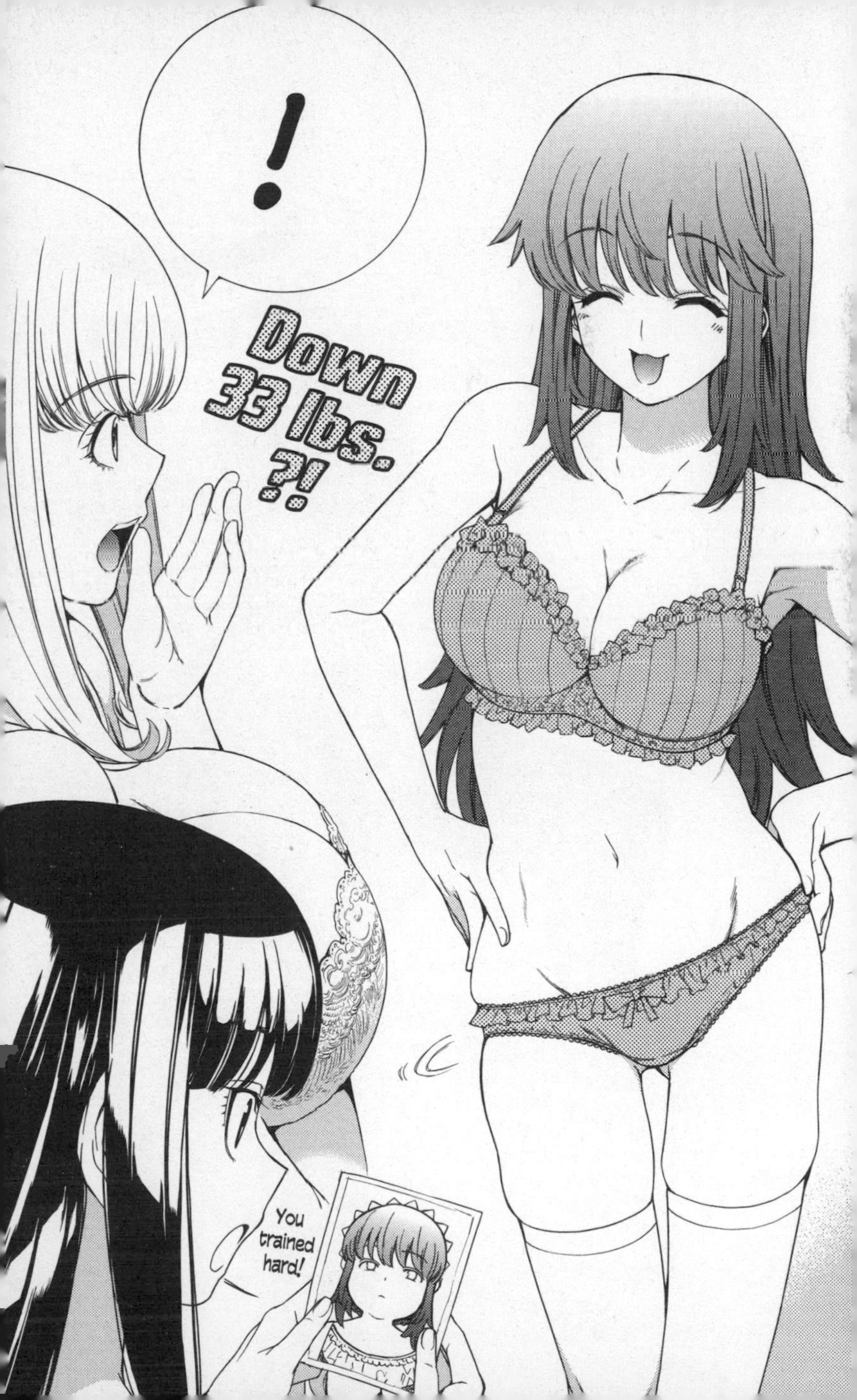
!
Down 33 lbs.?!
You trained hard!

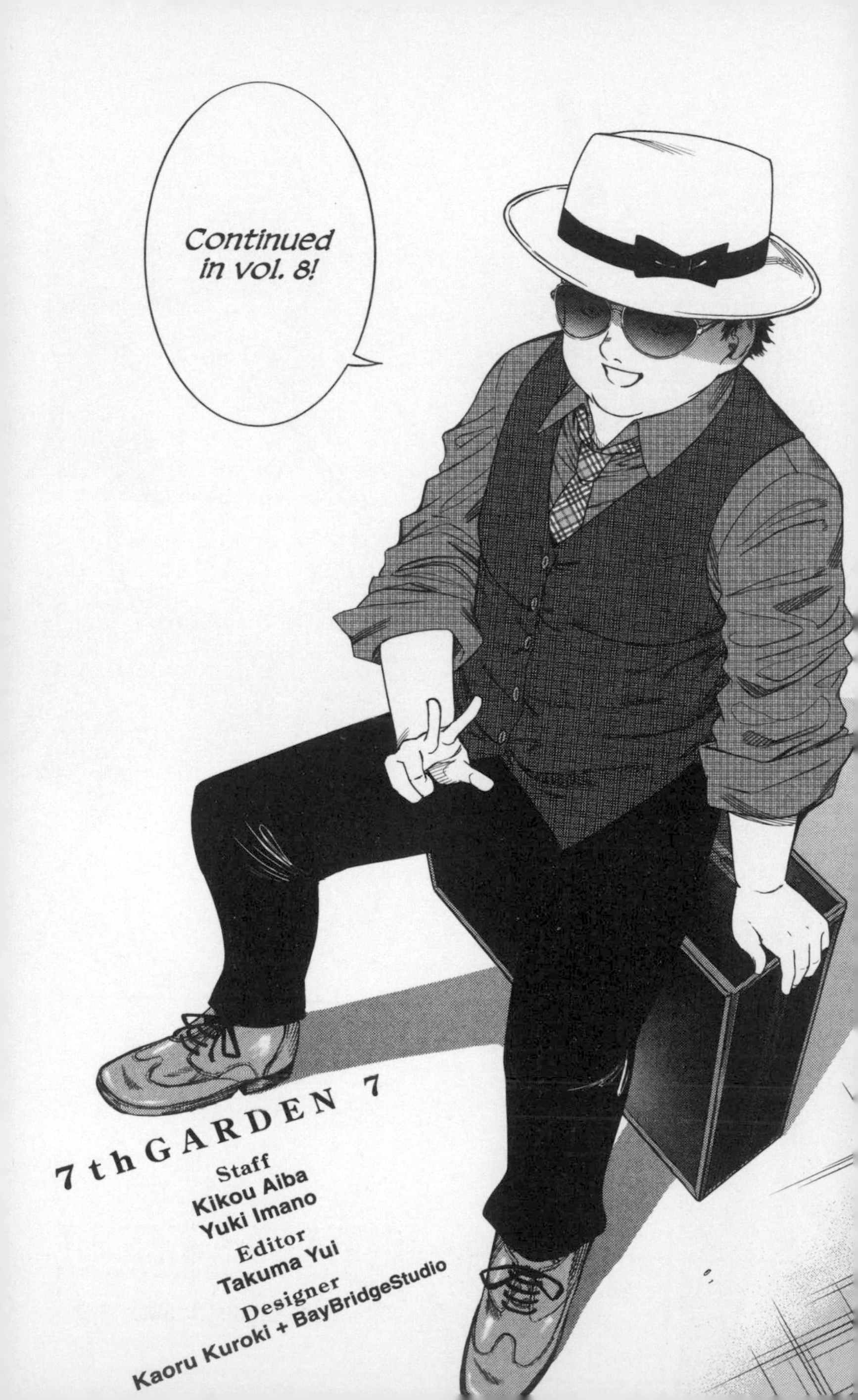
Continued in vol. 8!

7thGARDEN 7
Staff
Kikou Aiba
Yuki Imano
Editor
Takuma Yui
Designer
Kaoru Kuroki + BayBridgeStudio

7thGARDEN
7

SHONEN JUMP Manga Edition

Story and Art by Mitsu Izumi

Translation/Tetsuichiro Miyaki
English Adaptation/Annette Roman
Touch-Up Art & Lettering/Susan Daigle-Leach
Cover & Interior Design/Izumi Evers
Editor/Annette Roman

7thGARDEN © 2014 by Mitsu Izumi
All rights reserved.
First published in Japan in 2014 by SHUEISHA Inc.,
Tokyo.
English translation rights arranged by SHUEISHA Inc.

The stories, characters and incidents mentioned in this
publication are entirely fictional.

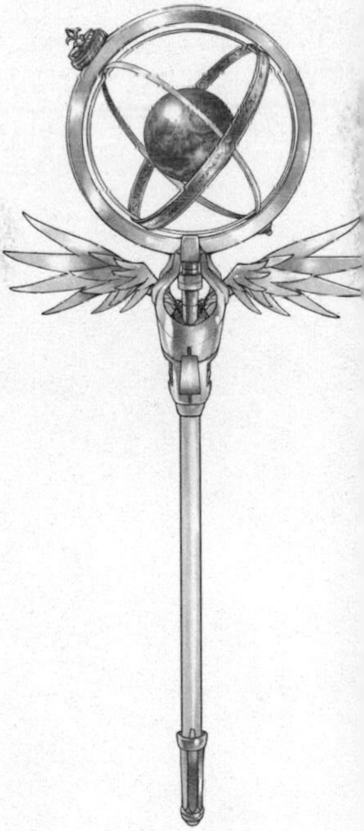

Printed in the U.S.A.

Published by VIZ Media, LLC
P.O. Box 77010
San Francisco, CA 94107

10 9 8 7 6 5 4 3 2 1
First printing, January 2018

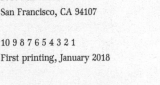

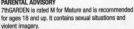

PARENTAL ADVISORY
7thGARDEN is rated M for Mature and is recommended
for ages 18 and up. It contains sexual situations and
violent imagery.
ratings.viz.com

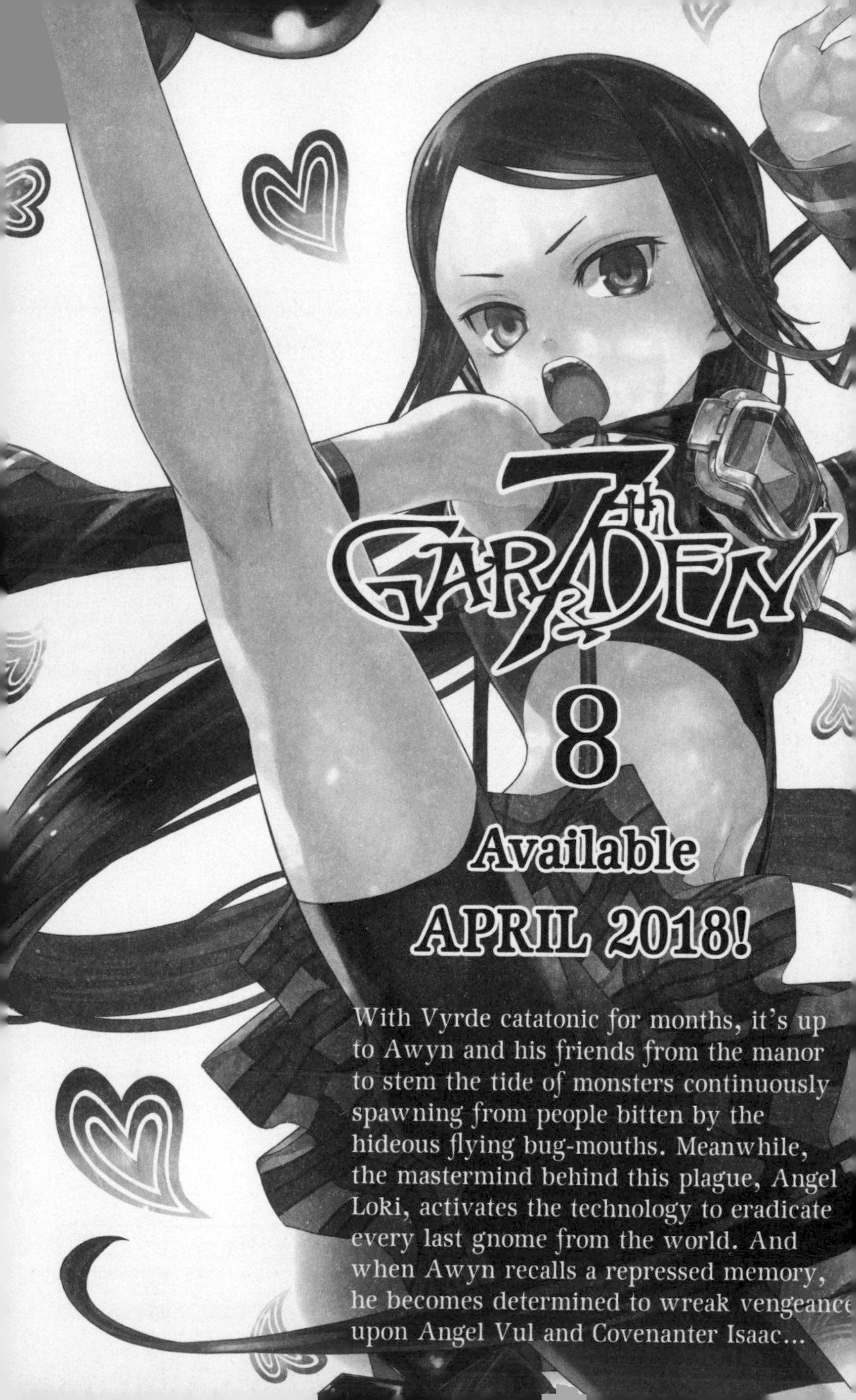
7th GARDEN
8
Available
APRIL 2018!
With Vyrde catatonic for months, it's up to Awyn and his friends from the manor to stem the tide of monsters continuously spawning from people bitten by the hideous flying bug-mouths. Meanwhile, the mastermind behind this plague, Angel Loki, activates the technology to eradicate every last gnome from the world. And when Awyn recalls a repressed memory, he becomes determined to wreak vengeance upon Angel Vul and Covenanter Isaac...

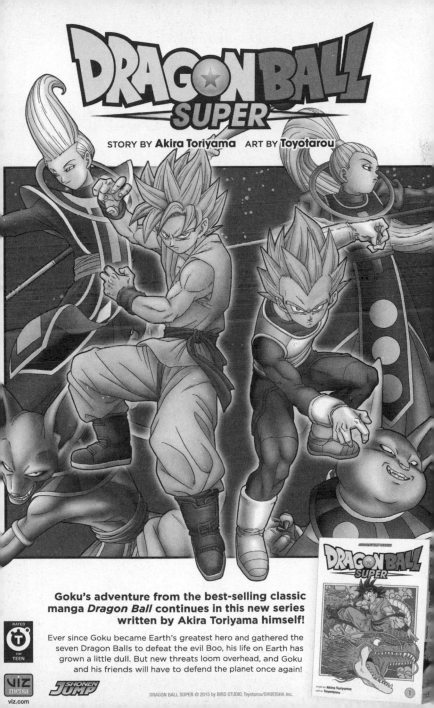

You're Reading in the Wrong Direction!!

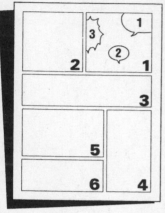

Whoops! Guess what? You're starting at the wrong end of the comic!

...It's true! In keeping with the original Japanese format, **7thGARDEN** is meant to be read from right to left, starting in the upper-right corner.

Unlike English, which is read from left to right, Japanese is read from right to left, meaning that action, sound effects and word-balloon order are completely reversed... something which can make readers unfamiliar with Japanese feel pretty backwards themselves. For this reason, manga or Japanese comics published in the U.S. in English have sometimes been published "flopped"—that is, printed in exact reverse order, as though seen from the other side of a mirror.

By flopping pages, U.S. publishers can avoid confusing readers, but the compromise is not without its downside. For one thing, a character in a flopped manga series who once wore in the original Japanese version a T-shirt emblazoned with "M A Y" (as in "the merry month of") now wears one which reads "Y A M"! Additionally, many manga creators in Japan are themselves unhappy with the process, as some feel the mirror-imaging of their art skews their original intentions.

We are proud to bring you Mitsu Izumi's **7thGARDEN** in the original unflopped format.

For now, though, turn to the other side of the book and let the adventure begin...!

—Editor